FAITH
UNDER PRESSURE

FAITH UNDER PRESSURE

A Study of Biblical Leaders in Conflict

Michael S. Moore

LEAFWOOD
PUBLISHERS

FAITH UNDER PRESSURE
A Study of Biblical Leaders in Conflict
published by Leafwood Publishers

Copyright © 2003 by Michael S. Moore

ISBN 0-9714289-1-3
Printed in the United States of America

Cover design by Rick Gibson

For information:
Leafwood Publishers, Siloam Springs, AR
1-877-634-6004 (toll free)

Visit our website: www.leafwoodpublishers.com

03 04 05 06 07 08   9 8 7 6 5 4 3 2 1

ACKNOWLEDGEMENTS

I want to thank all the people who have taken the time to read portions of this manuscript and make comments. Many students have left their fingerprints on this material over the years as together we have wrestled with these stories in class. Lorelei Hillman, David Steinbrenner, Adriene Buffington, Mary Long, Rod Tussing, Christine Stephenson, Chris Chandler, Cameron Jorgenson, Jim Graham, and many others have offered wonderfully fresh perspectives on these texts which have challenged me to rethink my positions and examine my own interpretations. Editors Terry Muck, John Walton, Bob Hubbard, Tremper Longman, and Andy Dearman offered helpful suggestions on how and where to begin the project. Leslie Allen, Jim Butler, Joel Hunt, Don Benjamin and John Goldingay have given much helpful guidance over the years on how to read the Bible holistically.

The influence of my teachers Herb Huffmon, Jim Roberts, and Baruch Levine colors all my work, and I am happy to remain their student. Mark Smith and John Day offered incisive comments on matters of comparative history. James Thompson and A. van der Kooij gave editorial guidance at critical points in the research. Carey Newman and John Kutsko helped shape the book's final form by insisting on structural clarity and economic prose. The comments and prayers of Paul Halley, Garth Nash, Bob Crawford, Kent Giboney, and Pastor Gayle Parker have gone a long way toward making sure that this book at least tries to address the needs of contemporary believers. The encouragement of colleagues like Tom Parker, Rich Erickson, Will Stoller-Lee, Kim Anderson, Curt Longacre, Karl Wolfe, David Parris, Cliff Anderson, Sylvia Newman, Grayson Carter, and Art Patzia can never be repaid. Cheryl Austin-Brown, Jeff Braucher, Diana Beskind, Bob Freeman,

Pat Rexroat, Joel Gereboff, Jeff Braucher, and Carol Eaton have all been constant sources of blessing and encouragement. Leonard Allen's clear editorial eye has vastly improved the book's final draft.

I am grateful to each of these colleagues and friends for all their help, but a special thanks goes to my wife Caron for (a) putting up with me generally, and (b) allowing me the time and freedom to write about the Bible: "they seemed to him but a few days because of his love for her" (Gen. 29:20).

Michael S. Moore

TABLE OF CONTENTS

ABBREVIATIONS

Abbreviations and transliterations follow the *SBL Handbook of Style.*

AB	*Anchor Bible*
ABD	*Anchor Bible Dictionary (ed. D. N. Freedman)*
ABRL	*Anchor Bible Reference Library*
AJ	*Antiquities of the Jews (by Josephus)*
AJA	*American Journal of Archaeology*
AJSL	*American Journal of Semitic Languages*
Akk	*Akkadian*
ANE	*Ancient Near East(ern)*
ANET	*Ancient Near Eastern Texts Relating to the Old Testament (ed. by J. Pritchard; Princeton: Princeton University, 1969).*
Arab	*Arabic*
Aram	*Aramaic*
ARM	*Archives royal de Mari (Akkadian texts)*
b.	*Babylonian Talmud (followed by tractate reference)*
B. Qam.	*Baba Qama*
Sanh.	*Sanhedrin*
BA	*Biblical Archaeologist*
BAR	*Biblical Archaeology Review*
BASOR	*Bulletin of the American Schools of Oriental Research*
BBR	*Bulletin of Biblical Research*
BDB	*Brown, Driver, & Briggs (Hebrew and English Lexicon of the Old Testament)*
Bib	*Biblica*
BR	*Bible Review*
BS	*Bibliotheca Sacra*
BTB	*Biblical Theology Bulletin*
BWANT	*Beiträge zur Wissenschaft vom alten und neuen Testament*
BZ	*Biblische Zeitschrift*
BZAW	*Beihefte zur Zeitschrift fur die alttestamentliche Wissenschaft*
CAD	*Chicago Assyrian Dictionary (ed. A. L. Oppenheim)*
CBQ	*The Catholic Biblical Quarterly*
CC	*Christian Century*

CEJ	*Christian Education Journal*
CMHE	*Canaanite Myth and Hebrew Epic* (by F. M. Cross; Cambridge, MA: Harvard, 1973).
CML	*Canaanite Myths and Legends* (trans. & ed. by J. C. L. Gibson; Edinburgh: T. & T. Clark, 1977).
CSR	*Christian Scholars Review*
CT	*Christianity Today*
DAT	*Deir `Alla Texts* (ed. J. Hackett)
DeVries	S. DeVries, *1 Kings* (WBC 12; Waco, TX: Word, 1985).
DNWSI	*Dictionary of North-West Semitic Inscriptions* (eds. Hoftijzer & Jongeling)
Dtr	deuteronomistic (having to do with the theology of Deuteronomy)
EA	*Die El-Amarna Tafeln* (ed. J. Knudtzon)
EAEHL	*Encyclopedia of Archaeological Excavations in the Holy Land*
Eccl. Rab.	*Ecclesiastes Rabbah*
EEC	*Encyclopedia of Early Christianity* (ed. E. Ferguson)
EI	*Eretz Israel*
Emar	*Recherches au pays d'Astata, Emar VI* (ed. D. Arnaud; Paris, 1987)
EMQ	*Evangelical Missions Quarterly*
EQ	*Evangelical Quarterly*
ERT	*Evangelical Review of Theology*
ET	*Expository Times*
FH	*Fides et Historia*
FRLANT	*Forschungen zur Religion und Literatur des alten und neuen Testaments*
GEH	*A Grammar of Epigraphic Hebrew* (by S. L. Gogel)
Gk	Greek
GKC	Gesenius-Kautzsch-Cowley (*Gesenius' Hebrew Grammar* [Oxford: Clarendon, 1910]).
Gray	J. Gray, *I & II Kings* (OTL; Philadelphia: Westminster, 1970).
HBT	*Horizons in Biblical Theology*
HBD	*Harper's Bible Dictionary* (ed. P. Achtemeier)
Heb	Hebrew
HS	*Hebrew Studies*
HSM	*Harvard Semitic Monographs*
HTR	*Harvard Theological Review*
HUCA	*Hebrew Union College Annual*
IBMR	*International Bulletin of Missionary Research*
IDB	*Interpreter's Dictionary of the Bible* (ed. G. Buttrick)
IEJ	*Israel Exploration Journal*
Int	*Interpretation*
IRM	*International Review of Mission*

JAAR	*Journal of the American Academy of Religion*
JANES	*Journal of the Ancient Near Eastern Society*
JAOS	*Journal of the American Oriental Society*
JBL	*Journal of Biblical Literature*
JBQ	*Jewish Bible Quarterly*
JBR	*Journal of Bible and Religion*
JCS	*Journal of Cuneiform Studies*
JETS	*Journal of the Evangelical Theological Society*
JNES	*Journal of Near Eastern Studies*
JNSL	*Journal of Northwest Semitic Languages*
JPT	*Journal of Psychology and Theology*
JQR	*Jewish Quarterly Review*
JR	*Journal of Religion*
JSOT	*Journal for the Study of the Old Testament*
JSOTSup	*Journal for the Study of the Old Testament Supplement*
JSS	*Journal of Semitic Studies*
JTS	*Journal of Theological Studies*
KAI	*Kanaanäische und aramäische Inschriften* (eds. H. Donner & W. Röllig)
KB	Kohler-Baumgartner (*Hebräisches und Aramäisches Lexicon zum Alten Testament*)
KTU	*Die keilalphabetischen Texte aus Ugarit* (eds. Dietrich, Loretz, & Sanmartin)
KUB	*Keilschrifturkunden aus Bogazköy* (Hittite texts)
LCL	*Loeb Classical Library* (Cambridge, MA)
LXX	Septuagint (Greek translation of the Old Testament)
m.	Mishnah (followed by tractate)
MBA	*Macmillan Bible Atlas*
MC	*Modern Churchman*
MT	Masoretic Text (The Hebrew Bible)
NCBC	*New Century Bible Commentary*
Nelson	R. Nelson, *First and Second Kings* (Interpretation; Louisville, KY: John Knox, 1987).
NIBCOT	*New International Biblical Commentary* (Old Testament)
NJPS	New Jewish Publication Society (Tanakh)
NT	*Novum Testamentum*
NTS	*New Testament Studies*
OBO	*Orbis Biblicus et Orientalis*
OTL	*Old Testament Library* (Westminster)
OTP	*Old Testament Parallels* (ed. by V. Matthews & D. Benjamin; New York: Paulist, 1997).
OTS	*Oudtestamentische Studien*

PEQ	*Palestine Exploration Quarterly*
Phoen.	*Phoenician*
PJ	*Palästina-Jahrbuch*
Provan	I. Provan, *1 and 2 Kings* (NIBC 7; Peabody, MA: Hendrickson, 1995).
PSSD	*A Compendious Syriac Dictionary* (ed. R. & J. Payne Smith)
Rab.	Midrash Rabbah (the "Great Midrash")
RB	*Revue Biblique*
RLA	*Reallexicon der Assyriologie*
RQ	*Restoration Quarterly*
RRR	*Review of Religious Research*
SAA	*State Archives of Assyria*
SBLSS	*Society of Biblical Literature Semeia Studies*
SBT	*Studies in Biblical Theology*
Sem	*Semeia*
SJOT	*Scandinavian Journal of the Old Testament*
SJT	*Scottish Journal of Theology*
SR	*Sociology of Religion*
SSI	*Syrian Semitic Inscriptions* (ed. J. C. L. Gibson)
Sum	*Sumerian*
Syr	Syriac translation of the Old Testament
TB	*Tyndale Bulletin*
TDNT	*Theological Dictionary of the New Testament* (ed. R. Kittel)
TDOT	*Theological Dictionary of the Old Testament* (ed. H. Ringgren)
TE	*Theological Education*
TS	*Theological Studies*
TT	*Theology Today*
TZ	*Theologische Zeitschrift*
UF	*Ugarit Forschungen*
Ug	Ugaritic
UNP	*Ugaritic Narrative Poetry* (ed. S. Parker)
UT	*Ugaritic Texts* (ed. C. H. Gordon)
Vg	Vulgate (Latin translation of the Old Testament)
VT	*Vetus Testamentum*
VTE	*Vassal Treaties of Esarhaddon*
VTSup	*Vetus Testamentum Supplement*
Walsh	J. Walsh, *1 Kings* (Berit Olam; Collegeville, MN: Liturgical Press, 1996).
WMANT	*Wissenschaftliche Monographien zum alten und neuen Testament*
WTJ	*Westminster Theological Journal*
ZA	*Zeitschrift fur Assyrologie*
ZAW	*Zeitschrift fur die alttestamentliche Wissenschaft*

INTRODUCTION

Every generation has its "theme" songs. My grandparents loved *Ain't We Got Fun*, by Gus Kahn, Raymond Egan and Richard Whiting.[1] My parents danced to the "swing" music of *Take The A Train* and *Moonlight Serenade*.[2] When my kids were teenagers, they listened to stuff like Pearl Jam's *Jeremy* and the grunge anthem by Nirvana, *Smells Like Teen Spirit*:

> With the lights out it's less dangerous
> Here we are now
> Entertain us
> I feel stupid and contagious
> Here we are now
> Entertain us.[3]

Perhaps Billy Joel's *Pressure* best describes my generation:

> You have to learn to pace yourself – Pressure
> You're just like everybody else—Pressure
> You've only had to run so far, so good
> But you will come to a place
> Where the only thing you feel
> Are loaded guns in your face
> And you'll have to deal with Pressure

You used to call me paranoid— Pressure
But even you can not avoid Pressure

You turned the tap dance into your crusade
Now here you are with your faith
And your Peter Pan advice
You have no scars on your face
And you cannot handle pressure
All grown up and no place to go
Psych 1, Psych 2
What do you know?

All your life is Channel 13
Sesame Street
What does it mean?
Pressure
Pressure
Don't ask for help
You're all alone—Pressure
You'll have to answer
To your own Pressure

I'm sure you'll have some cosmic rationale
But here you are in the ninth
Two men out and three men on
Nowhere to look but inside
Where we all respond to Pressure.[4]

The themes in this song reflect the pressures of being an American baby boomer. Fear. Fatigue. Inexperience. Triviality. Hypocrisy. Violence. Loneliness. "Peter Pan" advice. Seems like all of my contemporaries are under some kind of pressure or another. Pressure to produce. Pressure to achieve. Pressure to give in. Pressure to opt out. The pressure of finding oneself "all alone." *Pressure.*

The title of this book has a double-meaning. *Faith Under Pressure* is first and foremost a book for believers. Having been a preaching minister for over two decades, I think I have something to say to believers about the life of faith. I know from firsthand experience how hard it is to preach the Word with passion and excitement week after week, year after year. I know firsthand the joys and the sorrows of serving the Lord under this kind of pressure, and I will share some of my experiences in this book. I want to encourage believers and help them grow in the Faith.

As a seminary professor I am also concerned about the life of faith as a vocational calling. Not many of my students tell me they want to work full-time with the Church anymore, and this bothers me. Even among those who do go into full-time ministry, too many give up after that first "bad experience," and I am concerned that too many of my students have an overly naïve view of the faith *vocation*. As an Old Testament instructor I want to help students access what I think is the best of all faith resources—the Bible. I want to help them understand the struggles of the believers who've gone before them, and I want to help them catch a passion for helping others grow in the Faith.

The book of Kings addresses all these concerns because here God comes to discouraged believers like Elijah and renews their vision. Here Elisha mentors student-ministers while working with the hungry and the lost and the brokenhearted. Here prophets like Nathan negotiate with the powerful on behalf of the powerless, and prophets like Micaiah show us when and how to confront idolatry.

Kings is fascinating for many reasons, not least because readers bring such different reading strategies to it.[5] Historians study Kings in order to learn more about the historical context in which these episodes take place.[6] Literary critics study it to learn more about the stories themselves—their structure and complexity and characters and themes.[7] Religion scholars read Kings to investigate the religious beliefs of the peoples responsible for producing these stories.[8] Preachers read it to figure out how to make these stories come alive for everyday people.

Believers have another reason for reading Kings, however—one often overlooked in contemporary discussion. Believers come to Kings for the same reason we come to Isaiah or Esther or Paul's letter to the Romans. We need help in living the life of faith. Faith is difficult. Faith requires growth. Faith needs constantly to be empowered, and though some may question it, the Bible is still our primary source of spiritual energy. This means that disciples aren't just "readers." Disciples are believers who take seriously the question, "Have you not read?"[9] For us, it's critically important that we learn how to read the Bible in ways which lead to genuine spiritual growth.

Between History and Narrative

When we look at the text seriously, the first thing we note is that Kings is one of two anthologies designed to record the history of Israel over a formative time—the age of Solomon and the divided monarchy.[10]

The other anthology is the book of Chronicles, yet where Kings frames its stories within an explicit prophetic framework, Chronicles does not. Chronicles focuses on the history of the Davidic monarchy—its covenant, its dynastic hopes, its amazing successes. Kings, however, focuses on the pitfalls of apostasy, the dangers of elitist hierarchy, the terrifying consequences of disobedience to the prophetic Word. Put another way, Kings focuses on the Mosaic covenant while Chronicles focuses on the Davidic covenant.[11] This means not only that the concerns in Kings are different from those in Chronicles, but that Kings may not go down well with audiences allergic to words like "sin" and "obedience" and "judgment."[12]

To overcome this reaction, I think we need to develop pastoral reading strategies which make these stories more "user-friendly." The purpose of this book is to propose such a strategy. Here is my thesis: I believe that Kings is a carefully-designed anthology in which the individual episodes parallel, reflect, and shape one another in order to formulate more explicitly the narrator's theological concerns. What do I mean by this?

First, I mean that a relevant, successful reading strategy will be holistic. Literary critics are interested only in the "world of the text," often downplaying the text's reliability as an historical resource. Many feel strongly about this. Robert Alter, for example, begins his most famous book on the subject by claiming that "the circumstances of intellectual history…have prevented (the Bible's) essential literary dimension from being sufficiently observed."[13] He feels, in other words, that too many people read the Bible—when they read it at all—as dry history. William Dever, on the other hand, is an archaeologist and historian who feels that the pendulum has swung too far to the other extreme—that too many readers are marginalizing the text's legitimate historical witness. In his book, *What Did the Biblical Writers Know, and When Did They Know It?*, he accuses several of them by name, chiding his colleagues for misunderstanding and mistreating Kings' historical witness.[14] These scholars represent opposite sides of a vigorous debate.

Yet there is a big difference between dialogical debate and allergic reaction. Academic debate is certainly important, but it does believers little good when it (a) unfairly devalues Kings' legitimate historical value and/or (b) unfairly devalues Kings' marvelous literary structure. The truth, of course, is that both approaches are necessary for holistic interpretation, and most interpreters recognize this. The structuralist Diana Edelman, for example, recognizes and emphasizes the importance of legitimate historical criticism, while evangelical scholars like David Dorsey are reemphasizing the fact that "all literary compositions have structure."[15] This dialogue is encouraging.

Second, I mean that a successful reading strategy will be both *inter-textual* and *intratextual*. What do these terms mean? In this book I will use these words as methodological, not ideological terms. By "intertex-tual" I will refer to the comparative reading of narrative episodes *between* biblical (and some non-biblical) books in order to clarify the meanings of each passage. I will use the term "intratextual," however, to describe the comparative reading of narrative passages *within* biblical books (like Kings).[16] Here's an example.

Writing in the venerably evangelical *Tyndale Bulletin*, Philip Satter-thwaite argues that the narrator of Kings deliberately structures the Elijah-Elisha traditions in order to reflect the theology of the Moses-Joshua tra-ditions.[17] In fact, Kings gravitates to these older traditions because the nar-rator wants to show that Elisha (Joshua) successfully completes the "con-quest" begun by Elijah (Moses). By structuring his material this way, he wants to show his readers not only that he's aware of the earlier traditions, but that he can and will use them to reinforce his theological point: heal-ing follows redemption. This is an example of intertextual interpretation.

The stories in Kings readily lend themselves to intratextual interpre-tation as well. The Nathan-David encounter, for example, is the first of several prophet-politician encounters in Kings which, when interpreted altogether, lay out a complex thematic trajectory about the *pressures of prophecy*. Most of these prophet-politician encounters come to a head in the Elijah-Elisha narratives, but read as a trajectory, they range in mood from quiet manipulation to violent confrontation, from angry denuncia-tion to wary inquiry, from desperate pleading to bizarre divination.

These stories can be approached from a variety of perspectives, not just as literature or just as history. But when we approach them from an intratextual perspective, we raise a whole new set of questions. Why is David's physical impotence at the beginning of Kings paralleled by Jehoiachin's political impotence at the end? Why do the last days of David's kingdom so obviously parallel the last days of Judah's "final four"—Jehoahaz, Jehoiakim, Jehoiachin, and Zedekiah? Why do the characters in Elisha's world (like the Shunammite woman) look so much like the char-acters in Elijah's world (like the Zarephath widow)? Why does Kings end, as Samuel predicts, with God's people crying out for deliverance (1 Sam 8:18), and Yahweh refusing to give it to them (2 Kings 24:20)? What is the writer saying theologically when he structures his work this way?[18] Historical approaches cannot answer these questions. Nor can traditional literary approaches. Questions like these must be explored through Kings' densely-textured, fascinatingly-structured intratextuality.

Here's what I mean. Kings opens up with a Davidic kingdom paralyzed, uncertain, and in deep crisis. Aware of this crisis, David's son,
Adonijah, declares himself David's successor—and dies for trying.
Solomon takes advantage of this situation, through Bathsheba's mediation, and displaces his older brother. This behavior may look ruthless, but
careful readers know from the context that there is an intertextual pattern
here, and this pattern is congruent with the previous material in Samuel.
In Samuel-Kings, to be blunt, power never flows easily from David to his
sons—not to Amnon (2 Sam 13:29), nor to Absalom (18:14), nor to
Adonijah (1 Kings 1-2). It is no surprise that Solomon's reign begins the
way it does, because the intertextual context prepares us for it. Solomon
succeeds to the throne through violence and trickery because the
prophetic narrator wants us to focus our attention on what he feels is a
much deeper problem—the corrupt nature of the monarchy itself. As
Martin Noth observed long ago, Kings' critique of the monarchy is relentless. From the first internal challenge of a Hebrew prince (Adonijah), to
the last external challenge of a Babylonian tyrant (Nebuchadnezzar),
Kings is a frontal assault on the monarchy.[19]

Generational power struggles are not unique to Samuel-Kings, yet the
fact that Kings *begins* with a grisly power struggle is both intertextually and
intratextually significant. It sets the tone for the whole book.[20] Like all
tragedies, this one does not so much develop as degenerate. In the beginning, Yahweh graciously allows the Davidic dynasty to continue, but only
because of David's historical obedience (2 Sam 7:1-17; 1 Kings 2:4; 8:25;
9:4-5). Eventually this changes, however, as Yahweh's reactions to disobedience become more and more pronounced (1 Kings 11:36; 15:4; 2 Kings
8:19). The David-Solomon power transition is certainly bumpy, but after
Solomon's death, things really start sliding downhill. Jeroboam's rebellion
bisects the kingdom into north-south factions. Syria slides into the vacuum
created by their developing intramural conflict, and Ahab's kingdom disas-
trously experiments with Phoenician Baalism. Watching from the sidelines,
Assyria bides its time until it can attack Samaria and devour the carcass.
Judah survives Sennacherib's invasion a few decades later, but the reprieve
is short-lived. Babylon soon arrives and destroys the Temple.

Were this our only reading angle, Kings would rank as one of the
Bible's gloomiest laments. Indeed, many still view it from this perspective,
and this is doubtless why so few preachers dare to preach from it today.
Gerhard von Rad, however, was one of a few post-war readers who challenged this one-sided interpretation.[21] He recognized that Kings is indeed
about the wrath of God, but it's much more than this. Over and over again

these stories show us a God who moves in the midst of violence, who saves in the midst of chaos, who sustains in the midst of despair, who challenges in the midst of complacency. Israel's self-inflicted disasters cannot stop this God from doing what he does best, whether it's saving kings or strengthening servants, saving prostitutes or encouraging royal stewards. The book of Kings may begin like Billy Joel's *Pressure*, but along the way we also hear echoes of Fanny Crosby's *A Wonderful Savior*.[22]

How Shall We Read?

Appropriately interpreted, then, these stories hold enormous spiritual potential. Inappropriately interpreted, they remain locked away from spiritual view, lifeless and inert. Are these texts designed for clinical dissection or spiritual empowerment? Are they meant to empower or condemn, entertain or encourage? None of these characters is sinless, as the narrator repeatedly points out, but many are faithful, and this theme desperately needs developing today. Can the God of Elijah still work wonders through broken clay pots? Can the prophetic Word still save?

Kings intratextually cycles and recycles the same themes over and over, creatively reinterpreting them, constantly reinforcing them. Kings, as James Sanders memorably puts it, is a book quite "full of itself."[23] This holds true for the Bible as a whole, to be sure, but nowhere is it more true than in Kings. So the question begs asking: Is this a disjointed anthology of individual episodes disconnected from one another and the rest of the Bible? Or is this rather a carefully structured anthology of intra-connected, prophetically-framed episodes designed to empower faith under pressure? The answer to this question begins to become clear as we take a closer look at the book's main trajectories.

The Pressure of Injustice

Kings are supposed to provide justice (Jer 22:16), but often they do not, and the episodes on this trajectory deal with various responses to injustice. David listens to Bathsheba plead for her child's salvation (1 Kings 1:11-31), two prostitutes beg Solomon for justice (3:16-28; 4:29-34), Ahab seizes Naboth's land and murders him for griping about it (21:1-29), an unnamed Israelite king (Jehoram? Jehoahaz?) gives a Shunammite woman back her land (2 Kings 8:1-6), and Manasseh murders countless children through ritual sacrifice (21:1-26).

The Pressure of Subversion

The episodes on this trajectory focus on the problem of internal subversion. In order of appearance, they include Adonijah's attempt to seize the throne (1 Kings 1:5-53), Solomon's judgments against his adversaries (2:13-46), Solomon's attempt to change Israel's tribal leadership structure (4:1-28), Solomon's moral subversion at the hands of his wives (11:1-13), the subversion of Rehoboam at the hands of his cronies (12:1-24), Jeroboam's subversion of Yahwism (12:25-33), chaos in the south (14:21-15:24), chaos in the north (15:25-16:34), and Ahab's attempt to subvert Israel altogether (18:16-46).

The Pressure of Prophecy

The episodes on this trajectory describe relatively hostile degrees of encounter between the prophets of Yahweh and various political leaders. In order of appearance, they include Nathan's encounter with David (1 Kings 1:11-45), Elijah's encounter with Ahab (18:1-15), two unnamed prophets vs. Ahab (20:1-43), Micaiah vs. Ahab (22:1-28), and the Jehoash-Amaziah conflict (2 Kings 14:1-22).

The Pressure of Famine

Famine is a recurring theme in Kings and the problems generated by hunger drive a number of its episodes. Among these are the story of Elijah's miraculous feeding of a starving widow (1 Kings 17:1-24), the story of two miraculous feedings in Gilgal (2 Kings 4:38-44), and the fascinating story of Samaria's siege (6:24-7:20).

The Pressure of Frailty

Physical frailty is the primary challenge in the opening vignette about David's impotence (1 Kings 1:1-4), Ahaziah's injury (2 Kings 1:1-18), the story of Naaman (5:1-27), Elisha's "resurrection" (13:1-24), and Hezekiah's miraculous recovery (20:1-11).

The Pressure of Foreigners

The episodes on this important trajectory focus on Israel's struggle with Phoenicians, Edomites, Moabites, Arabs, Ammonites, Syrians, Egyptians, Assyrians, and the Babylonians. In order of appearance, they include Solomon's covenant with Hiram (1 Kings 5:1-13-7:12), the Sabean Queen's visit (10:1-13), Solomon's "edifice complex" (9:10-28; 10:14-29), Solomon's conflict with his adversaries (11:14-43), Elisha's encounter with Hazael (2 Kings 8:7-29), Israel vs. Assyria (14:23-29; 15:8-31; 17:1-6),

Judah vs. Assyria (15:1-6, 32-28; 16:1-20; 19:1-37), and Judah vs. Babylon (20:12-20).

The Pressure of Yahweh

Yahweh makes a personal appearance several times in Kings, twice in the Solomon cycle and twice in the Elijah cycle. The Solomon cycle is in fact bracketed by Yahweh appearances: first in a dream promising a blessing to the young king (1 Kings 3:1-15), finally as a warning to him about sin and judgment (9:1-9). Two theophanies bracket the Elijah stories too: the first in the private conversation between Yahweh and Elijah (19:1-18), and the second in Elijah's dramatic ascension into heaven (2 Kings 2:1-25). Yahweh's final "appearance" occurs in a summary diatribe where, in first-person speech, Yahweh soberly explains the exile, defends his actions, and warns Judah to change its ways or suffer Israel's fate.

The Pressure of Reform

Alongside stories of external repression and internal subversion, several episodes lay out a series of variously motivated, variously structured, and variously successful reform attempts. These include Solomon's Temple prayer (1 Kings 8:1-44), the ministry of the Judahite man-of-God (13:1-34), Ahijah's oracle against Jeroboam (14:1-20), Joash's restoration of the Temple (2 Kings 12:1-21), Hezekiah's decision to "trust" Yahweh (18:1-16), and Josiah's attempt to reform Judah (22:1-23:25).

The Pressure of Violence

Several episodes occur at the beginning, middle, and end of Kings, each designed to articulate something about Israel's struggle with the problem of violence. They include the story of David's dynastic decision, after experiencing the deaths of two sons and the rebellion of a third (1 Kings 1:28-2:12), the story of Joram's salvation (2 Kings 3:1-27), the story of two mothers fighting for their children's lives (2 Kings 4:1-37), the Aramean farce (6:1-23), Jehu's coronation and purge (9:1-10:36), Athaliah's reign of terror (11:1-21), and the final judgment of Judah's last four kings (23:36-25:30).

Why This Approach?

All this may sound "new," but the rabbis—to cite only one of the Bible's constituencies—have been practicing such methods for millenia.[24] Contemporary readers recognize Kings' intertextuality because the book itself often alludes to earlier biblical tradition. When Samaria falls to Assyria, for example, the narrator says:

> All this took place because the Israelites had sinned against
> Yahweh their God, who had brought them up out of Egypt from
> under the power of Pharaoh king of Egypt. They worshiped other
> gods and followed the practices of the nations Yahweh had driv-
> en out before them, as well as the practices that the kings of Israel
> had introduced (2 Kings 17:7-8).[25]

Another intertextual connection occurs from the other direction, in
Deuteronomy's famous "law of the king":

> The king, moreover, must not acquire great numbers of horses
> for himself or make the people return to Egypt to get more of
> them, for Yahweh has told you, 'You are not to go back that way
> again.' He must not take many wives, or his heart will be led
> astray. He must not accumulate large amounts of silver and gold.
> When he takes the throne of his kingdom, he is to write for him-
> self on a scroll a copy of this law, taken from that of the priests,
> who are Levites. It is to be with him, and he is to read it all the
> days of his life so that he may learn to revere Yahweh his God
> and follow carefully all the words of this law and these decrees
> and not consider himself better than his brothers and turn from
> the law to the right or to the left (Deut 17:16-20).[26]

But this does not mean that Kings only has intertextual structure. That
two houses have similar roofs says nothing about the furniture inside.
Likewise the mere presence of similar language in Kings and Deuteronomy says little about the structure or contents of the books themselves.
To minimize all intertextual comparison to this particular intertextual comparison inappropriately keeps alive a reading strategy which relies less on
the text itself than older European dichotomies about "history-vs.-faith."[27]
To help contemporary believers learn from these stories today we need
better, more helpful exegetical tools. In particular, we need to insure that
discussion about Kings' external "roof" (deuteronomistic language at critical points, particularly in the speeches) does not overly predetermine all
discussion about its internal "furniture" (the book's overall theological
thrust, for which the stories—as a whole—are the primary evidence).[28]

Intratextual approaches have been around a long time too. For those of
us already familiar with this exegetical tool, the nine trajectories suggested
above will not map out the entirety of Kings' intratextuality to everyone's

liking. But this is relatively unimportant. What is more important is the challenge before us to learn how to apply some sort of intratextual approach to these stories, so that newer generations of believers can rediscover them. All studies bring to the Bible their own ideological and methodological biases, and this one is no exception. For me, Kings speaks very effectively to the needs of (post)modern readers when read though an intertextual/intratextual lens. Tired attempts to segregate Kings' historical context from its literary structure are leading readers to overlook one of its most important theological themes: how to keep the faith under pressure. I believe we need to turn this around, because there's an awful lot at stake. The legacy of the maximalist/minimalist debate ought to be clear by now: we rarely hear these stories preached anymore, and when we do, often what we hear instead of the stories themselves are rationales for the destruction of Jerusalem,[29] or historical explanations for the exile,[30] or ideological explanations for God's judgment against sin.[31]

The time is ripe to release these stories from their cages. Intratextual approaches are not the final answer to our dilemma—to make such a claim would be arrogant. But they can make us more aware of Kings' intricate structure and awesome spiritual potential. By allowing these stories to interpret themselves, we can aim them more intentionally at struggling believers—not just professional scholars, but preachers and elders and Bible teachers and counselors and youth workers and worship leaders and chaplains and seminary students and all the other gifted people trying to serve Elijah's God. Kings is not simply about a God who punishes those who break his promises. It's also about how to keep the faith when we're pressured to break ours.

Notes

1. Gus Kahn, Raymond B. Egan, and Richard Whiting, *Ain't We Got Fun* (1921).

2. Billy Strayhorn, *Take the A Train* (1941); Glenn Miller, *Moonlight Serenade* (1939).

3. Pearl Jam, *Jeremy*, from the album *Vs* (Epic Records, 1995); Nirvana, *Smells Like Teen Spirit*, from the album *Nevermind* (DCG DCGD-24425, 1991).

4. Billy Joel, "Pressure," from the album *The Nylon Curtain* (CBS Records, 1982).

5. In this study, 1-2 Kings is simply "Kings."

6. See, e.g., V. Phillips Long, *The Art of Biblical History* (Grand Rapids: Zondervan, 1994).

7. See. e.g., M. Sternberg, *The Poetics of Biblical Narrative* (Bloomington, IN: University of Indiana, 1985) 431; G. Savran, "1 and 2 Kings," in R. Alter and F. Kermode, eds., *The Literary Guide to the Bible* (Cambridge, MA: Harvard, 1987) 146-64; J. T. Walsh, *1 Kings* (Berit Olam; Collegeville: MN: Liturgical Press, 1996) xi-xxi.

8. Responding to the critics of a previous generation, A. Heschel (*The Prophets*, vol. 2 [Peabody, MA: Prince, 1999; originally pub. in 1962] 195) pointedly asked whether it was "plausible to regard an utterance such as 'thus says the Lord' or 'the word of the Lord is like a burning fire in my bones'" merely as a "literary device." Heschel's spirit influences the present book.

9. Matt 19:4; 22:31; Mark 12:26 and passim.

10. This book is designed to be read with or without footnotes. Footnotes can be a help or a hindrance, depending on one's needs, and the footnotes below are given to serve the needs of those who want to go deeper into the discussions behind my discussion.

11. G. von Rad, *Old Testament Theology* (New York: Harper & Row, 1962; trans. from 1957 German ed.) I:334-47.

12. S. Grenz, *A Primer on Postmodernism* (Grand Rapids: Eerdmans, 1996).

13. R. Alter, *The Art of Biblical Narrative* (New York: Basic, 1981) 3.

14. W. G. Dever, *What Did the Biblical Writers Know, and When Did They Know It? What Archaeology Can Tell Us About the Reality of Ancient Israel* (Grand Rapids: Eerdmans, 2000) 23-52.

15. D. Edelman, "Doing History in Biblical Studies," in *The Fabric of History: Text, Artifact, and Israel's Past*, ed. D. Edelman (Shefield: JSOT Press, 1991) 13-25; David A. Dorsey, *The Literary Structure of the Old Testament: A Commentary on Genesis-Malachi* (Grand Rapids: Baker, 1999) 15.

16. George Lindbeck's philosophical work on "intratextuality" (*The Nature of Doctrine: Religion and Theology in a Postliberal Age* [Philadelphia: Westminster/John Knox, 1984]) is not the concern of this book.

17. P. Satterthwaite, "The Elisha Narratives and Coherence of 2 Kings 2-8," *TB* 49 (1998) 1-28.

18. Kings' ending is quite different from the ending of Chronicles. In Kings, Judah is still in Babylonian captivity (2 Kings 25:22-30), but in Chronicles Judah hears from Cyrus a gracious invitation to return home (2 Chron 36:22-23).

19. M. Noth, *The Deuteronomistic History* (Sheffield: JSOT Press, 1981; trans of 1943 German ed.) 80.

20. See my "David and His Teenagers," in *Reconciliation: A Study of Biblical Families in Conflict* (Joplin, MO: College Press, 1994) 49-60.

21. G. von Rad, *Studies in Deuteronomy* [SBT 9; Chicago: Henry Regnery, 1953] 74-91.

22. Fanny Crosby, *A Wonderful Savior* (New York: Hope Publishing, 1918).

23. J. Sanders, "Intertextuality and Dialogue," *BTB* 29 (1999) 35-44.

24. M. Fishbane, *Biblical Interpretation in Ancient Israel* (Oxford: Clarendon, 1985).

25. Pauline Viviano ("2 Kings 17: A Rhetorical and Form-Critical Analysis," *CBQ* 49 [1987] 548-59) recognizes that many see this passage as later justification for the fall of Samaria.

26. G. Knoppers ("The Deuteronomist and the Deuteronomic Law of the King:

A Reexamination of a Relationship," *ZAW* 108 [1996] 329-46) thinks that the presentation of Solomon in 1 Kings 1-10 revises the "antimonarchical stance" of Deut 17. Most other scholars see it the other way around.

27. J. Goldingay ("The Patriarchs in Scripture and History," in *Israel's Past in Present Research,* ed. V. P. Long [Downers Grove, IL: InterVarsity, 1999] 37-39) traces the maximalist/minimalist debate to the older *Heilsgeschichte* debate in 19th century European scholarship.

28. A good place to begin this discussion is the anthology edited by G. Knoppers and J. G. McConville, *Reconsidering Israel and Judah: Recent Studies on the Deuteronomistic History,* Sources for Biblical and Theological Study 8 (Winona Lake, IN: Eisenbrauns, 2000).

29. G. von Rad (*Studies in Deuteronomy,* 74-91) sees Kings as an attempt to explain why Yahweh, a God of infinite grace, postpones judgment for so long.

30. M. Noth (*Überlieferungsgeschichtliche Studien* [Halle: Niemeyer, 1943] 91, 95) sees Kings as a document written to justify the necessity of the exile.

31. H.-W. Wolff thinks ("Das Kerygma des deuteronomistischen Geschichtswerk," *ZAW* 73 [1961] 171-86) that the purpose of Kings is to show that "repentance works."

ONE

THE PRESSURE OF INJUSTICE

BATHSHEBA'S PLIGHT (1 Kings 1:11-31)

Bathsheba plays a pivotal role in the effort to make Solomon king, yet the contours of her character remain blurry. Certainly she plays the role of mediator in the prophet-politician encounter between Nathan and David, and this is not unusual given the other mediator-figures in Kings, not to mention the roles played by female mediators generally in the ancient Near East.[1] But this is not the only role she plays. By suturing two verses together, we can ascertain (a) that she is the daughter of a man named Eliam (2 Sam 11:3), and (b) that a man named Eliam is the son of Ahithophel, one of David's royal counselors (23:34). Whether these "Eliams" are one and the same person is not easily determined, however, and to complicate matters further, the only name we have in Chronicles is "Bathshua" (1 Chron 3:5). In other words, we simply cannot say for sure whether Bathsheba, as some confidently argue, is in fact the granddaughter of Ahithophel, regardless of how this might heighten the drama of this episode.

Faced with such sketchy details, many simply colorize her character. Alice Ogden Bellis, for example, portrays the young Bathsheba as "an innocent victim of (David's) lust."[2] Jon Levenson and Baruch Halpern view her not as a "victim," but as a shrewd conspirator who entraps David, then replaces him with the fruit of their sexual relationship.[3] Ken Stone takes an anthropological approach, suggesting that David's seizure of Bath-sheba is a classic example of a king abusing a subordinate (Uriah).[4] Gale Yee simply wonders whether the ambiguity in this text might not be part of the narrator's strategy; i.e., to force readers into making a judgment about her character.[5]

Initially, in 2 Samuel, Bathsheba is a "flat" character (Adele Berlin calls her an "agent") whose function is simply (a) to be a married woman and (b) to have adulterous sex with David.[6] Later, however, as Abishag replaces her (the new "agent" in David's life), her role matures from "sex-ual partner" to "favored wife" to "queen mother." This, Berlin feels, is why the second mention of Abishag the Shunammite attending him in 1 Kings 1:15 so strongly contrasts with the paragraph's opening description: "Bathsheba, who was once young and attractive like Abishag, is herself now aging, and has been, in a sense, replaced with Abishag, just as she comes for the purpose of replacing David with Solomon."[7] Later, when Adonijah comes to Bathsheba to ask for Abishag as a "consolation prize" (or more likely, as his "agent" to help bid for the throne), Bathsheba's response is measured and cautious. Either she is naïve, or indecisive, or, like Medea in Euripides' famous play, she intentionally plots revenge to try to cripple David.[8]

Intratextual Reflection

All these interpretations are interesting, but we need to examine them carefully against the story's intratextual context. Reading this story in this context allows us to see something which we would not otherwise see—that the story of "Bathsheba's Plight" is indeed the story of Bathsheba's *plight*. What many interpretations fail to observe is that this episode lies on a definable trajectory alongside several other episodes, each address-ing in some way the *pressure of injustice*. Not all of these stories are iden-tical, of course, yet the issues raised in "Helping the Homeless" (2 Kings 8:1-6), "Naboth's Vineyard" (1 Kings 21:1-29), and "Your Ears Will Tingle" (2 Kings 21:1-26) all resonate deeply with the issues raised here. Unlike the stories of Israel's neighbors (Hittite, Canaanite, Mesopotamian), bibli-cal stories take us deep into the lives of socially marginalized people as well as rich, powerful people.

Both Bathsheba and the homeless Shunammite, for example, are powerful women forced by tragic circumstances to beg for help. The par-allels are remarkable. Both women lose their sons: Bathsheba at the hands of Yahweh (2 Sam 12:18); the Shunammite via an unnamed illness (2 Kings 4:21). Both women find themselves marginalized by circumstances beyond their control: the Shunammite by famine; Bathsheba by Jerusalem's ever-shifting political winds. Both women work alongside Yahweh prophets to get their message through to the king: Bathsheba with Nathan; the Shunammite with Elisha. Both women have their sons' lives prophetically saved: Elisha miraculously; Nathan politically. Like Naomi, the Shunammite has to figure out how to deal with issues involving the preservation and maintenance of her ancestral land (Ruth 3:1). Like Esther, Bathsheba has to figure out how to save innocent blood-kin from impending destruction (Esth 4:11).

The point of deepest parallel (and deepest pain) comes when each mother has to summon up her courage and go before the king. Having just lived with the Philistines for seven years, the Shunammite returns to Israel only to find herself thrust into an unjust situation, the loss of her ancestral estate. Bathsheba's plight is even more desperate. Waiting for David to keep his promises, she wakes up one morning to find herself thrust into the dangerous role of "rival queen mother." The "son of Haggith" (Adonijah) and the "son of Bathsheba" (Solomon) cannot occupy the same throne at the same time.

Clutching at straws, she apparently decides that the only way out of her dilemma is to beg for mercy. Otherwise both she and her son will become criminals (lit., "sinners," *hatta'îm*). This story unflinchingly shows us the harsh realities of an unjust situation. Life can become hard when promises are ignored and land is seized, when children are sacrificed and covenants are broken. This theme is a raw nerve in Israel's collective memory, throbbing constantly, nagging persistently. Bathsheba's plight is the same as Naboth's, the peasant farmer who stands up to his powerful king. Her pain is the same as that which engulfs all those parents who watch in horror as Manasseh kills their children in ritual human sacrifice. Preservation is what motivates this mother, not aspiration.

Theological Reflection

I know another mother who is fighting hard, like Bathsheba, to save her son. She wants to save him from many things: financial bondage, social ruin, spiritual death, marital anguish—all the demons which haunt young people today. The odds against her are daunting. Her ex-husband, the boy's biological father, is physically abusive, religiously fanatic, sexually perverse, and emotionally disturbed. Instead of providing for his son, he stalks him like a predator. Between bouts of drunkenness and joblessness, he shows up to harrass his ex-wife and frustrate his son, even when court orders are supposed to keep him away.

This son loves his mother very much and wants to love his father, but he is so full of rage, he doesn't know what to do. Because of this rage, no one really knows what to do with him, either. Our church has tried valiantly to incorporate him into the youth group, but it's not working. He picks too many fights with the other kids. Other parents are asking his mother and the youth minister to "do something" about him—but no one really knows what to do. He has enough rage inside him to fuel twenty teenagers.

In addition to this, Mom is dying of a terminal disease. Many doctors have pronounced her incurable, and many times her friends have taken her to the emergency room. Her only wish now is to see her son graduate from high school, a request she puts before the Lord every day. Her plight poignantly reminds me of Bathsheba's plight, and leads me to suggest the following possibilities for interpreting this text.

First, life isn't always fair, and stories—especially biblical stories—don't always have contrived happy endings. We need to be honest. To argue otherwise is to live in a fantasy world, not the world of Scripture. Who knows what Bathsheba is thinking when she first receives that summons from David? Who knows what she feels when she first hears the news about Amnon's murder, then Absalom's rebellion, then Adonijah's coronation? Certainly David's death does not consign her to a future as hopeless as, say, Hindu widows who throw themselves on their husband's funeral pyres (the rite of *suttee*, "widow-burning").[9] Yet does she ever in her wildest dreams imagine that she will have to plead for her son's life from his own father?

Second, justice is often postponed. To put it another way, people do not always do justice on our timetables. As in the story of Tamar, sometimes there's a long wait (Gen 38). As in the story of Jesus, sometimes justice fails to be meted out in this life at all. Naboth's relatives watch helplessly as Ahab and Jezebel get away with murder. The parents in Manasseh's kingdom lose their children to the horrors of child sacrifice. "They did not see the things promised; they only saw them and welcomed them from a distance" (Heb 11:13).

Third, God remains faithful. One of the members of our church, for example, has anonymously taken on this family as a special project. Checks arrive monthly to pay for rent and food and court costs and medical bills and anything else she needs. Just as Nathan helps Bathsheba, so God uses a Christian businessman to save his sister. Faithfully and regularly the checks come, even as his own children need college tuition and mortgage down-payment money. He doesn't just talk about serving; he serves. He doesn't stand around complaining about the "irrelevancy of the Church."

PHENOMENAL WISDOM (1 Kings 3:16-28; 4:29-34)

Immediately after his encounter with God, Solomon receives the opportunity to move from promise to practice. Where Yahweh promises him a "listening heart" at Gibeon (*lêb shômê`a*), here he gets a chance to exercise this heart. This sequence, *promise > practice*, is familiar to readers of the Bible. Immediately after Saul becomes king (1 Sam 10), for example, Nahash the Ammonite challenges him (1 Sam 11), and this gives Saul the opportunity to prove his mettle. David too, after Samuel's anointing (1 Sam 16), immediately confronts Goliath (1 Sam 17).

Here Solomon faces quarreling prostitutes.

Interesting choice. From all the stories at his disposal—and there must have been several—the narrator chooses this story to showcase Solomon's remarkable intellectual gifts. His leadership challenge comes not through the conceit of an Ammonite or the arrogance of a Philistine. It comes through the heart of a mother in pain. Like all great stories, this one can be interpreted in several ways: "traditional folktale,"[10] "mystery story,"[11] "anecdote,"[12] "common tale,"[13] "detective story,"[14] "kidnap story,"[15] "riddle."[16] These are just some of the more frequently suggested.[17] Structurally, however, this episode can be viewed as a series of ever-widening circles, each generated by the introduction of a new character. The first comes in the allegations of the first prostitute. The second comes in her roommate's response. The third comes in Solomon's decision. And the fourth comes in Israel's reaction.

The action starts in a mother's heart. Nothing pejorative is said about her status as a "prostitute" (*zônâ*).[18] More important is her status as a "mother" (*'êm*). When she speaks to Solomon, she tells her side of the story in raw language, uncensored and unvarnished. The allegations she makes are serious; kidnapping is a very serious offense. Yet beneath all the emotion, we can deduce from her testimony little factual information. A child has died. We do not yet know whether it's her baby or her friend's. We do not know if the death is from negligence or malevolence.

While passing on her testimony, the narrator reveals something pivotal in the line, "But when I looked at him closely...." Up to this point, this lady has not realized what has happened, but this changes as soon as she stands back and reflects on the facts. The word here is an important one in the Solomonic tradition. "Look closely" (*NIV*) is a translation of the Heb verb *bîn*, "to discern, gain insight," and it's one of the key words in Proverbs: "The proverbs of Solomon son of David, king of Israel: for attaining wisdom and discipline; for understanding words of insight" (Heb *lehabîn…bînâ*; lit., "for discerning…discernment," Prov 1:1-2).

That it is reflexive here (*'etbônen*) implies that the act of looking repeatedly at the dead baby causes her to rethink her situation. This language is intentional because the narrator is suggesting that her "sudden" realization is not all that sudden. Discernment is essential to the decision-making process, whether one speaks of the business of government or the business of family. Discernment is hard to come by, especially when truth is obscured beneath competing agendas wrapped in slick layers of rhetoric. At such times, one really needs a "listening heart."

Yet discernment is incomplete without faith. Summoning up this faith, she takes her case to court. She pleads her case to the king, and though there are gaps in her testimony, she mounts a compelling argument.[19] Before she can conclude it, however, the second prostitute butts in. The king listens to her testimony, too, and when he commands the remaining child's death, she seems perfectly willing to comply: "Neither yours nor mine shall he be. Cut!" Offering no alternative to the first woman's testimony, she simply agrees with the king's "solution."[20]

All eyes now look to Solomon. What should he do? To believers, this dilemma feels familiar, because the response here looks so much like Jesus' response when he asks Jerusalem's leaders: "John's baptism—was it from heaven, or from men?" (Mark 11:30). Like Solomon's "test-decision," Jesus' penetrating question cuts through the rhetoric of his plaintiffs and forces them to decide their priorities. Solomon does the same thing. Refusing to take sides, he calls for a decision—a life-or-death decision, a now-or-never decision. Boldly he slices through his audience's presumptions about "truth." Everyone here realizes that only one of these plaintiffs can be the child's mother. So, like Christ, he calls their bluff. He brings these women to the precipice of their lives and dares them to jump. That's when we hear the true mother cry out, "Please, my lord, give her the living baby! Don't kill him!"

No wonder Israel stands in awe. Discernment like this is rare.[21] The people who hear the Sermon on the Mount walk away dumbstruck too. According to Matthew's account, they walk away "amazed" (a word which can also mean "panic-stricken," or "astonished").[22] Likewise Solomon's audience experiences "fear" (*yare'*) before "the king's face" (*mippenê hammelek*). Underlining this further, the narrator concludes his story by setting it in an historical context. What Solomon receives from Yahweh is not just "insight," it's "exceedingly great insight" (*tebûnâ harbeh me'od*, 4:29). Solomon's discernment is able to encompass liturgy and ethics, individuals and nations, the arts and the sciences. In fact, it's superior to the wisdom of all the men of the East and all the wisdom of Egypt.

Intratextual Reflection

Powerful and moving, this story is but one voice in a larger chorus. Understanding who these voices are and how they harmonize with each other can help us appreciate more fully the meaning of this particular episode.[23] We can read this episode alongside other wisdom narratives in the Old Testament.[24] We can also read it alongside other episodes in Kings. Previous interpretation of this text tends to focus on Solomon and exclude the story's other characters, but an intratextual reading will go in a different direction. In many ways this mother is the story's main character, not Solomon. This person has a lot in common with other mothers in Kings, like Bathsheba (1 Kings 1:11-21), the widow of Zarephath (17:17-24), the prophet's wife (2 Kings 4:1-7), the Shunnamite woman (4:8-37), and the Samarian mothers (6:26-29).

Perhaps the closest parallel, however, is the story of Naboth (1 Kings 21:1-29). Even as Ahab steals Naboth's inheritance, so this prostitute has her inheritance stolen. Just as Naboth suffers at the hands of a cruel woman (Jezebel), so this woman suffers at the hands of a cruel woman (her roommate). What kind of person steals another person's baby, then lies about it? Human cruelty can be obstinate and pervasive, yet the story's ultimate purpose is to generate hope. Just as Israel eventually witnesses Jezebel's death, so this mother eventually receives justice.

Theological Reflection

Once I conducted a wedding in which two sisters had not spoken to each other in a decade. Seems that one of them had become pregnant out of wedlock while her sister, happily married, could not get pregnant. Working out their dilemmas together, they hastily decided that the barren sister should adopt the fertile sister's child. So, without thinking, they signed the papers. Two weeks later, the child's biological mother experienced great pangs of conscience and demanded her baby back. This created an enormous rift, and this was tragically compounded by the baby's death a few months later from Sudden Infant Death Syndrome (SIDS).

Now their little sister was getting married, and she wanted both of her sisters to participate in the wedding. Bravely she asked them to read a famous passage of Scripture together—Paul's poem on *agape*-love in 1 Corinthians 13. At rehearsal, everyone wondered what would happen. Would they do it? Would they work together? It was a tense moment. I'll never forget the feeling in our hearts when both sisters stood up on cue and hit their marks. Nor will I ever hear Paul's words the same way again: "Love is patient, love is kind. It does not envy, it does not boast, it is not proud. It is not rude, it is not self-seeking, it is not easily angered, it keeps no record of wrongs. Love does not delight in evil but rejoices with the truth. It always protects, always trusts, always hopes, always perseveres" (1 Cor 13:4-7).

The women in 1 Kings 3 could have chosen the path of forgiveness and reconciliation, but one of them chooses to cocoon herself in the role of "victim," and this forces the other, after an experience of discernment, to stand up and fight for justice. What can we learn from this story?

First, we might approach it as a text about justice. Repeatedly we see this theme in Kings, and repeatedly we see it in contemporary life. Whether it's a mother fighting for her cancer-stricken son to graduate with his class,[25] or a mother pleading for her baby before "ethnic-cleansing" butchers,[26] this kind of story always hits hard. Maternal suffering is only one kind of suffering, certainly, but it's one of the most universal. Sometimes it's a grandmother having to decide whether to fight for the life of her unborn grandchild.[27] Sometimes it's a mother forced to watch terrorists murder her children.[28] The psalmist knows well our need to see justice:

> They sit in ambush in the villages; in hiding places
> they murder the innocent (Psa 10:8, *NRSV*).

Second, we might focus on "the least of these." God's people take seriously the needs of the poor and the marginalized, like this prostitute. As I write these lines I am ashamed of my own culpability. Years ago I gave a lecture series at a colleague's church, and ran into a lady I did not recognize at first. Then, after remembering her name, I asked her about her husband, a student of mine from years past. Her face changed color. "You haven't heard?," she asked. "He's in prison for embezzlement." Shocked by the news, I could only stammer out, "Where?"—to which she replied, "Not far from where you live. Will you go visit him? Please?" Well, I promised her I would, but her hastily scrawled request has not yet found its way to my daytimer. Why haven't I kept my promise? Perhaps I don't think I have the time. Perhaps I don't want to take the time. Perhaps I don't see the relevance of Jesus' words, "I was in prison and you came to visit me." My behavior is different from Solomon's. He doesn't just promise justice. He delivers it.

Third, we might focus on the theme of mission. The pursuit—not just the awareness, but the pursuit—of justice is central to our Mission. Addressing himself to pious, yet ignorant people, Jesus once says: "Woe to you, scribes and Pharisees, hypocrites! For you tithe mint, dill, and cummin, and have neglected the weightier matters of the law: justice and mercy and faith. It is these you ought to have practiced without neglecting the others. You blind guides! You strain out a gnat but swallow a camel!" (Matt 23:23-24). By climbing Calvary, Jesus proves to us that he's no camel-swallower. Similarly, Solomon proves that he's no ivory-tower geek. Solomon has a mission, the one Yahweh gave him at Gibeon, and he intends to fulfill it. That's why he gets involved in what a lesser leader might consider smarmy or vulgar.

NABOTH'S VINEYARD (1 Kings 21:1-29)

Jezreel is a tiny village nestled in the rolling hills of Issachar (Josh 19:18). Saul prepares for his final battle here (1 Sam 29:1), Solomon barely mentions its existence (1 Kgs 4:12), and Pharoah Shishak doesn't mention it at all in his lists of captured cities.[29] Anonymity is one of its primary attractions. Jezreel is a rustic hideaway off the beaten path, a place where harried kings like Ahab can "get away from it all." Jezreel is Ahab's "Camp David," if you will, a place to get away from the pressures which make kings like Ahab "sullen and angry" (20:43).

What happens on this particular "getaway weekend," however, makes Ahab very "sullen and angry" (21:4).[30] Having just concluded a real estate deal in Damascus (20:34), Ahab comes home to find that he can't even close a simple land deal with his next-door neighbor. The way he treats Naboth stands in sharp contrast to his treatment of Ben-Hadad (1 Kings 20). With the Syrian king he shows "grace" and "mercy" (at least his version of it). But not Naboth. Why?

Kingly hubris is not a minor biblical theme. David commits adultery with Bathsheba and murders her husband to cover it up. Saul destroys an entire village out of pure rage. Solomon ignores Yahweh's warnings about idolatry and wanders off into the worship of foreign gods. Manasseh burns Israel's children in the fires of pagan sacrifice. Jehoiakim attacks Jeremiah by shredding his oracles into pieces and burning them.[31] Yet the story in this passage stands in a category all its own. Compared

to other examples, this one shows us a king who not only murders innocent people in cold blood, he actually involves a whole community in it.
He turns Naboth's neighbors into a lynch mob. This behavior is so
depraved, it's hard to find anything else quite like it in Scripture.[32]

Plutarch, however, tells a similar story about a certain Athenian politician named Pausanias.[33] Pausanias is famous for expelling the Persians
from Greece, but in the process he alienates many of the very Athenians
he wants to save. Athens is embarrassed by him because his treatment of
others is vicious and cruel. Misrepresenting all that is good about Greece,
he makes Athens look like another famous city, Rome—a city Paul
describes as "foolish, faithless, heartless, and ruthless" (Rom 1:31).

To highlight his depravity, Plutarch contrasts him with one of his gen-
erals, Cimon. Where Pausanias "holds treasonable conference with the
barbarians, writes letters to the king, treats the allies with harsh arrogance, and displays much wantonness of power," Cimon "receives with
mildness those who bring their wrongs to him."[34] In his arrogance,
Pausanias summons a young virgin to his bed. She consents to go, but
only on the condition that all the lamps in his bedroom be extinguished
(probably so she won't have to see what's about to happen to her).
Drawing near in the dark, she accidentally stumbles against one of the
lamps and knocks it over. Pausanias leaps up from sleep and instinctively stabs his "attacker," murdering an innocent girl whose only "crime" is
to be in the wrong place at the wrong time.

In other words, Pausanias is very much a Greek version of Ahab, and
Plutarch tells this story because he wants his students to recognize the
fundamental differences between moral and immoral leadership. For
kings in the ancient world, it is "evil...to be wanton" (Plutarch),[35] and two
of the most relevant biblical texts in this vein are Deut 17:18-20 (the "law
of the king"—see the Introduction), and Ezek 46:18: "The prince must not
take any of the inheritance of the people, driving them off their property. He is to give his sons their inheritance out of his own property, so that
none of my people will be separated from his property."

Men like Pausanias and Ahab care less about ethics than they do
about power, and this is why prophetically-minded writers like Plutarch
and this biblical narrator so ardently oppose them. Where Pausanias
"holds treasonable conference with the barbarians," Ahab makes back-
room deals with the Syrians. Where Pausanias writes libelous letters,
Jezebel writes libelous letters. Where Pausanias "displays much wantonness of power and silly pretension," Ahab pouts like a child when he
doesn't hear the answer he wants. Where Pausanias murders an innocent

victim, Ahab murders an innocent victim. The main difference between these stories is that in lieu of a counterbalancing protagonist (Cimon), the biblical story defers its protagonist until later (Jehu), choosing instead to show us three overlapping layers of conflict.

First, Ahab and Naboth disagree over how to define "worth" (*mehîr*, v. 2). To Naboth, "worth" is an idea rooted in covenant inheritance (*nahalâ*). To Ahab, "worth" is a variable commodity generated by the ups and downs of the real estate market. To Naboth, "worth" is a theological idea anchored in historical tradition. Israelites like Naboth recoil from the argument that Israelites might buy and sell "ancestral land" (*nahalâ*) like any other kind of "land" (*'erets*). Where Naboth believes that ancestral *nahalâ* is "price-less," Ahab believes that everything has a "price" (*mehîr*)—land, inheritance rights, slaves, personal responsibility. Everything is for sale in Ahab's world.

That's why Elijah condemns him. Josephus thinks him guilty only of "killing a citizen unjustly, contrary to the laws of his country,"[36] but this analysis is more Roman than Hebraic. The Hebrew text is very clear about this king's behavior and the motives behind it. Elijah condemns Ahab because he "sells himself" into evil (v. 25): "There was never a man like Ahab, who sold himself to do evil in the eyes of Yahweh." Later, in the programmatic summary of 2 Kings 17, all Israel is condemned for "selling itself into evil-doing." In other words, it's not the murder, nor is it the "selling" *per se* which so angers the prophets. It's the desire to sell "evil" (*ra`â*) under the guise of religion ("Proclaim a fast...he has cursed both God and the king"). This is what nauseates the prophets.

Second, Ahab and Jezebel disagree over what it means to "act as king." Ironically, the question she puts to her husband is a good one: "Is this how you act as king over Israel?" Should a leader withdraw and pout when things don't go right? Jezebel knows what makes an effective leader. Like Pausanias (or Lady Macbeth, or Hamlet's mother Gertrude), Jezebel is a "get-it-done," "ends-justify-the-means" kind of leader. To her, how one closes a deal matters little. What's important is to close the deal, even if means cutting an innocent man's throat and covering it up with religious red tape. Jezebel responds to her husband's distress by delegating his problem to Jezreel's town council, the elders and the nobles. For Jezebel, this is how one "acts as king." This is how one takes control. We have already seen how her oath alone can terrify the prophets (1 Kings 19:2); writing a few nasty letters and stamping them with the royal seal is not going to be a problem. This is how one "acts as king," even when it alienates people.

Third, Elijah and Ahab disagree over the meaning of "justice." To Ahab, "justice" is an unrealistic expectation generated by religious fanatics enslaved to a mythological past. We see this in Obadiah's dealings with Elijah (chap. 18). Perhaps Ahab, like Obadiah, suspects Elijah of being a "religious flake," a weakling who cannot survive in the "real world" of hardball politics. Maybe he thinks that the "real world" is a place where the rules have to be broken now and then. In the film *Liar, Liar*, attorney Fletcher Reade (Jim Carrey) tries to explain this principle to his son: "Adults have to lie, Max. Otherwise, how is Daddy going to make partner?"[37]

Elijah doesn't buy it. Ahab is a murderer and a thief, and no amount of smoke-and-mirror plea-bargaining is going to change this fact. Just like the scene on Mt. Carmel ("How long will you limp between two opinions?"), Elijah here asks another pivotal question: "Have you not murdered a man and seized his property?" Ahab has not "executed" a criminal (Heb *qatal*)—he's "murdered" a brother (*ratsah*). Jeremiah uses this word in his temple sermon, along with a few other words from the Ten Commandments (Exod 20:1-17): "Will you steal (*ganab*) and murder (*ratsah*), commit adultery (*na'ap*) and perjury, burn incense to Baal and follow other gods you have not known, and then come and stand before me in this house, which bears my name, and say, 'We are safe'—safe to do all these detestable things?" (Jer 7:9-11)

We could compare this story with its echo in 2 Kings 9:21-26, but even if one version can be proven to be dependent on the other (and it can't), such a theory would not necessarily imply that the narrator wants to "exonerate" Ahab here.[38] The more balanced view is that Kings gives us synoptic accounts of this tragedy—one focusing on Ahab's role (2 Kings 9), the other on Jezebel's (1 Kings 21). From 1 Kings 21, we do not know whether Ahab already knows about his wife's plot—all we know is how gleefully he reacts to the news of Naboth's death. He jumps out of bed and runs to "inherit" (*yarash*) his new vegetable garden. He does not mourn or grieve. He does not chastise or question his wife. Fresh cucumbers are more important to this man than human life.

When Elijah confronts him, Ahab seems to grieve in response, but the text is ambiguous. Does he humble himself (*nikna`*) out of grief, or out of the frustration of getting caught? Humbling can be quite involuntary (Lev 26:41). As with Job's response to Yahweh (Job 42:6), it is problematic to call every fearful response to the deity "repentance."[39] Yahweh eventually ameliorates Ahab's punishment by postponing it, but this says more about Yahweh than it does about Ahab. Yahweh ameliorates Solomon's punishment too (1 Kings 11:34-39). The literary point is that Ahab's response to Elijah looks very much like his response to Naboth. Again he "lies down" (*shakab*, vv. 4, 27) and "fasts"/"refuses to eat" (*tsûm, lo' 'akal,* vv. 27, 4). Ahab nowhere "admits sin" (*hattâ*) or "pleads" (*baqash*) or "worships" (*yishtahû*) or contemplates "changing course" (*shûb*). His response, in other words, is an exact opposite of David's (1 Sam 12:16-20; Psa 51:4, 14).

Intratextual Reflection

Yahweh is a God of justice. True prophets emphasize this, and false prophets deemphasize it, marginalize it, or simply ignore it. To say this is a central prophetic theme is the "mother of all understatements." Micah, for example, castigates those who "covet fields and seize them, who defraud a man of his home, a fellowman of his inheritance (*nahalâ*)" (Mic 2:2). Isaiah condemns the "stubborn-hearted" who choose to live "far from justice" (Isa 46:12). Jesus warns his disciples that unless their justice "surpasses that of the Pharisees and the teachers of the law," the Kingdom will remain nothing more than a well-intentioned idea (Matt 5:20).

"Naboth's Vineyard" is one of several episodes on a trajectory including stories like "Bathsheba's Plight" (1 Kings 1:11-31), Solomon's "Phenomenal Wisdom" (3:16-28; 4:29-34), "Helping the Homeless" (2 Kings 8:1-6), and "Your Ears Will Tingle" (21:1-26). Each of these episodes shows us a God who is deeply concerned about the problem of justice, but perhaps the closest parallel is "Helping the Homeless" because the theme common to both these stories is the problem of land. What generates land disputes? How are land disputes to be adjudicated? What do such adjudications say about a given culture's value-system?

In 2 Kings 8, a Shunammite leaves her land on Elisha's advice and goes to live with the Philistines (like David in 1 Sam 27:7). Here Naboth "leaves" his land, too, though the famine driving him away is a famine of justice, not food. When the Shunammite returns, she discovers that her land is no longer hers, and this causes her to "cry out" (*tsa'aq*, vv. 4, 5). In the Covenant Code, this word has special meaning: "Do not take advantage of a widow or an orphan. If you do and they cry out (*tsa'aq*) to me, I will certainly hear their cry. My anger will be aroused, and I will kill you with the sword" (Exod 22:22-24). Where the Israelite king successfully repatriates the Shunnamite, however, Naboth suffers permanent expatriation—not just his physical death, but the destruction of his children's inheritance. Both of these cases highlight contrasting Israelite responses to injustice, and each illustrates the tenuousness of Israel's grand socio-economic experiment with land.[40]

One obvious application is to ask, "To what lengths should we go to fight against injustice today when it means involving ourselves in messy land disputes on behalf of the poor?" Hernando de Soto argues persuasively that the international poor have considerable financial assets, but that they're simply not legally recognized; stubborn bureaucracies in developing countries are too interested in preserving their own power to allow those "outside the system" to experience financial prosperity.[41] Davie Napier thinks the Church has yet to face this question seriously because we first have to face the larger question behind it—what he calls the question of "adjacency." Adjacency occurs when A and B are adjacent parties. B's property, which is B's by inheritance, becomes in its adjacency an object of desire on the part of the more powerful A. Often A simply takes over B, either by changing the law or bankrupting the owner or some other legal means. Thus, Ahab's seizure of Naboth's vineyard is like Iraq's seizure of Kuwait in 1990, or the systematic seizure of land from aboriginal Americans in the 1800s. This problem "is perennially acted out in this remarkable human family of ours with demonic craft by the powerful, in an absolutely dazzling array of forms, upon well-established but shamelessly fraudulent justification, usually in the broad sense religious and sometimes even specifically theological."[42]

There are exceptions, of course, but it's distressing to see so many wealthy Christians participating in adjacency, particularly when we do it "according to God's holy ordinance...even in the name of Jesus Christ.... You know, in God we trust."[43] Napier is not the only believer embarrassed by this shameful history. Olive Shreiner feels the same way about the behavior of the old South African government: "We know, none so well, how stained is our African record; we know with what envious eyes the Government of English Ahabs eyes the patrimony of Black Naboths and takes it, if necessary, after bearing false witness."[44] In North America, however, the problem generates little more than a yawn:

> In common practice in organized religion in the United States we have let our Jezebels set the stage for the effective dispossession of the inheritance of land, resources, productivity, and human dignity of weaker neighbors declared to be adjacent to us all around the globe. The vast majority of us in the Church are able to live like relative Ahabs because Jezebel is scheming schemes and working works around the clock—in our name and, as it works out, also to our profit.[45]

Strong words. Biting words. Whether we agree with them or not, covetousness is not something from which anyone can claim immunity. The tenth commandment, after all, specifies several kinds of covetousness (Exod 20:17), and most have more to do with power than money. "If necessity is the mother of invention, then covetousness and lust are the parents of ingenuity."[46] What covetousness is not is simply a matter of political preference or ideology, as if somehow "capitalism equals covetousness," therefore "socialism equals compassion." Equations like these are dangerously simplistic. The truth is that the ownership of property has always been a problem for believers.[47] The problem is acute, however, because as "Americans grow wealthier and wealthier, money is becoming a kind of narcotic for us. We hardly notice our own prosperity or the poverty of so many others."[48]

When interpreting this story we therefore need to be clear that private property is not in itself an avenue to "virtue." Naboth is not automatically virtuous because he has a *nahalâ* to defend. At Qumran, the sectarian Essenes wrestle mightily with this problem, though contrary to popular belief, communalism was not a universal practice there. More likely "use was communal, but ownership was private."[49] And lest we forget, we need to remember that the Church's first recorded crisis comes out of the conflict between private property and corporate governance (Acts 5:1-11). Obviously this is an old debate, but Naboth dramatizes its contours in a powerful way, forcing us to face these questions head-on.

Theological Reflection

The film *Hurricane* tells the story of Rubin "Hurricane" Carter, a man sent to prison for a crime he claims not to have committed.[50] In the early 1960s, Carter is an up-and-coming middleweight contender, but on June 17, 1966, someone murders three white men in a New Jersey bar, and the authorities arrest Carter for it. He goes to jail for the crime, and while there he begins writing an impassioned autobiography, *The Sixteenth Round*.[51] Every time it looks as if he might get out of prison, a white judge sends him back to prison, usually on grounds based more on "racism rather than reason" (according to one federal judge).

Yet far away from his prison three Canadian friends befriend an illiterate black teenager in Brooklyn. Eventually they bring this teenager to Toronto to help him with his education, and while learning to read, Lesra picks up a copy of *The Sixteenth Round*. The book touches his heart, and he gets involved in a crusade to get Carter out of jail. Finally, after many legal, social, and racial obstacles, Lesra and his Canadian friends succeed in springing Carter from prison. Bob Dylan sings about Carter's ordeal in his song, "Hurricane," and in a way which angrily criticizes the justice system. Like Naboth's Vineyard, Carter's story teaches us two important truths.

First, evil people are not stupid. Jezebel does not call in the "Jezreel mafia" to do her dirty work—she goes after Naboth through "proper legal channels." The Ku Klux Klan does not destroy Hurricane Carter's life—the federal court system does. Judges and lawyers know how to bend the law to suit their own purposes. In their haste to "act as king," many simply lose their balance and paint themselves into a moral corner. Some admit it. Some don't. Injustice is most often perpetrated by good people who decide to do nothing in the face of evil. "Shallow understanding from people of good will is more frustrating than absolute misunderstanding from people of ill will."[52] Paul tells Timothy that the law (*nomos*) is good, but when fame-hungry people "handle" (1 Tim 1:8) it unlawfully, faithful leaders have to rise up and defend the flock. Some of Timothy's contemporaries, for example, are "shipwrecking" the faith (1:19). That is, they are focusing on peripheral matters like "genealogies" and "myths" instead of important matters like justice and mercy. Both of these texts, one from the OT and one from the NT, need constantly to be preached if we are to remain clearheaded about the Gospel.

Second, leaders like Ahab are going to face "payday someday." Veteran preachers will recognize this catchy phrase immediately, because it's the title of a famous sermon by the great Baptist preacher R. G. Lee. Lee characterizes Naboth as "a devout Israelite…who abhorred that which was evil." Ahab is a "vile human toad who squats upon the throne of his nation…a mean and selfish rascal." Jezebel is a "painted viper…a beautiful and malicious adder coiled upon the throne of a nation." Elijah is "God's tall cedar wrestling with the pagan cyclones of his day without bending."[53]

Of course, these are "flat" characterizations of complex characters, and though we might quibble with their rigidity, Lee's sermon still punches home a prophetic truth: God sees, God remembers, and "the wages of sin" is still "death" (Rom 6:23). We can stop preaching these texts when dictators stop abusing the poor, when CEOs stop sacrificing their employees on the altar of greed, when land developers stop bribing local officials to "see things their way," and when seminary professors stop putting academic fame ahead of their students' needs.

HELPING THE HOMELESS (2 Kings 8:1-6)

Though it may not seem immediately obvious, Kings is filled with stories about desperate women. It's a rather long list—Bathsheba, the two prostitutes, a Sabean queen, Jeroboam's wife, the Zarephath widow, the Phoenician princess Jezebel, the preacher's widow, the wealthy Shunammite, the starving Samarian mothers, the queen-mother Athaliah, the prophetess Huldah. Each of these characters is complex and fascinating and easily caricatured by interpreters in a hurry.[54] What's interesting about this particular woman, however, is her sudden reappearance. We've seen her before. This is the well-to-do woman from Shunem (2 Kings 4:8). Here she's "the woman with the restored son," and the titular distinction is important because the king only knows her by the latter title. That he really doesn't know *her* is the irony driving the whole episode. Elisha does know her, and his concern for her situation is what motivates him not just to resurrect her son, but to fight for his inheritance.

When Elisha advises her to leave the country, we know from the Naboth story that this is hard for an inheritance-minded Israelite to do.[55] Yet she obeys her prophet, even though a decision to leave one's inheritance is a decision to jeopardize the name of one's ancestors.[56] In fact, not only does she leave, she takes up residence with the Philistines, undergoing a major shift in her social status—from "great woman" (*'ishâ gedôlâ*) to "legal alien" (*gêr*).[57] By doing this, she demonstrates her faith in the prophetic Word, and thus becomes an example for all believers.

When the famine lifts, she returns to Israel to take back her land, but like Naomi (another refugee), she has to find a creative way to argue her case. Like Naomi, she lives in a paternalistic culture with which she has lost touch—resettlement is a problem because (a) geographical mobility is not easy to factor into pre-monarchical economics, and (b) monarchical economics shifts attention away from the built-in safety-nets previously provided by the Mosaic Code. The prophets complain about this often. Leaders—even transitional leaders—have a responsibility to take care of widows, not marginalize and oppress them.[58] Many prophetic oracles warn about this (Isa 1:17; Jer 7:6; Zech 7:10; Luke 18:3), but here the warning comes to us in a memorable narrative about a woman who falls from "great woman" to "homeless refugee" status.

Re-entering Samaria, she overhears Gehazi conversing with the king about the many great things for which Elisha has become famous. This conversation, of course, only camouflages and postpones the conversation which needs to take place. By split-screening the action, the narrator wants us to contrast the king's academic interests with the interests of this woman. It's one thing to talk about great things. It's another to do great things. It's one thing to "make others live." It's another to help them stay alive.

Intratextual Reflection

This story resonates with at least three others. First, it resonates deeply with the stories of Naomi and Tamar (Ruth 1:1-4:18; Gen 38:1-30). Like the Tamar story, this episode is about a man who needs to decide whether he wants to be a man of integrity. Just as Judah has to decide whether to help his daughter-in-law, so this king has to decide whether to help this Shunammite. Both men eventually respond positively, of course, but not without difficulty. Judah does the right thing only after Tamar tricks him into it. This king helps the Shunammite woman only after she cries out. Like Naomi, she has to endure a lot of pain first—a theme common to the stories of "Bathsheba's Plight," "Naboth's Vineyard," and "Your Ears Will Tingle."

Leaders often camouflage reluctance behind various sorts of façades. Once an elder came to me frustrated by the fact that so many profession-al women were leaving our church to find church homes elsewhere. He just couldn't understand their problem. "Why are they leaving?" he would ask. "What's their problem?" When I tried to explain to him that he would leave, too, were he forced every week into humiliating silence, he looked at me as if I had suddenly started speaking in Latin. He just doesn't real-ize how unjust it is to treat Christian sisters like second-class citizens in the name of "biblical submission."

Of course, overreaction is as undesirable as under-reaction. Contemporary debates over whether there might be "several goddesses" or just "One Goddess," for example, would be incomprehensible to this Shunammite.[59] The heroine of this story is not considering renouncing Yahwism altogether. On the contrary, what she wants is what the prophets want—covenant justice. She understands that the Hebraic faith is different from the polytheism of its neighbors—seven years among the Philistines has no doubt convinced her of that! She simply realizes that Lady Wisdom's (Prov 8:23) only real competitor is Lady Stupidity (9:13)—not Lady "Narcissus" or Lady "Victim."[60]

Second, this story raises critical issues about land reform. In Phoenix, where I live, land developers are as plentiful as gecko-lizards. People make and lose fortunes daily in the land business. Church foyers are full of talk about land pricing, land availability, land financing, land speculation, land development, but rarely is there much talk about land reform. I know at least one realtor, however, who thinks this ought to change. Speaking to my ethics class one evening, he described an incident in which he helped a destitute single mother buy her first home. He made all the financial arrangements for her. He set up her mortgage. He convinced the bank to take a chance on her. He contacted the title company and pulled a few strings. He went far beyond the call of duty with this lady, shelling out hundreds of dollars of his own money.

Then one day he got a letter from her lawyer, stating that she was suing him for "failing to keep the home properly maintained." This lady actually went behind his back and sued him because he had not fixed a leak in the roof—the roof he had just put over her head! When the class heard this, they just sat there in shock. They couldn't believe it. Here was an individual actually trying to do justice, and the homeless person he was trying to help was kicking him in the teeth.

"What did you do next?" someone asked. "How did this make you feel?"

"I felt like I was serving Christ," he replied.

"Did this make you wary of helping anyone else?" someone asked, irritated by his placid response.

"Wary, yes," he said, "but using our gifts to serve others is not an option for us."

"You mean … you'd do it again?" someone squeaked.

"Do it again?," he laughed. "I'm doing it now." Then he told us about the work he was doing in Mexico, building houses for homeless people in shanty towns like Tecalote and Tijuana. In spite of our bad experiences, he urged us passionately, we must remain dedicated to the principles of biblical justice.

Third, many of the Elisha stories have intertextual echoes in the NT, and this one is no exception. In Luke 18, Jesus tells a parable to his disciples "to show them that they should always pray and never give up." He tells a story about a widow whose constant persistence drives a grizzled magistrate into doing the right thing. He emphasizes that it's not the magistrate's disinterestedness which needs emulating, but the woman's persistence. Finding justice takes persistence and patience and prayer, and the point of Christ's parable is that we should "never give up."

Christianity does not concern one small aspect of our lives, leaving the rest unaffected—it is about bringing our entire existence, the way we think and the way we act, into line with the model given to us in the crucified and risen Christ. Far from being just the basis of a 'private' or 'interiorised' religion, the Cross opens the way to a radical and authentically Christian approach to ethics and politics.[61]

Theological Reflection

Some time ago one of my students, a physically-challenged lady who jets around in a wheelchair, had a run-in with the Social Security Administration. This government agency exists to help people who can't work full-time. In this lady's case, she could work, but when she discovered that her paycheck was exceeding the limit set by the S.S. Administration, she duly reported it, and, receiving confirmation of her report, continued to work at the legal income level. Years later she got a terse letter not only revoking all her benefits, but demanding $47,000 from her as "over-payment."

When the seminary community found out about this injustice, we took up her cause. We posted her name on the e-mail prayer-chain. We started calling meetings and asking for donations. We got some wonderful Christian attorneys involved. The outpouring of concern so overwhelmed this lady, she literally did not know how to respond—nothing like this had ever happened to her before. Like the Shunammite, she cried out for justice—and she got it. Eventually we got a settlement from the S. S. Administration, and we learned several things from this experience.

First, when faced with a breakdown of "the system," nothing replaces faith. More specifically, nothing replaces faith-community. The resurrection of the Shunammite's son helps launch her faith, but the crisis of her homelessness brings Elisha into the picture. The benefits of practicing faith under pressure are incalculable, but not just for homeless refugees. After years of fighting with hostile white judges, for example, attorney Fred Gray writes in his autobiography about how "grateful" he is "for the unusual opportunities...to enjoy intellectual contact with the finest representatives of the white race"—and this from the lawyer who represented Rosa Parks in the 1955 Montgomery boycott.[62]

Second, we need to learn how to demand justice in culturally appropriate ways. Sometimes it's more effective to take a collection than call in a TV reporter. Sometimes it's more appropriate to engage in intercessory prayer than ideological tirades. Better to be patient and persistent. Better to focus on the Dream instead of the Enemy.

YOUR EARS WILL TINGLE (2 Kings 21:1-26)

Jerusalem falls prey to the Babylonians, in part, because Manasseh succumbs to the detestable practices of the nations (*tô`abôt haggôyim*). With priestly rigor the narrator lists several of these practices, most of which we can see in earlier chapters. Some think that he unfairly scapegoats Manasseh by ignoring the tradition of his repentance and restoration recorded in 2 Chron 33:11-18.[63] Others suspect that the Chronicler's memory is too clouded by a desire to rescue the Davidic house from "pollution."[64] This is an old debate. All we will point out here is that Kings' narrator offers his audience a prophetic explanation for Jerusalem's destruction, and that this explanation focuses on Manasseh as a typical "evil leader."[65] Kings is less interested in rescuing David's reputation than in underlining the connection between detestable practices (*tô`abôt*) and exile (*gôlâ*).

Tô`abôt is not a rare word. Elsewhere it denotes the detestable practices of homosexuality (Lev 18:22; 20:13), covetousness (Deut 7:25), idolatrous worship (12:31; 13:15), cross-dressing (22:5), non-kosher eating habits (14:13), prostitution (23:19), defective sacrifice (17:1), divination/sorcery/witchcraft (18:12), and moral bankruptcy (25:16). Both priestly and prophetic writers use the term some 116 times in the Hebrew Bible, and the phrase we find here, *tô`abôt haggôyim* ("detestable practices of the nations"), resonates loudly in prophetic Yahwism's "Holy-of-Holies" passage: "When you enter the land Yahweh your God is giving you, do not learn to imitate the detestable practices of the nations" (*tô`abôt haggôyim*, Deut 18:9).[66] At any rate, the narrator uses this term to describe the detestable practices of three Judahite kings: Rehoboam (1 Kings 14:24), Ahaz (2 Kings 16:3), and Manasseh (21:2). The Chronicler ameliorates the legacies of these kings, but Kings reminds us that Manasseh is neither the first, nor the only Judahite king to succumb to the detestable practices of the nations (*tô`abôt haggôyim*).

In Chronicles, Manasseh is a "prodigal son" character.[67] By repenting and praying, he becomes a role model for every other Jew trying to find the way "home." This, in fact, is the Chronicler's main point: if Manasseh can repent and change, then any Jew can. Yet we know more about his historical context than we do about him. According to Kings, after Sennacherib leaves Jerusalem and returns to Nineveh, he falls prey to an assassination plot. Like Absalom and Adonijah, Sennacherib's sons Adrammelech and Sharezer plot against their own father: "One day, while he was worshiping in the temple of his god Nisroch, his sons Adrammelech and Sharezer cut him down with the sword, and they escaped to the land of Ararat." Then a third son lunges into the power vacuum: "And Esarhaddon his son succeeded him as king."[68]

Esarhaddon tells us "the rest of the story." From his perspective, Sennacherib (his father) overlooks him and gives unfair precedence to his older siblings. After Sennacherib's death, however, the gods (especially Ishtar) confirm Esarhaddon as king, and this empowers him to fight for the throne against his siblings. Ishtar encourages him to do this through numerous divination-inquiries, because his brothers "forsake the gods, trust in their own haughty deeds, and hammer out evil plans."[69] Obviously this is propagandistic jargon, but still it shows how bad things are in 7th century Nineveh. The biblical writer focuses on Sennacherib's hubris and aggression, while the cuneiform sources show us what's going on behind the scenes. While Sennacherib is away, Adrammelech and Sharezer succeed, according to Esarhaddon, in "angering my father's gentle heart toward me...though deep in his heart he felt compassion for me and remained intent on my assuming the throne."[70] Very much like the David-Amnon-Absalom-Adonijah-Solomon succession, the Sennacherib-Adrammelech-Sharezer-Esarhaddon succession is a chaotic mess.

How can this help us explain Manasseh? Well, we know from Esarhaddon's annals that Manasseh participates with 22 other vassals in transporting building material to Assyria (*ANET* 291), and we also know that he gives tribute to Esarhaddon's son, Assurbanipal (*ANET* 294). But where his grandfather (Ahaz) tries to emulate Assyrian religion, Manasseh apparently ties to emulate Assyrian law. We know this from the Vassal Treaties of Esarhaddon (*ANET* 534-41), which, when examined alongside the curses in Deut 28, show similarities so remarkable, it's hard not to see direct literary dependence between these documents.[71] How exactly this happens—and what role Manasseh plays in it—this narrator does not elaborate because his concern is to portray Manasseh as just another wicked king. Instead, what we have are three barbed metaphors aimed at Manasseh's Judah—a construction metaphor, a housework metaphor, and a communication metaphor:

> I will stretch out over Jerusalem the measuring line used against
> Samaria and the plumb line used against the house of Ahab.
> I will wipe out Jerusalem as one wipes a dish, wiping it and turn-
> ing it upside down.
> I am going to bring such disaster on Jerusalem and Judah that
> the ears of everyone who hears of it will tingle.

Intratextual Reflection

Ever hit an inside fastball so far up the handle, it stings your hands? How about the "funny bone?" Ever hit that tiny crevice on your forearm just below the elbow, and feel the voltage shoot up to your shoulder like a bolt of lightning? Apparently Judah knows the feeling because they have a word for it—*tsâlal*. English translations usually translate it "tingle," but this word can mean much more than just "tingle." It can mean "shock" or "dismay" or "wonder" or "amazement."

Construction Metaphor. Few people enjoy job evaluations. Many of us would rather have a root canal than a job evaluation. When I worked in a Connecticut shipyard, everyone hated it when the guys in the light blue hats showed up—the inspectors. Even though we knew that their job was to examine our work and tell us whether to replace this valve or repressurize that system, their work still annoyed us. But what happens when inspectors don't inspect?

The results can be disastrous. On Aug 14, 2000, for example, the Russian nuclear submarine Kursk went down in the Barents Sea in over 400 feet of water. None of the 118-man crew survived. Hundreds of Russian mothers and fathers bitterly lamented the loss, recognizing it as one more sign of an increasingly incompetent military machine. Why, they ask, is our once-mighty Russian navy falling apart at the seams? Why are Russian boys going to their deaths in deathtrap machines?

Tough questions. Here's a few more.

Why do some preachers think that their preaching will automatically improve? Why do some counselors think they can become better healers without reading a single book or undergoing a single peer-evaluation? Why do some youth pastors think that zeal alone qualifies them to mentor troubled teenagers? Why do some lay leaders think that, because they've successfully built a business, this automatically qualifies them to pastor churches? What kinds of plumb lines are we using? Are they appropriate? Do they work?

Housework Metaphor. The other day our dishwasher sprang a leak, a "disaster" we discovered when the carpet started turning brown. What a mess! I did not grow up in a home with a dishwasher, but it didn't take me long to realize that I hadn't washed dishes by hand in a while. Washing dishes is hard work! Sometimes you actually have to soak a dirty dish overnight in order to loosen up the cooked-on grime.

This is what prophetic theology does—loosens up the grime. Prophetic theology is like hot dishwashing liquid, the stuff we use for the grimiest dishes and the filthiest silverware. Jesus once illustrated it this way: "Woe to you, teachers of the law and Pharisees, you hypocrites! You clean the outside of the cup and dish, but inside they are full of greed and self-indulgence. Blind Pharisee! First clean the inside of the cup and dish, and then the outside also will be clean" (Matt 23:25-26). Jesus emphasizes that righteous leaders will clean up the inside as well as the outside of their lives, and the reason he does is because so many of us believe we can do one without the other.

Communication Metaphor. Ever hear a message so prophetic it makes your ears tingle? Once I heard Mike Yaconelli attack hypocrisy within the Church in a way that made my ears tingle for days.[72] First, he listed what many in the Church want youth ministry to be—a "safe place for kids," a "training ground for future adult Christians," a "place to have fun." Then he dared to talk about what youth ministry ought to be—a place to discover Christ, a place to be disturbed by the Gospel, a place to foment counter-cultural community. Afterwards I asked a student what she thought about the speech, and her response was memorable: "He made me see my sin." What a simple, clear definition of prophetic theology. Prophetic theology is supposed to make me see my sin. Here are a few ways to apply this truth.

Theological Reflection

First, we need to start listening more intentionally to our consciences. Manasseh doesn't suffer from a "wavering heart," like Solomon. Manasseh suffers from a calloused heart, like Jezebel. Once I asked a friend to meet me for lunch because I had solid evidence from several reliable sources (his daughters, his sons-in-law, his friends and co-workers) that he was having an extra-marital affair. Arriving at the restaurant first, I asked God for wisdom: "How do I minister to this brother? How do I help him deal with this sin? How do I help this marriage?" Soon he showed up, and for the first 15 minutes or so, all he wanted to talk about was his new church—its possibilities, its problems, its needs, its programs. Valiantly he resisted every effort I made to steer the conversation back to his marriage and its needs. Finally, I just looked him in the eye and asked him whether there was anything he wanted to tell me. Staring back, he said "No"—and to this day he has never told me the truth about his affair. He's going to a different church now—they always do—but to my knowledge he has not yet made things right with the people he has wounded.

Second, we need to stop marginalizing the Mission. We need to stop confusing "our needs" with Christ's claims. We need to stop passing our children through the fires of negligence. We need to stop listening to the soothsayers of self-indulgence and self-recrimination. When I enrolled in college, I signed up to be a music major my first year because I was convinced that music was my calling. One of my professors, a visiting missionary, took it upon himself to challenge the wisdom of this choice. He asked me to go to Brazil with him that summer and work with some of the new churches he had planted. "This way," he said, "you can really find out what God wants." To his constant invitations, however, I kept giving him the same excuse: "I have to work this summer and save money for school next fall. I can't go with you on some wild-eyed mission!"

Finally he said, "I'll make a deal with you. If you will call your home church, and they refuse to help you, I'll leave you alone. I'll never mention Brazil again." Well, that seemed fair enough. "Knowing" my home church, I walked over to the pay phone outside the library and called one of the elders, a man I had known since my childhood.

"Mr. Wells?"

"Yes?"

"Can you do me a favor?"

"Sure. What do you need?"

"Well, I've got a problem. I have this teacher, see, and he keeps bugging me about going to Brazil with him this summer. I've already told him I can't go, but he won't leave me alone. In fact, he ..."

Mr. Wells interrupted—"How much do you need?"

Tingle.

"Excuse me? Mr. Wells, you don't understand. I'M NOT GOING! I DON'T EVEN WANT TO GO! I'm just calling you because if you tell me you can't help, then he'll leave ..."

Mr. Wells interrupted me again, pronouncing the words more slowly this time:

"How ... much ... do ... you ... need?"

I almost dropped the phone. Not knowing what to say in response, I simply mumbled out the price of the airfare, and the voice on the other end of the line said (I'll never forget it!),

"Where do I send the check?"

TINGLE.

Have you ever had an experience so powerful, it makes your ears tingle?

Truth be told, my ears are still tingling over that one.

Notes

1. See my "Wise Women in the Bible: Identifying a Trajectory," in C. D. Osburn, ed., *Essays on Women in Earliest Christianity*, vol. 2 (Joplin, MO: College Press, 1995) 87-103.

2. Bellis, *Helpmates, Harlots, Heroes: Women's Stories in the Hebrew Bible* (Louisville: Westminster/John Knox, 1994) 149. Bellis, however, distinguishes between the "flat" character in 2 Samuel and the "developed" character in 1 Kings.

3. J. Levenson and B. Halpern, "The Political Import of David's Marriages," *JBL* 99 (1980) 507-18.

4. K. Stone, *Sex, Honor and Power in the Deuteronomistic History* (JSOTSup 234; Sheffield: Sheffield Academic Press, 1996) 102-7.

5. G. Yee, "'Fraught with Background': Literary Ambiguity in 2 Samuel 11," *Int* 42 (1988) 240-53.

6. A. Berlin, "Characterization in Biblical Narrative: David's Wives," *JSOT* 23 (1982) 69-85.

7. A. Berlin, *Poetics and Interpretation of Biblical Narrative* (Winona Lake, IN: Eisenbrauns, 1994) 28.

8. Commentators are divided. A. Berlin (*Poetics*, 29) sees Bathsheba as "cunning" and "jealous" of Abishag. David Gunn (*The Story of King David: Genre and Interpretation* [JSOTSup 6; Sheffield: JSOT, 1978] 137) thinks this is ludicrous. J. P. Fokkelman (*Narrative Art and Poetry in the Books of Samuel*, vol. 1 [Assen: Van Gorcum, 1981] 394) tries to find a middle ground between these extreme opinions.

9. E. Thompson, *Suttee: A Historical and Philosophical Enquiry into the Hindu Rite of Widow-Burning* (London: G. Allen & Unwin, 1928).

10. Nelson, *Kings*, 37.

11. Walsh, *Kings*, 78.

12. DeVries, *Kings*, 57.

13. W. Brueggemann, *1 Kings* , Knox Preaching Guides (Atlanta: John Knox, 1982), 13.

14. M. Sternberg, *The Poetics of Biblical Narrative* (Bloomington, IN: Indiana University, 1985) 167.

15. H. C. Brichto, *Toward a Grammar of Biblical Poetics: Tales of Prophets* (New York: Oxford, 1992) 50-51.

16. S. Lasine, "The Riddle of Solomon's Judgment and the Riddle of Human Nature in the Hebrew Bible," *JSOT* 45 (1989) 61.

17. H. Gressmann ("Das salomonische Urteil," *Deutsche Rundschau* 130 [1907] 212-14) lists no fewer that twenty-two variants of this story in several literatures from several cultures.

18. Some rabbis speculate that these women are "spirits" (on the supposition that real harlots would care nothing about offspring). Others think they are "sisters-in law" (*Cant. Rab.* 14).

19. If she is asleep, though, how does she know for sure that it's her housemate who switches the babies? See E. & G. Leibowitz, "Solomon's Judgment," *Beth Mikra* 35 (1989-90) 242-44.

20. Gary Rendsburg ("The Guilty Party in 2 Kings 3:16-28," *VT*[1998] 534-41 argues

that the first prostitute is the offending party.

21. S. Lasine, *Knowing Kings: Knowledge, Power, and Narcissism in the Hebrew Bible,* Semeia Studies 40 (Atlanta: Scholars, 2001) 1-38.

22. Matt 7:28. The Gk word is *exeplêssonto,* from the verb *ekplêsso.* The English word "plague" (lit., a "striking") comes from this word.

23. G. Knoppers thinks (*Two Nations Under God* [HSM 52; Atlanta: Scholars, 1993] 1.80) that the text's intention is to show "not simply that Solomon is wise in a specific way, but that his wisdom, encompassing many different dimensions, renders him an incomparably successful king."

24 G. W. Coats ("The Joseph Story and Ancient Wisdom: A Reappraisal," *CBQ* 35 [1979] 285-97) sees a parallel with the Joseph story because in both stories the central hero appears faultless. Coats thinks that such stories seek to demonstrate to future administrators the proper way to manage difficult situations.

25 L. Baker, "Teen Gets Commencement OK, Honorary Diploma," *The Arizona Republic* (April 14, 1999, www.azcentral.com/news/0414dvwin.shtml).

26 M. O'Connor, "Serbs in Kosovo Said to Rely Now on Arrest and Torture," *New York Times* (Dec. 11, 1998, http://www.nytimes.com/library/world/europe/121198 cosovo-milosevic.html).

27 C. W. White ("Why Abortion Matters Most," *CT* 33 [1989] 33-37) argues passionately that Christians should not be more concerned with things like education and the testing of anti-satellite weapons than with the fates of unborn babies.

28 This is what happened to the family of Pastor Aleksandr Kulakov in the village of Groznya, Chechnya ("Prayer Update," *Fresh Fire Ministries,* Vol. 2, Issue 15, for the week of 4/11/99 [e-mail newsletter from fireministries@hotmail.com]).

29 B. Mazar, "The Campaign of Pharaoh Shishak to Palestine," *VTSup* 4 (1957) 37–66.

30 The narrator uses the phrase *sar weza`ep* ("sullen and angry") as a catchword bridge linking Ahab's misfortunes at Aphek (chap. 20) to this incident (chap. 21).

31. 2 Sam 11; 1 Sam 21; 1 Kings 11; 2 Kings 21; Jer 36.

32 H. Rand ("David and Ahab: A Study of Crime and Punishment," *JBQ* 24 [1996] 90-97) thinks that the main difference between this story and Uriah's murder is the way in which this leader seduces an entire town into his crime. Notice that the elders (*zeqenîm*) and nobles (*horîm*) here play roles similar to the silly bureaucrats in 1 Kings 20.

33. Plutarch (50–120 AD) is a Greek scholar from Chaeronea, a little town approximately eighty miles northwest of Athens. His *Lives* represent some of the earliest (and best) biographies of Graeco-Roman leaders. Shakespeare, for example, bases his Julius Caesar on Plutarch's biography of Caesar (B. Perrin, ed. and trans., *Plutarch's Lives* [LCL; Cambridge, MA: Harvard, 1914–26]).

34. Plutarch, *Cimon* 6.2.

35. Plutarch, *Cimon* 6.2.

36. Josephus, *AJ* 8.13.8. D. Marcus ("Civil Liberties Under Israelite and Mesopotamian Kings," *JANES* 10 [1978] 53-60) argues that the abuses by David in the Bathsheba affair and by Ahab in the taking of Naboth's vineyard both illustrate laws to which kings must be subject. Both Israelite and Mesopotamian kings are subject to *kînatû,* "correct behavior" (*CAD* K, 383-84).

37. Directed by Tom Shadyac (Universal Pictures, 1997).

38. A. Rofé ("The Vineyard of Naboth") argues for the priority of the story in 2 Kings 9:21-26, but M. White ("Naboth's Vineyard and the Legitimation of a Dynastic Extermination") argues for the primacy of the story in 1 Kings 21.

39. See my "Job's Text of Terror," *CBQ* 55 (1993) 674-75.

40. L. R. Bailey, "Exodus 22:21-27," *Int* 32 (1978) 286-90.

41. H. de Soto (*The Mystery of Capital: Why Capitalism Triumphs in the West and Fails Everywhere Else* [New York: Basic, 2000]) reckons that the "undocumented holdings" of the poor are worth more than $9.3 trillion.

42. Davie Napier, "The Inheritance and the Problem of Adjacency: An Essay on 1 Kings 21," *Int* 30 (1976) 8-9.

43. Napier, "Inheritance," 5.

44. O. Schreiner, *A Track to the Water's Edge: The Olive Schreiner Reader* (H. Thurman, ed.; New York: Harper & Row, 1973) xxvii.

45. Napier, "Inheritance," 10.

46. Napier, "Inheritance," 5.

47. J. Sobran, "Christians and Private Property," *Center Journal* 2 (1983) 79-84.

48. W. Brueggemann, *Deep Memory, Exuberant Hope* (Minneapolis: Fortress, 2000) 69.

49. L. Schiffman (*Reclaiming the Dead Sea Scrolls* [New York: Doubleday, 1994] 110) suggests a similar explanation for the behavior in the early Church (Acts 5:1-11). A. Malherbe ("The Christianization of a Topos (Luke 12:13-34)," *NT* 38 [1996] 123-35) sees parallels in Graeco-Roman sources, like Dio Chrysostom, to explain Luke's views on covetousness.

50. Directed by Norman Jewison (Universal Pictures, 2000).

51. Published in 1974, *Sixteenth Round* is presently out-of-print. Meanwhile see J. S. Hirsch, *Hurricane: The Miraculous Journey of Rubin Carter* (Boston: Houghton Mifflin, 2000).

52. Martin Luther King, Jr., "Letter from the Birmingham Jail" (http://almaz.com/nobel/peace/MLK-jail.html).

53. Robert Greene Lee, *Payday Someday and Other Sermons* (Nashville: Broadman and Holman, 1995) 16-18. Lee died in 1978.

54. The literature on women in the Bible is vast; see the bibliography in *Joshua, Judges, Ruth* (NIBCOT 5; Peabody, MA: Hendrickson, 2000). Comparatively little work has been done on how the deuteronomistic historian portrays women, however, and more specifically, how Kings portrays women.

55. Precisely how long one can retain ownership while absent is an oft-debated question among the rabbis (e.g., *b. B. Qam.* 60b).

56. T. J. Lewis, "The Ancestral Estate (*naḥălat 'elôhîm*) in 2 Samuel 14:16," *JBL* 110 (1991) 597-612.

57. F. Spina, "Israelites as *gerîm* ('Sojourners') in Social and Historical Context," in *The Word of the Lord Shall Go Forth: Essays in Honor of David Noel Freedman* (eds. C. L. Meyers & M. O'Connor; Winona Lake, IN: Eisenbrauns, 1983) 321–35.

58. W. Brueggemann, "The Liturgy of Abundance, the Myth of Scarcity," in *Deep Memory, Exuberant Hope* (Minneapolis: Fortress, 2000) 69-75.

59. A. Long, "The One or the Many: The Great Goddess Revisited," *Feminist Theology* 15 (1997) 13-29.

60. C. Camp, *Wise, Strange and Holy: The Strange Woman and the Making of the*

Bible (Sheffield: Academic Press, 2000). See also my "Wise Women or Wisdom Woman? A Biblical Study of Women's Roles," *RQ* 35 (1993) 147-58.

61. A. McGrath, *The Mystery of the Cross* (Grand Rapids: Zondervan, 1988) 19.

62. F. Gray, *Bus Ride to Justice* (Montgomery, AL: Black Belt Press, 1995) 355.

63. B. Halpern argues ("Why Manasseh Is Blamed for the Babylonian Exile: The Evolution of a Biblical Tradition," *VT* 48 [1998] 473-514) that Kings blames Manasseh for the catastrophe of the Babylonian exile.

64. W. Schniedewind argues ("The Source Citations of Manasseh: King Manasseh in History and Homily," *VT* 41 [1991] 450-61) that 2 Chron 33:11-18 reworks the account of Manasseh's "repentance" in the same way 2 Chron 12:6-8 reworks the account of Rehoboam's "repentance."

65. C. Evans, "Naram-Sin and Jeroboam: The Archetypal *Unheilsherrscher* in Mesopotamian and Biblical Historiography," *Scripture in Context II: More Essays on the Comparative Method,* ed. W. W. Hallo, J. C. Moyer, L. G. Perdue (Winona Lake, IN: Eisenbrauns, 1983) 114, 124.

66. S. Grenz has a discussion in *Welcoming But Not Affirming* (Louisville: Westminster/John Knox, 1998) 36-47, and I have a review in *BBR* 10 (2000) 143-46.

67. J. Charlesworth preserves the text of his apocryphal prayer in *The Old Testament Pseudepigrapha*, vol. 2 (New York: Doubleday, 1985) 625-27.

68. 2 Kings 19:37. Esarhaddon means "Assur has given a brother."

69. *ANET* 289-90 preserves R. Campbell Thompson's 1931 translation, but S. Parpola (*Assyrian Prophecies* [SAA 9; Helsinki: Helsinki University, 1997] lxxii-lxxv) uses Rykle Borger's 1956 translation.

70. Ibid.

71. The evidence is impressive: (1) The same curse motifs occur in the same sequence in VTE § 39, 40, 42 (*ANET* 538) and Deut 28:27-30 (skin-disease, darkness, and violated wife); and (2) The same kinds of motifs occur in VTE §§ 63-64 (*ANET* 539) and Deut 28:23-24 (sky and earth made of metal, rain transforms into coal and ashes). That there are parallels between motif sequences and curse combinations shows that these are not random parallels.

72. Christian Communication Network broadcast, Sept 7, 2000, "Youth Pastor's Forum with Mike Yaconelli."

Two

THE PRESSURE OF SUBVERSION

THE ANXIETY OF AMBITION (1 Kings 1:5-10, 41-53)

David's attitude creates a leadership vacuum into which Adonijah finds himself reluctantly drawn. Amnon and Absalom have already perished here (Amnon at the hands of Absalom, 2 Sam 13:29; Absalom at the hands of Joab, 18:14), so one might imagine that Adonijah ("Yah is my lord") has learned something about this peculiar danger. Apparently he has not, however, because he too "lifts himself up" and gathers around himself the requisite horses, chariots, and "fifty men to run" (like Absalom, 2 Sam 15:1). Power vacuums can be irresistibly strong.

A rabbinic legend says that Adonijah's coup fails because "he attempts to fit the crown on his head, but it won't fit" (*b. Sanh.* 21b). The Canaanites also preserve a legend in which a god, Athtar, is found hilariously unfit to replace Baal, though unlike the rabbinic Adonijah, Athtar's problem is with his feet, not his head. He cannot fill Baal's shoes, literally, because his legs are too short (*UNP* 154). The Greeks tell similar stories about Zeus vs. Prometheus and Oedipus vs. his sons.[1]

Compared to such characters, David Marcus thinks, Adonijah looks like an unwitting "dupe"[2]—but this may be pushing the meaning of the text too far. All the text actually says about their relationship is that "his father never interfered with him by asking, 'Why do you behave as you do?'" More precisely, the MT says "his father never *grieved* him (`atsab*),"[3] and this is a very interesting word. Isaiah portrays Israel, for example, as a wife with a "grieving spirit" (Isa 54:6, `atsûbat rûab*), and Daniel's king calls out to him in a "grieving voice" (Dan 6:20, *qol `atsîb*). Perhaps David does not want to "grieve" Adonijah because he thinks him too emotionally damaged to handle parental discipline, given the rape of his sister and the violent deaths of his brothers.

Whatever his reasons, David's parenting strategy backfires, and this leads his family into a tragedy of Olympian proportions. Several parallels can be drawn, for example, between David's relationship with Adonijah and Apollo's relationship with his son Ion.[4] In Euripides' famous tragedy, Apollo ravishes Kreousa, an Athenian princess. In Kings, David ravishes Bathsheba (2 Sam 11:3; 23:34), possibly the granddaughter of one of his advisers (Ahithophel). In *Ion*, Apollo shows a passive-aggressive response to his son. In Kings, David expresses passive-aggressive behavior as well, and not just toward Adonijah—prior to this we see a *pattern* of passive-aggressive behavior toward his children. In this story it's hard to know whether the greater tragedy lies in David's passive-aggression or Adonijah's adolescent desperation.[5]

At any rate, Adonijah apparently believes he can succeed where his brothers have failed. He enlists the aid of David's old guard because he needs their help to consolidate power. By excluding Benaiah and Zadok in the process,[6] however, and most significantly, Nathan, he makes a fatal mistake. Instead of sitting down with *all* of his advisers and hammering out a vision, he retires to a "smoky back room" and tries to manipulate the situation. David responds by making Solomon his successor, and Adonijah learns of this decision in a typically indirect way. Just as Philistine warriors learn of the ark's arrival by distant shouting (1 Sam 4:6), so Adonijah learns of his rival's coronation from a distance. Panicking, he runs to the horns of the altar for sanctuary, but this gesture proves as ironic as it is pathetic. These horns are designed to tie down live victims for sacrifice.

At this point Solomon makes his first official appearance by responding to Adonijah's plea. "If he shows himself to be a worthy man, not a hair of his head will fall to the ground; but if evil is found in him, he will die." Like all of his pronouncements, Solomon's words are presented to us as a careful balance of wisdom and mercy.

Intratextual Reflection

Several stories address Israel's subversion problem, and each is a secret passageway into a huge subterranean cave. In other ancient histories this cave is usually left unexplored, but Kings not only explores it, it invites us to go along for the ride. Like all leaders, Israelite monarchs spend a good deal of time worrying about their positions. Take, for example, the various intrigues surrounding Sennacherib, the Assyrian king who traps Hezekiah "like a bird in a cage" (*ANET* 288). Eventually he becomes trapped by his sons, who assassinate him (2 Kings 19:37). One also thinks of Herod, the Idumean puppet who murders not only the babies of Bethlehem, but also his own wife and children.[7] Shakespeare dramatizes this tendency in *King Lear*, the story of an aged monarch who desperately cries out for release from "ingrateful" men.[8]

One might, therefore, after reading such stories, muster up *some* sympathy for Adonijah because, after all, *his* subversive behavior seems tame when compared to other leaders in Kings. Yet all of these stories stand on the same trajectory, and taken together, they reveal to us a side of Israel we would probably rather not see. Each story pulls us deeper and deeper into the bowels of a decaying institution. Each stands as a sequential fulfillment of Samuel's original woe-oracle (1 Sam 8:18-19). Israel's leadership problem is deep, and it gets deeper every time a king resists the prophetic Word. With every selfish intrigue, with every backroom deal, with every whining sycophant, with every terrorist attack, the narrator wants us to reflect on the implications of this behavior.

Compare, for example, the story of Adonijah with the story of Athaliah (2 Kings 11:1-21). Each of these stories is a commentary on the other. Adonijah is foiled by a female relative, Bathsheba; Athaliah is foiled by a female relative with a similar-sounding name, Jehosheba. Adonijah is outmaneuvered by a concerned religious official, Nathan; Athaliah is outmaneuvered by a concerned religious official, Jehoiadah. Adonijah is unseated by Hebrews who appeal to David for help; Athaliah is unseated by Hebrews using "the spears and shields that belonged to King David."

The parallels are striking, but there's more beneath the surface. In the first story, Adonijah declares himself king and withdraws to the countryside, taking with him his father's aging cronies. The first of Kings' subversion stories, the tone of this opening episode seems almost gentlemanly. A callow young prince follows the advice of his friends and leads a bloodless coup "for the good of the country." That he refuses to consult the will of Yahweh or gauge the political backlash to this decision seems almost comical in retrospect.

Not so the Athaliah story—this is a text of terror. What looks like a bloodless transition with Adonijah turns into a genocidal bloodbath under Athaliah. All of the main components of the earlier story repeat themselves here, yet this usurper responds to her power vacuum by going on a bloody rampage, not a countryside retreat. Here the climate is ruthless, not civil. To read these stories in intratextual sequence is to recognize that subversion eventually becomes an "acceptable" succession strategy in Israel, and once this happens, bloodless revolutions turn into genocidal massacres. What are the implications of this development?

Theological Reflection

Years ago one of the catchers on my Little League team was a 12-year old boy with a Johnny Bench physique and a *prima donna* attitude. He looked like a catcher, but he was such a whiner, none of the other kids wanted to play with him. Whenever he took the field, he gave his usual 60% effort (!), but whenever he sat the bench, he whined and sulked like…well, like a peacock prince in search of a throne. His father was the prototypical "nightmare-parent." Often showing up to games drunk, this guy would scream and yell like an idiot whenever someone struck out or blew a play. He never praised. He just screamed at mistakes—and his decibel level really increased whenever his son sat the bench. One time, in the middle of a close game, he actually flew down from his seat in the stands and poked the befanged noses of his two Dobermans through the chain link fence (I'll never forget the feel of those cold snouts on my back!). By means of such pathetic displays he tried to force us to play his son.

Harry Hagan sees the Adonijah story like this. Like my Little League story (which I've told and re-told so many times, my wife is sick of it), this story has all the earmarks of a classic farce: "the dotty old king, the proud peacock son, the wily prophet, the distraught mother.., the reign which lasts the length of a feast." Hagan sees this episode as something "written by an ideological ancestor of Molière,"[9] yet what we have in this story is much more than mere entertainment. What we have is a prophetic commentary on Israelite leadership.

First, whether we view these events as fulfillments of Nathan's prophecy or not (2 Sam 12:10), this story makes a significant contribution to the question of parental leadership. Contemporary discussion about how to parent children is lively and animated. On the one hand, conservatives like James Dobson argue for a hierarchical approach.[10] Others, however, think this is too narrow, and recommend instead that parents give more consideration to long-term goals before deciding on this or that parenting style.[11] In Cameron Lee's opinion, for example, parental discipline should focus on at least (a) the relationship between "discipline" and "discipleship," (b) the relational context of discipline, (c) the multi-dimensional nature of parenting, (d) the importance of involving both parents, and (e) empathy for the child's needs.[12]

Children don't need perfect parents, Bill Cosby preaches, just parents who are "there."[13] In a culture where most children are being raised in single-parent families, this can be a politically incorrect position today. Yet David Blankenhorn still pleads for the father-involved family, and argues eloquently (to anyone who will listen) that the father-deprived family is nothing but a radical social experiment, sociologically untested and historically unprecedented.[14] In point of fact, most of the changes of the past fifty years were already foreseen by the great anthropologist Bruno Malinowski, who argued in 1962 that

> the most important moral and legal rule concerning kinship is that no child should be brought into the world without a man— and one man at that—assuming the role of sociological father, that is, of guardian and protector, the male link between the child and the rest of the community. I think that this generalization amounts to a universal sociological law and as such I have called it in some of my previous writings the principle of *legitimacy*.[15]

Why, then, are so many parents ignoring the sociological evidence and marginalizing the biblical evidence? Why are so many, like David, "afraid" to "grieve their children"?

Second, this story shows us what can happen when a leader tries to short-circuit the corporate decision-making process. Management consultants talk about this constantly. In 1938, for example, Chester Barnard laid out a clear strategy: "The fine art of executive decision consists in not deciding questions that are not now pertinent, in not deciding prematurely, in not making decisions that cannot be made effective, and in not making decisions that others should make."[16] Fifty years later, Tom Peters and Bob Waterman offer an incisive update:

> Leadership is many things. It is patient, usually boring coalition building. It is the purposeful seeding of cabals that one hopes will result in the appropriate ferment in the bowels of the organization….It is being visible when things are going awry, and invisible when they are working well. It's building a loyal team

at the top that speaks more or less with one voice. It's listening carefully much of the time, frequently speaking with encouragement, and reinforcing words with believable action.[17]

All leaders need to take the decision-making process seriously, and most do. But much can be done to improve the process, and one of the most overlooked resources in the contemporary discussion is the Bible—hence the need for the present study.

Third, this story is a warning about what can happen when subversion becomes an acceptable leadership strategy. Unfortunately, we live in a world filled with Adonijahs and Athaliahs, and often it's hard to tell whether they're interested in us or only their careers. Reinhold Niebuhr once remarked that "if there were a better understanding of human nature in the church today...there would be fewer captains of industry living under the illusion that they are good enough and wise enough to hold irresponsible power and exercise it for the good of the community."[18] Put another way, leaders like Adonijah do not seem to understand that the door to subversive leadership is a Pandora's box. Once it's open, it's *very* difficult to close. So the question remains. Is subversion an acceptable political strategy in my organization/family/church? Should we address this issue seriously, and if so, how? If Kings is a reliable guide to what can happen when we ignore this problem, then what are the consequences of doing nothing? Could David have avoided this problem?

It's but a short distance from Adonijah to Athaliah.

LEADERSHIP UNDER STRESS (1 Kings 2:13-46)

It's one thing to be warned. It's another thing to see the warning come true. Solomon's father has warned him about the dangers of becoming Israel's new king. Now David is dead, Solomon is alone, and the vultures are circling. Even before he has time to set up his mother's throne (v. 19), they begin to plot his demise. No honeymoon period for this king. This young man has to fight for his life from day one.

The first challenge comes from Adonijah, his recently-ousted older brother. Like Nathan, Adonjah too decides to approach the king through a proven, safe avenue—Bathsheba. Unlike Joab and Shimei, however, he acts more like a whiny adolescent than a serious rival. Assuming that Israelite leaders define their power by the size of their harems,[19] and assuming that the women housed in these harems are designated solely for the king (*b. Sanh.* 22a), Adonijah's plea looks pathetic. What does he intend to do with Abishag? What does he expect to accomplish by this strategy? The text doesn't say. Whether he thinks he can win Bathsheba over, or whether he genuinely cares about Abishag, all we know is that Solomon explodes when he discovers what's happened. "What Adonijah desired was not given him, and what he possessed was taken from him."[20]

The second challenge comes from Abiathar, the priest whose decision to join Adonijah forever disqualifies him from further service. Refusing to execute David's old friend, Solomon decides to let him pack up his things and head home, to Anathoth. Even though he sees him as a "man of death" (v. 26),[21] Solomon spares his life, probably because (a) Abiathar carried the Ark for David, and (b) Abiathar shared in David's sufferings. Reflecting on his father's dying words, Solomon decides that expulsion is punishment enough, thus fulfilling the man of God's prediction in 1 Sam 2:30-35.

The third challenge comes from Joab, Solomon's most dangerous adversary. On the one hand, Joab is an effective warrior (2 Sam 10:12; 11:1), a loyal servant who follows orders (11:6-17) and supports his king (14:1-33). Joab, however, is a "violence addict," and his addiction is so deep, David publicly despairs about it at one point: "What do you and I have in common, you sons of Zeruiah?" (2 Sam 16:10). Joab is a great warrior, but he's a volatile combination of Robin Hood and Hannibal Lector,[22] and Solomon decides he's not worth the risk. Note also that his death occasions no state funeral or mourning period, and the narrator underlines this with an innocuous phrase, "and when Joab heard" (v. 28). Apparently Joab "hears" things *second*-hand because so few are willing to trust him with anything first-hand.

The fourth challenge comes from Shimei, a character introduced by another clever play on words. In Nathan's prophecy to David (2 Sam 7:5-16), the Heb word *bayit* wonderfully and intentionally oscillates between the meanings "national temple" and "spiritual home." To David's desire for a physical "house" (*bayit*), for example, Yahweh promises him instead an eternal "dynasty" (*bayit*).[23] Here the wordplay continues. Because Shimei desires to destroy David's "house," Solomon allows him to build a "house" (not a "dynasty," just a "house"). Should he ever leave this "house," he will forfeit his right to live in *Solomon's* "house" (the Davidic kingdom). Thus, when Shimei violates the agreement, the king makes good on his promise. David's "house" therefore stands above all its rivals—the "houses" of Adonijah (1 Kings 2:24), Eli (2:27), Joab (2:33), and Shimei (2:36).

Intratextual Reflection

This is no random list, but the first of many warnings about how important it is to practice Yahweh-centered leadership. Judging from its frequency, the *pressure of subversion* trajectory is central to Kings, and how we choose to interpret it will have an enormous impact on how we interpret any story within it. Here Solomon successfully defends his kingdom against its internal adversaries, and this clears the way for a Solomonic "golden age." Similarly, the entire book of Kings begins with a number of "success" stories followed by a string of ever-more-depressing "failure" stories, both in Israel (2 Kings 15:17-31) and in Judah (18:17-37).[24] The intratextual context shows that this story is a microcosm of the rise and fall of the monarchy itself.[25]

Compare, for example, the story here with the story of Hezekiah (2 Kings 18:1-37). Both narratives show us Judahite kings under tremendous stress. Solomon faces down Adonijah, Abiathar, Joab, and Shimei—four internal rivals from his family, his priesthood, his army, and the former royal family. Hezekiah's external enemy, on the other hand, is a coalition of three high-ranking Assyrian officers. The problem facing Solomon is his adversaries' desire to unseat him. The challenge facing Hezekiah is his enemies' desire to crush him for rebelling against Sennacherib. Hezekiah's response is to take the belligerent letter of the Assyrians before Yahweh and pray for help. Solomon's response is to mete out justice in measured doses.

Each of these narratives, in other words, shows us a different response to a leadership crisis. Sometimes the response can be judicial (1 Kings 2:13-46), sometimes economic (2 Kings 15:17-21). Sometimes it can lead to skin-of-the-teeth survival (2 Kings 18:17-20:11), sometimes to unmitigated disaster (1 Kings 22:29-50). Only by reading Kings through an intratextual lens can we see this variety, and apply these stories more intelligently to contemporary crises.

Theological Reflection

The last decades of the twentieth century have witnessed the rise of another Adonijah-like figure—Udai Hussein, the son of Saddam Hussein, the Iraqi dictator. Like Adonijah, Udai is a prince whose "father never grieves him by asking, 'Why do you behave as you do?'" At age 24, Udai and his henchmen once crashed an official party in Baghdad for Suzanne Mubarak, the wife of Hosni Mubarak. In front of Egypt's horrified first lady, Udai and his thugs clubbed a man to death named Kamal Hana Gegeo, Saddam's personal valet. Udai had become suspicious of Gegeo's influence over Saddam for reasons much like Adonijah's.

Gegeo was Saddam's "spin doctor," the man in charge of making Saddam look good in front of an admiring public. This was a difficult job, because at the time Saddam was involved in a sexual affair with Samira Shahbander, the daughter of an influential Iraqi family. Udai, however, was the son of Sajida, Saddam's first wife. Thus, threatened by the possibility of displacement, and angered by Gegeo's attempts to cover up the affair, he murdered his father's press secretary for doing his job.

The Iraqi public was outraged, and Saddam had to put Udai on "trial." Simultaneously he put pressure on Gegeo's family, who took the hint and pleaded publicly for Udai's pardon, claiming that he had been "unfairly provoked." The strategy worked, and Udai became the "persecuted crown prince." After only a few months in exile, he came back to head up the Iraqi Olympic Federation and become the manager of a major television network.[26]

Political intrigue isn't new. It's as constant today as it's ever been. What's new is the way we think about it. Solomon might have tried meting out the same sort of "faux-punishment" to Adonijah as Saddam did for Udai, but (a) Adonijah's father is very different from Udai's father, and (b) David's deity is very different from Saddam's god. King David is not Saddam Hussein, and David's God shows him repeatedly—and painfully—that a king must pay a price for abusing his position.[27] A king's job is to serve his people, particularly the miserable and oppressed and impoverished. When one's deity is Naked Power, words like "wisdom" and "justice" no longer have any meaning, and this raises a number of questions.

First, leadership always involves having to deal with hostile resistance, whether overt or covert. Failure to understand this has led many a well-intentioned leader to organizational disaster. Barbara Brown Zikmund, for example, did not realize the mess she was inheriting when she became president of Hartford Seminary.[28] During her first year she tried to invest her energies in casting vision and creating infrastructure. Soon, however, she realized that all the vision in the world is meaningless until or unless one learns something about the stakeholders in the organization. Realizing this, she changed her strategy and began focusing her attention on learning about the needs of her staff, faculty, board, and other stakeholders.

Second, effective leaders operate from a clear understanding of human weakness, and constantly search for ethical ways to deal with these weaknesses. Solomon does not deal with Shimei, for example, in the same way he deals with Joab. Nor does he deal with Abiathar in the same way he deals with Adonijah. Each challenge to his authority is of a different kind—thus the variation in response. This is critically important. Nowhere in this story, for example, do we find a systematized theory of "monarchical leadership"—no flow-charts, no quarterly goals, no back-up plans for "any contingency." Kings is not a left-brain leadership manual, and effective leaders understand that decisions must be handled on a case-by-case basis.

Third, leaders can and do fail. Some learn from these failures; some don't. Going to Bathsheba to ask for Abishag has to be one of the stupidest decisions imaginable. Had Adonijah not tried to go behind Solomon's back, he might not only have saved his life, he might have become a respected statesman, like Jonathan. Jonathan, too, might easily have tried to wrest the kingdom away from David through intrigue and subversion, but he refuses to engage in such behavior, even in the midst of Saul's demands that he do so. The problem is not simply stubbornness. The problem can be our stubborn unwillingness to recognize our limitations. To pretend, as triumphalist, death-denying cultures do, that failure is avoidable is to create a culture of shame, not a culture of faith.[29] Cultivating a realistic approach to failure is absolutely necessary to growing a healthy faith. Of course, this should not be overemphasized—self-flagellation is not faith, either—but the antidote to depression is not more self-love. The antidote to depression is an informed faith.[30]

RESTRUCTURING FOR CHANGE (1 Kings 4:1-28)

The information presented here represents the first detailed evidence of Solomon's determination to transform Israel's intertribal confederacy into a centralized monarchy. The first of these lists catalogues no less than nine cabinet positions within his inner circle. Tantalizingly little is known about these cabinet-level ministers, but these are Israel's new leaders. The second list, with its registry of "district governors," documents the replacement of Israel's tribal leadership model (based on inheritance) with a bureaucratic leadership model (based on appointment). Who are these people, and what exactly do they do?

The Hebrew term *sarîm* ("officials," *NIV*) has parallels in several cognate languages.[31] Studying these parallels can help us learn more about officials elsewhere in the ancient Near East, but tells us little about the day-to-day functions of these particular officials. Solomon's cabinet may remain a mystery, but it seems obvious that he is willing to delegate power. Like David, Solomon is an expansionist, and he accomplishes much by the way he restructures his administration.[32] Comparing his inner circle with

David's (2 Sam 20:23-26), we can see right away that several of his men are former employees of David. Zadok, for example, continues on as "priest" (*kohen*), and is now joined by Azariah his son (also called "priest" in v. 2).[33] Jehoshaphat, son of Ahilud, continues on as "recorder" (*mazkîr*),[34] and this may be the brother of the district governor in v. 12.

New leaders appear over old departments as well. Benaiah moves up from captain of the king's bodyguard to general of the army, replacing Joab. Sheva the "secretary" (*soper*) is replaced by two new secretaries, Elihoreph and Ahijah. Most interesting are the two new administrative positions. The job of "palace manager" goes to a man named Ahishar, who becomes the first of many to hold this job.[35] The important job of "liaison" between Solomon and his newly-appointed district governors goes to one of Nathan's sons, Azariah (doubtless as reward for Nathan's earlier loyalty). Not only does Azariah have to report to the king, he also oversees the work of twelve district governors.[36]

In the Babylonian period these *sarîm*-officials become a powerful lobby in Jerusalem with headquarters in the Temple (Jer 35:4), playing a variety of roles in Jerusalem politics: "prosecutor" (26:11), "defense attorney" (26:16), "protector" (36:19), "jailor" (37:15). Later, they become so powerful, even the king himself "can do nothing to oppose" them (Jer 38:5, 25), but here at the beginning of Kings they appear only in lists.

The primary job of the district governors (lit., "standing ones," *netsabîm*) is to implement the policies established by the king through these *sarîm*-officials. Little is known about these governors except that two of them are sons-in-law of the king. Their primary duty is to supply the palace with everything it needs. Each governor has to provide supplies for one month of the year.[37] To make it all work, Solomon has to take power out of the hands of the tribes and give it to the governors, because, like an ant colony, oriental despotism cannot function without a rigidly centralized administration.[38] Socioeconomically this means a new system of taxation and military conscription. Politically it means scrapping the old power-flow-chart of give-and-take between Jerusalem and the tribes. Militarily it means building new chariot cities for the king's standing army.[39] All of this is Solomon's legacy, and though his restructuring plan appears sensitive to the needs of older Israelites, Israel's political life is never again the same.[40]

Archaeologists have unearthed a great deal of corroborative evidence to confirm this restructuring, predominantly in hundreds of jar-handles bearing the king's royal seal (*lmlk*, "belonging to the king"). Apparently these jars all come from the same pottery, and apparently these district

governors used them to gather taxes of oil and wine and other food-
stuffs.[41] Both biblical and archaeological sources confirm the success of
Solomon's restructuring effort. But why does the narrator extol Israel's
"happiness" in the midst of this change, when only a few verses later it
becomes painfully clear that Israel is not at all happy? Deeper concerns
("Who's paying for this?" "How does this affect the average Israelite?"
"What are the spiritual ramifications of this power-shift?") may be conspicuously left unaddressed, but perhaps we should not be overly critical. This is Israel's golden age, a time of brilliant creativity in Israel. Many
scholars believe that the first comprehensive draft of the Pentateuch
begins in this period, as well as the first drafts of both the Psalms and the
Proverbs.[42] Even Norman Gottwald, normally a harsh critic of Solomon,
recognizes this as an "optimistic" time in Israel's history.[43]

Intratextual Reflection

Subversion here is less overt than in other *pressure of subversion* stories,
but it's still here, standing offstage like a character actor waiting for his cue.
Compare, for example, Solomon's political accomplishments alongside the
accomplishments of Jeroboam (1 Kings 12:25-33). Jeroboam does several
things to anger this narrator, but none more provocative than his restructuring of the cult. In clear violation of the Law, he sets up two cultic altars
for regular religious sacrifice in Dan and Bethel. He constructs two golden
calves and commands Israel to worship them. He sets up an idiosyncratic
priesthood and an unauthorized festal calendar. Solomon is not nearly so
brazen. He limits himself only to transforming the old tribal system, and
even here he keeps many of David's old cronies in their jobs. If LXX preserves an authentic tradition, he appoints a cabinet-level official (Eliab) to
respond to the resistance of northern tribal leaders.[44] His methods, in other
words, are more cautious and sophisticated than Jeroboam's. Both monarchs succeed in accomplishing their goals, but Solomon's leadership is less
radical. Biblical leaders use a variety of means to effect change.

The point is that Israel is on a journey. Not everyone wants to go on
this journey, and not everyone is prepared to go on this journey. Ideologically it means having to find new ways to solve old problems. Politically
it means having to replace worn-out structures—"new wine for new wine-
skins." Administratively it means having to find new ways to streamline
old procedures. Theologically it means having to recontextualize Yahwism
for an up-and-coming generation. All this is demanding work, requiring
enormous energy—and not everyone is willing to expend this energy.
Solomon, at the beginning of his reign, successfully restructures his gov-

ernment to create a culture where education, literature and the arts become more important than politics, legislation and war, and these lists preserve the skeletal substance of this accomplishment. But soon there will be a conservative backlash, and Israel's "golden age" will come to an ignominious end.

Theological Reflection

Written and directed by the Wachowski brothers, *The Matrix* is a film about man-vs.-machine. Set in the distant future, humanity has developed a race of artificially intelligent (AI) computers—intelligent enough to conquer and domesticate the human race. They need a steady source of energy to survive, however, so they develop an entire industry devoted to breeding human beings in hive-like pods. The energy produced by each pod is then systematically harvested to meet the energy needs of this machine race.

To keep their charges in line, the AI computers create a virtual-reality framework which each human being perceives through an implanted neural stimulator. While their unconscious bodies hum along, their placated brains now imagine existence in a "virtual world." Yet this "virtual world" is not real. It's only an insidious brainwashing program—the Matrix. The climax of the film occurs when a small band of revolutionaries succeeds in breaking free from the Matrix under the leadership of a messianic figure named Neo.

Sometimes the "Mother Church" is obedient to Jesus, but other times she's like the Matrix. Sometimes she degenerates into a bureaucracy where conformity is rewarded and creativity is punished, where machinated believers decide that liturgy is more important than Christology, that administration is more important than prayer. Some believers feel that there is no difference between the structure of the Church and its mission, that ecclesiastical forms are just as important as theological content (*contra* Paul, 1 Cor 9:19-23). Others believe that deep spiritual piety and serious intellectual reflection are somehow antithetical, that Christ's command to love the Lord with both mind and heart is impossible (Mark 12:30). This sort of "folk theology" operates via

> unreflective believing based on blind faith in a tradition of some kind…a kind of theology that rejects critical reflection and enthusiastically embraces simplistic acceptance of an informal tradition of beliefs and practices composed mainly of clichés and evangelegends….Deep spiritual piety and intellectual reflection are considered antithetical within folk theology….Folk theology encourages

gullibility, vicarious spirituality and simplistic answers to difficult dilemmas that arise from being followers of Jesus Christ in a largely secular and pagan world.[45]

Believers succumbing to this matrix of traditions and evangelegends often find contemporary life...*unsettling.* Like Israel's tribal traditionalists, they prefer to bristle at the changes around them, not address them. Like the conservatives at Qumran, they prefer to disengage from the world rather than challenge it with a Kingdom Dream. They prefer to imagine nostalgically a time when life was "perfect"—though such a time has never existed.[46] They prefer to envelop themselves in old denominational cocoons, and hide within religious security blankets. They avoid the messiness of real ministry in the real world. Some even prey on the apocalyptic fears of others in the name of Christ.[47]

For disciples, however, these are exhilarating times, times of tremendous hope and dizzying possibility. What will the Kingdom look like in this new millenium? How will God reformulate the Creation into his image? As medical science continues to push the bioethical envelope, for example, what will Christian medical ethics look like? Will it keep pace with the conversation? Will it help set a new moral tone?[48] Ron Brown and Tony Wesson dream of a time when theologians and scientists will learn to work together on these questions.[49] Dan Shaw dreams of a day when the Church will responsibly address the questions raised by postmodern seekers, a day when church-planters will begin to anticipate these changes, not just react to them.[50]

Change is coming, though, and relatively few believers are prepared for it. Structurally the Church is creaking and groaning under the weight of an antiquated tribal confedecary. Theologically it's choking on a diet of elitist pedantry in the First World, matched by a diet of desperate violence in the Third World. Morally it's failing to deal with a sexual revolution already gone way beyond anything imagined by Moses or Paul.

Dealing with these changes will call for wisdom of Solomonic proportions.

A MATTER OF THE HEART (1 Kings 11:1-13)

Here the problems hinted at earlier in Solomon's life now break out into the open. On the surface, Solomon's apostasy seems due to his many pagan wives, but to conclude that Solomon's apostasy is due merely to the behavior of his wives is to miss the deeper point of this episode. As

Yahweh makes clear in his rebuke, the deeper problem is inside Solomon himself. At first glance, the narrator's emphasis seems to be on the king's love for women, on the fact that they are "foreign women," on the fact that they are "many foreign women."[51] Yet these women are but the needle through which the virus spreads, not the virus itself. Closer attention to matters of context and structure will show us that Solomon's deeper problem is his heart, not his wives. Four times in this text Solomon's heart "turns" (*leb natâ*, vss 2, 3, 4, and 9), and each time it does the narrator offers us a more damning explanation, repeatedly contrasting Solomon's heart to the heart of his father David.

The first of these contrasts occurs after a citation from the Pentateuch: "You must not intermarry with them, because they will surely turn your hearts after their gods." This is not a direct quote—the word for "turn" (*natâ*) is not the same word used in Deut 7:4 (*tsûr*). Nor is the idiom for "intermarriage" the same. Deuteronomy prohibits the *hatan*, the ancient Near Eastern institution of "son-in-law-making,"[52] while this writer simply warns Israel not to "go into them." Limiting the point only to intermarriage, in other words, is too narrow.[53] Granted, Solomon's contempt for the sexual boundaries laid out in Mosaic Yahwism is prophetically unacceptable. When David violates these boundaries with Bathsheba, he asks—no, begs—Yahweh to repair them (Psa 51). But Solomon prays no such prayer. Scripture contains no Solomonic equivalent to the 51st psalm. Instead, Solomon chooses to "hold fast" (*dabaq*, "cling")[54] to his sins, and when he does, his heart turns—the same heart which used to *listen* to God (*leb shome`â*, 1 Kings 3:9).

Second, this turning comes to a climax at the time of Solomon's old age. Dutifully recording his large harem of "princess brides" (*nasîm sarôt*) and "concubines" (*pilagshîm*), the text focuses on the effect of their influence over time. It's one thing to resist idolatry for a few weeks or months; it's quite another to have to resist it for years. Comparing Solomon to David, the narrator tells us why he eventually succumbs to them: "his heart is not fully devoted to Yahweh his God." The peculiar power of this statement does not come across in any of the translations because what we have here is an ingenious pun on Solomon's name. *Shelomô* ("[his] peace")[55] is no longer *shalem* ("whole, complete, fully devoted"). Should the word's Arabic cognate have a say in translation, one might even say that Solomon apostasizes because he is no longer *muslim* (i.e., "wholly devoted, wholly submissive," from Arab *slm*).[56] Solomon's heart used to be *shalem* ("complete"). Now it has become *lo' shalem* ("incomplete").

Third, the result of this change is twofold: (a) after Solomon decides not to follow Yahweh completely, he then (b) decides to follow other gods. The second decision is dependent on the first. Yes, his construction enterprises continue, but no longer for Yahweh's glory. Solomon is now preoccupied with erecting "high places" for his wives' gods. In fact, the new construction site becomes popularly known as "The Hill of Corruption" in prophetic circles (2 Kings 23:13). To imagine that he has a third choice—not to follow a deity at all—is absurd. Only a (post)modern reader would imagine such a possibility. Of course he's going to "follow" a deity—the only relevant question is "which one?"[57] From a political perspective, he doubtless rationalizes his behavior by imagining that the worship of his wives' gods *alongside* Yahweh is simply "good politics"—a necessary evil, a perfunctory duty. From a Yahwistic perspective, however, Solomon becomes an idolater. In spite of two heavenly warnings, Solomon has turned (*natâ*) away from Yahweh.

To drive his point home, the narrator actually gives us the names of Solomon's "new" gods, names for which we now have a good deal of extra-biblical confirmation. In the Canaanite myths, for example, the goddess here called Ashtoreth is most likely the Canaanite goddess Athtirat, the consort-wife of the patriarch-god El.[58] Chemosh is the Moabite deity on the famous Moabite Stone, who there shares power with Ashtoreth.[59] For Molech (v. 7) we have considerably less inscriptional evidence, yet enough biblical evidence to conclude that Yahwists find him "detestable" (*siqquts*, vv. 5, 7).[60]

Fourth, Yahweh responds. He becomes enraged at the king's behavior and condemns it. Characteristically this judgment breaks down into several stages. First, he renounces Solomon's attitude; lit., he condemns "this (way) with you," a rather interesting expression.[61] Nowhere does he say anything about Solomon's wives, nor does he castigate his "new" gods. The focus stays completely on Solomon's heart. Second, he focuses on the immediate result of this attitude, viz., his failure to "keep my covenant and my decrees, which I commanded you." Like Jesus, Yahweh operates on the presupposition that law-breaking is a symptom, not a cause (Matt 5:21-48). Third, he pronounces judgment, defining for Solomon what his covenant-breaking behavior is going to cost: "I will most certainly tear the kingdom away from you and give it to one of your subordinates." Leadership is a privilege, not a right. When Solomon decides to abandon the covenant, he abdicates this privilege. Fourth, Yahweh ameliorates his judgment, revising it for application in three stages:

(a) He reminds Solomon of his earlier covenant with David: "nevertheless, for the sake of David your father, I will not do it during your lifetime." Though Solomon is unfaithful, Yahweh is not. Yahweh is a God who faithfully keeps his promises, especially the promise of an "eternal house" to David (2 Sam 7:15).

(b) He states the precise time when this judgment will come: "I will tear it out of the hand of your son" (i.e., Rehoboam). The fact that divine judgment can extend to succeeding generations is not new (Exod 20:5), but what is new is Yahweh's decision to use a long-range hubris-management strategy with the line of David.

(c) He delimits the judgment's geographical extent: "I will not tear the whole kingdom from him, but will give him one tribe." All of these ameliorations occur because Yahweh is a God who keeps his promises.

In short, this is a tragic episode, painful to read, even more painful to apply. Like Solomon's response to his rivals (1 Kings 2:25-46), Yahweh's response to Solomon is measured and temperate. He does not overreact, nor does he underreact. He responds in a manner befitting his nature, always giving him a way out, always leaving a door of escape. It's a common pattern in Kings. A king chooses to "cling" (*dabaq*) to something besides the Law (in this case, "foreign wives"). The effect of this decision leads to an awful irony—in this case, the "complete one" becomes "in-complete." *Shelomô* becomes *lo' shalem*, and, since nature abhors a vacuum, the process cannot stop there. Behavior like this can and does lead to full-blown apostasy, putting tremendous strain on the king's covenant-partner, Yahweh of Hosts. This obligates Yahweh to respond. The only question is, "how?" How will Yahweh respond to such flagrant idolatry? How will he maintain his covenant in the face of such determined apostasy?

Intratextual Reflection

Subversion comes in many forms. In Adonijah's case it comes in a desire to become king, to the point of fomenting coup-plots. In Rehoboam's case it's just the opposite. Inheriting the kingdom from Solomon, he chooses not to listen to the wiser voices in his environment. In Jeroboam's case subversion becomes a rallying cry for revolution. When Rehoboam rubs his nose in his out-group status, this fuels inside him a whole series of counterattacks against things Davidic.

Subversion is a major theme in 1 Kings, but note carefully its conspicuous absence in 2 Kings. After the story of Micaiah ben Imlah, this theme dies out as "subversion" gives way to "survival" as the book's dominant theme. Internal subversion in 1 Kings is replaced by the threat, and later the reality, of external invasion in 2 Kings. Yahweh watches as Israel's leaders make their decisions. He sends prophets to warn them of the consequences. He allows the kingdom to divide via civil war. But eventually he stops sending warnings. Eventually he does something so unbelievable even the prophets will have difficulty understanding it. Yahweh will "raise up" (*qûm*, 1:6) the Assyrians and the Babylonians to "disinherit" (*yârash*, 1:6) and "devour" his own people (*'âkal*, 1:8). He will use the ruthless and the godless to save a nation which has itself become ruthless and godless. This is perhaps the deepest mystery of the Old Testament, and with Habakkuk and the rest of the prophets we might wonder how this will lead to Israel's repentance.

Theological Reflection

"I'm not doing anything wrong! You can't tell me what to do! My daddy's a deacon in this church!"

"Painful" doesn't begin to describe it. The young lady screaming in my face is an unhappy wife. Faced with reality for the first time in her life, all she knows is that she doesn't like it, and that she wants someone to "fix it." Her husband knows practically nothing about how to grow a healthy marriage, but he truly wants to help her raise their three boys, and he wants to try to make the marriage work. Her father, a deacon in our congregation, is a good man, but one who lacks both the gifts and the skills to do competent marriage counseling, particularly with his own daughter.

She doesn't realize it, yet, but the man she's chosen to marry is the exact opposite of her father. Unlike him, this young man refuses to cave in and grovel before every temper tantrum. He stands up to her incessant narcissism. So, in response, she's decided to move in with a new lover and take the kids with her. Words cannot convey the embarrassment this is causing her family, yet embarrassing as it is, she's now decided to raise it up a notch. She's decided to bring her new lover to church with her, planting herself in the second pew. Confronted by the minister, she's refusing to listen to any argument which does not begin and end with her. "Why can't I bring my boyfriend to church with me? Why is this 'wrong?' Maybe it'll make my husband 'come around,'" she says with a straight face. Then, wielding her twenty-year Sunday School education like a sword, she parries,

Maybe God doesn't want me to stay in a marriage where I'm not happy. Maybe it's wrong for the Church to expect so much from me. What's wrong with bringing my boyfriend to Church? He's good to my kids. He wants to make me happy. What's your problem? I'm not doing anything wrong! You can't tell me what to do! My daddy's a deacon in this church!

Political subversion is emotionally draining. Ask any pastor who's been in the trenches. Most are painfully familiar with the usual cast of characters: the adolescent "church-leader's-kid" who never grows up; the well-meaning parent/grandparent who wants to "fix things" rather than address the moral and ethical implications of their child's behavior; the weary pastor who wants to stay true to God and still keep his/her job; the congregation who agonizes from a distance over their corporate responsibility. Most of these character-types appear here as well, in this biblical episode. Like the stories of Adonijah's ambition and Athaliah's genocide, Solomon's wavering heart is an outrageous example of foolish idolatry. Yet, since he's the king, it's difficult to know how, exactly, to deal with it. How does one walk the line between divine integrity and human sinfulness? How can we communicate a text like this to believers today who are trying to do the same thing?

First, the clear focus here, as in Scripture generally, is the heart. The conflict in this text is not between Solomon's Yahwism vs. his wives' "paganism," though Christians have long read it this way. Cyprian, for example, lays virtually all of the blame for Solomon's apostasy at the feet of his wives.[62] Tertullian laments the fact that he becomes "a prey to foreign women."[63] These are shallow readings. The deeper conflict is the way Solomon's heart contrasts with David's heart. Both David and Solomon sin greatly against Yahweh, yet only one of these kings turns his heart away from God. Certainly political and religious factors have a place in explaining this behavior, yet the ultimate reason seems obvious enough. Some people have a heart for God, and some do not.

Ysabel de Andia reminds us that a pure heart is one whose sole purpose is to love God, whose greatest desire is to live for God. Purity, uprightness, and simplicity are indicators of genuine "wholeness" (Heb *shalôm*).[64] Greg Salyer reminds us that Jesus unflinchingly focuses on the heart because he knows that this is the only way to establish the Kingdom.[65] Alison and Davies agree that the central theme of the Sermon on the Mount is the heart. Matt 5-7 has a clear end in view: to help disciples learn how to think like God (Matt 5:48). If disciples today would desire the same thing, then we must learn how to develop moral qualities like poverty of spirit, love of enemy, and purity of heart.[66]

Our hearts can become troubled, foolish, darkened, even calloused. When we refuse to accept the Word in our hearts, we become double-minded. We become experts at honoring God with our lips while keeping our hearts "safely" miles away. Our hearts can become diamond-hard...but they can also be made soft again. We can refuse to become hardened cynics. We can enable our hearts to become depositories for God's good things, not just havens of rest from the "big bad world." Even the most troubled among us can learn, like Jean Valjean in Victor Hugo's *Les Miserables*, to cultivate hearts which do good in the face of evil. As the Talmud puts it, "better is one self-reproach in the heart of a man than many stripes" (*b. Ber.* 7a).

Second, even in situations of flagrant apostasy, the punishment needs to fit the crime. Yahweh's judgment is balanced, not arbitrary. God's response to Solomon, though severe, is more lenient than his response to the apostasy of, say, Ahab. Yahweh finds himself torn between his love for Israel and his righteous character. His righteous judgment at first prevails and Israel's future looks grim. Yet God resolves this dilemma by looking beyond the present age, enabling a remnant to survive even when the present is characterized by the most despicable idolatry. Knowing this future, Yahweh's judgment stays patient and measured and wise and persistent. So should ours. We need to be clear about God's judgment, but we also need to make sure we temper it with faith in his (future) grace. This God wants to save his children, not damn them—even deacon's daughters who refuse to grow up.

Third, "bad company corrupts good morals." It's one thing to fantasize about sin. It's another thing to be enslaved by it (Rom 6:16). In Scripture, intermarriage with foreigners is a persistent problem, but the texts prefer to couch it in ethical, not ethnic categories. The problem of intermarriage illustrates Israel's perennial conflict between the centripetal and the centrifugal, between trying to stay pure and trying to stay missiologically active (Gen 12:1-4).[67]

William Eichorst thoughtfully reflects on this tension with regard to Ezra's tough stance against intermarriage (Ezra 9-10).[68] Eichorst questions Ezra's decision (1) because Israel previously tolerates intermarriage (e.g., Jer 29:6), (2) because it creates problems by breaking up established families, (3) because it's most unfair to the wives and children, and (4) because it lacks clear Mosaic sanction (that Ezra 11:2 only paraphrases instead of quotes Deut 7:3-4 may be an indication of flexibility in the earlier history of tradition). He also supports Ezra's decision, however, (1) because Israel needs to correct violations of explicit priestly prohibitions against inter-marriage, (2) because intermarriage is a threat to Israel's theocracy at this fragile point in its history, (3) because Israel's religious leaders are hardly guiltless (e.g., Gen 38), and (4) because it occurs after careful seeking of God's will through prayer and study.

In other words, Ezra has to choose between what is desirable and what is necessary. Some rabbis confuse the two by hardening the *form* of Ezra's decision and deemphasizing its theological *substance*. The book of Jubilees, for example, uses this text and Lev 18:21 to prohibit intermarriage under any and all circumstances. Philo even extends the prohibition in Deut 7:3-4 to all Gentiles for all time.[69] There are good reasons for, say, Paul's admonition to the Corinthians to avoid becoming "unequally yoked to unbelievers" (2 Cor 6:14), just as there are good reasons for the narrator of Kings to begin his condemnation of Solomon with a warning against intermarriage. But we need to be careful not to take these passages out of their contexts and woodenly apply them to all situations at all times. Some Christians are strong enough to live in places where Kingdom ethics and Christian theology become "tangled and dark."[70] Others, however, are not, and learning how to contextualize this passage to specific contemporary contexts will always be challenging.

LEADERSHIP NAIVETÉ (1 Kings 12:1-24)

Strategically located between Mts. Ebal and Gerizim, Shechem is noted for its famous confrontations. Jacob's sons, for example, experience a major conflict here with the Canaanites who "humble" their sister, Dinah (Gen 34:2).[71] From the Amarna correspondence we know of a Shechemite warlord named Labayu who attacks and generally frustrates everyone in this vicinity.[72] Very possibly this same Labayu is responsible, at least indirectly, for the erection of the Ba`al Berit temple during Abimelech's reign (Judg 9:4). From Scripture we know that Shechem is one of Israel's earliest religious centers. Joshua initiates a covenant cere-mony here (Josh 24), and Abimelech attempts to have himself declared "king" here (Judg. 9:8).

In other words, Rehoboam and Jeroboam are not the first Syro-Palestinians to come to Shechem looking for peace. Nor are they the first to fail. One can only wonder how much of this history Rehoboam understands when he makes the decision to leave Jerusalem and meet with Jeroboam on his own turf. It's tempting to place all the blame for the division of the kingdom on him, but we need to be careful not to overemphasize his role. Other factors are at work here as well:

> The empire of David and Solomon could not stand the strain imposed on it by a natural polarization toward north and south... combined with a strong Egypt and a hostile Aram. This strain gave rise to squabbling over allocation of government funds, over government organization, and over priorities in foreign and domestic policies.[73]

Blame for Israel's division into Israel (north) and Judah (south) cannot fairly be laid at the feet of any one man, because to do this is to ignore the larger political, economic, social, and theological factors involved. The breakup of Israel is a complex matter, and it needs to be analyzed from several angles.

From a literary angle, though, Rehoboam's naiveté is the focus of this particular episode. In fact, this is a story of classical characters acting out classical roles focusing on classical themes. Something so significant as the division of Israel cannot be relegated to a line or two of colorless prose. Instead, it deserves to be housed in brilliant narrative comprised of the following themes: (a) the "oppressed laborers" theme; (b) the "dueling counselors" theme; (c) the "rebels-with-a-just-cause" theme; and (d) the all-important theme of "prophetic validation."

First, when Rehoboam comes to Shechem, he does not come to negotiate. He comes to see to it that "all the Israelites make him king." This is his first opportunity to prove himself (like Solomon in 1 Kings 3:16-28), and all he has to do is listen to the advice of his counselors and tribal leaders. But this man is not interested in listening to his people's anger over the "harsh" policies of his father. He cares little about redistricting, taxation, and the most hated Solomonic policy of all—forced labor.[74] Contrast this with the leadership of, say, Cyrus the Persian. When Cyrus conquers Babylon, one of his first official acts is to recognize publicly the suffering of its people, a shrewd strategy which wins him many disciples: "I abolished the yoke which was against their (social) standing. I brought relief to their dilapidated housing, putting an end to their complaints."[75] Moses does something similar in preparation for the exodus. Repulsed by the "hard labor" of fellow Israelites (Exod 2:11), he eventually wins them over and leads them out of slavery, and so important is this event, the prophets cite it to every new generation of potential Rehoboams (Amos 5:11; Jer 22:3).

Second, antecedents to this scene are ubiquitous in the ancient Near East. In the Sumerian epic of Gilgamesh vs. Agga, for example, dueling councils of "young"-vs.-"old" counselors advise Gilgamesh on how to respond to a war ultimatum from Agga, the neighboring warlord (*ANET* 44-47). Gilgamesh wants to launch a pre-emptive strike against Agga, but this goes against the advice of his elders. Dissatisfied, he then turns to a younger council, "the men of the city," and they advise him to be bold and attack. In each story, therefore:

(a) a beleaguered young ruler seeks the advice of opposing councils;

(b) one of these councils is older than the other;

(c) the king rejects the counsel of the older for the counsel of the younger;

(d) the "winning" council uses a proverbial phrase in its advice to the king;

(e) each proverbial phrase deals with similar motifs: "fastening ropes" in Sumer (*ANET* 45, line 7); "whips" in Israel (1 Kings 12:11).[76]

Third, Israel does more than just voice opposition to Rehoboam. Israel takes swift action in three stages:

(1) Ten of Israel's tribes secede from the kingdom of David. Even though the narrator tries to prepare us for it, this still takes us by surprise. The battle cry of the north, "To your tents O Israel!" is a verbatim repetition of Sheba's earlier cry against the house of David (2 Sam 20:1). Here, however, in contrast to Sheba's rebellion, the primary conflict is not clan/ethnic (Saulide/Benjamite vs. Davidic/Judahite leadership), but ideological/political. Rehoboam thinks he can continue a political policy of harsh labor and heavy yoke even though he has never proven himself worthy of the throne.

(2) The seceding tribes execute Adoniram, the bureaucrat in charge of forced labor. Tragic as this is, it's hard to read about it without thinking immediately of the Maccabean revolt centuries later—another rebellion sparked by the arrogant fiscal policies of a foolish king (1 Macc 2:25).[77]

(3) The seceding tribes crown Jeroboam as their new king. Not only does this decision put teeth in their opposition to the house of David, it also fulfills the prophecy of Ahijah (1 Kings 11:31). But this is not the first time an Israelite is "made king" at Shechem. The same verb appears earlier in the story of Abimelech's "kingship" (Judg 9:6). The main difference is that Abimelech's "kingship" does not receive prophetic validation.

(4) This underlines, fourth, the centrality and importance of prophetic validation. That God ratifies Jeroboam's kingship predictively through Ahijah and confirms his decision through Shemaiah is in many ways the point of the story, for it is here that Yahweh's will most clearly comes to expression. The prophetic message is not unclear. The God of Israel cares deeply about the plight of the oppressed. Earlier this compassion peeks through the genteel conversation between Rehoboam and his elders: "If today you will be a servant to these people and serve them and give them a favorable answer, they will always be your servants" (v. 7). Here it bursts forth with political ramifications. Ahijah and Shemaiah speak not in the language of sage counsel, but the language of divine indignation. Warning Rehoboam through Shemaiah, Yahweh intends to send a clear message. This God is adamantly opposed to the imposition of raw power on the poor, not just because it corrupts Davidic leaders, but because it reflects so poorly on David's God. Shemaiah's oracle reminds us that Yahweh always opposes "the proud gods and commodores of this earth."[78]

Intratextual Reflection

Rehoboam tries to subvert the dreams of the northern tribes only to discover, through Shemaiah, that Yahweh is the One who validates their cry for lighter burdens and easier yokes. From one perspective, this looks much like Jeroboam's later behavior (1 Kings 13-14). Granted, Jeroboam's creation of subversive cults in Dan and Bethel goes way beyond the bounds of the Mosaic covenant, yet both kings squander some golden opportunities. Like Rehoboam, Jeroboam completely wastes his opportunity to have his own kingdom and his own "house."

Looking to the broader context, however, this story foreshadows what is yet to come in the Elijah-Elisha cycles. The issues involved in the Rehoboam-vs.-Shemaiah conflict will come up again in the Ahab-vs.-Elijah and Elisha-vs.-Hazael conflicts. In fact, these first skirmishes introduce a pattern around which these later conflicts will intentionally operate: (a) a king tries to subvert the will of Yahweh, and (b) Yahweh sends a prophet to reestablish the delicate balance between admonition and exhortation. We can trace the contours of this pattern in Hittite, Greek, and Israelite prophecy as well, and when we do this we quickly realize that the prophet-king relationship is not just political, but about the difficulty of integrating the opposing dynamics of prophecy and politics into a nation's identity.[79]

Theological Reflection

In *Finding Time for Fathering*, Mitch and Susan Golant tell a funny story about their daughter.[80] When she was five, Cherie and her friend Doug were playing with a ball in the den of the house when Doug hit a "home run" into the bathroom. *Crash!* The ball destroyed a fancy light-globe over the guest bathroom sink, shattering it into pieces. Terrified, Doug ran home in tears while Cherie went upstairs to tell her father what happened. Moments later, Doug showed up at the front door with *his* father. "Doug, don't you have something you want to say to Mr. Golant?" After some coaching, little Doug finally blurted out, "I'm sorry for breaking your house!"

The Golants tell this story not just to get a laugh, but to illustrate the differences between authoritarian, permissive, and authoritative leadership. Had Doug's father been overly permissive, Doug would have "gotten away with it," because his father would have adopted a *laissez faire*, "hands off" philosophy toward his son's behavior—and little Doug would have had to look elsewhere for "wise counsel." Had his father been too authoritarian, though, the scene at the door might have looked like this:

> (Doorbell rings, and Mitch answers the door) Yes?
>
> Doug's father: Mr. Golant?
>
> Mitch: Yes?
>
> Doug's father: Well, I just want you to know how sorry I am that my son damaged your property. It'll never happen again, because I'm grounding him for the next 5 years. In addition to this, here's all the pennies I could pull out of his piggy bank, and here's his teddy bear…(etc., etc.).

Authoritative parents, on the other hand, understand that being a good parent means going into the "coaching business." Effective parents know how to give wise counsel to their children because they know how to lead them between the prophetic pole of vision and the priestly pole of boundary-setting (Ahijah gives Jeroboam a vision of the future; Shemaiah tells Rehoboam where the boundaries are). How can we communicate this "coaching" model more effectively, and how can this text help us?

First, Rehoboam pays dearly for ignoring his elders' advice—not simply because it comes from his elders, but because the kind of leadership they advocate is servant leadership. Servant leadership is incarnational. Servant leaders do not lord themselves over the flock. They do not avoid laying down their lives for others (1 Pet 5:3; John 10:11). Besides this, one can make the pragmatic argument that servant leadership is the only kind of leadership that actually works, particularly with people who feel alienated and marginalized and ignored by "the system."

"Leaders don't inflict pain; they bear pain."[81]

"Leadership is a foul-weather job."[82]

The parable of Jotham (Judg 9:8-15), Samuel's critique of the monarchy (1 Sam 8:11-18), the stories of Solomon, Naboth, and Jehoiakim—all are preserved to teach us that peacemakers and servants are more effective than demagogues and lone rangers.[83] Disenfranchised people find it hard to ignore this kind of leadership. Broken people simply do not respond well to "harshness" (*qashâ*) and "heaviness" (*kabed*): "What makes a leader a servant is not temperament, strength or energy. What makes a leader a servant leader is first and foremost the type of motivation in the leader….A person who is not a servant leader will tend toward more mixed motives in leading, striving to lead out of pride, manipulation, and force."[84]

Recently I heard a church leader say publicly, "I don't know where we're going, but with God's help, we'll get there." With all due respect, statements like this often betray more ignorance than competence. Servant leadership is not synonymous with "visionlessness." Nor is it synonymous with "blind faith." To be fair, either (a) this leader is a humble man who, while using his gifts to help cast vision for the congregation, simultaneously trusts in God to "provide the increase"; or (b) he works from ill-thought-out motives, confuses "management" with "leadership," and tries to cover over the results with a patina of prayer.[85] Not to question the need for prayer, the point here is that too many churches suffer from a kind of "leadership" which fails to understand what Rehoboam's God really expects.

Second, wise counsel is crucial. Commendably, Rehoboam goes through the motions of seeking out wise counsel, but (a) he chooses the wrong place to look, and (b) he does not know how to respond to it when he hears it. One group counsels him to adopt a leadership style based on manipulation and coercion. The other counsels him to develop a style more in tune with the covenant. Why does he reject the wise counsel for the foolish? Perhaps he fears for his life. Perhaps he fears that servant leadership is too hard. Perhaps he fears that it takes too much effort to make the changes necessary to support the groups and individuals in his realm who feel threatened by change.

Third, God uses prophets to communicate, incarnate, and accomplish his Vision. Sometimes these prophets, like Ahijah, inspire us to dream great dreams for God. Other times they stop us, like Shemaiah, from taking on impossible tasks and dead-end projects. The balance between exhortation and admonition is a delicate one. Does God still plan similar turns of events today (v. 15)? Spurgeon thinks so: "Do not think that you are married to Rehoboam, who will beat you with scorpions, for you are joined to a greater than Solomon. Do not fancy that your heavenly Bridegroom is a beggar."[86]

RELIGIOUS DIVISION (1 Kings 12:25-33)

Having dodged a disaster, Jeroboam immediately goes to work to build up his defenses. Perhaps he remembers the stories about the civil wars against Benjamin (Judg 20-21) and David (2 Sam 15-18).[87] Perhaps he wants to protect the seceding ten tribes from foreign attack. Simultaneously, Rehoboam initiates his own defense strategy, positioning the lion's share of his forces not in the north (against Jeroboam), but in the south, protecting his suddenly truncated kingdom from the Egyptians (2 Chron 11:5-12). This strategy fails, however, because Pharaoh Sheshonq I has some expansion plans of his own (11:12).

Yet Jeroboam is the shrewder leader—too shrewd to believe that military power alone will solve his problems. Like Solomon (his former employer), he knows only too well how a people's "allegiance" (*leb*, "heart," 1 Kings 12:27) can change, and change quickly. He also knows that the fastest way to securing this allegiance is to address his people's needs. He knows that kings have neither the responsibility nor the training to deal with such matters, because these are matters of the cult and need to be addressed in traditional cultic ways by traditional cultic specialists. Having severed all ties to the Jerusalem cult, Jeroboam needs to come up with some kind of a functional substitute, and fast.

Thus, the first step he takes is to construct new religious icons—golden calves. Of all the images at his disposal, bull-images are particularly useful because they so universally represent divine power, and Jeroboam wants to associate himself with this power. These images offend Yahwists because they so deliberately aim at blurring the line between creation and Creator. Jeroboam encourages this, bathing his new cult in traditional Yahwistic language and linking these images to "the God who brought you up from Egypt" (Exod 20:2).[88] Whether one agrees with his theology or not, his politics are shrewd. Where David incorporates both Aaronid and Mushite priesthoods into the Jerusalem cult (2 Sam 8:17), Jeroboam *de*-centralizes the cult so that the temples at Dan and Bethel can become the first of several non-Jerusalem Yahweh temples. This opens the door for other temples later: Josephus records the building of one at Gerizim (*AJ* 11.8.1), and the Talmud mentions one at Leontopolis (in Egypt, *b. Men.* 109b).

Bethel is a tiny village situated on the border between Benjamin and Ephraim. It has a long history of association with important figures—Abraham, Jacob, Deborah, Samuel (Gen 12:8; 28:10-22; Judg 4:5; 1 Sam 7:16). Dan also has a sacred history, and more to the point, a venerable priesthood going all the way back to Moses himself (Judg 18:30-31). The golden calves can be interpreted either as idolatrous Canaanite images or as "footstools" for Yahweh (like the ark in Jerusalem, Psa 132:7). Most scholars lean toward the latter of these opinions, but not all,[89] and this explains the differing translations one finds of Jeroboam's call to worship: "Here is/are your _?_, O Israel." Some translate *'elohîm* in the singular ("God"), others in the plural ("gods").

Second, Jeroboam installs "new" priesthoods at these cult sites. "New" needs to be put in quotation marks, however, because the biblical evidence shows that Dan has a priesthood in place long before Jeroboam: "Jonathan son of Gershom, the son of Moses, and his sons were priests for the tribe of Dan until the time of the captivity of the land" (Judg 18:30). Some argue that it's the rivalry between old priesthoods which causes the tragic schism between Israel and Judah, not just Rehoboam's naiveté.[90] Whether this is true or not, Jeroboam may be trying to revive a more egalitarian way of life in order to pull his people back from the hierarchical excesses of urban monarchy. From the narrator's perspective, however, Jeroboam is simply a heretic, and not just because he's decentralizing Yahweh worship. He's a heretic because he's challenging the validity of Davidic Yahwism—which the narrator perceives as Judah's last, best defense against divination (*qosêm qesamîm*) and sorcery (*me`ônen*).[91]

Third, he establishes "new" festivals to compete head-on with the festivals in Jerusalem. Alongside the new spatial innovations (new temples at Dan and Bethel), Jeroboam also introduces some temporal changes. He boldly changes the religious calendar, the backbone of ancient religious life. If the calendar changes, so must everything else. Calendrical conflicts affect everybody, not just the priesthoods who create them. At Qumran, for example, calendrical conflicts are bitterly divisive because the Jews at Qumran haggle constantly with their brothers in Jerusalem over whether to use a solar calendar or a lunar calendar.[92] To a lesser extent this continues into early Church disputes over the use of Julian vs. Gregorian calendars.[93]

Intratextual Reflection

In other words, Jeroboam intentionally subverts the whole religious system begun by Moses, modified by David, and solidified under Solomon. One can only imagine the impact this has on average Israelites. Jeroboam is forcing thousands of people to weigh convenience against loyalty, and economic expense against religious conviction. It's one thing for the government to feud and divide—it's quite another for one's religion to crack down the middle. Israel does not just split into two nations, but two religious cults with two priesthoods organized around two calendars. The impact of these changes is incalculable.

Jeroboam is not the only leader to use religion for political gain—compare his behavior with that of Jezebel's. Yet where Jeroboam tries to make life more religiously convenient for the northern tribes of Israel, his real goal is to wean them away from Davidic Jerusalem. Where Jezebel tries to teach her husband about how to "make a kingdom" (1 Kings 21:7), her real goal is to convert him to Tyrian Baalism. Jeroboam is not so bold. Where Jeroboam lives in constant fear of being murdered (12:27), Jezebel strikes fear into the hearts of her enemies (like Elijah, 19:3), and traditions like these are recorded to show us what can happen when political power takes precedence over the prophetic Word.

Theological Reflection

As we reflect on how to apply this text, it's helpful to see, first, that religious division is nothing new. Religious groups struggle with division all the time and on several levels. Eishun Ikeda, for example, laments the many institutional conflicts which divide both lay and professional organizations within Asian Buddhism.[94] That's right. Buddhists wrestle just as much with division as do Christians and Muslims. The problem is profoundly human. No one can read the Qur'an and not immediately see its polemical character. No one can read the New Testament and not appreciate how difficult it is for Gentiles and Jews, men and women, slave and free, to leave their old allegiances and unite together under One Head (Eph 4:4). In the American Orthodox Church, just to cite one contemporary example, division is practically paralyzing this denomination. Traditionalists and progressives are using all kinds of regulations and procedures to dictate the form, type and even the mode of worship, to the point that anyone who disagrees over form is susceptible to excommunication.[95] Jeroboam's behavior has a very familiar ring to it.

Second, religious division goes hand in hand with political and ethnic strife. "The break-lines of (world) conflicts," Eckart Otto observes, "run again and again on the border-lines between different religions."[96] Politicians still use religious people and religious causes to advance their own political agendas. Ephraimites and Judahites are not the only tribes who quarrel and fight under religious banners. One thinks, for example, of the religiously motivated Hundred Years War,[97] or the explosive growth of the African Independent Church—a movement as much indebted to ethnic division as missionary effectiveness.[98]

Third, religious division is a painful and debilitating experience for laypeople. America is still a very religious place, and emotions run very high on this issue. Mention any controversial question—abortion, euthanasia, clergy pedophilia, terrorism—and someone with a microphone is addressing it, often from an embarrassingly sectarian perspective. In Europe, sociologists have begun identifying the most volatile areas of division and are discovering, to their surprise, that Christians tend to divide over social issues more than purely religious issues.[99] In the United States, religious division occurs for a variety of reasons. In the past, these divisions were primarily denominational because American Christianity was highly denominational in character. Baptists disregarded Catholics because of their allegiance to the Pope. Methodists looked down their noses at Pentecostals because of their boisterous assemblies. Pentecostals looked down their noses at Presbyterians because their assemblies were not boisterous enough. Arguments like these are fading today because denominational loyalties are coming to mean little to a newer generation of believers, many of whom care more about Christology than ecclesiology. This does not mean that Christians no longer fight, of course. It means that they fight in different ways along different battle lines, and two of the more prominent today are biblical interpretation and worship style—the new golden calves of American Christianity.

Various prophets have been warning us for some time about the "hermeneutics wars." Well, now they're here, and Christian scholars are drawing lines in the sand over such "important issues" as "inerrancy," "structuralism," "deconstruction," "reader-response" criticism, and "gender-neutral" translations. Alarmed by the rancor of these debates, some scholars are beginning to suggest that the pursuit of "truth," when defined in such narrowly modernistic categories, is no longer profitable. Instead, we are exhorted to pursue (a) the text itself with (b) an appropriate variety of interpretive tools, taking into account (c) the living reader in the totality of his/her existence.[100] The jury is still out on whether this is a paradigm shift or a transitional fad.

Where scholars care passionately about hermeneutics, however, laypeople care about worship. Here the fights can get pretty brutal too, as many worshipers will attest. In some circles, "American churchgoers no longer sort themselves out by denomination, (but) by musical preference,"[101] and when American worship is vacuous—as it often is—many begin to wonder whether or how much it "operates out of the biblical vision of worship."[102] American Christians are in the midst of a no-holds-barred "worship war," a war comprised of two opposing camps—traditionalists vs. non-traditionalists. Among non-traditionalists, some also see two sub-camps: *reformers* working from within the church music tradition (driven by baby-boomer concerns), and *revolutionaries* who start from outside the church tradition (also baby boomers) to adapt popular music to religious settings.[103]

No one knows how these wars will turn out, and "golden calf" may not be the best metaphor for describing them. Yet the New Testament reminds us that the earliest churches also had people of different ages, different genders, different races, and different socio-economic levels—and somehow they found a way to transcend their differences and glorify Christ together.

We can too.

CHAOS IN THE SOUTH (1 Kings 14:21-15:24)

This is one of two transitional sections designed to set the stage for the Elijah/Elisha cycle at the heart of Kings. Yet this is not just "filler" information. Structurally a pattern develops here which is rather unique among ancient histories. Kings preserves not one, but two histories, side-by-side.[104] Through a series of staggered king-lists, the southern kings are critiqued right alongside the northern kings. Precisely how to reconcile the chronologies in these lists is not easy,[105] yet the motivation for preserving them has more to do with theology than synchronicity. This is a difficult time in Israel/Judah's history, a time when the kingdom is split into "two kingdoms within a single state,"[106] "two nations under God."[107] One of the narrator's goals is therefore to make sure that both nations have their respective histories preserved.

The narrator's overview of these three southern kings (Rehoboam, Abijah, Asa) tells us, first, that Judah's idolatries continue to damage her potential. Solomon's surrender to his wives' idolatries has opened the door to a religious nightmare in Judah. Rehoboam receives negative marks because he is the product of Solomon's union with a foreigner, Naamah the Ammonite (vv. 21, 31). But he's also castigated because he allows high places (*bamôt*), sacred stones (*matsebôt*), Asherah poles ('*asherîm*), and even male shrine prostitutes (*qadesh*) to operate—things which are detestable (*tô`abot*).

Abijah's reign continues this downward spiral, and the narrator tells us about it by shifting his emphasis from external critique to internal critique. Regardless of the results (cultically, ethically, militarily), Abijah's behavior is basically the same as Solomon's (1 Kings 11:4). Both kings suffer from "incomplete" hearts (*lo' shalem*). In spite of this, though, Yahweh graciously promises Abijah "a lamp in Jerusalem" (a favorite phrase of this narrator). This lamp is Asa, who has a "complete heart" (*shalem*), who expels the male shrine prostitutes (*qedeshîm*) from the land, and succeeds in cleansing Judah of "all the idols his fathers had made."

Here, then, is the *pressure of reform* trajectory. Things drift; religious apostasy develops; a king arises to bring reforms; these reforms seem helpful; yet in the final analysis they do not fully measure up to the narrator's prophetic standards. Even though the reforms of Hezekiah and Josiah are impossible to imagine apart from Asa's reform efforts, Asa is still not good enough—because he does not completely destroy the high places.

Second, foreign influence continues to be a problem. *Internally*, foreign influence has a corrosive, subversive character—the text twice names Rehoboam's Ammonite mother, Naamah, as an example. The same may hold true for Abijah's mother too (Maacah), but the fact that she is called "queen mother" (*gebîrâ*) may or may not be an indication of her foreignness.[108] The existence of queen mothers is more common in the south than it is in the north, but whether this is due to radical differences in northern-vs.-southern kingship ideologies is a matter of debate.[109]

Externally, Rehoboam and Asa have to face some tough international decisions. On Judah's southern flank, Shishak the Libyan pharaoh is mounting a successful campaign, ravaging Judah and cleaning out its treasuries.[110] Shishak's invasion not only devastates Judah, it also opens the door for several other invasions.[111] On Judah's northern flank, the Syrian Ben-Hadad forces Asa to go to these same treasuries in order to negotiate another military deal.[112] His immediate intention is to get Baasha off his back, but whether he is ultimately successful is left ambiguous. This is the first of many attempts to use the Temple treasuries as bargaining chips.[113]

Intratextual Reflection

Like other episodes on the *pressure of subversion* trajectory, this one forces us to look at what can happen when things are allowed to drift, when idolatry becomes, if not acceptable, at least unobjectionable. Subversive behavior, we should emphasize, is not always tied to idolatry. Often, in fact, it's a necessary component in prophetic reform. As the Elijah/Elisha stories demonstrate, subversion against Baalism is sometimes the only way Yahweh can pull his people back to himself. But when spiritual "drift" descends on a nation—or a family, or a business, or a congregation—to the point that "truth" becomes ambiguous, the results can be disastrous. The seeds of this disaster appear in "Adonijah's Ambition" (1 Kings 1:5-10, 41-53), "Solomon's Wavering Heart" (11:1-13), and "Jeroboam's Golden Calves" (12:25-33). Here we see the inevitable fruit. Each of these "subversion" stories shows us a king who fails because he allows foreign gods to sit on Yahweh's throne.

The NT reminds us that this is not just a problem for Judah: "We must pay more careful attention, therefore, to what we have heard, lest we drift away from it. For if the message spoken by angels was binding, and every violation and disobedience received its just punishment, how shall we escape if we ignore so great a salvation?" (Heb 2:1-3a). Just as Hebrew Christians have to sit down and figure out their Christologies,[114] so southern Judahites have to sit down and figure out their loyalties. Why are the first three post-Solomonic kings, with the partial exception of Asa, such poor examples of spiritual leadership?

First, this narrator thinks that conflict strategies involving "foreigners" are risky, dangerous, and tend to raise more problems than they solve. He states this theme, clearly and carefully, but he is careful not to overstate it because God can and does use "foreigners" to accomplish his will—xenophobia is never a desirable characteristic in the Bible.[115] But alongside the "blessing-of-foreigners" tradition, texts like this one remind us that interacting with *some* foreigners, particularly those who oppose Yahweh's divine claims, is a terribly risky business. Asa pays a high price for inviting Ben-Hadad into the intramural conflict with Baasha. Rehoboam too pays dearly for driving away four-fifths of his kingdom, especially while Shishak sits waiting on his southern flank. It's this kind of interaction Paul has in mind when he cautions the Christians at Corinth not to be "unequally yoked" (2 Cor 6:14). Great wisdom is needed when applying this principle to specific contexts today.[116]

Second, all believers have a tendency to drift. Judah's Davidic dynasty, while anchored to a great name, cannot automatically shield Judah from the ravages of idolatry. In fact, it can lead to a false sense of security. The same holds true for contemporary dynasties. Just because someone is the child of a denominational leader or seminary president does not mean that righteousness is somehow genetically transferrable. From a pastoral perspective, this means that we ought to expect idolatrous behavior in those places where it's least expected.

The Reformers realize this early on, and are not intimidated by it. After all, the Reformation occurs in one of the most religious places on earth—medieval Europe. On the 450th anniversary of Zwingli's death, some are calling for a return to the kind of prophetic preaching which changed Europe. Among Zwingli's many attributes—his expository preaching, his determination to preach from the original texts, his emphasis on personal and societal reform—perhaps his greatest accomplishment is his refusal to condone idolatry. Yet his example is hard to replicate today because preachers who try to follow it often find themselves standing before moving vans instead of filled pews.[117]

Theological Reflection

What this practically means is that realizing idolatry's subversive character is a good beginning, but it's only half the battle. Nancy Carmichael discovers this one morning while cleaning out her attic:

> Today as I cleaned, wavering between tossing an old letter or filing it, I thought, this is so like me! I have a tendency to cling to things with a tenacious grip. Not just physical things, but people. Positions. Memories. I heard someone once say, "The Lord will not fit in an occupied heart." I wonder—is my heart too crowded for Him...so full of my own agenda that there's no room for Him?[118]

Keen insight. Idolatry is not so much about confronting overt evil as it is about giving up otherwise good things when they cripple our witness. Bryan Chapell realizes this, and hosts a group of Christian businessmen who meet together once a month to ask each other some pretty pointed questions: "Did you stay pure on your last business trip? When you returned from your trip, did you stay honest on your expense reports?" Tough questions. Critical questions. Answering them honestly is not always easy, yet "it's not just a matter of fighting: it's a matter of fleeing. Look at 1 Cor 10:14: 'Flee from idolatry.' That's part of the battle. If you struggle with it, flee. Change the channel. Stay away from her."[119]

Idolatry will never be unappealing.

CHAOS IN THE NORTH (1 Kings 15:25-16:34)

This is the second of two paragraphs designed to prepare us for the Elijah/Elisha traditions, and though the similarities with the previous paragraph are obvious, the material here has a decidedly northern cast to it. Put in chart form, it looks something like this:

Name	Relationship	Length of reign	Location	Military?	Blood purge?	Prophet?
Nadab	son of Jeroboam	2 years	Gibbethon?	no	no	(Ahijah)
Baasha	usurper (Issachar)	24 years	Tirzah	no	yes	Jehu
Elah	son of Baasha	2 years	Tirzah	no	no	—
Zimri	usurper	7 days	Tirzah	yes	yes	—
(Tibni)	(son of Ginath [killed by Omri?])	—	—	—	—	—
Omri	usurper	12 years	Tirzah/Samaria	yes	yes	—
Ahab	son of Omri	22 years	Samaria	no	no	Elijah/Micaiah[120]

Northern Israel has its own character, in other words, and four components of this character include (a) Israel's stop-and-start attempts at dynasty; (b) the mobility of Israel's capital; (c) Israel's tendency to resolve political conflicts via military assassination; and (d) Israel's inclusion of prophets into the political process.

With regard to the question of dynasty, the narrator leaves no doubt: Jeroboam's attempt to create a "house of Jeroboam" is a failure. His son Abijah is dead, as predicted by Ahijah the prophet (1 Kings 14:10-16), and an otherwise unknown Issacharite, Baasha, assassinates another of his sons, Nadab. Instead of lamenting these tragedies, the narrator relates them dispassionately—this is just how things get done in the North. Like the old Mesopotamian king Naram-Sin, Jeroboam is very much the stereotypical "evil ruler."[121] Rarely does Kings portray him positively. Even the non-biologically-related kings who come after him fail "because of the sins of Jeroboam son of Nebat." In other words, no northern king will ever be able to do what David has done. Elah reigns two years. Zimri's reign lasts only seven days. Ahab's 22-year reign turns out to be the exception which proves the rule.

Second, several Israelite capitals come and go in this period. Before the monarchy of Saul, Shiloh and Shechem are the North's major centers of influence. No northern city has the prestige of a Jerusalem, but Tirzah, a city about which we know little, comes to prominence in this period. With the exception of Nadab, most of the kings in this period rule from Tirzah. Omri changes this. No one knows for sure, but Omri may decide to move the capital to Samaria because he hails from a clan called "Shemer," and he may be acting as Shemer's redeemer when he names his town "Samaria."[122] Kings' narrator tells us little about Omri, even though Mesha mentions him on the famous Moabite Stone as "oppressing Moab" and successfully "taking possession" of Medeba for "forty years" (*ANET* 320-21). Apparently he is a leader of some renown because the Assyrian king Shalmeneser III once refers to Israel as "Omri-land" (*ANET* 284, 285).

Third, Israel is different from Judah in its tendency to resolve conflicts via military assassination instead of political negotiation. Just as radical Protestants tend (emphasis on tend) to splinter instead of negotiate, so does northern Israel.[123] Baasha kills Nadab at Gibbethon. Zimri kills Elah. Omri forces Zimri to set fire to his palace (with himself in it). Tibnath's death, deftly understated ("So Tibni died") is probably Omri-provoked, or at least Omri-inspired. Israelite politics are a brutal mess after Jeroboam.

Perhaps most interesting, fourth, is prophecy's high profile in the midst of this chaos. Northern prophets seem to come out of nowhere in these texts. Some are persecuted for their faith (Elijah); others are left alone (Jehu ben Hanani). Poetic creativity is not their strongest characteristic. The prophet Jehu's prophetic oracle against Baasha, for example, is little more than a rehash of stereotypical threats and invectives. Further, not all prophets command the narrator's respect (e.g., the hundreds of prophets surrounding Ahab, 1 Kings 22:5-12).

Yet several prophets do rise up and condemn several northern kings for doing "evil in the eyes of Yahweh" (Nadab, Baasha, Zimri, Omri) and "provoking Yahweh, the God of Israel, to anger" (Nadab, Baasha, Elah, Omri). Two of the six merit the distinction of sinning more than all those before him (Omri, Ahab), and of these two, one marries the daughter of a king whose name (significantly) ends in -Baal (Ethbaal, Jezebel's father). Of these six kings, one sinks to the point of actually worshiping Baal (Ahab), and one sets up an altar for Baal in a Baal temple (*bêt habba`al*).[124] This is an incredible development, even by northern standards. Here kings actually encourage believers to sacrifice their children to foreign gods. Kings are not supposed to do this, but just as Ezekiel accuses Judah as a whole, this narrator accuses Ahab of making sin seem "trivial" (*qalal*, Ezek 8:17).

So strong is Baalism's pull, in fact, Yahweh eventually has to use Baal-jargon himself to communicate with his own people, evidently because this is the only religious language they understand. Rather than speak of himself as Creator or Redeemer, Yahweh speaks of himself as the One who controls the storms, as the One who brings dead things back to life, as the One who terrorizes Sea and Death. This is not the covenant language of Torah, and the fact that Yahweh himself uses it tells us a lot about the audience the prophets are trying to reach.[125]

Intratextual Reflection

If the previous paragraph invites us to reflect on Judah's problems with foreigners (Ben-Hadad, Shishak) and dynasties, this text sharply intensifies these themes. Ahab's marriage to the foreigner Jezebel, for example, goes beyond any alliance Asa makes with the Syrian Ben-Hadad. Ahab does not simply ask for occasional military help. Ahab embraces a foreign religious system.[126] Similarly, Judah's tendency to live in its dynastic past seems insignificant when compared to Jeroboam's shenanigans. Unflinchingly the narrator relates these sad truths in order to prepare us for the showdowns yet to come.

Baalism's primary appeal, according to Eugene Peterson, is its alluring combination of two things: subjective experience and psychological jargon.[127] So defined, contemporary Baalism is little more than a papier-mâché bridge precariously stretched over a deep canyon—the yawning chasm between Creator and creation—and unoffensive, self-centered, trivializing sensation is the glue holding together all its "planks." Contemporary as well as ancient Baalists do not and cannot imagine the divine will as something opposed to human will.

Robert Wuthnow has reflected on this phenomenon from a sociological perspective and, through careful research, has discovered that "small groups" sometimes become the vehicle through which Baalism enters the Church. Small group ministry is radically altering American Christian theology and culture. Small groups provide "community," but sometimes of a kind which is radically different from what we see in the NT. Small groups can have difficulty drawing people to the covenant God of the Bible because they often reimagine God more as an internal presence than a righteous king. Often such groups define the sacred only in personal, psychological categories, not canonical ones, and this hyper-personalizing of the sacred leads some to imagine that God himself can be domesticated.[128]

Wuthnow is quick to add that there are many positive things to say about small groups. Small groups can revitalize some sense of the sacred in a thoroughly secularized culture, and they can and do address deep religious yearnings. Yet because many small groups are ideologically committed to replacing theological doctrines with implicit norms, they pose a real danger to the spiritual health of the Church. Seldom do these kinds of small groups ever study anything objectively—not in a disciplined way—and this makes the people within them vulnerable to manipulation by strong-willed personalities.[129]

Theological Reflection

Political conflict in a church setting can cause people to question who God is, where God is, and, in some cases, whether God is. Joan, for example, is a lady in our church who always runs to this or that Baal (as defined above by Peterson) whenever she's confused or angry. Once, for example, we had an evening worship service in which the worship leader, in his enthusiasm for the new praise songs he was learning, simply erupted into praise for about fifteen minutes. Most of us tried to follow along, but this was just too much for Joan. It wasn't just the length of the eruption or even its contents. It was the tone she felt it reflected. "Why didn't someone tell us that we were going to do this?" From her perspective, the worship leader showed sheer disregard for the people he claimed to be leading.

She's not alone in her anger. Several worshipers walked out of our assembly that evening, and among those who stuck it out, several wrote angry letters. A few have never come back to worship with us again—they've gone somewhere else, somewhere more "safe." No one has fired the worship leader because in the final analysis this is not a "worship problem." It's a theological problem. Whether it's worship or budget-making or church-building or staff-hiring or anything else, there's a restlessness in the Church today, and a great deal of it stems from the Joans of this world and their devotion to Baal instead of Yahweh (as defined above). How can we address this theological problem more effectively?

First, we need to remember that leadership itself, particularly congregational leadership, is never static. Modes and types of leadership are always changing—in fact, some desperately *need* to change. Howard Clark Kee points out that the earliest of the Church was a time of tremendous change. Examining the Synoptic, Johannine, and Pauline traditions, he finds no uniform, sharply defined leadership roles in these texts, only a movement from spontaneity and improvisation to consolidation and order. What this might mean is that, depending on the types and ages of our congregations, we probably have more flexibility than we think—or that "Joan" would have us think.[130]

Second, the problem facing us is not "Baalism" *per se*. The deeper question is why people turn to "Baalism" at all. Maybe, like my friend Joan, they turn to "Baal" because they don't feel able (or don't want) to adapt to the changes being "sprung" at them. Corporate worship is often the flashpoint where this occurs because for immature believers this is their only contact with the Unseen world. On the other hand, for mature believers there's a growing desire to reach out to unchurched people who respond positively to creative worship. For such people contemporary worship is not disrespectful, but empowering. The problem is not stylistic, but theological. Craig Garriott reminds us that as our neighborhoods become more and more ethnically diverse, the Church is going to have to fight its battles on newer fronts, because each ethnic group has its own worship traditions. This means that we will have to learn how to consider theologies which are flexible enough to adapt to new multiethnic realities, yet anchored enough in the Word to call people back to Yahweh—not Baal.[131]

YAHWEH'S SHOWDOWN WITH BAAL (1 Kings 18:16-46)

Finally we come to the showdown for which we have been so carefully prepared. Complex and multi-layered, the contours of this episode become clearest when we unpack its layers and identify its salient features. Level One is the conflict between Elijah and Ahab. Level Two is the conflict between Elijah and Israel. Level Three is the conflict between Elijah and the Baal prophets. Level Four is the conflict between Yahweh and Baal. Underneath all of these levels lies a remarkable intertextual foundation anchored in the Gideon traditions. Gideon receives the name "Jerubba`al" ("Let Baal contend") because he tears down a Baal altar and destroys its accompanying Asherah pole (Judg 6:32). In response, his neighbors plot to kill him, but his father intervenes: "Are you going to plead Baal's cause? Are you going to save him? If Baal is God, he can defend himself" (6:31). Elijah uses a similar argument on Mt. Carmel: "If Yahweh is God, follow him; but if Baal is God, follow him."

Level one begins with a character slur: Ahab calls Elijah a "troubler" (`oker). Earlier Jonathan uses this word to describe Saul: "My father troubles the land" (`akar, 1 Sam 14:29), but here "trouble" is anything which goes against Ahab's agenda. Elijah defends himself with a definition akin to Jonathan's: "I have not made "trouble" for Israel...you and your father's family have!" The sequence is simple: one does not follow the Baals until one first decides to abandon the commands (*mitswot*). Canaanite Baalism may stand for many things, but this religion has nothing to do with "covenant" or "command." No archaeologist has ever found a tablet containing Baal's *mitswot* ("commands") or Asherah's *huqqîm* ("decrees"). Of the hundreds of Canaanite texts discovered— Ugaritic, Phoenician, Punic—we have yet to find a Canaanite equivalent to the Ten Commandments (Exod 20:2-17). This is significant.

Level two is the conflict between Elijah and Israel. Here the tone abruptly shifts from biting satire to pastoral sensitivity. Elijah does not speak to Israel the same way he speaks to Ahab. He "draws near unto them" (*nagash*, v. 21), speaking to them like the lost sheep they are. After he has their attention he asks them, "How long will you waver between two opinions?" To this pivotal question no one says a word in response. But Elijah does not give up on them. He lays down his contest rules and the crowd cheers: "Good (is the) word!" (*tôb haddabar*). Later, after the Baalists' marathon prayer session, he invites his people to "draw near unto him" again (same word, *nagash*, v. 30), and when they do, he does something quite telling. He repairs (lit. "heals," *rapâ'*) Yahweh's altar. Baal's altar stands primed and ready. Yahweh's altar lies in disrepair. This is significant.

The question Elijah asks is justifiably famous: "How long will you waver (lit., "limp," *pasah*) between two opinions?" (lit., "forks"). The scholarly discussion about what "limp" (*pasah*) might mean is intense, but more important is the fact that Elijah's question goes straight to the heart of Israel's dilemma. By asking it so publicly, he not only responds to the previous questions leveled at him about sin and death (chapters 17 and 18), but he challenges the twin-demons of spiritual ambivalence and moral fatalism. Elijah is more interested in rescuing Israelites than killing Baalists.

In level three, Elijah turns his attention back to his enemies, and his tone changes accordingly. To all Israel he *proposes*. To the Baal-prophets he *commands*, his earlier pleas with Israel turning into sharp imperatives: "Choose! Prepare! Call! Don't light!" Barking out orders like a drill sergeant, perhaps he speaks this way because he knows that *this* audience is too calloused to listen to any other kind of language. Whatever his intentions, the Baal prophets accept his challenge and gear up for battle. Turning on their religion machine, they dance around (*pasah*) Baal's altar for hours, and thanks to the Ugaritic texts, we can now imagine the contents of those prayers—e.g.:

> (28) O Baal, cast the strong one from our gates,
> (29) The warrior from our walls.
> A bull, (30) O Baal, we sanctify,
> A vow, O Baal, (31) we fulfill;
> A [first]-born (or: a [ra]m), O Baal, we sanctify,
> (32) A food-offering, O Baal, we fulfill,
> A drink-offering, O Baal, we make;

(33) We go up to the sanctuary of Baal,
We take the path to the temple of Baal.[132]

Nothing happens in response. Like everyone else, Elijah sees this, but instead of commiserating with his religious colleagues, he begins to taunt them (*yehattel*). The more he taunts, the more they rave. The more he mocks, the more they mutilate themselves with knives and spears. Still the result remains the same: no response (lit., no "sound," *qôl*), no answer(er) (`*oneh*),[133] no attention (lit., "evidence of life," *qasheb*). When we consider the fact that the root of this verb "taunt" (*htl*) is a lexical first-cousin to deceive (*tll*; hip`il: *htl*, "to deceive"),[134] Elijah's strategy looks more than a little intentional. When he suggests that Baal might be "deep in thought, or busy, or traveling...or sleeping" (*yshn*), Elijah appears to be using Baal's own epithets against him.[135]

All of this prepares us for level four, the final showdown. Here it's impossible to say much in detail, but obviously if fire doesn't fall, there's no reason to preserve such a story. Everything hangs on whether the fire actually falls. Yahweh's altar doesn't simply stand next to Baal's. Elijah saturates it in the commodity with which everyone is here concerned—*water*.[136] And when Yahweh's fire falls, it doesn't fall simply to "lick up" Elijah's sacrifice. It "licks up" Baal's false promises as well. It's not enough for Israel simply to say "Yahweh—he is God! Yahweh—he is God!" Israel must "bear fruits worthy of repentance" if it is to learn the meaning housed in this miraculous sign.

On Mt. Carmel, Elijah prays for an "answer," and fire falls from heaven. On Mt. Horeb, however, Yahweh again answers, but in a very different way (1 Kings 19). On Mt. Carmel, Elijah tells his servant to look to the sea for some sign of rain. When he comes back and says, "There is nothing there," this does not dissuade him from sending him back several more times. On Mt. Horeb, however, *Yahweh* is the one who keeps sending signs—tornado, earthquake, blazing fire—before his prophet finally decides to listen to his Word.

Intratextual Reflection

Most episodes dealing with subversion focus predominantly on political subversion (e.g., "Rehoboam's Naivete," "Adonijah's Ambition"). Only a few address the sensitive issue of religious subversion, and of those which do ("Jeroboam's Golden Calves," "Eye of the Storm"), "Yahweh's Showdown with Baal" is by far the most famous. This episode becomes intratextually significant, however, when we compare it with, say, the story of Micaiah ben Imlah (1 Kings 22).

First, both episodes have similar structures; i.e., both have similar layers of conflict within them. The Micaiah episode focuses on age-old conflicts between nations, prophets and kings. Micaiah, like Elijah, is a single Yahwist who stands alone against determined Baalist adversaries. Yet Ahab's pride is what falls in the Micaiah episode, not divine fire. Ahab's embarrassment pales in comparison with the events on Mt. Carmel. The theological conflict between Yahweh and Baal is more sophisticated at Ramoth Gilead. Where Micaiah sees a vision of the heavenly throne-room, Elijah sees fire fall from heaven. The implications of this should not be overstated, but neither should they be understated. With Ahab's pride Yahweh deals differently than he does with the Baal prophets.

Second, the prophet-prophet confrontation looks similar in each episode, but Micaiah's adversaries seem considerably less violent. Elijah's adversaries overtly connect themselves to the worship of Baal and the ideology of Baalism, but both traditions show prophets taking potshots at one another—Elijah through satire, Micaiah through "playful deception." Yet where the Micaiah incident ends with the protagonist in prison, the Elijah incident ends in a bloodbath. From a canonical perspective, the former is the more common ending to such confrontations (e.g., Jeremiah), but this only serves to render the incident on Mt. Carmel even more astonishing (from an intratexual perspective).

Theological Reflection
This is a public religious confrontation. It's difficult to recall the last time one of these occurred in North America. One can still find the occasional public religious debate today, but most are theologically esoteric, denominationally intramural, or just plain boring. Megachurches pull in "experts" every now and then to "debate" whether or not women should have the right to lead worship or whether or not Christ will return by a specific date. But rarely does "all Israel" show up to such affairs. What we usually see instead is a "naked public square" populated by religious demagogues and the occasional Christian bystander.[137]

Few of us have ever or will ever experience a public confrontation like this (what advertiser would televise it?). Israel's attitude looks like hardened conviction compared to the bland spiritual fog in which most Americans wander. Biblical illiteracy is part of the reason, for sure, but the deeper problem is theological disinterest, even among believers. In many churches it's best to avoid the word "theology" in polite discussion.[138] This makes stories like this one very difficult to preach or teach, because when Elijah gathers Israel to Carmel, he does so to make a public theological claim on their lives. There's something primal about this conflict, something unavoidably prophetic. This is no mock theological debate like the ones we used to have in seminary—this is the real thing!

E. B. Holifield reminds us that public religious debate used to be the primary way laypeople received a theological education.[139] Not any more, apparently. Too many have become too adept at segregating religion from the rest of the educational world. Even among Christians, commentators try to segregate Elijah's roles into separate categories. "Elijah cannot pastor doubting parishioners *and* challenge hostile enemies at the same time." "Israel cannot be intelligent and responsible enough to make up their own minds about God." This text challenges all such false dichotomies. One is tempted to say that it's about "spiritual warfare," but this is such a poorly-defined buzzword, it seems better to resist this temptation. Spiritual warfare is a biblical idea, properly defined, and Paul makes it very clear that the Ephesians' struggle is "against the powers of this dark world and the spiritual forces of evil" (Eph 6:12). But books like Frank Peretti's *This Present Darkness*[140] have bleached out the idea's biblical meaning and replaced it with a more acceptable folk theology—to be specific, a populist demonology. The result is that "spiritual warfare" is more closely aligned in the popular mind with practices like "prayer-mapping" and "territorial spirits"—two ideas which have nothing to do with Scripture. The Elijah traditions know nothing—absolutely nothing—about prayer-mapping or territorial spirits.[141] The central message of the biblical text is that Yahweh is more powerful than Baal, and if we focus squarely on *this* message, we can readily cull out from it a few relevant applications.

First, this episode is a studied contrast between reasoned history and frenzied experience. It does not go so far as to argue that reason should replace enthusiasm. It simply suggests that biblical worship begins and ends with theology—to be precise, Yahwistic covenant theology. Even as Gideon's father uses a single provocative question to stop a Baalist mob from killing his son, so Elijah uses a similar question to stop Baalist ecstatics from redefining Yahweh's character. If we are to follow Elijah's example, then we must keep raising this issue. We must be willing to ask people not only how they *feel* about God but precisely who they think God is.

Second, Yahwistic prophets are more interested in historical revelation than prayer technique. When Elijah rebuilds the altar, he uses twelve stones to represent the twelve tribes of Israel. He prays to Yahweh as the God of his fathers—Abraham, Isaac and Jacob—not as one god among a larger pantheon (Baal, Anat, Mot, Yam, El—the Canaanite pantheon). His actions demonstrate a clear knowledge of and commitment to Israel's theological history. It's the Baal-prophets who do the most praying here, not Elijah. Moreover, when Elijah finally does pray, he prays to request, not coerce. Yahweh is the one who sends the heavenly fire, not Baal, and Elijah is a prophet, not an exorcist.

Third, the Yahweh-vs.-Baal conflict is still with us. If the gulf between creation and Creator can be crossed via religious ritual alone, then sensory participation should rightly become the supreme expression of Christian worship (the more sensory, the better). But if worship is centered in the Word of a covenant-making God, then worship which deemphasizes or marginalizes or pushes a theology of the Word to the periphery should be rejected for what it is—Baalism. The divine will can be and often is opposed to human tastes and desires and perceptions, and Baalists will never understand this.

Notes

1. Hesiod, *Theogony*, lines 530-84; *Thebaid*, para. 2-3.

2. David Marcus, "David the Deceiver and David the Dupe," *Prooftexts* 6 (1986) 166-67.

3. MT ʿatsabô. Syr reads kl', "to hinder, restrain." LXX reads apekôlusen, "to hinder." Tg has 'klmyh, "to hinder, rebuke, put to shame." Vg has corripuit "to blame, rebuke, accuse."

4. Karelisa V. Hartigan, *Ambiguity and Self-Deception: The Apollo and Artemis Plays of Euripides,* Studien zur klassischen Philologie 50 (Frankfurt am Main: Peter Lang, 1991) 70.

5. Eugene McAfee suggests (*The Patriarch's Longed-For Son: Biological and Social Reproduction in Ugaritic and Hebrew Epic* [Th.D. dissertation, Harvard University, 1996]) that the epic of the "longed-for son" is a type of narrative in which sons cannot meet the expectations placed on them, and that the telling of such stories is designed to overcome logically, if not actually, the contradiction between children as conveyors of social continuity and children as agents of social change.

6. Benaiah first comes to David's court as the captain of the Kerethites and Pelethites (2 Sam 8:18), no doubt the "special guard" mentioned here. Zadok comes to the priesthood with the generation of Ahimelech, the son of Abiathar (8:17), and is a rather mysterious character. Some see him as a Jebusite priest only later subsumed to Davidic Yahwism. Others see him as an Aaronide priest and Abiathar as a "Mushite" priest, and that their separation represents an institutional rift between rival priestly houses (*CMHE* 208).

7. E. Schürer, *A History of the Jewish People in the Time of Jesus,* ed. Nahum Glatzer (New York: Schocken, 1961; trans. and abridged from 19th century German ed.) 137, 151-58.

8. *King Lear*, act 3, scene 2. The most thorough recent study of this issue is S. Lasine, *Knowing Kings: Knowledge, Power, and Narcissism in the Hebrew Bible,* SBLSS 40 (Atlanta: Society of Biblical Literature, 2001) 1-27.

9. H. Hagan, "Deception as a Motif and Theme in 2 Sam 9-20; 1 Kings 1-2," *Bib* 60 (1979) 321. Molière (1622-73) is a chronological and philosophical contemporary of Voltaire.

10. J. Dobson, *Dare to Discipline* (Wheaton, IL: Tyndale House, 1970).

11. J. Bartkowski and Christopher G. Ellison, "Divergent Models of Childrearing in Popular Manuals: Conservative Protestants vs. the Mainstream Experts," *SR* 56 (1995) 21-34.

12. Cameron Lee, "Parenting as Discipleship: A Contextual Motif for Christian Parent Education," *JPT* 19 (1991) 268-77.

13. Bill Cosby, *Fatherhood* (Garden City, NY: Doubleday, 1986) 158.

14. D. Blankenhorn, *Fatherless America: Confronting Our Most Urgent Social Problem* (New York: Basic, 1995) 222-34.

15. Bruno Malinowski, *Sex, Culture, and Myth* (New York: Harcourt, Brace, & World, 1962) 63.

16. Chester I. Barnard, *The Functions of the Executive,* 30th Anniversary Ed.. (Cambridge: Harvard, 1966) 194. Adonijah ignores all four of these criteria.

17. Tom Peters and Robert Waterman, *In Search of Excellence* (New York: Warner, 1982) 82.

18. R. Niebuhr, "The Ethic of Jesus and the Social Problem," in *Love and Justice: Selections from the Shorter Writings of Reinhold Niebuhr* (Louisville: Westminster/John Knox, 1992) 37-38 (first published in 1932).

19. K. Stone, *Sex, Honor and Power in the Deuteronomistic History,* JSOTSup 234; (Sheffield: Sheffield Academic Press, 1996).

20. *Gen. Rab.* 20.5. Some rabbis toss him into a biblical "rogues gallery" with Cain, Korah, Balaam, Doeg, Gehazi, Absalom, Uzziah, and Haman.

21. The phrase is *'is mawet*, the closest parallel to which is "son of death" (*ben mawet*) in 2 Sam 12:5. *NIV's* translation, "you deserve to die," misses this idiomatic parallel.

22. Hannibal Lector is the sociopathic antagonist in Thomas Harris's chilling novel, *The Silence of the Lambs* (New York: St. Martin, 1988).

23. L. Eslinger calls this conversation "verbal fencing," and "the wrangling of God and king" (*House of God or House of David: The Rhetoric of 2 Samuel 7,* JSOTSup 164; (Sheffield: JSOT, 1994] 6, 14).

24. Granted, Sennacherib fails to destroy Jerusalem (2 Kings 18:17-37), but this one bright moment is overshadowed by every other story on this trajectory except this one (the deliverance from Aram is muted and ambiguous in 2 Kings 13:1-9).

25. I am therefore in disagreement with Walsh ("The Characterization of Solomon in 1 Kings 1-5," *CBQ* 57 (1995) 483) when he styles 1 Kings 2:13-46 only as a "bloodbath" designed to "demonstrate his (Solomon's) control."

26. P. W. Roberts, *The Demonic Comedy: Some Detours in the Baghdad of Saddam Hussein* (New York: Farrar, Straus and Giroux, 1998) 46-84.

27. I am aware that Saddam is Muslim, but I am also aware that many of his brothers are embarrassed by his lip-service to Islam.

28. Barbara Brown Zikmund, "On Becoming a Seminary President: Reflections

on My Early Years at Hartford Seminary," *TE* 32 (1996) 153-76.

29. Susan Windley, "Success, Shame, and Illusion: American Culture Christianity and the God of Death-Denial," *CSR* 26 (1996) 55-71.

30. John R. W. Stott, "Am I Supposed to Love Myself or Hate Myself?" *CT* 28 (1984) 26-28.

31. Akk *sarru* ("king/leader"), Ug *sar* ("prince"), Arab *sar* ("head"), Aram *sr* ("official/functionary").

32. Whether or not he is consciously adapting Egyptian prototypes to Israelite needs is a matter of debate, though the arguments of J. Begrich are persuasive ("*Sofer und mazkîr*: ein Beitrag zur inneren Geschichte des davidisch-salomonischen Grossreiches und des Königreiches Juda," *ZAW* 58 [1940/41] 1-29).

33. Perhaps Azariah replaces David's "priest," Ira the Jairite, and perhaps Nathan's son Zabud becomes Ira's replacement as the king's personal adviser (lit., "friend"). Perhaps, on the other hand, Zadok and his son Azariah serve Solomon as co-priests in the same way that kings and princes operate as "co-regents."

34. Opinions are divided over the *mazkîr*. H. Reventlow ("Das Amt des *Mazkir*. Zur Rechtsstruktur des öffentlichen Lebens in Israel," *TZ* 15 [1959] 161-75) thinks of him as "the highest official in the land," while T. Mettinger (*Solomonic State Officials* [Lund: C. W. K. Gleerup, 1971] 52-62) sees him only as a "royal herald."

35. Other palace managers include Arza (1 Kings 16:9), Obadiah (18:3), Jotham (2 Kings 15:5), Eliakim (18:18, 37; 19:2), and Shebna (Isa 22:15).

36. LXX records yet another "official" in Solomon's inner circle, a certain "Eliab," whose job is to oversee Israel's "clans" (Gk *patrias*). What exactly this job might entail, assuming the reliability of LXX, cannot be ascertained, but the fact that such a position is mentioned at all shows that there is at least some awareness of the tension between tribal and federal governments.

37. A. D. H. Mayes, "Amphictyony," *ABD* 1.212-16.

38. Baruch Halpern writes definitively about this in his important study, *The Constitution of the Monarchy in Israel*, HSM 25 (Chico, CA: Scholar's Press, 1981).

39. Controversy exists over exactly where these cities might have been located (D. Ussishkin, "Was the 'Solomonic' City Gate at Megiddo Built by Solomon?" *BASOR* 239 [1980] 1-18).

40. "Insofar as this familiar model of the hierarchic city-state was totally contrary to the simplicities of previous Israelite social organization, it fueled intense resentment and grievance, and eroded the morale of the people" (N. Gottwald, *The Hebrew Bible: A Socio-Literary Introduction* [Philadelphia: Fortress, 1985] 323).

41. See my "The Judean *lmlk* Stamps: Some Unresolved Issues," *RQ* 28 (1985/86) 17-26.

42. For discussions, see J. Blenkinsopp, *The Pentateuch*, ABRL (New York: Doubleday, 1992) 25-28; R. Whybray, *Introduction to the Pentateuch* (Grand Rapids: Eerdmans, 1995) 18-27; Gottwald, *Hebrew Bible*, 137.

43. N. Gottwald, *Hebrew Bible*, 332. See also D. Jobling, "'Forced Labor': Solomon's Golden Age and the Question of Literary Representation," *Sem* 54 (1991) 57-76.

44. "Eliab son of Zaph was in charge of the 'clans' (*patrias*)" (1 Kings 4:6, LXX).

45. S. Grenz and R. Olson, *Who Needs Theology?* (Downers Grove: InterVarsity, 1996) 27-29.

46. R. Hughes and L. Allen write definitively about these issues in *Illusions of*

Innocence: Protestant Primitivism in America (Chicago: University of Chicago, 1988).

47. For example, "(Hal) Lindsey relentlessly turns the Bible into a manual of atomic-age combat" (P. Boyer, *When Time Shall Be No More: Prophecy Belief in Modern American Culture* [Cambridge: Belknap Press, 1994] 127).

48. M. McKenzie, "Christian Norms in the Ethical Square: An Impossible Dream?" *JETS* 38 (1995) 413-27.

49. R. Brown and A. Wesson, "Technology and Theology: Cooperation or Conflict?" *MC* 32 (1991) 16-23.

50. D. Shaw, "In Search of Postmodern Salvation," *ERT* 22 (1998) 48-60.

51. The Hebrew text is blunt: "The king, Solomon, loved women, foreign, many."

52. This institution may be originally rooted in circumcision ritual (E. Kutsch, "*hatan*," *TDOT* 5.274).

53. *NJPS*, for example, translates "none of you shall join them and none of them shall join you," implying that Solomon's problem is not just intermarriage.

54. This word often appears in Deuteronomy in explicitly theological contexts where the choice is between Yahweh vs. a foreign god (Deut 4:3-4) or a prophet's dream vs. Yahweh's word (13:5). Such choices are routinely set before Israel in order to test their "hearts" (13:3).

55. 1 Chron 22:9. T. Ishida challenges this etymology as late ("Solomon," *ABD* 6.105).

56. H. Wehr, *A Dictionary of Modern Written Arabic* (Ithaca: Cornell, 1966) 424-26.

57. Such faith choices are not limited to pre-moderns. Provan (*Kings* 8) reminds us that there is no such thing as unbiased, objective, faith-free historiography, only the choice between historiography which operates on one set of presuppositions vs. historiography which operates on another: "the noisy ejection of religious commitment through the front door of the scholarly house is only a cover for the quieter smuggling in...of a quite different form of commitment through the rear."

58. This goddess `ttrt is the Canaanite equivalent of Assyrian Ishtar, Greek Astarte, and Eblaite Ashtar, and is the "queen of heaven" to whom Jeremiah refers (Jer 7:18: 44:17-18).

59. *KAI* 181.5, 8, 12, 14, 17, 19.

60. Perhaps the best attempt to identify this shadowy deity is G. C. Heider, *The Cult of Molek: A Reassessment,* JSOTSup 43 (Sheffield: JSOT Press, 1985).

61. This is a literal translation of *ya`an 'asher hayetâ zo't `immak* in v. 11. The use of *`im* appears earlier in v. 9: "for his heart turned from being with (*me`im*) Yahweh."

62. Cyprian, *Three Books of Testimonies Against the Jews* 3.62.

63. Tertullian, *Five Books Against Marcion* 2.23.

64. Ysabel de Andia, "Purity of Heart," *Communio* 16 (1989) 32-53.

65. G. Salyer, "Rhetoric, Purity, and Play: Aspects of Mark 7:1-23," *Sem* 64 (1993) 139-69.

66. Dale C. Allison and W. D. Davies, "Reflections on the Sermon on the Mount," *SJT* 44 (1991) 283-309.

67. D. Senior and C. Stuhlmueller, *The Biblical Foundations for Mission* (Maryknoll, NY: Orbis, 1983) 316.

68. W. R. Eichhorst, "Ezra's Ethics on Intermarriage and Divorce," *Grace Journal* 10 (1969) 16-28.

69. Cited in S. J. D. Cohen, "From the Bible to the Talmud: The Prohibition of Intermarriage," *Hebrew Annual Review* 7 (1983) 23-39.

70. This is a line of a song by Bonnie Raitt.

71. Shechem (the person) is the son of Hamor, whose name means "donkey" (*hamôr,* Gen 34:2). Archaeologists have found, while excavating Shechem's east gate, the decapitated skeleton of a donkey with what appears to be the bones of an animal sacrifice (G. E. Wright, "Shechem," *EAEHL* 4.1083-94).

72. See *EA* 244.11; 245.6; 250.14.

73. B. Halpern, "Sectionalism and the Schism," *JBL* 93 (1974) 532.

74. M. Heitzer ("On Tithe Paid in Grain in Ugarit," *IEJ* 25 [1975] 124-28) shows that the Canaanite port-city of Ugarit has a well-developed taxation system as early as the 14th century BC. Taxes are paid in slave labor, in silver and agricultural products, and all able-bodied men have to work for the king. Solomon's taxation system appears little different. In fact, in 1980 N. Avigad ("The Chief of the Corvée," *IEJ* 30 [1980] 170-73) published a seal inscription which reads *lpl'yhw 'shr 'l hms,* "belonging to Pela'yahu who is over (in charge of) the forced labor." Paleographical analysis puts this seal in the 7th century BC, and this suggests that forced labor continued to be a state-organized institution in Judah long after Solomon's death.

75. *ANET* 316 (the Cyrus Cylinder). Note the same mention of the hated yoke in 1 Kings 12:4.

76. G. Evans ("Rehoboam's Advisers at Shechem, and Political Institutions in Israel and Sumer," *JNES* 25 [1966] 273-79), in response to A. Malamat, thinks that the *zeqenîm* ("elders") and the *yeladîm* ("young men") to whom Rehoboam successively goes for advice are not parallel to the two assemblies mentioned in Gilgamesh and Agga, but refer only to groups of older vs. younger men.

77. M. Hengel, *Judaism and Hellenism* (Philadelphia: Fortress, 1974) 18-32.

78. This line comes from Father Mapple's sermon at the beginning of Herman Melville's *Moby Dick* (Cutchogue, NY: Buccaneer Books, 1976) 61 (originally published in 1851).

79. K. C. Hanson, "When the King Crosses the Line: Royal Deviance and Restitution in Levantine Ideologies," *BTB* 26 (1996) 11-25.

80. M. and S. Golant, *Finding Time for Fathering* (New York: Fawcett Columbine, 1992) 88-91.

81. M. DePree, *Leadership is an Art* (New York: Doubleday, 1989) 9.

82. P. Drucker, *Managing the Non-Profit Organization* (New York: Harper-Collins, 1990) 10.

83. R. Klein, "Liberated Leadership: Masters and 'Lords' in Biblical Perspective," *Currents in Theology and Mission* 9 (1982) 282-90.

84. A. Nelson, *Leading Your Ministry* (Nashville: Abingdon, 1996) 78.

85. Management is "the process of keeping current systems functioning with a primary emphasis on efficiency," while leadership is "the process whereby changes are implemented with a primary emphasis on effectiveness" (Nelson, *Leading Your Ministry,* 86).

86. C. Spurgeon, "A Greater Than Solomon" (Sermon No. 1600, delivered on Feb 6, 1881 at the Metropolitan Tabernacle, Newington, England).

87. Deciding what to do with Benjamin is a problem because Ahijah promises Jeroboam only "one tribe" in 1 Kings 11:31-36, and this seems reinforced in 12:20:

"Only the tribe of Judah remained loyal to the house of David." Yet Rehoboam musters out two tribes in the very next verse, Judah and Benjamin (12:21). M. Noth suggests that the tribal reference in 12:20 originally refers to Benjamin, not Judah (*The History of Israel* [New York: Harper & Row, 1958] 234, nt. 1), but J. Bright rejects this solution, arguing that Benjamin probably tries to secede, but Rehoboam forces him back into the Davidic fold (*A History of Israel,* 3rd ed. [Philadelphia: Westminster, 1981] 233).

88. J. N. Oswalt ("The Golden Calves and the Egyptian Concept of Deity," *EQ* 45 [1973] 13-20) sees this as the reason for the bitter Yahwistic reaction to them, even up to the time of Amos.

89. N. Wyatt, for example, ("Of Calves and Kings: The Canaanite Dimension in the Religion of Israel," *SJOT* 6 [1992] 68-91) examines the two calf narratives (1 Kgs 12; Exod 32) and evaluates the theories concerning the identity of the god represented, concluding that the calf represents El, the Canaanite bull-god. Wyatt sees Jeroboam's reform not as a departure from a Yahwistic norm, but as a reversion to non-Yahwistic religion.

90. *CMHE* 195-215.

91. See my "Role Pre-emption in the Israelite Priesthood," *VT* 46 (1996) 316-29.

92. J. VanderKam, *The Dead Sea Scrolls Today* (Grand Rapids: Eerdmans, 1994) 175-76.

93. Eusebius, *Ecclesiastical History* 5.23-25; T. M. Finn, "Paschal Controversy," *EEC* 696.

94. E. Ikeda, "Teaching Assemblies and Lay Societies in the Formation of Modern Sectarian Buddhism," *Japanese Journal of Religious Studies* 25 (1998) 11-44.

95. B. Henderson, "Missing the Forest for the Trees: The Sickness of Jurisdictionalism in the Orthodox Church," *Epiphany Journal* 15 (1995) 13-23.

96. E. Otto, *Krieg und Frieden in der Hebräischen Bible und im Alten Orient* (Stuttgart: Kohlhammer, 1999) 9.

97. W. Walker, R. Norris, D. W. Lotz, & R. T. Handy, *A History of the Christian Church,* 4th ed. (New York: Charles Scribner's Sons, 1985) 399.

98. G. C. Oosthuizen, "Indigenous Christianity and the Future of the Church in South Africa," *IBMR* 21 (1997) 8-12.

99. S. Wydmusch, "La constellation protestante francaise," *Foi et Vie* 97 (1998) 71-91.

100. C. Mabee, "American Biblical Hermeneutics: A Simple Plea for Life in the Process of Reading the Bible," *Dialog* 35 (1996) 111-16.

101. M. S. Hamilton, "The Triumph of the Praise Songs," *CT* 43, 8 (July 12, 1999) 29.

102. R. Webber, *Signs of Wonder: The Phenomenon of Convergence in Modern Liturgical and Charismatic Churches* (Nashville: Abbott Martyn, 1992) 32-33.

103. Hamilton, "Praise Songs," 31-34.

104. For examples of other ancient king lists, see W. von Soden, *The Ancient Orient* (Grand Rapids: Eerdmans, 1994; trans. from 1985 German ed.) 42-46.

105. J. Hayes and P. Hooker, for example (*A New Chronology for the Kings of Israel and Judah* [Atlanta: John Knox, 1988] 12), reject all hypotheses about co-regencies (king-prince ruling together) in either Israel or Judah, especially when such hypotheses are used to harmonize conflicting numbers in these lists.

106. J. Hayes and P. Hooker, *Chronology*, 99.

107. G. Knoppers, *Two Nations Under God,* HSM 52 (Atlanta: Scholars, 1993).

108. S. Ackerman ("The Queen Mother and the Cult in Ancient Israel," *JBL* 112 [1993] 385-401) thinks that the queen mother fulfills both political and cultic roles in Judah.

109. Ackerman ("Queen Mother," 400) accepts the view of A. Alt ("The Monarchy in the Kingdoms of Israel and Judah," in *Essays on Old Testament History and Religion* [Sheffield: JSOT, 1989] 239-59; trans. of 1951 German article) and F. M. Cross (*CMHE* 219-73) that Solomonic kingship has less to do with prophetic kingmaking (the "ideology" of the northern tribes) than with the Canaanitish ideology of "divine adoption" (2 Sam 7:14; Psa 2:7; 89:20-38; 110:1-7). Cross styles these two ideologies "conditional covenant" (north) vs. "divine decree" (south).

110. K. A. Kitchen, "Shishak's Military Campaign in Israel Confirmed," *BAR* 15 (1989) 32.

111. N. Na'aman, "Shishak's Campaign to Palestine as Reflected by the Epigraphic, Biblical and Archaeological Evidence," *Zion* 63 (1998) 247-76.

112. W. Pitard, "Ben-Hadad," *ABD* 1.663-65.

113. Joash uses the treasury to pay off Hazael (2 Kings 12:18), Ahaz uses treasury money to pay off Tiglath-Pileser III (16:8), and Hezekiah uses treasury money to pay off Sennacherib (18:15). K. A. Kitchen ("Where Did Solomon's Wealth Go?" *BAR* 15 [1989] 30) shows that only three years after Osorkon's accession to Shishak's throne (ten years after Solomon's death), a lengthy inscription details numerous gifts to the temples of Egypt's gods including over 383 tons of precious metals—much of it likely taken from Jerusalem.

114. Mikeal Parsons ("Son and High Priest: A Study in the Christology of Hebrews," *EQ* 60 [1988] 195-215) sees the Christology of Hebrews as organized around the titles "Son of God" and "High Priest."

115. See my "Ruth the Moabite and the Blessing of Foreigners," *CBQ* 60 (1998) 203-17.

116. Bill Webb ("Unequally Yoked Together with Unbelievers: What Is the Unequal Yoke in 2 Corinthians 6:14?" *BS* 149 [1992] 162-79) presents no fewer than twelve possible interpretations of this passage.

117. W. Peter Stephens, "Zwingli's Reforming Ministry," *Expository Times* 93 (1981) 6-10.

118. N. Carmichael, "Spring Cleaning for the Soul," *Virtue* 21 (Feb/March 1999) 20.

119. B. Chapell, "How to Fight Temptation," *Men of Integrity* 2 (Jan-Feb 1999) Feb 20 devotional.

120. K. C. Hanson offers a more anthropological schema in his study, "When the King Crosses the Line: Royal Deviance and Restitution in Levantine Ideologies," *BTB* 26 [1996] 11-25).

121. Carl D. Evans, "Naram-Sin and Jeroboam: The Archetypal *Unheilsherrscher* in Mesopotamian and Biblical Historiography," *Scripture in Context II: More Essays on the Comparative Method,* ed. W. W. Hallo, J. C. Moyer, L. G. Perdue, eds. (Winona Lake, IN: Eisenbrauns, 1983) 114, 124.

122. B. Mazar, "The House of Omri," *EI* 20 (1989) 215-19.

123. This is not to suggest that Judah is assassin-free (Athaliah!)—only that Israel

permits it more often and more publicly (G. Wallis, "Jerusalem und Samaria als Königsstadte," *VT* 26 [1976] 480-96).

124. This is not the first Baal temple in Israel. Note the temple of Baal-Berith in Shechem, out of which Abimelech is paid for his services (Judg 9:4). The impulse to construct Baal temples has deep roots in Canaanite myth, where Baal complains loudly about not having a "temple like the (other) gods" (*KTU* 1.3 v 38; 1.4 iv 50-51; probably also in 1.3 iv 47 and 1.4 I 9-10). Apparently his devotees take this plea very seriously, if the ubiquitous temples to Baal and Hadad are any indication.

125. R. Chisholm, "The Polemic against Baalism in Israel's Early History and Literature," *BS* 151 (1994) 267-83.

126. I am aware that this view of Israelite religion is not universally held; see my "Role Pre-Emption in the Israelite Priesthood," *VT* 46 (1996) 316-29.

127. E. Peterson, "Baalism and Yahwism Updated," *TT* 29 (1972) 138-43.

128. R. Wuthnow, "Small Groups Forge New Notions of Community and the Sacred," *CC* 110 (1993) 1236-40; "How Small Groups Are Transforming Our Lives," *CT* 38 (1994) 20-24.

129. T. Stafford, "The Therapeutic Revolution: How Christian Counseling Is Changing the Church," *CT* 37 (1993) 25-32.

130. Howard Clark Kee, "Changing Modes of Leadership in the New Testament Period," *Social Compass* 39 (1992) 241-54.

131. Craig W. Garriott, "Leadership Development in the Multiethnic Church," *Urban Mission* 13 (1996) 24-37.

132. *KTU* 1.119.28-33 (trans. by D. Pardee and P. Bordreuil in *ABD* 6.708).

133. The Hebrew word is pointed in MT as an active participle, "answerer." In 18th-century Mesopotamia (Mari), there is a whole class of magico-religious specialists called "answerers" (Akk. *apilû*), and their primary job is to "answer" for the deity in rituals like these.

134. The hip`il form of Heb *talal* means "to deceive," and the loss of final reduplicated radicals on prefixed stems is common in Biblical Hebrew.

135. G. Rendsburg ("The Mock of Baal in 1 Kings 18:27," *CBQ* 50 [1988] 414-17) argues that this term means urine/excrement. H. Jacobson ("Elijah's Sleeping Baal," *Bib* 79 [1998] 413) suggests that Elijah's mocking words about a sleeping god reflect a famous passage in the ancient Near Eastern creation epic Atrahasis, where the nether deity Enlil is angered by men who make too much noise and keep him awake. H. Jagersma ("*Yshn* in 1 Könige XVIII 27," *VT* 25 [1975] 674-76) wonders whether Elijah might be mocking the Canaanite "sleep of death" associated with rituals for the first rainfall (*KTU* 1.3 ii 38-40). More likely, Elijah might be mocking the myth of Baal's "death" as he flees from the death-god Mot (*KTU* 1.5 v 5-17).

136. On a 1999 trip to Syria, I asked an officer in the Syrian army to choose what he thought was the most sensitive issue in international relations there. His answer came in one word: *water*.

137. R. J. Neuhaus, "The Naked Public Square," *CT* 28 (1984) 227-32.

138. Thus, the great title of the little book by Stan Grenz and Roger Olson, *Who Needs Theology?* (Downers Grove, IL: InterVarsity, 1996).

139. E. B. Holifield, "Theology as Entertainment: Oral Debate in American Religion," *Church History* 67 (1998) 499-520.

140. F. Peretti, *This Present Darkness* (Westchester, IL: Crossway, 1986).

141. C. B. Breuninger, "Where Angels Fear to Tread: Appraising the Current Fascination with Spiritual Warfare," *Covenant Quarterly* 53 (1995) 37-43, *contra* C. Peter Wagner, ed., *Breaking Strongholds in Your City: How to Use Spiritual Mapping to Make Your Prayers More Strategic, Effective, and Targeted* (Ventura, CA: Regal, 1993).

THREE

THE PRESSURE OF PROPHECY

CRISIS MANAGEMENT VALUES (1 Kings 1:11-45)

Nathan is the first Solomon-supporter to respond to Adonijah. Concerned that Adonijah has already "become king" in the eyes of many (v. 5), he knows only too well what the next step will be. Adonijah will seek to eliminate his rivals. Everyone knows how this process works, particularly those who have lived through the civil war generated by Absalom's rebellion. As Aeschylus puts it, "new-made kings are cruel."[1]

So Nathan crafts a crisis-management strategy, much like the one he uses with David (2 Sam 12:1-12). After Uriah's murder, Nathan approaches David through a subtly-worded story, the famous "ewe-lamb" parable.[2] Here he approaches the king in a similar way, indirectly, through a carefully orchestrated "Bathsheba strategy." Doubtless he chooses Bathsheba to "run interference" not just because she is the mother of Adonijah's rival, and not just because she is David's favorite wife. Nathan seems to believe that Solomon's life is in real danger. After Uriah's murder, Nathan exhorts David to make a decision in the imaginary world of the parable ("the man who did this deserves to die!" [2 Sam 12:5]) before confronting him directly in the real world ["thou art the man!" 12:7]). This is typical Oriental conflict resolution strategy: *parable + praxis*.[3] Nathan understands how important it is for kings to discover the truth "by themselves."

There are contrasts too, of course. After Uriah's murder no one except Nathan, Joab and David know the details. But here everyone seems to know what's going on except David. Nathan earlier speaks officially as a prophet of Yahweh, but here he operates more on his own authority. His reasons seem more overtly moralistic in the Uriah incident, yet here he seems driven by *Realpolitik*.[4] One could argue that justice is again his primary goal, but this is disputable: Josephus portrays Nathan merely as "prudent," not "prophetic."[5]

Antti Laato suggestively argues that Nathan's deepest concern is to "avoid destructive internal political struggles like those of Absalom,"[6] and this explains, for Laato, (a) why Nathan says nothing to Solomon after purging his kingdom, and (b) why he allows Solomon to install his sons into government jobs. What we can more certainly say is that Nathan does something unusual for an Israelite *nabî'* ("prophet"). Against the stereotype of what prophets do ("forthtell"/"foretell"), here he plays a role as "counselor" (*yo'ets*). Here he looks more like Ahithophel (2 Sam 16:23) than, say, Amos. He urges Bathsheba to take his counsel seriously, commanding her to "Save your own life and the life of your son Solomon!" English translations soften this, yet "Save!" is the second of four imperative commands from the mouth of this prophet: "Come! Save! Come! Go!" Nathan does not suggest, he commands Bathsheba to go to the king.

The really thorny question is, "Did David previously promise the throne to Solomon?" Is the narrator referring to some unrecorded promise, or is Nathan, through Bathsheba, planting an "embellished" promise in David's aging mind? Scholars are divided. Some see Nathan as a shrewd political operative manipulating the truth for his own purposes. Others see an unrecorded promise behind his request to David.[7] All we know is that after he enlists Bathsheba, he waits patiently for her to finish her assignment. He dares to ask the king not about *Adonijah's* "secret coup," but whether the *king himself* has been acting "secretly." Subtly, carefully, he shifts the focus away from Adonijah and on to David. Just like their "thou-art-the-man" encounter, he puts David on the defensive, and the narrator underlines this with a subtle pun. Nathan (a) tells Bathsheba that David "does not know" (*lo' yada'*, v. 11); then Bathsheba (b) tells David that he "does not know" (*lo' yada'ta*, v. 18); then finally, Nathan (c) asks David why he and his royal advisers "do not know" (*lo' hôdata*, v. 27). Not only is this strategic crisis management, it comes packaged in wonderfully textured prose.

Intratextual Reflection

The Nathan-David encounter is the first of several prophet-politician encounters and sets the tone for later collisions. Most of these encounters come to a head in the Elijah-Elisha narratives: two focus on King Ahab (1 Kings 18:1-15; 20:1-43), and another focuses on the encounter between Isaiah and Hezekiah (2 Kings 19:1-37). They range in mood from quiet manipulation to violent confrontation, from angry denunciation to wary inquiry, from desperate pleading to bizarre divination. This is one of Kings' most fascinating trajectories.

It's also one of its most Hebraic. Nathan is a *nabî'* ("prophet"), and, thanks to discoveries at Mari and Emar, we now know that Israel is not unique in its use of prophetic specialists.[8] At least three neighboring cultures—Mesopotamia, Anatolia, and Egypt—have similar specialists, who warn kings of possible attacks,[9] who advise them of their religious responsibilities,[10] and who challenge them to deal justly with the poor.[11] Prophecy is more complex in Israel because biblical prophet-king encounters come to us packaged in theologically intentional narratives, not personal letters or administrative reports. The portrayals in Samuel and Kings are much "rounder" than those in the cognate literature,[12] and the portrayals in the Former Prophets are considerably more complex than those in the Latter Prophets.

The intratextual context tells us more. First, in the parallel between the Nathan-David encounter (1 Kings 1:11-45) and the Elijah-Ahab encounter (18:1-15), each story shows us a prophet working through an intermediary. Nathan communicates to David through Bathsheba; Elijah works through the palace steward, Obadiah. Second, both prophets use their intermediaries in similar ways. Nathan uses Bathsheba to remind (?) David about his promise, while Elijah uses Obadiah to set up a meeting with Ahab. Third, both narrators use verbatim terminology. "Behold, Nathan!" (1:23) is clearly parallel to "Behold, Elijah!" (18:7). Fourth, both kings walk away from these encounters bested and chastened: David "loses" to Nathan just as surely as Ahab "loses" to Elijah.

There is, however, at least one major difference, and it has to do with the way in which each mediator theologically functions. In the Nathan story, Bathsheba obeys Nathan without complaint or question. Not so Obadiah. Even though he proves himself loyal, Obadiah cowers in fear instead of obedience. Why? Perhaps it's because Elijah is a more terrifying figure than Nathan. Perhaps it's because Obadiah thinks that Ahab is less worthy of respect than David. Iain Provan attractively suggests that the reason lies in Kings' emphasis on "cumulative sin." By this point in the narrative, a great deal of "bad blood" has built up between the prophets and the kings, and this "cumulative sin...puts (the Davidic) promise in its unconditional aspect under too much stress."[13] What does this imply about the overall character of this trajectory?

First, the conflict between prophets and politicians is persistent and inevitable, more perennial than occasional, more institutional than personal. Like all the other prophets, Nathan's intention is to confront David, not bless him. His motivation may seem hazier than that of, say, Elijah, but it's important not to segregate these encounters from their common trajectory. One twentieth-century prophet, Reinhold Niebuhr, argues that believers who ignore or underestimate the institutional struggle between prophets and politicians are bound to focus less on the doctrines of the Faith than the business of ladling out "syrup" to "mystics, monastics, martyrs, and mothers."[14] Niebuhr draws "a sharp distinction...between the moral and social behavior of individuals and social groups," arguing that "this distinction justifies and necessitates political policies which a purely individualistic ethic must always find embarrassing."[15] Nathan would probably agree with Niebuhr.

Second, this conflict is a mixture of political and moral elements. None of these encounters is purely political. None is purely moral. Always there is a mixture of both elements in this growing tension between the prophets and the kings. Nathan's strategy appears to be more political than ethical, but it's not, and prophetic ministry always involves addressing both elements squarely and clearly. The immediate context reinforces this because Nathan's performance contrasts strongly with the inchoate counseling performances of Hushai and Ahithophel (2 Sam 15-17).

Third, the means by which some prophets operate is more indirect than direct. Compared to other prophet-vs.-politician stories, Nathan's "confrontation" with David seems relatively mild. Only a few prophets in Kings use mediators, but the challenge facing Nathan is just as real as any other prophetic challenge. Should Nathan choose not to confront this king, the result will almost certainly be exile or death for Solomon. That he chooses to use a mediator to resolve it is significant, but ultimately less important than the fact that he, in fact, resolves it. Nathan does what all prophets do—he takes action by faith to address an unjust situation in the name of Yahweh.

Theological Reflection
Years ago I used to drive a cab. Once a distinguished-looking gentleman climbed into the back of my Checker and asked me to drive him to a

nearby address. When we arrived, the meter, as I recall, registered a whopping $2.10. Getting out, he walked around to the driver's side, reached into his Brooks Brothers pants pocket, and pulled out two crisp dollar bills. Grinning like a Cheshire cat, he neatly placed them into my hand and walked away. Naively I thought he was going inside his house to locate the remainder of the fare he owed me. I didn't realize he'd cheated me out of ten cents until he was already in the house.

Boy, was I angry! Fuming like a volcano, I grabbed the wheel, smashed the transmission into gear, and floored the accelerator, peeling out with as much Checker horsepower as I could muster. No one was going to steal a lousy dime from me and get away with it! If I couldn't punish him, I'd at least punish...*the cab!* About five minutes later, a voice crackled over the two-way radio: "Number 36. Number 36. Is there a wallet in your backseat? Your last fare called...says he's lost his wallet somewhere...would you take a look?"

Immediately I turned around...and there it was! Black leather. Money practically spilling out of the sides. Flushed with excitement, I pulled over and parked. My heart dared to imagine that this was a "reward" for the humiliation I had just "suffered." I imagined my discovery as "justice." Oh, how easy it would be to lie to my dispatcher and take this man's money. "Number 36. Number 36. Is it there? Did you find it?" The radio punctured my larcenous fantasies like a hot needle. "Uh, give me a minute. I'll call you back." I didn't know what to say. I mean—it was a *lot* of money. Like Tevya, the milkman in *Fiddler On The Roof,* I weighed my options. *"On the one hand,"* I was broke. Driving cab was barely paying the rent. I needed the money, and here was a treasure trove in my hands. This guy was an obvious jerk—who steals ten cents from a cab-driver? He *deserves* to suffer! *"On the other hand,"* what if I lied and took the money? How could I live with myself? However tempting, however attractive, how could I sink to becoming a common thief?

Kings is about how often Israel's politicians become paralyzed by the first voice, and how often the prophets speak to them in the second voice. The power of their message excels in direct proportion to the darkness within which it operates, involving at least the following concerns.

First, prophets are strategic and deliberate. Nathan has seen David at his worst. He's seen him commit adultery. He's seen him commit murder. He's seen him detach from his children. He's seen him postpone dealing with the problems in his administration. Still he tries to serve his king. Still he tries to tell him the truth he needs to hear rather than the propaganda he wants to hear. Prophetic preaching will continue to follow this example, focusing on (a) themes of relevance backed by a case for truth; (b) an understanding that conversion is a long process; (c) the finding of evangelistic pathways within the church itself; and (d) personal authenticity.[16] Prophetic preaching is strategic and deliberate, not reactionary and manipulative.

Second, prophets are not easily intimidated. Like the Reformers, they believe that God uses the preached Word to create pathways for The Word. David Buttrick argues for a return to this level of homiletical confidence,[17] and though some voice reasonable caution,[18] it's difficult to argue that overconfidence is a problem in the average Western pulpit. Nathan is careful, but he's confident—and this kind of confidence is sorely needed today.

ELIJAH AND THE KING'S STEWARD (1 Kings 18:1-15)

Where the previous chapter (chapter 17) begins with a prohibition, this one begins with a promise. After three years of "severe famine" Yahweh promises to send the rains. This promise is not fulfilled, of course, until the showdown on Mt. Carmel, but the first step is to "present yourself to Ahab" (lit. "make him see," *hera'ê*). Should Elijah do this, Yahweh promises, "I will send rain on the land." Seems easy enough. Yet the task of bringing this king together with this prophet proves difficult.

Kings is filled with "hiding." Elijah "hides" from Ahab (17:3); Obadiah "hides" a hundred prophets of Yahweh (18:4); Micaiah predicts that Ahab will someday have to "hide"; Jehosheba "hides" the young prince Joash (2 Kings 11:3). Like Rahab, Ahab's steward has a reputation for "hiding" people "secretly." Rahab hides Hebrew spies in Jericho; Obadiah hides Yahweh prophets from Jezebel. Rahab's act of faith makes it possible for Israel to begin the conquest (Josh 6:17); Obadiah's act of faith makes it possible for Israel to *stay* in Canaan. Obadiah, however, doesn't just hide a couple of spies—he hides a hundred Yahweh-prophets from a fanatical enemy bent on finding them. This act of faith makes it possible for Yahwism itself to survive, and the way it's introduced is significant.

Notice that the text does not introduce the royal couple directly. Instead, it takes an ordinary verb and makes a pun on it, the verb *karat* ("to cut off"). When we first meet Jezebel, in other words, we see a pampered queen spending her days "cutting off" the prophets of Yahweh (*karat*, v. 4). Ahab, on the other hand, spends his days looking for ways to keep his livestock from being "cut off" (*karat*). See the pun? With a single play-on-words, the narrator not only introduces us to the antagonists of Israel, he introduces us to a value-system gone berserk, a world in which domesticated "beasts" (*behemôt*) are of more value than God's prophets.

The narrator heightens the pun by having Obadiah and Ahab greet Elijah in practically identical ways:

> Obadiah: Is it really you, my lord? (*ha'attâ zeh 'adonî,* 1 Kings 18:7)
> Ahab: Is that you, O troubler? (*ha'attâ zeh `oker,* 18:17).

Morphologically and syntactically these phrases look identical, yet semantically they're worlds apart. One character respects the prophet deeply, calling him "lord" (*'adonî*). The other despises him deeply, calling him "troublemaker" (*`oker*). When Elijah seizes on the latter to launch his attack—"I have not made trouble for Israel, but you and your father's family have" (18:18)—the plot takes off and the fight heats up. By making each greeting look so similar, yet so dissimilar, the narrator cleverly pulls us into Elijah's greatest conflict.

Obadiah is just trying to do his job. The requirements of this job are simple: (a) keep the master happy, and (b) keep the master happy. When his master commands him to look for food, he immediately obeys and goes out, like Jeroboam, "alone" into the field (*lebaddô,* 1 Kings 11:29). Once he leaves Samaria, however, he soon "recognizes" Ahab's enemy, and this immediately puts him in a delicate position. Like the "chance" encounter between Jeroboam and Ahijah, this encounter also has to do with "chance." Perhaps he expects Elijah to ask him for sanctuary. Perhaps he expects him to help him look for fodder. Perhaps he expects a prophetic blessing.

Doubtless the last thing he expects is a request for a meeting with his boss. This is the only place in Scripture where Obadiah is mentioned, so all we know is that he "fears Yahweh exceedingly" (*yare' 'et yhwh me'od*), an impression which continues well into the post-exilic period ("greater praise was expressed of Obadiah than Abraham, since of Abraham the word 'greatly' is not used, while of Obadiah it is," *b. Sanh.* 39b). Yet if Obadiah is a righteous man, then why does he react so negatively to Elijah's request? This story suggests several possible reasons.

First, apparently he feels the need to educate Elijah. "Does Elijah not realize where ultimate power *really* lies? Does he not realize that King Ahab is in absolute control?" Obadiah fears Ahab, but more than this, he thinks Elijah should fear him too. Like the Zarephath widow, Obadiah is troubled by Elijah's demands. Both of these minor characters use the same language in their responses, words like "sin" and "death" instead of "faith" and "hope." Like the widow, Obadiah thinks that Elijah expects the "impossible," and this causes him great consternation.

Second, Obadiah seems to think that Elijah is...well, ...a bit of a flake. Doubtless he has no reason to doubt him, but he worries that Elijah will abandon him at crunch time. He worries that Elijah will try to hide, as religious flakes tend to do, behind feeble excuses like "the Spirit of Yahweh has changed my mind!" Whether or not the Spirit of Yahweh actually does change minds is not the point. The point is that Obadiah worries that Elijah will use this excuse to abandon him. This leads him to reject Elijah and his "impossible" request. Like the Zarephath widow, this man wants faith assurances, not faith challenges.

Third, when these arguments fail, Obadiah falls back on the "resting-on-my-laurels" argument. In so many words, he says to Elijah, "Don't you think it's enough that I've already saved ONE HUNDRED of you prophets? What else do you want me to do—risk my life, too?" Like the rich young ruler, Obadiah reminds Elijah that he has worshiped Yahweh "since my youth. Haven't you heard, my lord, what I did while Jezebel was killing the prophets of Yahweh? I hid a hundred of Yahweh's prophets in two caves, fifty in each, and supplied them with food and water. And now you tell me to go to my master and say, 'Elijah is here?' He will kill me."[19]

Elijah listens patiently to these excuses. Like Yahweh with Moses (Exod 3:11-4:12), he empathizes with Obadiah's fears and he offers him reassurances, even to the point of swearing another oath: "As Yahweh Almighty lives, whom I serve, I will surely present myself to Ahab today." Does he do these things because he thinks they will cause Obadiah to trust him? Does Elijah truly understand the depth of his fear? Perhaps Elijah does understand something about human fear because, after all, this is now the second person in his environment who seems paralyzed by it (the Zarephath widow being the first). That he takes an oath here (and not in Zarephath) may be evidence of this realization.

Intratextual Reflection

Ahab's steward faces a stiff challenge. Compared to other episodes, like "Making Tough Decisions" (1 Kings 1:28-2:12) or "Mothers Needing Miracles" (2 Kings 4:8-37), this story shows us another average Israelite under tremendous pressure, and the fact that we have such episodes testifies to the truth that Yahweh cares deeply about individuals as well as nations, about the frightened as well as the faithful. Stories like these show us how intensely God cares about saving us from our fears.

Compare this story, for example, with the story of "Mothers Needing Miracles" (2 Kings 4:8-37). Where Obadiah worries for his life, the Shunammite worries for the life of her son. Where Obadiah experiences a love-hate relationship with Elijah, the Shunammite experiences a love-hate relationship with Elijah's disciple, Elisha. Where Obadiah accuses Elijah of incompetence, the Shunammite accuses Elisha of "lying" (v. 16) and "misleading" her (v. 28). These are not atypical responses. Suffering people often find themselves paralyzed by worry and fear. Perhaps Yahweh's promises are so distant and so forgotten, they've simply lost their desire to believe them anymore. It's hard to hang on to your faith when you're in the midst of a famine, in the midst of competing prophets, in the midst of oppressive idolatry.

Theological Reflection

This leads us to two theological reflections. First, many people want to believe, but they live in the twilight zone between fear and faith. The 1987 film *Field of Dreams* illustrates this beautifully. The film's main character, Ray Kinsella, is a young husband and father facing a crossroads in his life. Like his deceased father, he dreams of being a major league baseball player, but also like his father, he settles for something different. He gives up on his dreams and becomes a corn farmer. There's nothing particularly wrong, of course, about becoming a corn farmer, but there's nothing particularly right about it either—especially for talented ballplayers like Ray. He realizes he's becoming just like his father, and it scares him.

Then a Voice comes to him when he's "alone" (1 Kings 11:29; 18:6). It challenges him. It prods him. It pushes him out of his comfort zone. Its message is urgent, persistent, mysterious: "If you build it, he will come." "Heal his pain." "Go the distance." Ray's response to the Voice is much like Obadiah's response to Elijah. "Do you have any idea how much this is going to cost me?" "How do I know you're telling the truth?" "How do I know I'm not going crazy?" Still, in spite of his fears, Ray obeys the Voice and plows under his cornfield. He weathers the ridicule of neighbors and family. He turns down his brother-in-law's offer to buy back the farm, and builds a baseball field on it instead. He learns to live by faith, and it changes his life forever.

Second, the biblical God has a habit of coming to people where they are. God works through Obadiahs as well as Elijahs. Like Elijah, Obadiah *fears* Yahweh, but the deeper question is whether he *trusts* Yahweh. Yahweh does not wait until he works everything out. Instead, he offers him the privilege of serving in the midst of doubt. The message is clear. If we wait for disciples to come to "perfect faith" before asking them to teach a class or visit a hospital or serve on an administration committee, we might soon discover that the volunteer pool has become a puddle. Like the Voice, God comes to us in the midst of our doubts. He asks us to "plow up our cornfields." He asks us to make appointments with "Ahab." He asks us to do the "impossible."

This God will surprise you when you least expect it.

DECEIVING A KING (1 Kings 20:1-43)

Israel's relationship with Syria is convoluted. Several Aramaic inscriptions offer us a glimpse into the history and culture of Israel's northeastern neighbor,[20] but the biblical evidence gives us more. We know that one of the earliest encounters between Israel and Syria is Saul's attack against the king of Zobah (1 Sam 14:47). His successor, David, defeats Hadadezer, another king of Zobah, and this victory gives David access to Damascus (2 Sam. 8:5-12). Solomon "overpowers" (*wayyehezaq*) the Syrian town of Hamath-Zobah early in his reign (2 Chron. 8:3-4), but a Syrian upstart named Rezon defies him and takes over (1 Kings 11:23-25). At Rezon's death, a Syrian king named Hezion establishes a dynasty of "Ben-Hadad" kings (15:18; 20), but in 843 BC Hazael (19:15) murders one of these "Ben-Hadads" and seizes power (2 Kings 8:28-29; 9:15; 10:32-33; 13:22). Jeroboam II's victory over Syria hastens Damascus' decline until its capture in 732 BC by the Assyrians.

"Ben-Hadad,"[21] like "Pharoah," is a title, not a surname. A certain "Ben-Tabrimmon," for example, uses this title to partner with Asa against the northern Israelite king Baasha (1 Kings 15:18-21). The "Ben-Hadad" here in 1 Kings 20 may be the same individual who later partners with Ahab against Shalmaneser III at the battle of Qarqar (*ANET* 278-79), but this is disputed. Another king named "Ben-Hadad" besieges Samaria during Elisha's time (2 Kings 6:24), and Hazael has him assassinated (2 Kings 8:7-15). Still another "Ben-Hadad" takes several cities away from King Jehoahaz of Israel (2 Kings 13:24-25). The history of Syria's relationship to Israel is complex and convoluted.

So is this episode. What otherwise might have been a perfunctory battle report in the hands of a lesser writer reads here like an adventure story, with a plot as complex as any in Kings.

• A Syrian king lays siege to Samaria and verbally assaults its king

- The Israelite king accedes to his demands
- The Syrian king pushes harder, claiming also the possessions of his enemy's officials
- The Israelite king consults with his advisers before refusing this second demand
- The Syrian king swears an oath against the Israelite king
- The Israelite king responds with a sarcastic rejoinder
- The Syrian king consults with his officials, who advise him to attack
- *First prophetic message:* a prophet strengthens and guides Ahab
- The Israelite king leads a surprise attack and routs the Syrian army
- *Second prophetic message:* a prophet advises Ahab to be vigilant
- The Syrian officials explain their defeat via a theological argument
- *Third prophetic message:* the Syrians' theological argument is false
- The Syrian king fails (again) to defeat Israel
- The Syrian officials advise their king to throw himself on Israel's mercy
- The Israelite king shows "mercy" to Syria, and the two kings renegotiate their relationship
- *Fourth prophetic message:* Ahab has misrepresented Yahweh's "mercy."

This story has suspense, dialogue, humor, even a surprise ending. Like the Adonijah narrative, it shows us not one but two peacock princes cackling and screeching at each other, looking for all the world like trash-talking wrestlers on cable TV. When their advisors get involved, though, things turn silly. The story's various levels come into focus when we shift our attention to the conflicts they represent: (a) king vs. king; (b) officials vs. officials; and (c) prophet vs. king. Like the showdown on Mt. Carmel, this is a highly textured piece of prose.

The underlying conflict is international. Samaria in this historical period is a *nouveau riche* city-state. Its traffic in "washed oil"[22] and ivory furniture (Amos 6:4-7) make it an obvious target for any predator, and Ben-Hadad's attack doubtless has several motivating factors behind it, preeminent among them simple greed ("Your silver and gold are mine"). Omri's military successes in Moab probably haven't gone unnoticed either (*ANET* 320-21), and this might mean that Ben-Hadad is trying to be preemptive with this attack—a "shot over the bow," so to speak.

Aramean coalitions are not uncommon, as the coalitions against Zakkur of Hamath (*ANET* 655-66) and the Assyrians (*ANET* 278-79) demonstrate.

What distinguishes this coalition, however, is its comic subtext—the episode's second level of conflict. Like most career bureaucrats, the officials in this encounter know how to massage royal egos and tiptoe through political minefields. On the one hand stand Ahab's advisers, who counsel him not to give in—ironically the same advice he receives from his prophets. On the other hand stand the Syrians, who offer Ben-Hadad disastrous counsel:

• *Their theological/geographical argument.* The argument beginning in v. 23 may look strange to Christians, but polytheists really do believe that different gods operate only within different cosmic arenas. Each deity is thought to control only a "section" of the universe. Astral deities, for example, communicate their will by projecting messages into the livers of sheep. Mountain-deities work only in the mountains. Plains-deities operate only on the steppes. Ben-Hadad's advisers hold unswervingly to this view of the cosmos.

• *Their theological/political argument.* When things go wrong, these officials do what bureaucrats everywhere do—they try to spin events their way. This not-so-hidden agenda is more political than theological, because what they really want is to take advantage of Ben-Hadad's situation and centralize power into their own hands. Under the pretext of re-arming Syria, they slyly recommend to the king that he replace the present feudal system (32 kings) with a more "efficient" one (officers). In other words, they want Ben-Hadad to do what Solomon has done—replace feudal confederacy with centralized monarchy.

• When this fails, they run out of advice. Twice stymied, all they know to do now is react to rumor—"we have heard that the Israelite monarchs are merciful." Gone now are the geographical and theological arguments, suddenly replaced by arguments of desperation and deceit. Ben-Hadad, they counsel, should try to trick Israel by disguising himself. Amazingly, he still listens to them, and even more amazingly, they succeed in tricking Ahab.

The third level of conflict is between prophet and king. Despite his battlefield "success," Ahab's behavior enrages Yahweh. Ahab pardons Ben-Hadad, but like Saul with Agag (1 Sam 15:11), he has not sought God's will in the matter. The problem is not that he shows Ben-Hadad mercy, but that he refuses to consult Yahweh. Worse, he ignores the advice of Yahweh's prophets. Four times in this paragraph a Yahweh prophet advises him not to let Ben-Hadad off the hook, and each time he spurns this advice.

• The first of these comes in a prophet-king dialogue, a rare thing in Kings. To the prophet's oracle of assurance, Ahab responds with a question about mechanics: "Who will do this?" Yahweh's answer—"The young officers of the provincial commanders will do it"—encourages him to follow the same advice offered by the Syrians ("use your subordinates wisely"). When Ahab asks, "Who will start the battle?," Yahweh answers, "You." The ultimate responsibility falls on the king, not on his officials—and certainly not on his junior officers. This contrasts sharply with the Syrians' behavior, and it hammers home the message that delegation does not equal abdication (v. 12).

• The second message comes in the form of a warning: "Strengthen your position and see what must be done, because next spring the king of Aram will attack again." Yahweh does not want Ahab to follow Ben-Hadad's example and get "drunk" on his own success. He wants him to be vigilant. He wants him to plan for the future. He wants Ahab to defend Israel in the face of mounting international tension. Vigilance is necessary because Ben-Hadad has (a) a clever and determined bureaucracy, (b) several capricious gods to placate, and (c) thirty-two kings to keep happy.

• The third prophetic message responds directly to the Syrians' theological statements. We do not know what these advisers think in detail; we can only marvel at their desire to "spin" Yahweh into some kind of minor grotto-deity. It's like…well, like asking someone with a plank in his eye to remove a dab of dust from his neighbor's eye. This is great comedy! Ben-Hadad's army has just lost to a vastly inferior army led by junior officers. As they figure out their next move over a few "tall ones," someone says, "Hey, this is not *our* problem. This is a *theological* thing. Once we get their army out of the mountains—where their god lives—they'll *have* to throw in the towel!"

Yahweh's answer is deafeningly immediate. Yahweh of Hosts is no plastic icon easily attached to one's dashboard; no colored ribbon easily pinned to one's lapel. Yahweh is Sovereign Lord of Creation. So astoundingly have the Syrians misdiagnosed him, they might as well be fighting this war from their offices in Damascus.

• The fascinating thing about the fourth encounter is not just its manic intensity, but the way in which this prophet's communication style sums up the absurdity of the whole episode. Knowing how Ahab is easily deceived, this prophet decides to trick him yet again. Because he wants to make sure that Ahab gets the message, it's not enough to put on a headband and look "wounded." These wounds have to be real. This parable has to entrap Ahab.

Intratextual Reflection

Of all these conflict-layers, perhaps the most intratextually significant is the prophet-vs.-king conflict. If nothing else, Kings shows us how difficult it is for prophets to preach the Word to equivocating politicians. Like "Nathan vs. David" (1:11-45) and "Elijah vs. Obadiah" (18:1-15), this story shows us no less than four attempts to get through to Ahab. At the beginning of Kings, David does not respond to the threat posed by Adonijah—not until Nathan pushes him. In chapter 18, Obadiah seems perfectly willing to resist Elijah's challenge—until Elijah brings all Israel to Carmel and forces the issue. So here the prophets demand that Ahab take a stand consistent with the Law: "When Yahweh your God has delivered them over to you and you have defeated them, then you must destroy them totally. Make no treaty with them. Show them no mercy" (Deut 7:2). That he ignores their advice and pardons the enemy anyway is more than just ironic. It's a tragic example of what can happen when leaders abandon the Word. Because of Ahab's idolatry, he makes poor judgments, and Yahweh has to respond.

Theological Reflection

For over thirty years John Geoghan was Father John Geoghan, a parish priest in the archdiocese of Boston. On Jan 9, 2002 his former cardinal, Bernard Law, held a press conference and apologized to all the victims Geoghan had sexually abused. The motivation for his apology, critics suspected, was a powerful exposé of the priesthood in the *Boston Globe* a week before, an indictment filled with undeniable evidence of Geoghan's pedophilia. This sparked several more stories in other dioceses, and eventually a national scandal in the Roman Catholic Church.[23]

People lose faith when they see such behavior—not just the pedophilia, but the shameless cover-up. The desire to "take care of one's own" is strong, and this is what Ahab does in the name of "mercy." He unwisely pardons a dangerous enemy, and by so doing he shows us that "evil comes…in countless respectable and seductive disguises."[24] Often, instead of "clear" consciences, Bonhoeffer argues, people are willing to settle for "salved" consciences. "Shakespeare's characters walk in our midst," and too many well-meaning believers have gotten into the habit of "consenting to the bad, knowing full well it is bad."[25] It's easy to say that Ahab should pardon Ben-Hadad, yet anyone who thinks this is an easy decision has probably never been in a leadership position. Here are some issues to ponder as we apply this text.

First, God-emptying theologies are misguided and dangerous. Yahweh of Hosts is never going to settle for a minor position in *anyone's* pantheon. Some years ago I tried to communicate this truth to a young father who left a promising teaching career to become a poker dealer in a local casino. I begged him to reconsider his decision. His wife begged him as well, fearing that it might lead him away from his family. Poker dealers work in environments which crassly promote the basest elements of human nature. But they make a lot of money. Tips alone can be upwards of $300 a night (as he proudly told me on several occasions). College-degreed and multi-talented, he didn't have to take this job. He had planned to become a high school math teacher—in fact, he helped my son pass 8th-grade algebra. But once he got used to the easy money, he wouldn't quit. If someone were to ask him today whether he believes in God, his answer would almost certainly be a resounding "yes." But this comes from a man who's divorced his wife (after cheating on her), and abandoned his children for the "good life."

Second, delegation does not equal abdication, and this principle is nowhere more applicable than in the field of Christian education. Two of the reasons for its decline in the Church today are (a) the lack of leadership over staff and volunteers, and/or (b) the micro-management of those who do volunteer. To revive Christian education, we need to consider a number of restorative strategies: (1) reaffirm the biblical base for Christian education; (2) rethink the traditional models; (3) adapt our programs to changing social structures; (4) emphasize local needs; (5) focus more on adult education; (6) respond to the need for lifelong learning; (7) deal with relevant life-related issues; (8) encourage lay leadership in congregational programs; (9) support all workers with adequate training and supervision; and (10) call all participants to higher standards of excellence.[26] The existence of the Church depends on whether we can successfully educate the next generation. Can we afford to confuse delegation with abdication in this crucial area of ministry?

Third, we all need to learn the difference between "covenant mercy" and "cheap grace." Sometimes it's difficult to know which is which, and this confusion is playing havoc with good people who mean well. Ahab's problem is not that he extends Ben-Hadad mercy, but that he so readily allows himself to be deceived. The Church has always struggled with this. Jesus tells his disciples to be "wise as serpents" (Matt 10:16), and many well-meaning believers are trying to figure out what this means. Well-meaning laypeople routinely promise the moon to people in need, only to see these folks become codependent on our food pantry instead of dependent on Christ. God's love is indeed intended for all people, but we need to make sure that we teach our new brothers and sisters how to distinguish Yahweh from all other gods.

The poor struggle with idolatry just as much as the rich.

EYE OF THE STORM (1 Kings 22:1-28)

This story sweeps over Kings like a cyclone. At the center of the storm stands a lone prophet about whom we know practically nothing. Unlike the prophet in 1 Kings 13, this prophet doesn't just hear the Word; Micaiah ben Imlah sees things, marvelous things. Unlike the Elijah/Elisha cycles, his prophecy does not come to us in a series of narrative episodes. This is the only episode we have about him, and this is the first time we see the Unseen World in Kings. "Who will go?," "I will go," "Go and do"—statements like these rarely occur on earth, at least not without agendas behind them. Not so in the Unseen World. This amazing story contrasts life in the Unseen World with no less than four types of earthly conflict: (a) Israel vs. Syria, (b) Ahab vs. Jehoshaphat, (c) Ahab vs. Micaiah, and (d) Micaiah vs. Zedekiah.

However difficult it may be to reconstruct the Israel-vs.-Syria relationship,[27] apparently Ramoth Gilead still remains—a full three years after the Samaria-Damascus treaty—a disputed territory (1 Kings 20:34). This is not all that unusual. That Ahab singles out this town for a battle may mean only that he wants to use it as a test case before deciding whether to declare war on all of Syria. The point is that the noise generated by this international conflict is the aural wallpaper against which all the other conflicts in this episode resonate.

This applies, second, to the Judah-Israel relationship. Jehoshapat is Judah's king, but why is he visiting Samaria? The last prior mention of Judah's dealings with Israel focuses on Asa's war with Baasha (1 Kings 15:16-22), and with the battle between Ahab and Ben-Hadad this intramural conflict comes again to the fore. Yet the narrator keeps us in the dark about the details. Perhaps Jehoshaphat visits Samaria because he wants to check on the status of his son's marriage.[28] Perhaps he's in town to confer with Ahab over Edom (v. 47; see 2 Kings 3:1-9). We don't know, even though Jehoshaphat is one of the Chronicler's parade examples of faithful leadership, a "torah-disseminator" (2 Chron 17:7-9) and "judicial reformer" *par excellence* (19:4-11).

These roles do not appear in Kings. Instead, like Cimon with Pausanias, Jehoshaphat functions only as a "moral reformer" to Ahab's "unrighteous despot."[29] To Ahab's initial request—"Will you fight the Syrians with me?"—

Jehoshaphat responds warily. When Ahab suggests that Jehoshaphat wear his royal robes into battle, he dutifully plays along. But when he suggests that they go to war on the advice of 400 hand-picked prophets, Jehoshaphat demurs. He wants to consult "another" (`ôd, v. 7) prophet first. Whether his hesitation comes out of tradition or experience is not clear. What *is* clear is that he reveres Yahweh *and* desires an alliance with Ahab, and this is not an easy place to be. Jehoshaphat is a man in the middle.

The third conflict is Ahab vs. Micaiah, the classic "king-vs.-prophet" conflict. Like Elijah's encounter with Ahab, Micaiah moves beyond critique to full-fledged satire.[30] Perhaps it's because Ahab is such an easy target. When Jehoshaphat initially requests the oracle, Ahab rounds up 400 prophets, an amazing thing to consider in light of what's just happened on Mt. Carmel. Apparently he still thinks, in spite of Carmel, that Yahweh's prophets are easily manipulated. Still, in honor of Jehoshaphat's request, he sends for Micaiah, and as the unnamed messenger escorts the prophet back, he gives him a little friendly advice about how to deal with Ahab. "Look, as one man the other prophets are predicting success for the king. Let your word agree with theirs, and speak favorably." This looks much like the advice of another timid bureaucrat, Obadiah (1 Kings 18), but whether his motivation is to spare Ahab embarrassment or spare Micaiah's life, the advice itself is idolatrous because it tries to exalt unity (`ehad, "as one man") over truth ( `emet, v. 16). Alongside Ahab's intransigence, in other words, this messenger represents the much subtler problem of complacency. His is the voice of the well-intentioned crowd whose message is always the same: "Go along and get along." "Don't make waves." "Keep your job."

Micaiah's response looks like that of the southern prophet in 1 Kings 13: "As surely as Yahweh lives, I can tell him only what Yahweh tells me." Reproducing it here underlines its centrality within the prophetic tradition. Interestingly, Ahab's messenger is the only person who hears it—everyone else hears only biting sarcasm. With Ahab, in fact, Micaiah chooses not to tell the truth at all—at least not on their first pass.

The fourth conflict is prophet vs. prophet—Micaiah vs. Zedekiah. Micaiah arrives at the threshing floor, and the first thing he sees is Zedekiah's dog and pony show. Obviously these prophets want to impress Ahab, who in turn wants to impress his new ally, Jehoshaphat. But as the show gathers steam, Zedekiah begins to move beyond proclamation to homeopathic ritual. He brings out symbolic cattle horns and ritually acts out Israel's "inevitable" victory. These are not just visual aids, but homeopathic images designed to coerce the gods into compliance—just like the self-mutilation rituals on Mt. Carmel.

Micaiah's response is a satirical masterpiece. First he surprises Ahab, then he baffles him. When Ahab hears him repeat verbatim what his 400 yes-men have just been "prophesying"—"Attack! Be victorious!"—he realizes immediately that he's been had. Aware that Jehoshaphat is witnessing his humiliation, he tries to save face: "How many times must I make you swear to me to tell me nothing but the truth in the Name of Yahweh?" Big mistake. The mention of the words "truth" and "Yahweh" causes Micaiah to take off the gloves and come out swinging. "I saw all Israel scattered on the hills like sheep without a shepherd, and Yahweh said, 'These people have no master.'" Micaiah puts some pointed questions to this leader. How can a nation go to war when it can't find its way home? How can a flock function without a shepherd? Boldly he lets Israel know that Israel's problem is not Syria. Israel's problem is that it has an idiot for a leader. Eating fresh vegetables is more important to this man than human life. Cocooning himself in "prophecy" is more important than seeking the truth.

When the scene suddenly shifts to the Unseen World, Micaiah reveals to Ahab how he knows what he knows. To Samaria's vacuum of leadership, Micaiah shows him a vision of effective leadership. To the raucous "worshiptainment" circus going on down at the threshing floor, Ahab suddenly hears nothing but silence: Lord Yahweh sits silently and transcendently upon *his* throne, surrounded by *his* servants, wearing *his* robes. To Ahab's repeated inquiries, "Should I go up and attack?" the king now hears another query: "Who will entice Ahab into attacking?" To the 400 prophets' incoherence, Ahab hears an orderly discussion: "One suggests this, another that." To Zedekiah's attempt to manipulate the gods, Ahab suddenly sees a heavenly spirit obeying the One God. To Samaria's dreary religion of lockstep conformity, the 400 prophets witness a burst of creative originality: "I will go out and be a lying spirit in the mouths of all his prophets." To the fearful spirit of political correctness, Micaiah hears a Word of divine encouragement: "You will succeed. Go and do it."

In other words, *everything* about this council is different—its leadership, its function, its creativity, its goals. Everything in heaven profoundly mocks everything on earth.

Intratextual Reflection

What a strange text! Of all the issues here, perhaps the most difficult to understand is Yahweh's decision to "entice" Ahab. Why would God want to "entice" someone, even someone like Ahab? Many scholars have wrestled with this question. David Clines and David Gunn try to answer it by softening the verb for "deceive" (*patâ*) to "persuade."[31]   Volkmar Hirth tries to answer it by locating Yahweh's "deception" in the mind of a pos-texilic editor, not the divine mind.[32] Neither of these solutions is attractive. Apparently the notion that God might entice someone is too difficult for some believers to take, perhaps because responding to it means that we will have to wrestle hard with the tension between two complementary biblical doctrines: determinism vs. free will. If God allows free will, then we have the freedom to do whatever we please, and this, by definition, can lead us to disaster.

> When any Israelite or any alien living in Israel separates himself from me and sets up idols in his heart and puts a wicked stumbling block before his face and then goes to a prophet (*nabî*) to inquire of me, I Yahweh will answer him myself. I will set my face against that man and make him an example and a byword. I will cut him off from my people. Then you will know that I am Yahweh (Ezek 14:7-8).

This is particularly true for prophets.

> If the prophet is enticed (*patâ*) to utter a prophecy, I Yahweh have enticed that prophet, and I will stretch out my hand against him and destroy him from among my people Israel. They will bear their guilt—the prophet will be as guilty as the one who consults him. Then the people of Israel will no longer stray from me (Ezek 14:9-11).[33]

Preaching to believers in Thessalonica, Paul conveys a similar sentiment: "For this reason God sent them a powerful delusion so that they will believe the lie and so that all will be condemned who have not believed the truth but have delighted in wickedness" (2 Thes 2:11-12).[34]

   If we genuinely have free will, God will allow us to believe whatever we want—but it's important to realize in the same breath that God does not send "strong delusions" to the faithful, only the faith-less. Were we not allowed free will, God would simply force us to "knuckle under" and "believe." But this would no longer be faith. Mere acknowledgement of God's existence does not equal obedient trust, as the Letter of James makes clear: "even the demons believe...and tremble" (James 2:19). Either God allows free will or he does not, and this means that the possibility always exists for some of us not to believe.

   And when this unbelief becomes a habit, a host of God-shaped substitutes can start springing up in our hearts. This is the message of "Solomon's

Wavering Heart" (1 Kings 11:1-13), and it's certainly the message here. Idolatry is the primary reason why Yahweh's prophets turn to pointed sarcasm and biting satire. We need to recognize Micaiah's audience for who they are. This is not a sermon preached to the saints on a Sunday morning. Micaiah is preaching to Ahab, the pouting husband of Jezebel, the bitter enemy of Elijah, the heinous murderer of Naboth,[35] the king known for selling himself into evil. Enticement is God's last, desperate act of grace for the Ahabs of this world.

Theological Reflection

Most of the characters in this story can be found in any congregation. I remember a particularly stormy meeting in which the leaders of our church gathered to discuss the needs of a poor family facing eviction from their apartment. The mother had lost her job and was behind in her rent. The father had long since abandoned the family, and the purpose of this meeting was to see what we could do to help.

As the meeting got under way, the chair listened patiently to the pros and cons about whether "this church ought to be in the real estate business," and whether "we can afford to set a precedent like this with the Lord's money." Whenever ethnic prejudice flared up (the family was Hispanic), the chair reminded us that the Kingdom was about "every nation and tongue and people and tribe." Whenever someone argued that "the budget won't allow this," the chair reminded us of Christ's command to give a cup of cold water in his name. Like Jehoshaphat, the chair was a faithful leader caught in the middle of a difficult situation.

Another participant had a different agenda, constantly throwing out stories like, "When I used to pastor...." For example, "When I used to pastor in Tennessee, this is what we did"; "When I used to pastor in Pennsylvania, this is what we found effective." Now and then he proposed a good idea, but most of what he had to say was canned and sterile. At no time did he ask a single question about this particular family. He preferred to live in the past, and he wanted us to live there with him. The suggestions he made were so tired, so mechanical, so completely out-of-touch with the situation before us, he seemed to believe that conjuring up past victories would automatically guarantee us "victory" in the present. Those who agreed with him that night—and there were several—went home convinced that devotion to tradition is the *real* goal of Christian service. Like Zedekiah, he knew how to "wear the horns" and put on a good show.

Another participant was like the "unnamed escort." Whenever the debate got heated, this man would wince, "Can't we all just get along?"

For him, unity was preferable to truth. Like Ahab's messenger, he was well-meaning, but he had no idea what to do for this family—he just didn't want anybody to get "hurt." Forget about the needs of this family. The "needs of the Church" come first.

Only a few looked heavenward. Opening their Bibles, they read to us the stories of Jesus—the healing of the blind man, the debate with Simon the Pharisee, the conversation with the Samaritan woman. Kindly but firmly, they critiqued the ideologies of the Ahabs and the Zedekiahs who sought to pull us away from the Mission. They weren't trying to be difficult, just faithful. Every church has prophets. They're the believers who refuse to sell out. They're the ones who know how to tell a good joke and defuse a tense situation. They're the ones always reminding us of our priorities.

Ultimately the council voted not to use church funds to help this family, but that didn't stop a few of us from holding another meeting in the foyer and raising the funds "un-officially."

BUSINESS AS USUAL (2 Kings 14:1-22)

After Elisha's death, Israel begins to drift. Left without prophetic guidance, Amaziah and Jehoash go through the motions of leadership, but they don't really lead. Like Ahab, Jehoash uses proverbial speech to poke fun at his opponents, lecturing Amaziah with a "thistle" parable much like the old parable of Jotham (Judg 9:7-15). Amaziah's behavior—his executions, his campaign against Edom, his interest in maritime commerce—all make him look like Solomon, the quintessential southern king. What's interesting, though, is not so much the predictability of their behavior as the gaps within the narrative.[36] In Kings, we really don't know (a) why Amaziah and Jehoash go to war, (b) why Amaziah issues the challenge and Jehoash the attack, (c) why Jehoash spares Amaziah's life, or (d) why Amaziah, like his father, falls victim to another assassination conspiracy.

We have to turn to Chronicles to fill in these gaps. According to 2 Chron 25, Amaziah hires Israelite mercenaries to help fight off Edom, but he summarily dismisses them when a prophet pronounces them "unfit." Humiliated and angry, Amaziah's mercenaries plunder and pillage their way back to Ephraim, and this astonishes Amaziah, so much so that he declares war against Israel. Yet Jehoash attacks first, and for a very "good" reason: Amaziah plans to introduce Edomite gods into Judahite worship. Yahweh therefore punishes Amaziah by (a) using Jehoash to defeat him in battle, and (b) permitting an internal conspiracy to harass him. Kings says nothing about any of this because the prophetic narrator wants us to focus on the impact of Elisha's death.

First, Elisha's death leaves a huge, prophet-shaped hole. Miracle stories notwithstanding, Elisha's death effectively brings to an end any hope for prophetic "succession," and it's difficult to over-emphasize the significance of this. In a few short years the southern prophet Amos will rise up and challenge Jeroboam II, but unlike Elisha, he will *deny* any connection to the *benê nebî'îm* ("sons of the prophets"). At Bethel, the priest Amaziah will try to label him a "seer" (*hôzeh*), but Amos will reject this role-label (Amos 7:14).[37] After Elisha, no prophet will ever again command the attention of the monarchy in quite the same way.

Second, in lieu of a prophetic oracle the narrator cites a biblical text—Deut 24:16 (almost verbatim).[38] This may not seem significant at first glance, but to cite a written text in lieu of a prophetic oracle is significant. When we look at this phenomenon in the Chronicler's work, what we begin to see is a new kind of prophet emerging, the "inspired messenger" who no longer *receives* the Word of God—only *interprets* it.[39] That this occurs already in Kings implies that this narrator is becoming aware of this paradigm shift. That he cites from the Law shows that Amaziah's behavior is as surprising as it is commendable.

Third, alongside this transformation of prophecy via the citation of a covenantal law, the narrator adds a memorable parable. Like Ahab, Jehoash uses parables to psych out his enemies. Ahab uses a parable with Ben-Hadad (1 Kings 20:11), and the Shechemite Jotham uses similar motifs in his famous parable (Judg 9:7-15). Jotham uses the image of a "thistle" to represent Abimelech's poor leadership, but "thistle" here symbolizes Amaziah's arrogance: "You have indeed defeated Edom and now you are arrogant. Glory in your victory, but stay at home! Why ask for trouble and cause your own downfall and that of Judah also?" It's a bit surprising to see these words on Jehoash's lips because this is the same king Elisha earlier criticizes for faithlessness (2 Kings 13:19). Once the battle starts, Jehoash goes on a rampage, much like Jehu's rampage against the Omrides (10:1-35). Where Jehu rages out of control, however, Jehoash reigns himself in. He captures Amaziah at Beth-Shemesh. He invades Jerusalem. He tears down a sizable section of Jerusalem's wall. But then he lets Amaziah go free, only keeping a few hostages to protect himself and his army from further reprisals.[40]

Intratextual Reflection

This all seems like business as usual, but perhaps there's more to this story than meets the eye. Once, when the Israeli government of Ehud Barak collapsed, the Knesset took a no-confidence vote because they were afraid that Barak might give away too much land to the Palestinians. Several in the Knesset even accused him of governing without the people's consent. To some Israelis, Barak was a courageous peacemaker. To others, he was a "thistle" in a long line of thistles. Like the Amaziah-Jehoash conflict, they polarized and paralyzed over what to do in the face of danger.[41]

Political conflicts perplex us because the parties involved seem so diametrically opposed. It's difficult to know how to respond to such conflicts. Should we pray? Should we send out missionaries? Should we involve ourselves in the debate? Should we take sides? Our desire, of course, is for genuine peace. This is why we Christians are sacrificing our lives in conflict-plagued hotspots all over the globe—Palestine and Kosovo and Ireland and China and Los Angeles and the Philippines and anywhere else we think we're needed. We know from experience that many of these places have no intention of turning to Christ, yet still we leave home to preach the Good News. We know that some conflicts are so ancient, so tradition-bound, so institutionalized, so emotionally rooted that even the message of Yeshu`a the Jew sounds like a foreign, Western idea.

Is it appropriate to give up the Gospel's broader implications and become isolationist in our thinking? Is it appropriate to act as if the ministry of reconciliation has no corporate political component? Politics and religion are inseparable in the prophetic literature. Kings is neither quietist nor activist. The question is not whether we ought to apply the book's theology to contemporary sociopolitical problems, but how.[42] The conflict between Jehoash and Amaziah is deeply, organically connected to Kings' other conflicts, like the conflict between Nathan and David (1 Kings 1:11-45), and Ahab vs. Ben-Hadad (20:1-43). Also on this trajectory stand the stories of Ahab's disaster at Ramoth-Gilead (22:29-50) and Isaiah's conflict with Sennacherib (2 Kings 19:1-37). What can we learn from this intratextual memory?

First, we can learn that politics is just as much an instrument of God's creation as preaching or counseling or teaching or chaplaining. Evangelicals especially need to hear this. We may want our leaders to be "above the fray," but none of them are. Indeed, none of them can be. The episodes on this trajectory are a strong reminder that we need to be wise as serpents, more realistic about leaders and leadership issues. These are not happyfaith sermons, nor are they Harlequin romances. These are gritty stories about frail leaders facing tough problems. They tell us the truth about how God's power *actually* works, and just as there are true prophets and false prophets, so there are true politicians and false politicians. Indeed, stories like these are designed to help us tell them apart.

Second, we can learn to recognize the distinction between political ideology and political method. Interpreters who fail to make this distinction often do some pretty crazy things with the Bible. Marxist interpreters, for example, tend to see class conflict and dialectical opposition behind every rock.[43] Premillennialists tend to side with everything modern Israel says and does—not because they've weighed Israel's behavior against Jesus' Kingdom ethic, but because they view the modern state of Israel as the "fulfillment" of "biblical prophecy."[44] Both positions confuse political ideology with political method. The book of Kings has a clear ideology. Kings is a prophetic, predominantly northern Yahwistic account of Israel's history over the course of the divided monarchy. To read it through some other ideological lens is to misinterpret its message and corrupt its theology. Kings' theological message is not apolitical. In fact, some of its stories (like this one) are almost purely political, because "the political instinct...is one of these things which (all people) hold in common."[45] To be appreciated fully, stories like Amaziah's conflict with Jehoash need to be laid alongside Isaiah's critique of Sennacherib or Nathan's behind-the-scenes encounter with King David. Intratextual interpretation can help us outgrow our religio-political naïveté. Kings is about good politicians and bad politicians, but rarely is it about no politicians.

Third, it's important to learn when and where to pick one's battles. Amaziah thinks that defeating Israel is going to be easy—as easy as, say, invading Edom. Even when he's given the chance to back away and cool off, he refuses to glory in his own victory and stay at home. Instead, he "asks for trouble." Amaziah doesn't know how to pick his battles, and in this he looks like another naïve leader, the academic Charles Van Doren. In Robert Redford's film *Quiz Show*, Van Doren makes the following speech to a Senate subcommittee investigating the television quiz show scandals: "I've stood on the shoulders of life and I've never gotten down into the dirt to build, to erect a foundation of my own. I've flown too high on borrowed wings. Everything came too easy."[46] Like Van Doren, everything came a bit too easy for Amaziah. Like Van Doren, Amaziah refused to "get down into the dirt to build," choosing instead to plow into something about which he knew little.[47]

Theological Reflection
Perhaps Jesus is reflecting on this episode when he remarks,

Suppose a king is about to go to war against another king. Will he not first sit down and consider whether he is able with ten thousand men to oppose the one coming against him with twenty thousand? If he is not able, he will send a delegation while the other is still a long way off and will ask for terms of peace. In the same way, any of you who does not give up everything he has cannot be my disciple.[48]

In Jesus' mind, preparing for discipleship is like preparing for war. War is a time for careful reflection, not petulance—a time for weighing options, not gambling the farm. Discipleship, like war, requires wisdom and patience and a sober willingness to count the cost. To negotiate peace from a position of weakness is one thing. To attack a stronger army unprepared is...well, like a *thistle* pretending to be a *cedar*. Here are two ways to apply this principle:

First, it may be time to take Jehoash's advice. Of all people, Christians should be wary of adopting uncritically the friend-or-foe, either-or rhetoric we see all around us. Culture-war rhetoric can lead us to distort others' positions and make our own sound hollow and naïve. Culture-war rhetoric can play us right into the hands of those who want to divide us. The bulk of the American public does not neatly divide into two giant sectors, "Right vs. Left." So why do so many of us act like it does? Why do we allow the culture-war rhetoricians to skew and distort our understanding? Do we not serve a Triune God who loves sinners? Do we not serve a Creator who cares about the entirety of the creation?[49]

Second, ideological war is constantly percolating within the Church itself. Both Catholic and Protestant communions, for example, are struggling today over how and where to "pick their battles." Among Catholics, Vatican positions on a number of issues continue to generate controversy and anger, even bitterness. Liberation theology, sexual ethics, abusive priests, women's ordination, mandatory celibacy—these are but a few of the battles being fought.[50] Mainline Protestants, meanwhile, are aligning into opposing camps over whether to restore the foundations of biblical theology in Church practice, or simply to reimagine the Church as a pluralistic community bound together by "love" and "tolerance."[51] Whether solid middle ground can be found between these positions is an open question, but one which becomes more difficult to address when we choose to settle for business as usual.

Notes

1. Aeschylus, *Prometheus Bound*, line 31.

2. 2 Sam 12:1-14; see my "Wise Women or Wisdom Woman? A Biblical Study of Women's Roles," *RQ* 35 (1993) 152-56.

3. See my "Wise Women in the Bible: Identifying a Trajectory," in C. Osburn, ed., *Essays on Women in Earliest Christianity*, vol. 2 (Joplin, MO: College Press, 1995) 97-98.

4. H. Cohen ("David and Bathsheba," *JBR* 33 [1965] 142-148) sees David not as a typical Oriental despot indulging himself, but as a mortal man engaged in a life and death struggle with the aging process.

5. Josephus, *AJ* 7.7.3.

6. A. Laato, "Second Samuel 7 and Ancient Near Eastern Royal Ideology," *CBQ* 59 (1997) 265.

7. Gray (*Kings* 88) thinks that Nathan is instructing Bathsheba to practice auto-suggestion on a senile old man. De Vries (*Kings*, 15) thinks "such subtle psychologizing (is) beyond the naïve art of the narrator, however much of it may possibly have motivated the historical Nathan." Provan (*Kings* 25) suggests that Adonijah uninvites Solomon to his feast precisely because the public already knows about his privileged status as David's designated successor. Nelson (*Kings* 16) suggests that Adonijah's feast may never have been intended as a "coronation" until the "wily Nathan" spins it into one.

8. In 1940, W. F. Albright argued that *nabî* should be taken as a passive form of the root *nb'*, "to call." The prophet, therefore, is "the one called." Daniel Fleming, however ("The Etymological Origins of the Hebrew *nabî*: The One Who Invokes God," *CBQ* 55 [1993] 217-24), has persuasively argued from the newer comparative evidence that *nabî* is better translated as an active form; i.e., "the one who calls/invokes"). The major argument against this newer etymology is the fact that *nabî* is a qatîl passive form.

9. An Anatolian "wise woman" warns of a city's possible destruction via an elaborate magico-religious ritual (*KUB* VII.60).

10. A *muhhutu* prophet speaks on behalf of the god Dagan to tell King Zimri-Lim to offer a funerary sacrifice for his father, Yahdun-Lim (*ARM* 3.40).

11. An Egyptian prophet bluntly tells his Pharaoh, "Egypt is in chaos. No order remains. No profit can be made. No one cares about the pain in this land.... Egypt is without direction" (*OTP* 313-14).

12. E. M. Forster, *Aspects of the Novel* (New York: Harcourt Brace Jovanovich, 1927) 72-73.

13. Provan, 13.

14. *Love and Justice: Selections from the Shorter Writings of Reinhold Niebuhr*, ed. D. B. Robertson (Louisville: Westminster/John Knox, 1957; reprinted 1992) 11.

15. R. Niebuhr, *Moral Man and Immoral Society* (New York: Scribner's, 1932) xi.

16. Tim Keller, "Preaching to the Secular Mind," *Journal of Biblical Counseling* 14 (1995) 54-62.

17. D. Buttrick, *A Captive Voice: The Liberation of Preaching* (Louisville: Westminster/John Knox, 1994) 21-23.

18. Craig C. Christina, "The Theology of Preaching: Is the Preaching Event the

Word of God?" *Journal of the American Academy of Ministry* 4 (1995) 37-61.

19. Compare Luke 18:18-27.

20. Scott Layton ("Old Aramaic Inscriptions," *BA* 51 [1988] 172-188) argues the consensus opinion that by the 7th century BC, Aramaic has become the *lingua franca* of the ancient Near East.

21. Ben-Hadad is the Hebraized version of Aramaic "Bir-Hadad," meaning "son of Hadad." Hadad is the most common epithet of the Syrian storm god, the Syrian equivalent of Canaanite Baal.

22. L. Stager, "The Finest Olive Oil in Samaria," *JSS* 28 (1983) 241-45.

23. W. V. Robinson and M. Paulson, "A 'Grieving' Law Apologizes for Assignment of Geoghan," *Boston Globe* (Jan 10, 2002) A1.

24. D. Bonhoeffer, *Ethics* (New York: MacMillan, 1955; trans. from 1949 German ed., based on manuscripts written between 1940-43) 3.

25. Bonhoeffer, *Ethics*, 5-6.

26. K. Gangel, "Ten Steps to Sunday School Revival," *Christian Education Journal* 11 (1991) 31-42.

27. See above on 1 Kings 20:1-43.

28. The problem of deciding Athaliah's precise relationship to Ahab centers on the simple genealogical phrase *bat `omrî* in 2 Kings 8:26. ASV reads "daughter," while NIV reads "granddaughter." Either reading is possible.

29. Plutarch, *Cimon* 6.2.

30. T. Jemielity, *Satire and the Prophets* (Lousiville: Westminster/John Knox, 1992).

31. D. J. A. Clines & D. M. Gunn, "'You Tried to Persuade Me' and 'Violence, Outrage!' in Jeremiah XX, 7-8," *VT* 28 (1978) 20-27.

32. V. Hirth, "'Der Geist' in I Reg 22," *ZAW* 101 (1989) 113-14.

33. Note that the reason for the first stipulation is Yahweh's desire to bring glory to his Name, while the reason for the second is Yahweh's desire to save those who "stray" *(ta`â)*.

34. G. L. Bahnsen argues ("The Crucial Concept of Self-Deception in Presuppositional Apologetics," *WTJ* 57 [1995] 1-31) that self-deception involves deception of the self, by the self, about the self, and for the sake of the self. All of this is included in the monotheistic phrase "God sends them a powerful delusion."

35. In fact, one rabbi suggests that "the spirit" which volunteers to entice Ahab is none other than Naboth himself (*b. Shab.* 149b).

36. M. Sternberg, *The Poetics of Biblical Narrative* (Bloomington, IN: Indiana University, 1987) 186-228.

37. Not everyone agrees with this interpretation. Z. Zevit ("A Misunderstanding at Bethel: Amos VII 12-17," *VT* 25 [1975] 783-90) thinks that Amos merely claims to be a prophet independent of royal patronage. H. J. Stoebe ("Noch Einmal zu Amos VII 10-17," *VT* 39 [1989] 341-54) thinks he's claiming a direct divine commission to prophesy, but that this is something entirely different from institutional "office." C. Levin ("Amos und Jerobeam I," *VT* 45 [1995] 307-17) thinks that Amos is, in fact, the Judahite "man of God" in 1 Kings 13.

38. The only differences are (a) the addition of a *kî 'im* clause near the end of the quote, and (b) the pluralization of the final verb *(mût)*. That 2 Chron 25:4 repeats verbatim 2 Kings 14:6 instead of Deut 24:16 demonstrates a greater likelihood of

dependence on Kings than on Deuteronomy.

39. W. Schniedewind, *The Word of God in Transition: From Prophet to Exegete in the Second Temple Period*, JSOTSup 197 (Sheffield: JSOT Press, 1995) 11.

40. M. Avi-Yonah, "The Walls of Nehemiah—A Minimalist View," *IEJ* 4 (1954) 239–48.

41. N. Sharansky, "Barak Took the Wrong Path for Israel," *New Perspectives Quarterly* 18 (Winter 2001) 34.

42. W. Brueggemann, "Together in the Spirit: Beyond Seductive Quarrels," in *Deep Memory, Exuberant Hope* (Minneapolis: Fortress, 2000) 32-4.

43. R. Boer, "Western Marxism and the Interpretation of the Hebrew Bible," *JSOT* 78 (1998) 3-21.

44. Tim Weber, "How Evangelicals Became Israel's Best Friend," *CT* 42 (1998) 38-49.

45. G. K. Chesterton, *Orthodoxy* (New York: John Lane, 1908) 42.

46. *Quiz Show*, directed by R. Redford, screenplay by P. Attanasio, based on a book by R. Goodwin (1994).

47. Van Doren eventually lost his teaching position at Columbia University and never taught again (K. Anderson, *The History and Implications of the Quiz Show Scandals* [Westport, CT: Greenwood Press, 1978] 71).

48. Luke 14:31-33.

49. J. Woodbridge, "Culture War Casualties," *CT* 39 (1995) 20-26.

50. P. Berryman, "The Battle for the Catholic Church," *CC* 106 (1989) 523-26.

51. J. Edwards, "At the Crossroads: The Battle for a Denomination's Soul," *CT* 41 (1997) 21-25.

FOUR

THE PRESSURE OF FAMINE

ELIJAH AND THE WIDOW (1 Kings 17:1-24)

Elijah is one of the most famous prophets in the Bible, yet the Elijah cycle begins with an oath, not an oracle. Elijah swears to King Ahab that the life-giving rains will dry up for the next few years. These words challenge Ahab's whole view of the cosmos because Ahab believes that Baal is the Divine Rainmaker, not Yahweh. Elijah delivers to Ahab the message that Yahweh is the God of the rain, not Baal, and because Ahab refuses to accept this truth, drought is coming, and with it famine, pestilence, and death.

Unlike Pharaoh, who responds positively to Joseph's warning (Gen 41:37-45), Ahab responds negatively to Elijah's warning. In fact, he puts out an all-points-bulletin on him, calling him "my enemy" ('*oyebî*). He's so angry, in fact, he tries to compel his neighbors to swear whether they've seen him or not. Much more is going on here than a personality conflict between two strong-willed leaders. This is a no-holds-barred, bare-knuckled brawl between two deities. Either Yahweh is God or Baal is God—but both cannot be God.

Thanks to the Canaanite myths from ancient Ugarit (in Syria), we now have a great deal of information about Baal and his cult. In the Canaanite pantheon, the father-deity El spawns several children, including Mot (god of death), Yam (god of the sea), Nahar (god of the rivers), and Anat (goddess of war). Baal is the fair-haired favorite. Baal is the rainmaker, the giver of life, the god who triumphs over all his siblings through a series of mythological adventures. Through a vigorous and sophisticated use of word associations and narrative allusions, the narrator of Kings constantly interacts with and challenges these myths.[1]

Famine therefore has deep ideological, even mythological connotations. Will Israel trust Yahweh or will they turn to Baal in times of famine? Hiding from Ahab, Elijah camps out in a wady called Cherith before he moves, at Yahweh's command, to a Sidonian suburb on the Mediterranean coast, a village called Zarephath. The pattern here is distinctively prophetic. Yahweh commands. Elijah obeys. Unlike the southern prophet from Judah (1 Kings 13:1-32), Elijah here shows no desire to disobey God.

The widow of Zarephath, though, is not so obedient. Yahweh "commands" her too, but Elijah has to persuade her to get involved in the prophet-feeding ministry. First, she laments that she has no food to give him. In fact, on the very day he arrives, her food runs out and she begins planning her death. Yet God gives her a choice. Will she help feed his prophet? Or will she decide not to help? Even in the midst of suffering, God invites her to live by faith. Fatalistic determinism is not an option, even for starving widows.

Second, when her son dies, she blames Elijah. Angry and distraught, she goes so far as to accuse Elijah of causing her son's death (the verb in v. 18 is causative, *lehamît*). Nowhere does she ascribe his death to the anger of Baal or the caprice of Asherah. Instead she blames Elijah. This becomes obvious when, after the resurrection of her son, she confesses, "Now I know that you are a man of God and that the word of Yahweh from your mouth is truth" (*'emet*, 17:24). This sort of scepticism saturates the entire Elijah cycle. Characters here frequently associate Elijah with "sin" and "death." This widow, for example, thinks that Elijah has come to "remind me of my sin and kill my son" (17:18). In the next chapter, Obadiah will repeat these same two words when he cries out, "What is my sin...that you hand over your servant to Ahab to be put to death?" (18:9). Not only is this reaction common, but a case can be made for a whole progression of accusations: (a) the widow doubts whether Elijah is a man of "truth" (*'emet*, 17:24); (b) the palace steward (Obadiah) wonders whether Elijah will abandon him to face the king alone (18:12); and (c) the king categorically labels him as a troubler of Israel (*'oker*, 18:17). In short, everyone wants a piece of Elijah—the poor, the middle class, the ruling elite—everyone.

Why? Is it because famine drives people crazy? Is it because Baalism has taken over their hearts? Is it because Elijah's words push his Canaanized audiences a bit too far? Whatever the possibilities, Elijah eventually recognizes the depth of this anger. At the beginning of his Mt. Carmel speech, he prays that "these people will know that you, O Yahweh, are God, and that you are turning their hearts back again" (18:37). In fact, Elijah's prayers even have a sequential structure. In his *first* prayer he cries out to Yahweh on behalf of a desperate widow. NIV translates, "Have you brought tragedy also upon this widow I am staying with, by causing her son to die?" (17:20), but this ignores the syntax in MT, which reads, "Are you again bringing evil upon this widow?" In other words, Elijah seems more interested in this widow's pain than God's actions. Elijah is alarmed that, in addition to her starvation (a tragedy in itself), this widow has to suffer the loss of her baby too. Like Jeremiah, this causes him to get stuck on the "why" question—a common reaction in such circumstances.

In his *second* prayer, Elijah asks Yahweh to demonstrate his power over Baal (18:36-37), while in his *third* prayer he says, "I have had enough, Yahweh...Take my life; I am no better than my ancestors" (19:4). Exhausted by ministry, Elijah's *fourth* prayer betrays the harsh realization that Israel's idolatrous heart is not going to change (19:10, 14). If we read these prayers in sequence, they look very much like Jeremiah's laments (Jer 11:18-12:6; 15:10-21; 17:14-18; 18:18-23; 20:7-18). Both prophets struggle with deep inner suffering. Both feel the pain of alienation, and both struggle with the mystery of theodicy.[2]

Intratextual Reflection

Intratextually, this episode sets the tone for the rest of Kings' famine-stories, especially "Mothers Needing Miracles" (2 Kings 4:1-37), "Death in the Pot" (4:38-44), and "Under Siege" (6:24-7:20). When we compare, for example, the episode in 1 Kings 17 with the one in 2 Kings 4:1-37, the parallels practically jump off the page. Both stories show us poor widows in distress. Both show us prophets trying to help them. Both show us a God miraculously intervening. These parallels are so close, many scholars view them as literary doublets of the same event. Without denying this as a possibility, we need to give more attention to the intratextual context.

First, what does "famine" mean? This becomes a relevant question once we examine "famine" in 1 Kings 17 vs. "famine" in 2 Kings 4. The first is a Yahweh-induced famine. The second is a famine of justice. The first is divinely caused. The second is humanly caused. The famine in the second story plays off the one in the first, but in doing so it highlights the fact that famine can be something very…avoidable. This in no way minimizes the second widow's pain—it simply causes us to ask deeper questions about what "famine" means.

Second, there is no hint in the Elisha narrative that the widow's problem is connected to the theological problem of Phoenician Baalism. The conflict between Baal and Yahweh is the driving force behind the Zarephath story, but crass materialism is the reason behind the second widow's plight. The prophet's widow falls into debt and almost loses her children not because she has no husband to pay off the creditors. This woman suffers disgrace because nobody is taking seriously the Law of Moses.[3]

Third, God truly loves the "least of these" (Matt 25:40). Elijah's God refuses to patronize the poor or make them sacrifice everything to some Canaanite fertility deity. No, Yahweh invites the poor to believe in him, like everyone else. Suffering widows need to live by faith just as much as rich kings and frightened stewards. The Zarephath widow may ask some disturbing questions about her plight, and she may make some rather naïve theological connections between sin and death, but at least she decides to stop thinking of herself as a victim. By faith, she offers Yahweh's prophet her last piece of bread—and God blesses her for it.

Theological Reflection

Years ago I got a frantic call from a young mother with whom I had begun a discipling relationship. Calling from an emergency room phone, she apologized for getting me out of bed, but would I come to the hospital and talk to her brother? *Her brother? Why her brother?* Never having met her brother before, I wondered why she wanted me to talk to him as I raced through our abandoned streets at 2:30 in the morning. Arriving at the hospital, the refrigerated air helped clear my head as I navigated my way toward the ER waiting room. There, in the middle of the room, this young mother and her brother were shouting at each other at the top of their lungs.

Never has a triage nurse been so glad to see a pastor. Separating brother and sister from the rest of the family (Mom and Dad and the brother's son, a young man in his early twenties), I whisked everyone away to the hospital cafeteria. From what I could gather, the young mother had been out earlier with some friends, leaving her 2-year-old daughter with her brother's son—her nephew. When she came home, she found her baby lying listlessly in front of the TV, her plastic pants swollen with blood. Terrified, she called the doctor, who immediately ordered her to bring the child into the ER. Along the way, the only thing her nephew would say about it was, "I dunno."

Everyone else arrived at about the same time the triage nurse came out with the shocking news: the baby's vaginal wall had been ruptured by a sharp object, probably a pen or a pencil. As soon as the word "pencil" fell from her lips this mother lunged at her nephew like an enraged tiger. Eyewitnesses testified later that they genuinely thought she would kill him. This, of course, provoked the father's intervention on behalf of his son and the ensuing melee. Already the victim of an abusive husband, this woman simply assumed that "another stupid man" had abused her family. *Obviously* that "bad man" was her nephew. Whether or not someone else might have been present that evening never entered her mind.

In point of fact, the police investigation found out that someone else had been there that evening, but that's irrelevant to the point we're making here. Whether the child of the Zarephath widow dies because of the Yahweh-induced famine is not really the point of the biblical story. The focal point is the widow's response. This Sidonian mother, like my friend in that ER waiting room, feels an overwhelming need to blame someone, whether that person is guilty or not. Such is the pain generated by unexplainable suffering. Like this young mother, the Zarephath widow jumps to an unwarranted conclusion—understandable, perhaps, but wrong nonetheless.

Situations like these are not going to go away, so we need to realize (a) that God wants us to minister to hurting people even when their questions are unanswerable; (b) that ministry is not limited by a pastor's (or anyone else's) perceptions; (c) that faith can enable us to recognize God's work in the midst of chaos; and (d) that there is always at least something we can do to help, however insignificant it may seem.[4]

DEATH IN THE POT (2 Kings 4:38-44)

Literary patterns are important, and one of them in the Elisha cycle is distinctive. Elisha's miracles tend to come in pairs. Not one, but two miracles inaugurate Elisha's ministry—one a blessing, the other a curse (2 Kings 2:19-26). Not one, but two mothers request and receive the salvation of their children—one from a creditor, the other from death (4:1-37). Not one, but two miraculous feedings address the needs of Elisha's disciples—one to *purify*, the other to *multiply* the meager bits of food at their disposal. That Elisha's miracles tend to come in pairs is a mystery, but this is a major distinction between the Elijah and Elisha cycles.

The first of these miracles is a miracle of purification. Elisha knows that his disciples are hungry, so he takes responsibility for feeding them. Gathering herbs for a communal meal, someone accidentally picks a "wild vine," a *gepen sadeh* (lit. "vine of the field"), then throws it into the pot with the rest of the food. No one knows exactly what it is or where it's from, but still it finds its way onto the community dining room table—and the results are devastating. The community food supply becomes contaminated and inedible—a particularly bad thing to happen during a famine. Just as Jericho's water supply becomes contaminated (2 Kings 2:19-22), so now the food supply at Gilgal.

Such a crisis might discourage someone else, but Elisha sees it as a teaching opportunity. Were it not for the famine, perhaps the "sons of the prophets" might have been more careful. Perhaps they might have thought twice about the relative (in)edibility of "wild vines." But hunger can do strange things to people. It can make us drop our guard and cut corners and do things we normally wouldn't do. It can tempt us into eating things about which we know nothing. It can so broaden the "acceptable" items on our menus, even donkey heads can start to look tasty (2 Kings 6:25).[5]

To purify the food supply, Elisha sprinkles a little flour (at Jericho he uses salt). Items like flour and salt are not uncommon in the average kitchen, but they're essential ingredients in the homeopathic arsenals of purification priests.[6] This does not mean that Elisha's use of flour, unaccompanied by incantation or other ritual, necessarily acts as a "demon prophylactic" in this particular incident, but it's unwise to pretend that such things don't exist in Elisha's world. Intratextually, two keywords link this story to the ones preceding. As in the story of the preacher's widow, salvation comes here via something "poured out" (*yatsaq*), and just as Elisha "knows" (*yâda`*) nothing about the Shunammite's distress, so no one here "knows" anything about this wild vine.

The second of these miracles is a miracle of multiplication. Apparently the famine is localized to Gilgal because a man from Baal Shalishah (only 25 km north) brings Elisha a sampling of first ripe grain and garden produce (*karmel*; "new grain"). Elisha and his disciples welcome the help, but this man has doubts about whether so little food will satisfy so many disciples. Elisha can see a way out of this "impossible" situation, so he says to his visitor, "Give it to the people to eat." When he balks at this command, Elisha repeats it: "Give it to the people to eat."

It's significant that in both of these cases Elisha delegates the actual job of feeding to others. Like any good mentor, he empowers others to learn by doing, not just watching. In the first case, he lets a servant take care of the disciples, and he fails miserably. After purifying the pot, however, Elisha gives him a second chance, commanding him (again) to "pour it out." One can only imagine the look on the disciples' faces when they see this same servant ladling out a second helping of stew. Whether *they* give him the same benefit of the doubt as Elisha does we cannot know, but Elisha definitely knows how to mentor students.

In the second miracle, Elisha repeats this pedagogical pattern: "Give it to the people to eat." Elisha's faith in Yahweh's provision stands undeterred, yet he wants the man from Baal Shalishah to learn something about leadership. So confident is he of the outcome, in fact, he strips his response down to two infinitives: *'âkôl wehôter* ("Eat and leave over!"). One can only imagine the look on this man's face when he too realizes that God can do miraculous things with meager resources.

Intratextual Reflection

This story holds several themes in common with its intratextual counterparts—the pain of famine, the temptation to despair, the wonder of Yahweh's power. Each of these stories shows us a different divine response to the horrors of famine. The widow of Zarephath despairs for her life when she meets Elijah, but Yahweh responds to this despair with the promise of nourishment. The famine in Samaria comes in response to a Syrian siege, but the response to it there is as multiplex as the characters involved—two mothers kill and eat their own children; the king wears sackcloth under his clothing; a cynical lieutenant voices bitter skepticism; four lepers throw themselves desperately on the mercy of their enemies. With each of these characters Yahweh responds in a different way.

Here the stress of famine trips up the sons of the prophets and one of them makes a foolish mistake. The challenge for his mentor is to teach him how to learn from this mistake. This mentoring theme continues in the second miracle as Elisha teaches an inexperienced layman how to do ministry—even when it looks impossible. Where the miraculous element predominates elsewhere on the *pressure of famine* trajectory, here the main emphasis is on education. Elijah does not teach the Zarephath widow how to minister to others, but Elisha does teach the sons of the prophets and the visitor from Baal Shalishah. Like any good teacher, he seizes on their mistakes not to judge them, but to help them "fail forward."[7]

Theological Reflection

We don't have Elisha's lesson plans in front of us, but sanctification and multiplication are not peripheral educational goals. It's no accident that all four of the Gospels model their versions of the "feeding of the five thousand" after this OT narrative. In both Testaments we find (a) two kinds of food, (b) a leader teaching disciples how to serve, (c) disciples questioning their abilities, (d) a teacher promising results, and (e) a salvation miracle. In fact, the Gospels rely strongly on this intertextual foundation to build up a Christology of Jesus as Provider.[8]

Theologically speaking, the Holy Spirit is both "salt" and "flour." The job of the Spirit is to take inedible food and undrinkable water and transform them into nutrients for the Body. Sanctification is the process by which the "water" grows sweeter and the "food" more nourishing. Were it not for the Spirit, we could not neutralize the "death in the pot." The world is filled with "wild vines," and some of them fall into the educational food supply now and then. No one, particularly those of us who know a little about the curriculum of cooking, ever sits down to bread and cucumbers without (a) being invited, and (b) recognizing the power of the Provider. This is important. We cannot feed the hungry by ourselves—there are just too many mouths to feed. Only the Spirit can purify the food we eat and multiply its benefits.

One Monday my administrative assistant came into my office hopping mad.

"If you don't get that man out of my office, I'm going to scream!"

"What's the matter?" I asked.

"He keeps trying to tell me how to do my job, and I'm sick of it!"

The man to whom she was referring had been a prominent leader in another church before transferring to ours. He was used to being in control. He was used to telling church secretaries what to do. His immediate concern was the absence of the names of the church's lay leaders on our weekly bulletin. In his previous church, not only the names, but even the photographs of these men were regularly displayed, so the fact that the same didn't happen here could "mean only one thing"—we did not sufficiently respect our lay leadership.

That was just the tip of the iceberg. This brother didn't like the way we did much of anything. His goal, therefore, was to transform our congregation into the image of the one he had just left, and regular visits to the church secretary were a deliberate part of his strategy. Though his teaching consisted of a rather simplistic legalism, he packaged it in just enough contemporary jargon to make it look "cutting edge." His method was to praise the pastor in public, then privately question his credibility to anyone who would listen.

We tried everything within reason to deal with this individual. It didn't take long to realize, however, that he had no interest whatsoever in serving Christ with us. What he really wanted was to change our vision to suit his. In short, he was a "wild vine" in our congregational stew, and our pastoral strategy transitioned from ministering to his needs toward bringing "healing" to the "pot." First we tried the salt of human kindness. Several of us invited his family over for lunch after church—not once, but several times. Since he had teenagers, we tried to get him involved in the youth group.

When that didn't work, we tried sprinkling a little "flour." We asked him whether he was aware of the impact his behavior was having. He seemed surprised to learn of this problem. We asked him why he felt he had the authority to pressure our administrative assistant into doing things outside of her job description. His answer was classic: "Well, in *our* church the secretary doesn't seem to have near the power that yours seems to have...." When we informed him that we were not talking about his former church, that's when light finally began to dawn. From that point on, he refused to talk about the matter at hand, and tried to change the subject to matters of theology and church by-laws and other "important" matters. We were not successful in persuading this brother to change his behavior, but we did help purify the food supply for the rest of the flock.

What might have happened had we not taken seriously our pastoral responsibility to guard the congregation's food supply? Well, perhaps the same thing that happens in a lot of churches. Paralysis. Fanatic adherence to unhealthy tradition. Biblical illiteracy. Theological extremism. Political powermongering. Name them what you will, but such things bring death to a church. Such attitudes bring immeasurable harm because when we allow such "wild vines" to put down roots, the Christian faith can very quickly turn into something inedible. Left unchallenged, these wild vines make it impossible for hungry people to find their way to the messianic banquet table—and this is unacceptable. Jesus condemns his enemies because they refuse to remain in the Vine (John 15:1-8). Athenagoras warns his congregation of their "too keen appetite" for "taking in...with food something poisonous."[9] Tertullian warns pastors that the privilege of feeding Christ's flock can be lost whenever we choose to focus on the needs of "swine" instead of "sheep."[10] Marva Dawn has spoken with passion about the embarrassingly pagan curricula upon which many believers habitually feed.[11]

Jesus says that good shepherds are known not simply by their willingness to feed sheep, but by their willingness to guard sheep (John 10:11). Wolves prowl constantly, and they're not always easy to spot.

Sometimes they attack the sheep head-on, fangs bared. More often than not they simply sidle up in sheep's clothing and try to steal our lambs away, one-by-one. Good shepherds lay down their lives for the lambs. This may mean throwing a little flour into the pot every now and then. Or it may mean waiting patiently until the Day when the Father separates the wheat from the weeds.[12] Whatever the situation, it's not appropriate to turn tail and run every time a wolf appears (or a weed, or a "wild vine"). Nor is it appropriate to go into the weed-pulling business. Finding the right balance between feeding and guarding is a challenge for which we constantly need the Spirit's help.

UNDER SIEGE (2 Kings 6:24-7:20)

"Siege" is an ugly word. Ancient writers have only to use the metaphors of siege warfare, and this is enough to terrify their audiences. Homer immortalizes the Greek siege of Troy, for example, with epic poetry of great beauty—yet no couplet can camouflage the horror of a prolonged siege.[13] One of the longest sieges on record is the famous siege of Alyattes—over twelve years long.[14] Alexander the Great is known for an unusually large number of sieges, particularly in Syria-Palestine. In the Bible, Nebuchadnezzar's siege of Jerusalem is the best-known, but lest we think it a pagan custom, Israelite kings are known for the practice as well (2 Kings 24:11).

Slavery is the primary goal of a siege. In Hammurabi's time, Mesopotamians were so afraid, they sold their families into slavery just to ward off a siege[15]—in fact, one of Assurbanipal's sieges so traumatizes one woman she sells herself into slavery.[16] The Arameans are not as ruthless as the Assyrians with respect to the siege, but they certainly know about this unique form of terrorism. In Hadrach (250 miles north of Samaria), for example, the Aramean chieftain Zakkur manipulates his enemies' tribal disunity in order to survive their siege,[17] and afterwards he gives credit to the god Baalshamayin for saving his life.[18]

In other words, Samaria is not the only ancient city to suffer the horrors of a Syrian siege.[19] What distinguishes this one, however, is the way in which this Hebrew narrator works into the story a number of motifs and character-types from earlier episodes. In 1 Kings 3:16-28, for example, two prostitutes come to Solomon for help. Each claims the same child as her own, but each disputes with the king over who is going to cook and eat their remaining child. Both narratives have to do in some way with children, but the second one is horribly grisly: "Give up your son and we will eat him." Pondering these stories intratextually, it's impossible not to see the narrative connections. When the Samarian mother cries out, "Save me!" (*yâsa'*), the narrator seizes on this word to reprise the main theme of the Elisha cycle—*salvation*. When the king responds with a shrug—"if Yahweh has chosen not to save, how can I save?"—he articulates this same theme, even through his doubts.

Frustration and anger are understandable responses to pain and suffering—we've seen them earlier in the Elijah cycle. Yet this king ratchets it up a notch. He tries to scapegoat Elisha and blame him for this siege. Why? Is he angry because Elisha has allowed a Syrian army squadron to go free in the previous paragraph? Or is this simply what Omride rulers do at moments of crisis—scapegoat prophets? The text doesn't say, but apparently the feeling from Elisha is mutual because his immediate response is to label this king a "murderer." Like Micaiah with Ahab, what he has to say is very specific and very focused, but interestingly he does not predict the end of the siege, nor does he predict the end of Syria. He simply predicts the end of inflation, and this sets up the heart of the episode:

> Lepers suffer at city gate
> > "What have we got to lose?" questions
> > > Testing and discovering the truth
> > > > "This is a day of good news!"
> > > Testing and discovering the truth
> > "What have we got to lose?" questions
> Officer trampled at city gate[20]

When we focus our attention on the parallels in this chiasm, what we see first is that these four lepers, like their cannibal-sisters, feel like they have nothing left to lose. Stuck at the bottom of the food chain, these men are despised by their own people and hated by their enemies. If they go into the city they'll die because nobody has any food for them. If they stay at the gate they'll die because the siege prohibits anyone from exiting or entering. Their only remaining option is to go to the Syrians. From a chiastic perspective their suffering parallels the "suffering" of the unbelieving officer—both scenes occur at the city gate. Though they suffer in hope, the officer suffers in cynicism. Though they come up with a plan for survival, the officer bathes himself in waves of self-pity.

Second, the utilitarian questions of the lepers find a parallel in the utilitarian questions of the king. Where the lepers learn to ask good questions, however, the king does not. In fact, his questions lead him into ever-deeper canyons of cynicism. He trusts no one—not his officers, not his messengers, and certainly not a bunch of lepers raving on about good news. By so obviously paralleling the utilitarian questions of the king with the questions of the lepers this narrator wants to emphasize not only that it's important to ask questions, but that it's important to ask the right kinds of questions.

Third, the turning point comes not when the lepers discover the Syrians' treasure, nor even when the siege lifts. The turning point comes when the lepers realize the depth of their sin. To hoard food while others starve is wrong. Good news must be shared. The disease of leprosy may be debilitating, but it doesn't have to become dehumanizing. Suffering does not inevitably lead to criminality. Certainly these lepers have good reasons for hoarding their new-found treasure, but whatever the reasons, it's impossible to justify them in a context of famine. Thus they do what the Prodigal Son does—they come to themselves. They stop burying loot and start sharing Good News. Yahweh will not bless mothers who eat their own children, nor does he bless officers who slander the prophets. But he does bless sufferers who dare to look up from their suffering and share the Good News with others, even those who've mistreated them.

Intratextual Reflection

Intratextually this story parallels two other famine narratives: "Death in the Pot" (2 Kings 4:38-44) and "Elijah and the Widow" (1 Kings 17:1-24). When Elijah challenges the Zarephath widow, her response is very much like that of the cannibal-mothers. She blames Elijah for bringing sin and death into her life. The cannibal-mothers take this a step further: they bring death to their own children. Both responses are fatalistic—the difference is simply one of degree. Fatalism also colors the characters of Obadiah (1 Kings 18:1-16) and this cynical officer. Obadiah doesn't trust Elijah because the prophet, he fears, might abandon him to Ahab. The cynical officer here trusts no one, though we're never really told why. The point is that these are not just literary foils, but *types* of sufferers.

Philip Yancey understands why this happens. In fact, it's one of the dominant themes of his writing. Yancey understands how someone under pressure might be tempted to say, "I wish we could just scrap the whole metaphor of God as a judge. I don't think it's a very helpful image these days. To me, the most helpful image is God as a physician, a wise physician, who gives us advice in the Bible, which we may not like, but it's for our own good."[21] Yancey illustrates this with a visit to the doctor:

"I had surgery on my foot a year ago, and I couldn't put any weight on it at all for a week. Then I had crutches for two weeks and a plastic boot for six weeks.... So I went to the doctor and said, 'I really like to play golf. I've been very good, I haven't put any weight on my foot. And I've actually been practicing a golf swing where I don't use my left foot at all. I keep all my weight on my right foot.'"

The doctor listens patiently to this, then says, "'You would make me very unhappy if you played golf this weekend.' I said, 'Well, you must not be a golfer.' He said, 'Oh, I am a golfer. I play every Wednesday. That's why I would be unhappy.'" Reflecting on his response, Yancey asks himself,

> "Why should I care whether he's unhappy or not?" The (answer) is, the only reason my doctor would be unhappy is because he has my best interests at heart. He knows that if I started too soon, then I would risk my health in the long term. Instead of wagging his finger at me and saying, "Now you listen to me, young man! Don't you get out there and play golf!'—which would make me want to go and do just that, just to disobey him—he expressed his concern in a very compassionate way. The more I read the Bible, the more I think that's a helpful model to illustrate that God's way is actually the best way. It's good news, truly good news.[22]

Theological Reflection

Suffering people have a tendency to give up—on others, on God, on themselves, on everything. Pain does this to people. Often when we suffer, we lapse into denial, and when this occurs it can be very difficult to keep faith alive and healthy. Once an older believer came into my office and said, "I don't know what to do," then downloaded on me as much anger and bitterness as I've ever heard at one sitting. Bile poured out of his heart like an ugly green ooze. He pulled out stuff he'd hidden away for years—every little hurt, every little disappointment. Had I not put up a boundary, he would still be venting on me. I don't remember everything he said, but I do remember his stubborn refusal to deal with it through the eyes of faith. To every attempt I made to point him upward, he steadfastly refused to lift his head.

After listening to this for some time, I finally asked, "Don't you *want* to believe?" The question caught him off-guard. He never answered it, not directly, yet I still believe it was appropriate to ask this question. I have met several people like this man in the course of my ministry—

"cynical officers" who prefer to ridicule the faith of others rather than grow their own. Religiously they go to church and "do their duty." But spiritually they're dead branches hanging precipitously from a Living Vine because they prefer anger over hope, ignorance over learning, cynicism over faith.

Another challenge is the problem of pragmatism. Instead of appealing to the Kingdom Dream, evangelists sometimes appeal to our more utilitarian values. Sometimes the "what have you got to lose?" questions take precedence over the Kingdom Dream itself. We are encouraged to attend this or that church because "there's a good youth group there, and you don't want your teenagers doing drugs, do you?" We are invited to attend this or that assembly because "the music is so … 'uplifting' (read: 'entertaining')." We are invited to this or that social function because "you don't want to be lonely, right?"[23]

These are "leper-questions," all boiling down to one basic question: "What's in it for me?" The text is clear. These lepers do not preach Good News because of their great faith. They share the Good News because they're afraid of what might happen to them if they don't: "if we wait until daylight, punishment will overtake us." The question is, Is this *faith*? Is this sort of "faith" going to empower us to "go into all the world" and "preach the Gospel to every creature?"

We need to decide whether we want to plug in and serve or clock out and hoard.

Notes

1. Several allusions occur, for example, between the description of famine's devastation here and in the Canaanite myths. Both Ahab and the Canaanite hero Daniel, for example, send out search parties to find green grass (*UNP* 70).

2. I deal with this more thoroughly in my "Jeremiah's Progressive Paradox," *RB* 93 (1986) 386-414.

3. The Mosaic prohibitions are designed to ward off just such a circumstance as we see here: a desperate widow in debt through no fault of her own. Jeremiah sees Jerusalem's willingness to tolerate such injustice as another example of "profaning the Name" (Jer 34:16).

4. R. Doebler, "Ambassador for an Inscrutable God," *Leadership* 12 (1991) 26-30.

5. J. D. Douglas reminds us ("The Bible on Hunger—A Source of Discomfort?" *CT* 20 [1976] 1064-66) that there are nearly two thousand references in the Bible to the phenomenon of hunger, many of them here in the Elijah-Elisha traditions.

6. See my *Balaam Traditions* (Atlanta: Scholars, 1990) 23-32, 36-8.

7. John Maxwell, *Failing Forward* (Nashville: Thomas Nelson, 2000).

8. A. Mayer ("Elijah and Elisha in John's Signs Source," *Expository Times* 99 [1988] 171-73) argues that the Elisha cycle is a better source for the "feeding of the five thousand" than the story of the manna (Exod 16:31).

9. Athanagoras, *Treatise*, § 6.

10. Tertullian, *On Modesty*, § 9.

11. M. Dawn, *Reaching Out Without Dumbing Down: A Theology of Worship for the Turn-of-the-Century Culture* (Grand Rapids: Eerdmans, 1995).

12. R. K. McIver, "The Parable of the Weeds among the Wheat (Matt 13:24-30, 36-43) and the Relationship between the Kingdom and the Church as Portrayed in the Gospel of Matthew," *JBL* 114 (1995) 643-59.

13. Homer, *The Iliad*.

14. G. McMahon, "Anatolia," *ABD* 1.235.

15. M. Dandamaev, *Slavery in Babylonia from Nabopolassar to Alexander the Great* (DeKalb, IL: Northern Illinois University Press, 1984) 175.

16. E. F. Weidner, "Keilschrifttexte nach Kopien T. G. Pinches," *Archiv für Orientforschung* 16 (1952/53) 37.

17. *SSI* 2.8-12.

18. W. Pitard, *Ancient Damascus* (Winona Lake, IN: Eisenbrauns, 1987) 174.

19. Rick Moore (*God Saves: Lessons From the Elisha Stories* [Sheffield: JSOT Press, 1990]) thinks that Aramean militarism is the primary historical factor behind the Elisha cycle.

20. Scholars call this kind of paralleling structure a chiasm.

21. P. Yancey, "Putting Faith in Doubt," *U.S. Catholic* 66, 2 (Feb 2001) 19.

22. Ibid., 20.

23. Robert Webber, *Signs of Wonder: The Phenomenon of Convergence in Modern Liturgical and Charismatic Churches* (Nashville: Abbott Martyn, 1992) 32-33.

FIVE

THE PRESSURE OF FRAILTY

DEALING WITH IMPOTENCE (1 Kings 1:1-4)

As Kings picks up the story-line from Samuel, David's monarchy meanders before us as a kingdom in decline, a government reflecting the deteriorating health of an aging leader. King David is nearing the end of a long, fascinating life. Having entered Israel's history as the courageous shepherd-boy who stands up to Goliath, he begins his rise to power as the mighty warrior who successfully fends off the Philistines. He masters the ins-and-outs of Israelite politics as the up-and-coming army lieutenant who displaces his father-in-law from the throne. Eventually he becomes the shrewd empire-builder responsible for uniting Israel's tribal confederacy.

Then, of course, there's his non-public side. One of the strongest proofs for the reliability of Scripture is the fact that it preserves stories so scandalous, even later biblical historians avoid them: the story of David the roving philanderer who steals a loyal lieutenant's wife; the story of David the cold-blooded politician who commits murder to cover it up; the story of David the absentee father who only perfunctorily responds to the rape of his daughter (Tamar) and the murder of his firstborn (Amnon). The book of Chronicles preserves none of these stories.

Now we see the old warrior at the end of his life, and with old age comes a new irony. David the former philanderer now only celibately sleeps with a young woman.[1] David the former activist now passively sits idle while others initiate the action all around him. David the former poster-boy for virility becomes a decrepit old man whose body can barely maintain a healthy pulse.

Like the book of Esther, Kings starts off with a "beauty contest." Both books begin with royal servants frantically searching for the "perfect virgin" to satisfy the needs of the king. This is classical Oriental literature. In literature like this, the king's needs are paramount. It's not enough, for example, for a scribe to report, "the king was successful on his hunting trip." No, one should rather say, "he killed seven lions by shooting in the completion of a moment. He carried off a herd of twelve wild cattle within an hour" (*ANET* 243).

Women must be treated with special discretion in this literature. Whereas Esther, for example, eventually becomes the woman to assuage Ahasuerus' embarrassment (Esth 2:9), Abishag becomes the woman to alleviate David's, and how she does so is not a little mysterious. We cannot say for sure what she actually does for David because the narrator uses a rather rare Hebrew word to describe it. Abishag is a *sokenet*, a "helper" of some kind. Isaiah uses the masculine form (*soken*) to describe Shebna, the "manager" of the king's palace (Isa 22:15, 19), and perhaps the narrator uses it here to connote, however discreetly, something of Abishag's power. This is confirmed by Adonijah's attempt to take her away from Solomon later.[2]

Yet the rabbis have difficulty accepting David as an impotent old man. Defending his virility, some rabbis argue that David refrains from sex with Abishag not because he has to, but because he chooses to. To "prove" their point, they cite a crude legend in which Abishag taunts him with the proverb, "When courage fails the thief, he becomes virtuous," and David responds by performing his conjugal duties thirteen times with Bathsheba (*b. Sanh* 22a). In other words, David, like Moses, must maintain his physical power until the very end, because the thought of an old, impotent David is just too much to bear.[3]

Such rose-colored revisionism, however, leads us to overlook the intratextual possibility that David's impotence is a foreshadowing of things to come. Not only can Israel's greatest king not initiate a sexual encounter with a beautiful young woman; he can't even control the actions of his sons or his wife or his court. Kings begins with a political vacuum because this book is very much a study in political vacuums. Political vacuums cannot remain unfilled. Something always has to fill them, whether that something is messy and violent or righteous and stabilizing. The following story of

"Adonijah's Ambition" addresses this theme directly, but the whole book is practically obsessed with it. Sometimes political vacuums are internally filled up (Athaliah's reign of terror, 2 Kings 11:1-21); sometimes they're externally filled up (Tiglath-Pileser's invasion, 15:17-31). Sometimes they attract abysmally poor leadership (Rehoboam, 1 Kings 12:1-24); sometimes they attract relatively righteous leadership (Josiah, 2 Kings 22:1-23:25).

Intratextual Reflection

Intratextually this story parallels several others about sickness and frailty, each roughly equidistant from its counterpart. One of these occurs near the beginning (David, 1:1-4), two near the middle (Ahaziah, 2 Kings 1:1-18; Naaman, 5:1-27), and two near the end of Kings (Elisha, 13:1-24; Hezekiah, 20:1-11). What binds them together is the way in which they portray individual leaders struggling with various physical limitations. Kings is filled with fascinating stories about ordinary people facing extraordinary situations, but the stories on this trajectory focus on leaders under pressure.

David, for example, has to deal with the problems associated with aging, a problem faced by all mortals, yet one which puts kings under a special kind of stress. It's one thing for someone's grandfather to die; it's quite another when one's grandfather is the king. Naaman is a military leader who has to deal with leprosy, a disease characterized by social isolation as well as physical pain. He responds to it by searching the countryside for help, and finding it in the strangest of places—the memory of a Hebrew slave. Ahaziah responds to his frailty by taking the idolatry route, sending messengers to inquire of Baal-Ekron (instead of Yahweh). Hezekiah responds by doing something kings only rarely do: he prays to Yahweh.

In other words, comparing David's response to the other responses on this trajectory is a very revealing exercise. Do these leaders respond differently because of the peculiarities of their personalities, or does the narrator want to say something about the consequences of physical frailty, something for which these leaders are woefully unprepared?

Theological Reflection

Bill Cosby finds a good deal of humor in growing old. "It is not a pretty sight to see a man jumping a tennis net and going down like something snagged by a lobster fisherman." "As the (expert) of sock-putting on, let me tell you how I do it. I raise my leg as high as I can; and then, for the second or two that my foot is quivering at its peak, I quickly bring down the sock over my toes. When my foot hits the floor, I finish pulling up the sock."[4]

Cosby hits a nerve with this book because his audience is aging at a rapid rate. Never before have so many Americans been so old. The numbers are revealing. In 1900, only 4% of the population was over 65. Today this figure is closer to 15%, and projections for the year 2030 go as high as 22%.[5] The usual explanations for this are better awareness of personal health needs, better health care technology, and the demographic reality that millions of baby boomers are "coming of age." Yet quantity of life does not mean quality of life. More elderly people are suffering today from more painful diseases than ever before. Like David, many are dealing with these problems the best way they can. Yet chronic depression is common among the elderly, and "parent abuse" is an ugly new phrase in the social worker's lexicon. Assisted suicide is now recognized by some states as an appropriate "solution" to the problem of aging. How can the story of David's impotence address these new realities?

First, this transparently human story can remind us that aging and death are inevitable. Even virile leaders like David eventually become impotent old men. Death-denying cultures are adolescent and dysfunctional because they refuse to deal with this truth. In North America, for example, whole subcultures are loathe even to talk about death, much less plan for it. This attitude stands in stark contrast to the opening story of Kings. In the Talmud, the words "old man" and "invalid" can be synonymous (see *b. Pes.* 101b), and though it's sometimes comical to poke fun at the forgetful, Rab Judah admonishes us to "be careful (to respect) an old man who has forgotten his knowledge through no fault of his own" (*b. Ber.* 8b).

Second, this story reminds us that even our most respected leaders— even our "King Davids"—will one day have to be replaced, and this means that leadership transitions can be notoriously difficult.[6] Sometimes they're duplicitous and ragged; seldom are they quick and painless. Sometimes they're well-planned and smooth; sometimes they're unplanned and violent. The book of Kings illustrates all of these and more, but the fact that the very first transition is so violent is significant. It sets the tone for the whole book.

Alfredo Nanez documents and discusses this problem in a major mainline denomination which, like most others, struggles mightily with the problem of leadership transition.[7] On a congregational level, everyone knows how difficult it can be for a congregation to do something as "simple" as change pastors. The problem is so difficult, in fact, an entire literature has sprung up to deal with it, focusing on issues like "how to shepherd congregations through transition," and "how to help new pastors adjust."[8] Michael Blaine, for example, advises new pastors in their first year to make sure that they attend to the following concerns: (1) affirm people's feelings about the previous pastor; (2) recognize and facilitate the grief process; (3) accentuate the continuities between past and present; (4) seek to understand the reasons for the predecessor's success; and (5) accept oneself and one's own style of leadership.[9]

Third, in its intratextual context this story shows us that there's more than one way to respond to frailty in our leaders. Compared to Naaman and Hezekiah, David's response looks passive-aggressive, but the fact that it is does not imply that this need be normative. The *pressure of frailty* trajectory shows that this is not how all leaders respond when confronted by their limitations. Guided by the intratextual context, we can do a great deal to help people who struggle with this issue.

INJURY TO INSULT (1 Kings 22:51-2 Kings 1:18)

Just as the catch-phrase "sullen and angry" (*sar weza`ep*) links Ahab's misfortunes at Aphek to his problems at Jezreel (1 Kings 20:43; 21:4), so also the catchword "wound" (*halâ*) links Ahab's misfortunes to those of his son Ahaziah (1 Kings 22:34; 2 Kings 1:2). Both father and son are profoundly wounded leaders.[10] Ahaziah's has to do with the fact that he does evil in the eyes of Yahweh, walking in the ways of his father and mother and in the ways of Jeroboam son of Nebat, who caused Israel to sin. Yet lest there be any question about his religious beliefs, "he served and worshiped Baal and provoked Yahweh, the God of Israel, to anger, just as his father had done" (1 Kings 22:52-53). Unfortunately, Kings does not give us much information about Ahaziah, nor do we know why he fails so miserably to connect with his heritage. All we have are a few details about the major characters in his life—Ahab, Jezebel, Jehoshaphat, and Elijah—and a study of these relationships can help us reconstruct at least something about his character.

Ahaziah asks Jehoshaphat to partner with him in the shipping business (1 Kings 22:49) because he wants to exchange some of Israel's seafaring technology for a percentage of the gold trade. After all, if there can be a "treaty" (*berît*) between Israel and Phoenicia (1 Kings 5:12), why not an "alliance" (*habar*) between Israel and Judah?[11] Jehoshaphat, however, has good reasons to balk at this proposal. Still smarting from the

Ramoth-Gilead defeat, he doubtless suspects that doing business with the Omrides is too risky. Further, with Ahab's death, Jezebel becomes Israel's widowed queen mother, and thus the major influence in Ahaziah's life. Jezebel is a powerful queen-mother, and to survive the world of paternalistic politics she has to develop the ability to manipulate situations to her own advantage. Savvy and smart, she has to learn how to "spin" things the "right" way—like the Naboth incident (1 Kings 21:8-10).[12]

Therefore these three factors—Jehoshaphat's snub, Ahab's death, and Jezebel's influence—combine to help explain Ahaziah's decision. Yet several questions remain. Does Ahaziah not know who Yahweh is at all? Is he not aware of the very recent, very public showdowns at Mt. Carmel and the Samarian threshing floor? Is his rejection of Yahweh for Baal-Zebub simply another illustration of Israel's addiction to Baalism? The deity to which Ahaziah turns, Baal-Zebub, has a name which means "lord of the flies." This name may be a distortion of an original divine title, Baal-Zebul ("Prince Baal"), a title well-known from the Canaanite myths.[13] Evidence from the Bible (1 Kings 8:13; Isa 63:15; Hab 3:11; Psa 49:15), the Dead Sea Scrolls (1QM 12:1–2; 1QS 10:3; 1QH 11:34), and the rabbis (b. Rosh ha-Sh. 17a; t. Sanh. 13.5), moreover, suggests that zebûl may refer to a place as well as a person (especially the "exalted place"— "heaven").[14] Thus it's difficult to know which theory is the more plausible. Either (a) Baal-Zebub is a corruption of an original "Baal-Zebul," or (b) this title refers to a precursor of a sky-deity very popular in the Hellenistic period—Baalshamayin.[15] What interests us, however, is the way this divine name structures the whole episode, repeated no less than four times (vv. 2, 3, 6, & 16).

The first occurrence comes in Ahaziah's initial command: "Go and consult Baal-Zebub, the god of Ekron, to see if I will recover from this injury. Like all polytheists, Ahaziah wants to cover his spiritual bases—that's why he goes outside his inherited religious tradition to consult another.[16] This is not an uncommon decision. Just as Balak the Moabite sends messengers to fetch Balaam (Num 22:5), so Ahaziah sends messengers to Ekron, a Philistine city some 60 km southwest of Samaria. Just as Balak elicits a foreigner's knowledge about "the gods," so Ahaziah consults foreign magico-religious specialists about his illness, and Naaman seeks help in Israel after exhausting his resources in Syria. According to one tablet, the Hittite king Tudhaliya III employs magico-religious specialists from as far away as Egypt. None of this behavior is unusual.[17]

Yahweh, however, doesn't like "sitting the bench" while Ahaziah plays ball with the "lord of the flies." The Ten Commandments' first prohibition is against having "other gods before me," but unlike Micaiah's intervention with his father Ahab, Yahweh sends no prophet to Ahaziah, nor does he send an ecstatic vision (Solomon), nor does he try to "coax" him back into the Yahwistic fold.[18] He simply condemns him to death: "You will not leave the bed you are lying on. You will certainly die!" The judgment is more severe because the apostasy is more severe.

One can only imagine the look on the messengers' faces when they hear this oracle from Elijah. Concerned and alarmed, they nevertheless obey the prophet and take his words back to the king: "This is what Yahweh says: Is it because there is no God in Israel that you are sending men to consult Baal-Zebub, the god of Ekron? You will not leave the bed you are lying on. You will certainly die!" But Ahaziah, at first, does not seem to know how to receive this message. He questions them sharply— "Who is this man?" They answer dutifully: "We don't know…but he was 'covered with hair' (lit., "he was a *ba`al* of hair"). Not only does he learn, then, that the source of his challenge is his father's old nemesis, but he learns of it via a not-so-subtle pun on the very word "B/baal."

Instead of inviting Elijah to Samaria, however—as his father did with Micaiah—he orders him picked up like a common criminal. Where Ahab graciously invites Micaiah to Samaria—even sending him an escort— Ahaziah sends out a posse: "Man of God, the king says, 'Come down!'" This strategy repeats itself several times before somebody finally realizes it's not going to work. Even as Balaam's donkey takes several beatings from her master (Num 22:21-33), so Ahaziah's commanders take several beatings from Elijah.

Finally, assured by a "Fear not" oracle,[19] Elijah summons up his courage and goes before Ahaziah, where he delivers the same oracle we've already heard three times: "This is what Yahweh says: 'Is it because there is no God in Israel for you to consult that you have sent messengers to consult Baal-Zebub, the god of Ekron?' Because you have done this, you will never leave the bed you are lying on. You will certainly die!"

Intratextual Reflection

Both 1 and 2 Kings begin with "fragile leader" stories because the issues in these texts so immediately introduce us to the limitations of human leadership, particularly when it's placed under pressure. When it comes to physical illness, ancient Near Eastern peoples do not view sickness the way modern Westerners do.[20] For Ahaziah, sickness is not a matter of germs and microbes, nor is it even about faithfulness to the Law (Deut 27:27-28). Sickness is the work of unseen beings, and the only acceptable response to their attacks is priestly liturgy, not modern medicine. The character of this liturgy depends on (a) the type and intensity of the illness, (b) the theology of the priest performing the incantation, and (c) the expectations of the client paying for it.[21]

When David gets old, no one thinks of sending for an exorcist or consulting one of the Baals (Baal-Zebub or otherwise). His attendants simply find him a young virgin to help keep him warm. They find a "helper" (*sokenet*), not a "diviner" (*qosem*). When Hezekiah gets sick, Isaiah tells him, "Put your house in order" (lit., "command your house," *tsab lebêtekâ*), because you are going to die; you will not recover" (2 Kings 20:1). Naaman the Syrian expects Elisha to heal him miraculously ("wave his hand over the spot and cure me," 5:12), but eventually he obeys the prophetic Word and experiences the healing he seeks.

Ahaziah's behavior stands out sharply against this intratextual context. Like other sufferers, Ahaziah realizes he cannot survive without divine help. What he doesn't seem to realize is that Yahweh is that divine help. He ignores the fact that Yahweh has proven his power over Baal several times. He ignores the fact that Mosaic covenant theology is worlds apart from Phoenician animism. He rejects Yahweh as his Healer and Savior, and turns instead to Baal's professional specialists.[22]

Theological Reflection

Dialysis wards are unpleasant places. The process is so dehumanizing, very few can survive it unscarred. I am familiar with this world because of Kenny,[23] a twenty-eight-year-old man dying of cardiomyopathy. Kenny's question is the perennial one: "How can a good God allow innocent suffering?" Unable to answer this question, Kenny often uses his visitors as theological sounding boards. Sometimes the anger inside him drives him to ridicule the life of faith altogether. "Sure, it's easy for you to say that God cares, that God wants the best for us. But I dare you to say this after you've been strapped to a machine! I dare you to trust in God after your feet turn brown and the surgeons start cutting off your toes. Then we'll see what you believe!" Kenny was raised in a Christian home, but like many believers, he never learned to think seriously about the problem of suffering.

Now Kenny talks to anyone who will listen, anyone representing any "god" or "spirit" or "higher power." I remember arriving at his room one evening as a self-proclaimed "healer" was winding up his pitch, promising to heal Kenny for a thousand dollars ("...now most of that is for expenses"). Another time, a lady with blue hair promised him a cure for only four hundred dollars ("...now you can wire that directly to my daughter in San Diego"). Chatting about them afterwards, Kenny always noted the strange correlation between "price" and "jargon" in his erstwhile healers—the weirder the jargon, the higher the price. Three of his questions interface directly with the story of Ahaziah.

First, "Where do I go when I'm wounded"? Often I have wondered what to say to sufferers in response to this question. Often I've wondered how to minister to people who struggle with illness or depression or grief or impending death. And often I've seen them choose "Baal-Zebub" instead of Christ. When people are suffering, it's sometimes hard to realize that Christ's suffering has healing power: "Communion with the Lord is no mere talk with some of us. We have known it in the chamber of affliction; we have known it in the solitude of many a night of broken rest; we have known it beneath discouragements and under sorrows and defamations, and all sorts of ills."[24]

It's hard to draw neat and tidy boundaries between doubt and apostasy when we're wounded. In fact, as Thomas Aquinas puts it,

> apostasy…happens in various ways according to the different kinds of union between man and God. For, in the first place, man is united to God by faith; secondly, by having his will duly submissive in obeying His commandments.…Though a man may apostatize in both the above ways, he may still remain united to God by faith.…But if he give up the faith, then he seems to turn away from God altogether: and consequently, apostasy simply and absolutely is that whereby a man withdraws from the faith.[25]

In other words, Ahaziah's decision to choose Baal-Zebub over Yahweh has several factors behind it, and we have tried to imagine what they might be (his bad relationship with Jehoshaphat, his codependent relationship with Jezebel). But the bottom line is that his decision leads him into a twilight zone in which the Spirit and human experience bear witness to the same truth: wounded people often make desperate religious decisions when pain relief becomes God.

Second, "When will my suffering be over?" This question often throws us back, kicking and screaming, into the blurry twilight zone between doubt and faith. No one likes doing time in what C. S. Lewis calls "the shadowlands," yet the call to ministry is often a call to this very place. Human pain cannot simply be wished away, and Yahweh's character does not change with the ups and downs of physical or emotional health. Like Hezekiah or Naaman, Ahaziah too has the option to turn to Yahweh for help. But he does not, and it's important that we recognize this decision for what it is.

Third, "How can I lead sufferers to the Healer?" This, of course, is the most pressing pastoral question. John Wesley, for example, records a particularly frustrating "Ahaziah" in his journal: "I had much satisfaction in conversing with one who was very ill and very serious. But in a few days she recovered from her sickness...and from her seriousness."[26] Whether Elijah's exact strategy can be (or should be) reproduced today is not nearly so relevant a question as whether we need to plan out some sort of pastoral strategy in response to the problem of suffering. When we fail at this—and fail we will—it's important to remember that every sufferer has a choice. Sometimes people choose Baal as the way out of their pain. Sometimes they choose Christ. Ultimately every sufferer has to make this decision.

LET'S TAKE A DIP (2 Kings 5:1-27)

This story is an intratextual echo of the Ahaziah story. Where Ahaziah is an Israelite seeking healing from a foreign god, Baal-Zebub, Naaman is a Syrian raised in the Baalist tradition[27] seeking healing from Yahweh. See the irony? The prophets love this kind of irony. In the *pressure of frailty* trajectory it's Naaman, not Ahaziah, who makes the "good confession": "I know that there is no God in all the world except in Israel." Thus Jesus cites Naaman as an example of saving faith (Luke 4:27), not Ahaziah, and similar interpretations animate the reflections of Chrysostom, Luther, Calvin, and Moody.[28]

Here also the theme of purification continues from passages immediately prior to this one (2 Kings 2:19; 4:40), only now it's reworked into a much more sophisticated narrative. Even as Yahweh purifies water of "evil" (*ra*) and food of "death" (*mâwet*), so he purifies the skin of a foreign leper (lit., "your flesh will return to you, and clean," v. 10). The structure of this text is another chiasm in which we see a fascinating series of actions and reactions. The slave-girl pities the leprous general. The Aramean king empowers his general to search for this cure. The Israelite king reacts negatively to this search. The Yahweh prophet reacts negatively to the Israelite king's negativity. The general at first reacts negatively, then obeys the prophetic Word. Elisha refuses Naaman's thanksgiving gift as he commends Naaman for his decision to renounce idolatry. Gehazi reacts negatively to Elisha and runs after Naaman, and Elisha throws Naaman's leprosy onto him. Diagrammed sequentially, the story looks like this:

Naaman's reaction to the Israelite slave-girl's suggestion
  The Aramean king's reaction to Naaman's request
    The Israelite king's reaction to the Aramean king's letter
      Naaman's bi-leveled reaction to Elisha's command
    Elisha's reaction to Naaman's gift
  Gehazi's reaction to Elisha's reaction
Elisha's reaction to Gehazi's deceptive behavior

These parallels narrow down more and more until we're finally faced with the story's main theme. Naaman's reaction to the slave-girl parallels Elisha's reaction to Gehazi. The Aramean king's reaction to Naaman parallels Gehazi's reaction to Elisha. The Israelite king's reaction to the Aramean king's letter parallels Elisha's reaction to Naaman's gift. The parallels bracket and highlight the episode's central message: *even a foreign leper can obey the prophetic Word.*[29]

In the first parallel, the narrator introduces us to Naaman—not the mighty Syrian warrior (*gibbôr hayil*), but the suffering human being. Unfortunately we cannot say much about the etiology of his disease (*tsârâ'*): mycobacterial leprosy probably does not arrive in Syria-Palestine until the invasion of Alexander,[30] so what he suffers may be a continuously painful case of shingles.[31] Whatever it is, no one in Syria can cure it, and no one can take away the physical pain and the social shame. Like the devout centurion Cornelius (Acts 10), this foreigner is desperate to hear a word of hope.

By structuring the plot chiastically, the narrator contrasts the slave-girl's compassion with Elisha's indignant reaction to the behavior of Gehazi. We do not know the origin of Naaman's leprosy, but we certainly know the origin of Gehazi's. Gehazi contracts leprosy for the same reason Miriam does—willful rebellion (Num 12).[32] Gehazi's problem is not just greed. His sin is like Achan's, another Israelite who tests Yahweh's patience (Josh 7). Compared to Achan (and the southern prophet from Judah, 1 Kings 13), Gehazi's punishment seems tame—he only contracts leprosy, not death. But by chiastically paralleling Gehazi's greed with Naaman's faith, the narrator sets up a well-known polarity. The Bible often contrasts unfaithful Israelites with faithful foreigners, and Jesus tells us why: to challenge the complacency of the chosen people (Luke 4:24).[33]

The second contrast is between the Aramean king's desire to empower Naaman and Gehazi's desire to exploit him. When Naaman goes to the king and expresses new hope, the king responds enthusiastically. "By all means, go" is the NIV's translation of two imperative verbs: *lêk bô'* ("Go!

Go!"). So Naaman does go, and with him goes a glowing letter of recommendation. Now, sending recommendation letters to counterparts is not particularly noteworthy, but what is extraordinary here is that a Hebrew narrator is so obviously praising an Aramean king at the expense of an Israelite king. This should not be overemphasized, in light of the murky historical context, but neither should it be underemphasized. Gehazi's sin stands out boldly and obviously against Gentile righteousness, and Jesus seizes on this contrast in his Nazareth sermon (Luke 4:24-27). In the chiastic structure the Aramean king is a positive foil to Gehazi's negativism. Where the Aramean says, "Go! Go!," Gehazi says, "Wait! Wait!" Where the Aramean releases funds for his friend, Gehazi covets these funds for himself. Where the Aramean sends a letter of recommendation, Gehazi concocts a lame story about poor prophets needing new clothes. Where the Aramean asks that his friend's leprosy be "removed" (*'âsap*), Gehazi himself "removes" Naaman's treasure to a secret place.

In the chiasm's third level of comparison, the narrator pushes the contrast a step further, comparing the reaction of the Israelite king to Naaman with the reaction of Elisha to Naaman. At first glance, there seems no earthly reason for the king to react as intensely as he does to Naaman's request. Certainly war makes enemies suspicious, and the history between these two enemies is less than friendly. But why does this Israelite king complain to this non-Israelite foreigner about "not being God"? Why does he lament his inability "to kill and bring back to life"? The answer can only lie in the chiastic parallel. This is a very clever narrator. Instead of criticizing the Israelite king directly, he critiques him indirectly. He shows that in contrast to the "man-of-God," this king is in no way "God." In fact, he does not even understand "God"; thus having him spew out shallow "God-talk" like this is brilliant satire. It highlights even more Elisha's statement of faith: "Why have you torn your robes? Have the man come to me and he will know that there is a prophet in Israel."

With Elisha's reaction to Naaman the narrator returns to the same theme enunciated earlier (1 Kings 13). Occasionally it's appropriate for a prophet to accept "gifts"—Elisha accepts a guest-room from the Shunammite, for example—but as a general rule Yahweh's prophets must be very careful when it comes to money. Indeed, they must stand guard against a whole genre of financial traps and get-rich-quick schemes, all having the potential to cut them off from the Source of Life. Sometimes they must say "no" to innocent-looking dinner invitations, whether they come from kings (Jeroboam) or colleagues (the Ephraimite prophet; 1 Kings 13:34). Sometimes they must say no to more obvious attempts at bribery—it's only a short step from accepting unsolicited gifts to preaching only "peace" to those who pay the preacher's salary (Mic 3:5).

Doubtless Elisha is touched by Naaman's sincerity, but he also knows that Naaman needs to learn something about grace. Grace is not for sale—if it were, it would no longer be grace. In fact, it cannot even look like it's for sale. Thus Gehazi's decision to take Naaman's monetary gift undermines Elisha's attempt to teach this foreigner about Yahweh's unfathomable grace. The narrator intertwines Gehazi's story with Naaman's because he wants to show us what can happen when we forget this basic tenet of the Faith. Instead of following Naaman's example and renouncing idolatry, Gehazi presumes upon the grace of Yahweh. To offer Naaman "real miracles, sensibly priced" is a decision to deny him the grace of God altogether.[34]

Now we come to the crux of the matter, the center of the chiasm. By the time Naaman arrives at Elisha's house, this poor sufferer has traipsed through the courts of two kings and traveled hundreds of miles to find relief from his pain. That he would expect great things from "the great prophet" should not be surprising. Like Elijah on Horeb, he apparently expects some unmistakable divine signal: "I thought that he would surely come out to me and stand and call on the name of Yahweh his God, wave his hand over the spot and cure me of my leprosy. Are not Abana and Pharpar, the rivers of Damascus, better than any of the waters of Israel? Couldn't I wash in them and be cleansed?"

Like Yahweh with Elijah, however, Elisha throws Naaman a theological curve. Yahweh comes to Elijah in a still, small voice (1 Kings 19), and Elisha sends Naaman a simple, short command: "Go. Wash yourself seven times in the Jordan." Naaman can't believe what he hears. To his servants he asks, "You mean, this guy won't even come out of his house and receive me personally? Does he have any idea how far I've come? Does he have any idea how much I'm suffering?" Doubtless he stomps off in a rage because he's been conditioned to imagine "healing" as something always spectacular—in our jargon, as something more at home in a circus tent than a prayer closet. Perhaps he expects Elisha to launch into a series of anti-demonic incantations, like the preachers back home in Syria.[35] Perhaps he expects him to build wooden altars and sacrifice live animals on them—the more, the better (like Balaam, Num 22-24).

It is at this crucial point that another minor character intercedes on behalf of a major character, reasoning with Naaman via the "what-do-you-have-to-lose?" argument.

"What do you have to lose?"

"Can't hurt to try."

"Hope this works."

"How many times did he say to dip in the water...?"

Intratextual Reflection

In the NT, Jesus intratextually connects the character of Naaman with the Zarephath widow (Luke 4:25-27—showing that Jesus is quite aware of this interpretive technique), but we might extend his comparison to include the Queen of Sheba as well, because (a) both are "devout foreigners," (b) both are seeking help, (c) both are willing to change, and (d) both respond positively to Israel's God. The Sabean comes to Jerusalem hungry for truth (*'emet*); the Syrian comes to Samaria hungry for healing. The Sabean has the "wind/spirit (*rûah*) knocked out of her"; the Syrian has "his flesh return" (*yâshab besârô*). The Sabean says "Blessed be Yahweh" (*yhwh 'elôhekâ bârûk*); the Syrian says, "Now I know that there is no God in all the earth except in Israel."

The primary difference lies in the nature of each confession. The Sabean does not come for physical healing, but she does pay "tuition" (gifts), and Solomon reciprocates by giving her all that she desires (1 Kings 10:13). Nowhere does she renounce her gods or question the tenets of her religion. Naaman, however, does this very thing, promising no longer to offer burnt offering or sacrifice to any god except Yahweh. In fact, he goes so far as to renounce the cult of Rimmon (Hadad/Baal), and the fact that he asks for forgiveness in the meantime beautifully echoes Solomon's Temple prayer:

> Likewise when a foreigner, who is not of your people Israel, comes from a distant land because of your name —for they shall hear of your great name, your mighty hand, and your outstretched arm—when a foreigner comes and prays toward this house, then hear in heaven your dwelling place, and do according to all that the foreigner calls to you, so that all the peoples of the earth may know your name. (1 Kings 8:41-43)[36]

Theological Reflection

In the early Church, Naaman's cleansing becomes a baptismal symbol and 2 Kings 5 a favorite baptismal text. Ephraim the Syrian, for example, parallels Naaman's cleansing from leprosy to the "cleansing (of) the secret misdeeds of the soul."[37] Yet a chiastic intratextual reading shows that there's much more going on here theologically, and it's amazing that each of these contrasts touches on a nerve of contemporary concern.

Faith vs. Cynicism. Croatian theologian Miroslav Volf has experienced firsthand the pain of violence. Growing up in a culture of hate, he now dedicates his life to challenging it. Why should we demonize others over differences in race or culture or economic status or religious belief? Why is revenge preferable to reconciliation? By asking such questions, Volf hopes to provoke a debate, but what he really wants is reconciliation—to bring victims and oppressors to repentance and healing.[38] Gehazi refuses this path. He thinks Elisha treats Naaman too easily, and this drives him to "correct" his teacher's "mistake." The heart of cynicism is self-centeredness.

Empowerment vs. Exploitation. That the Syrian king empowers Naaman does not mean that he surrenders all authority to him. Money can be a means of exclusion or inclusion, a means of exploitation or empowerment, and it's very easy to become like Gehazi when dealing with these narcotics. Empowerment is something over which believers profoundly disagree. One study, for example, concludes that the perceptions of congregants and pastors are vastly different: congregants tend to see much less evidence of empowerment in the Church than do their pastors.[39] This should not be surprising: thirty years ago Richard Salzmann prophesied that the Church would have to change its attitude toward lay empowerment, even abolish tired labels like "clergy" and "laity."[40] Why? Because for every "Aramean king," there's a "Gehazi," and it's almost impossible to overemphasize the rage average Christians feel over the growing problem of clerical exploitation.

Nor is this the only kind of exploitation about which we should be concerned. Lorin Baumhover and Colleen Beall document the systematic exploitation of the elderly.[41] Toby Marotta documents the shameful way children are treated in the sexploitation industry.[42] Caroline Moorehead documents the exploitation of children in the workforce.[43] John Freie criticizes self-help movements for offering what he calls "counterfeit community" in lieu of genuine *koinônia*.[44] John Gonsiorek documents the rising tide of sexual misconduct by health care professionals and clergy.[45] In short, "Gehazi" is still milking "Naaman" for all he's worth—and people are getting fed up with it.

Hypocrisy vs. Authenticity. In many ways this is the most subtle, yet the most important polarity in this text. Hendrik Hart, among others, tries to apply it to the study of theology itself, arguing that the Enlightenment liberalism which bases itself on rational consensus is no longer possible—not in a postmodern environment.[46] Rational thinking isn't even possible in some circles, because in its place now stands a diverse plurality of religious beliefs. According to Alasdair MacIntyre, this explains why contemporary

Western culture is becoming morally paralyzed, because "there is no rational way of securing moral agreement in our culture."[47] Hart's response to this problem is evangelically unacceptable, however, because he interprets this new situation as an excuse for despair. Hart advocates giving up trying to articulate religious ideas in terms of Christology or soteriology and focusing instead on (a) a person's ability to tolerate other commitments, and (b) a person's ability to engage others in solving problems.

But biblical stories like this one scream out the truth that suffering people hunger for genuineness, not tolerance. We're tired of the cafeteria-approach to religion. We're tired of the empty rhetoric, the shallow "God-talk." We're tired of scratching at the leprosy of polytheism, salving over the eczema of agnosticism. We want to be healed. More than anything else we want to be saved, really saved. We need more Elisha-prophets to say "no" to our idolatries. We need more leaders to empower us and mentor us and pastor us—and care about us. Truth is getting harder to find in our culture because (a) so few are willing to search for it, (b) so few are willing to sacrifice for it, and (c) so few are willing to define it in personal terms, as something knowable in a person. When Jesus says, "I am the truth," how many believers really understand what this means?[48]

Faith vs. Works. Naaman's dilemma is not just leprosy. Pride is his deeper problem—pride in his country, pride in his religious belief-system, pride in himself. He wants to be healed, but on his own terms. He wants Elisha to heal him, yes, but he expects Elisha's God to work in ways with which he's already familiar—the hoary categories of Syro-Palestinian magic, the rivers of his own country. It's not easy for people like Naaman to live by faith, much less faith in a "foreign" God.

The Green Mile illustrates this powerfully. In one of the book's most powerful scenes, inmate John Coffey succeeds in pulling "evil" (a brain tumor) out of his warden's sick wife.[49] Usually when he effects a healing, Coffey simply sucks the evil out of a suffering person, then expels it harmlessly into the air. With this healing, though, he can't expel the evil. Instead, it just rattles around inside him, unable to find its way out. Falling back into his cell, he comes into physical contact with the true perpetrator of the murders for which he's been convicted, and this allows the evil inside him to find a way out. It rushes into the soul of a sadistic guard, who then pulls his gun and executes the true murderer. Just as the evil inside Coffey invades the true murderer, so the leprosy on Naaman invades the skin of the self-centered Gehazi.

The point, of course, is that we are all just like Naaman, just like Gehazi. We imagine that our lot in life is to receive some great thing from God. As scholars, we dream of writing the most important books. As teachers, we dream of teaching only the brightest students. As preachers, we dream of preaching the most powerful sermons before the largest congregations. As worship leaders, we dream of blending that perfect mix of song and drama and preaching and prayer. As mystics, we dream of bliss-filled reunion with our Beloved One. As missionaries, we dream of whole nations laying down their idols and turning to Christ.

But how do we know these are God's dreams? Are we sure, absolutely sure, that this is what God wants? What if God's dreams are different? What if God's dreams go in a different direction? What if God simply wants us to "take a dip" and wait for further instructions?

STRIKE THE GROUND (2 Kings 13:1-24)

This story contains one last powerful vignette about Elisha—and it's a strange one. The idea that a prophet's bones might somehow make a corpse stand up on its feet is, well, a little weird, to say the least. Most contemporary scholars label this story a "legend."[50] One Hellenized reader imagines behind it a cosmic conflict in which Elisha's soul sends a long-distance call to his dead body,[51] and a few rabbis see here the fulfillment of Elisha's double-spirit request to Elijah earlier (2 Kings 2:9).[52] What's literarily and theologically fascinating, though, is the way in which the narrator weaves earlier Elisha motifs into (a) the paragraph as a whole, and (b) Kings' broader prophetic tradition. This text is something of an Elisha "memorial,"[53] and to maximize its impact, the narrator plops it down into one of Kings' dreariest contexts.

"Dreary" may be an understatement. After Jehu's death, Jehoahaz takes over his father's throne and proceeds to relax his father's militant Yahwism. In Samaria he permits the Asherah pole to stand again, along with the ubiquitous high places. He stands by passively as the Syrians slowly gobble up his standing army. The Syrian usurper Hazael continues to ravage and oppress,[54] but the only action he takes in response is to seek Yahweh. Yahweh dutifully sends a "savior" (*môshî`a*) to bail him out, but the mood is perfunctory and passionless. Israel's candle is nearing its very last flicker. Jehoash knows the right words to say—"My father! My father! The chariots and horsemen of Israel!"—but unlike Elisha, his voice lacks any measure of conviction or resolve.[55] Elisha ritualistically leads him through a victory over Aram, using a homeopathic bow-and-arrow procedure, but the king's response is tepid and lukewarm. Jehoash is a tired leader in a dying nation suffering the final stages of corporate arthritis.

No one seeks double portions anymore. No one wants to pick up the mantle and lead.

Jehoahaz seeks Yahweh, but the narrator does not describe this "seeking" via the common Heb verb *dârash* (e.g., 1 Kings 22:5). Instead he uses the much rarer term *hâlâ*, a word usually associated with "illness," as in the phrase, "Now Elisha was suffering from the illness (*hâlâ holyô*) from which he died." As Elisha weakens physically, so Jehoahaz weakens politically. In fact, Jehoahaz is like all the other weak kings in Israel—Jeroboam (1 Kings 13:6), Abijah (14:1), Ahab (22:34), Ahaziah (2 Kings 1:2), Joram (8:29). All the pressures of the monarchy find an easy target in the character of Jehoahaz.

Anger, second, is another reprised motif. Yahweh's "anger burns" (*yihar 'ap*) against Israel; Elisha's anger burns against Jehoash. Jehoash recites an ancient adage about the chariots of Israel and its horsemen, but this exclamation comes right after the decimation of his father's horse-and-chariot corps, and that this parallel is intentional seems clear from the repetition of *râkab* ("to ride"). In other words, Elisha does not just put his hands on the king's hands (NIV), he "rides" them on the king's hands (*râkab*). Jehoash "stands up" (*`âmad*) after striking the ground three times, and the narrative cleverly ties this to the corpse's "standing up." One entity "stands up" after contacting a dead prophet; the other "stands up" uncertainly before a still-living prophet. One "stands up" in strength; the other "stands up" in weakness and indecision.

Puns like these subtly link this episode to its context while two other motifs link it to the larger prophetic corpus. "Elisha" means "my God saves," and Elisha's God does save—the strong as well as the weak, the rich as well as the poor. Elisha's God saves when other gods do not. Mirroring its protagonist, this salvation theme runs throughout the Elisha cycle like a scarlet thread. Yahweh sends a "savior" (*môshî`a*) to deliver Israel from Aram, but unlike Elisha, the power of this savior does not extend beyond the grave.

Lingering over these contrasts, the narrator subtly ties in another sacred tradition to memorialize Elisha. In 1 Kings 13, a lion "throws down" (*shâlak*) the corpse of a Judahite prophet. Here another corpse is "thrown down" (*shâlak*), but not in an open, unprotected place. On the contrary, someone throws down this corpse into a protected, sacred space—Elisha's tomb. In 1 Kings 13, the Ephraimite prophet commands his sons to "lay my bones beside his bones." Does he do this to memorialize his own name? Does he imagine that the power of this prophet's bones will energize his own bones well beyond the grave?[56] Whatever his motivations, when

Josiah later comes across the tomb of the Judahite prophet, he commands his men not to disturb his bones (2 Kings 23:18). In other words, what we have here is a prophetic trajectory which begins and ends with "after-death stories" (1 Kings 13; 2 Kings 13)—just as 1 and 2 Kings begin with "frailty" stories.

Intratextual Reflection
Of course, there is no full-blown doctrine of resurrection here, only a primitive prophetic response to the problem of human frailty. The twist here is the way in which the narrator overtly parallels the frailty of Elisha with the frailty of Israel. Even though he's dying, Elisha is the strongest person here. Everyone around him is tentative, ambivalent, faithless, or indecisive. Even Elisha's dead bones are healthier than the kings of Israel. What are we to make of these contrasts?

First, wartime is no time to be tentative. Robert Rodat explores this theme in two of his screenplays. In *Saving Private Ryan*, he creates a character named Corporal Timothy Upham,[57] a quiet, nervous man who gets drafted into action as a translator behind enemy lines. When he sees the horrors of war for the first time, this crisis drives him to question the ethics of his superiors. He talks a lot about "good" and "evil" and "right" and "wrong"—until he's put under pressure. Then he has to make decisions about it. In one of the film's final scenes, a buddy cries out for help against a German attacker, and Upham freezes in his tracks. He starts to run up the stairs and save his friend, but then he becomes paralyzed with fear. Even as he hears the grisly sounds of his friend's death, he can bring himself to do nothing to save him. Like Jehoash, he's good at saying the words, but that's about as deep as his faith goes.

In *The Patriot*, "Corporal Upham" becomes the conflicted lead character.[58] Benjamin Martin is a single parent with seven children and a shady past. Having experienced the horrors of the French and Indian War, he wants no part of war with the British, and he says so publicly. Only when the Revolutionary War comes directly to his door does he finally respond, though in the process Rodat keeps us guessing whether he fights the British as a parent or as a patriot.

No one likes war. No one even likes conflict. Paul makes it clear, though, that we "fight not against flesh and blood, but against the rulers, against the authorities, against the powers of this dark world and against the spiritual forces of evil in the heavenly realms" (Eph 6:12). Apart from genuine commitment to this war, the Church will never accomplish its Mission. The enemy is just too strong, too determined. The difference between Elisha and Jehoash is the difference between an effective pastor and a hireling. Only one will fight for the flock; the other will not. The difference between a father and a weekend boyfriend is that one will fight for his children; the other will not. Courage under pressure is the acid test of commitment.

Second, God hears prayer. Amazed by Jesus' prayers, the disciples ask him to teach them how to pray, and he tells them a parable:

> Two men went up to the temple to pray, one a Pharisee
> and the other a tax collector. The Pharisee stood up and
> prayed about himself: "God, I thank you that I am not like
> other men—robbers, evildoers, adulterers—or even like
> this tax collector. I fast twice a week and give a tenth of all I get."
> But the tax collector stood at a distance. He would not
> even look up to heaven, but beat his breast and said, "God,
> have mercy on me, a sinner." (Luke 18:10-13)

The problem with the Pharisee is that he misuses his religious tradition to exalt himself over others. The problem with the tax collector is that he never goes beyond lamenting his sin to doing something about it. Like Jehoahaz, he prays, but whether or not this prayer leads to action is conspicuously left unsaid.[59]

Still, Christ calls him "justified" and this gives every praying sinner hope. Prayer is not always easy. Some of us come from traditions where we've been taught to work, but not to pray. Some of us come from situations in which we've inadvertently developed attitudes of independence rather than God-dependence.[60] Some of us can really identify with Jehoahaz, and we marvel that God listens to our rote petitions and tenuous whinings. Some of us have come to realize that the point is not whether we pray eloquently, but whether we pray when all our horses are gone, when all our chariots are wrecked, when all the pressures of life are threshing us to dust.

Third, God's power is greater than death. Not to see this is to surrender this text to a hollow naturalism. Postmodern agnostics will always challenge this teaching, but prayer-less interpreters have been challenging this for a long time: "On the bones of Elisha one dead man revived, but when our Savior descended to the abode of the dead, He quickened many and raised them up."[61] Over-zealous believers have to avoid taking it to the extreme—Christian resurrection does not stand behind every word of the Old Testament. Stories about reviving corpses do not equate to the Easter story, but they do raise important questions about life and death—which to Christian believers find an answer in the Easter story. Personally I believe that God wants the entire Creation to stand up on its feet and proclaim his Name, but I know that not everyone shares this faith. Henry James, however, expresses pity for those who try to have it both ways:

> Think of a spiritual existence so wan, so colourless, so miserably dreary and lifeless...presided over by a sentimental deity, a deity so narrow-hearted, so brittle-brained and putty-fingered as to be unable to make godlike men with hands and feet to do their own work and go their own errands....These creatures could have no life. At the very most they would barely exist. Life means individuality of character; and individuality of character can never be conferred...but must be inwardly wrought out by the diligent and painful subjugation of evil.[62]

Elisha becomes angry because the king of Israel models before his people despair instead of hope, *anomie* in place of conviction. Yahweh is not going to confer a blessing on Jehoash simply because he is king. Nor is he going to confer one on me simply because I live in a "Christian nation." Just as he expects this king to strike the ground more than three times, so he expects me to commit myself to something more than weekend spirituality.

Theological Reflection

"So this is how it's going to be?"

Carl and I are sitting quietly in the ICU waiting room, and Carl is in the mood to talk.

"Do you think I should just...quit?"

"I don't know," I respond cautiously. "Do you think you can adjust to this guy's leadership style?"

Staring off into space, he mumbles, "I don't know. I just don't know."

Carl is the last remaining pastor on a transitioning church staff. The new senior pastor, high-powered and entrepreneurial, has been shaking things up, and Carl is upset by the changes. The pastor has been calling in his staff and (as he put it to me later) "clearing out the deadwood." Prior to his coming, the statistics were indeed grim. Attendance and contribution were in a free-fall. The congregation was floundering for lack of direction. Now attendance is up. Contribution is up. Excitement is up. We're becoming a growing church again.

Carl has survived the transition so far because he complements well the senior pastor's gift-set. He likes to pray with people and visit the hospitals. He likes recruiting teachers for the church's educational programs. He likes all the "people-person" tasks of ministry, and this is why the senior pastor has kept him around—until today. Today he's just challenged Carl to put on his desk by next week a plan for reaching the unchurched community in a more intentional way—and Carl is bristling at the assignment. In so many words, this pastor is challenging Carl to "strike the ground," and Carl doesn't know whether he wants to or not.

Every congregational vision has two sides. On one side stands the missiological imperative. On the other stands ecclesiological reality. New churches tend to grow because they haven't been tested yet. They're still young and outward-oriented, still working to build themselves up to critical mass. Older churches tend to have stronger identities, but unless they've stayed mission-minded over the years they often tend to coast instead of soar, meander instead of march. Every congregation lives in this tension, and for those who engage it honestly, ministry can be a rewarding experience. Missiologically speaking, "Victory over Aram!" ought to be every congregation's war-cry. Translating this into contemporary language might sound something like "Victory over racism!" or "Victory over adultery!" But every church has to have a war-cry. All of us need victory over something.

Carl has to decide whether he wants to strike the ground or leave the battlefield.

I WILL HEAL YOU (2 Kings 20:1-11)

Like many kings before him, Hezekiah becomes ill (*ḥālâ*).[63] We don't know exactly what this illness is; we only know that it's a life-threatening boil (*shehîn*; rabbinic tradition imagines at least twenty-four kinds of boils, *Gen. Rab.* 41.2). If this boil is anything like the festering boils cast upon Egypt (Exod 9:9-11), then no wonder Isaiah pronounces Hezekiah's doom! In Job, the *satan*-adversary strikes Job with painful boils (Job 2:7, lit. "evil boil" [sg.], *shehîn ra*`), but unlike the Joban narrator, nowhere does this narrator offer a cosmic rationale for his protagonist's distress. The precise nature of this illness is unimportant.

What is important is the fact that it gets Hezekiah's attention—and what really takes him by surprise (and us) is the curtness of Isaiah's response: "Put your house in order. You are going to die. You will not recover." After everything that's happened to Hezekiah, this is hard to hear. Hearing it doubtless makes everyone in the room ask the same painful question: What kind of a God is this? First he saves, then he condemns. First he calls, then he leaves. As with Balaam, first he gives a green light, then he gives a red light (Num 22). As with Abraham, first He gives life, then he commands that it be taken away (Gen 22). As a hospital chaplain, I was trained never to use such language—it violates every principle of Clinical Pastoral Education.[64] Yet Isaiah uses it here.

Stammering and sputtering, all Hezekiah can think to do in response is recite his résumé. He turns his face to the wall and prays, but this prayer is not at all like his earlier prayer (2 Kings 19:14-19). This prayer is decidedly more anthropocentric. Where his first prayer focuses on defending God's Name from blasphemy (2 Kings 19:15-19), this one focuses on the king—his "faithfulness," his "complete heart." Hezekiah never asks God to change—he simply lists his character traits and tacks on an imperative verb: "Remember!"

What we need to recognize is that this is formulaic language rooted in the Davidic Zion tradition. In Yahweh's original promise to David, David thanks him for speaking words of truth (*'emet*) and promising him good things (*tôb*, 2 Sam 7:28). Here Hezekiah relies on this same promise, and apparently it works, because Isaiah stops dead in his tracks and turns around in obedience to Yahweh. Through Isaiah, Yahweh promises the king fifteen more years, but when he predictably asks why he should believe the latter oracle over the former one, Yahweh gives him a sign so show-stoppingly spectacular it takes his breath away. Is Hezekiah's "righteousness" the reason for God's change of heart? No, Yahweh responds "for the sake of my servant David." Doubtless Hezekiah's tear-stained plea influences the divine response, but in no way does it determine it. Yahweh keeps covenant regardless of human behavior, whether good or evil, faithful or faithless (1 Kings 3:6; 11:13).

Intratextual Reflection

This is not the first time a king turns his face to the wall and weeps. Ahab weeps in his "hour of distress" too (1 Kings 21). Where Ahab cries over the loss of a vegetable garden, though, Hezekiah prays more maturely. People like Ahab don't pray—not really. They cry a lot. They complain a lot. They whine a lot. But they rarely pray. In the previous episode, Hezekiah's prayer is overtly theocentric—"that all kingdoms on earth may know that you alone, Yahweh, are God" (2 Kings 19:19). Here he prays for more personal reasons, but regardless of his motives, we need to recognize that he turns to God out of faith, not petulance. Hezekiah has just survived one of the worst crises of the ancient world—an Assyrian siege. Yet before he can celebrate his deliverance, he has to deal with another "siege," and in v. 6 the narrator covertly links this siege (the king's disease) with Jerusalem's siege (Sennacherib's invasion).[65]

Physicians and exorcists, diviners and healers, soothsayers and mediums—all these specialists try to deal with the problem of frailty the best way they can, using abysmally poor diagnostic tools.[66] To (post)moderns, this looks like superstition, yet the fact that the book of Kings has an entire trajectory devoted to the *pressure of frailty* is not accidental. Human frailty is the portal through which the prophets offer their theology of healing.

Theological Reflection

To sufferers, no words are sweeter than "I will heal you," and the fact that the God of the Universe would condescend to hear and heal is both amazing and inspiring. Yet desensitized believers often forget this basic human need. "Why all this talk about healing?" they ask. Good question. Why is "healing" so constantly discussed on talk shows, in books, in contemporary films, on CNN? Why do some films satirize it (*Leap of Faith*, *Elmer Gantry*), while others practically divinize it (*Rainman*, *Ghost*, *The Green Mile*)? Why does Jesus make the ministry of healing absolutely central to his Mission (Matt 4:23, *therapeuō*)?[67]

Westerners rarely think about healing because, compared to the rest of the world, we don't have to. Paul Brand blames this amnesia on the seductiveness of affluence.[68] In fact, Dr. Brand thinks that the West is a difficult place to experience either pain or pleasure. Though no society in history has ever succeeded so well in eliminating pain, we still struggle with the question, "Is contentment the absence of discomfort or the avoidance of pain?" Pain, Dr. Brand argues, is one of the most misunderstood aspects of the human body. Without it, no body can survive. With it, every body becomes aware of its connectedness to its environment.

Having conquered most infectious diseases, Brand argues, the West is now substituting new health problems for old. Where malaria, polio and smallpox ravaged a previous generation, the new diseases in the West have significantly more to do with choice of lifestyle: heart disease, hypertension, stomach ulcers, cancers associated with toxic environments, AIDS and other STDs, emphysema, lung cancer caused by smoking, alcohol and drug abuse, diabetes and other diet-related disorders. Regardless of what we're being told, many of the diseases now killing us in the West we bring on ourselves.

Kierkegaard addresses this issue in theological language in a famous study, *Fear and Trembling*.[69] In Gen 22, he argues, the tradition of the Aqeda ("binding" of Isaac) is a forerunner of Christ's "binding" on the Cross. Immanuel Kant, however, rejects a biblical atonement theology for a religion based on reason alone, and many (post)modern interpreters support Kant's proposal because they too believe that pain avoidance is the Ultimate Good. Thus for some readers Yahweh is a child abuser because he inflicts pain on Abraham and Job and Christ.[70] But what these scholars fail to see is what Isaiah wants Hezekiah to see: faith must be tested or it cannot be faith. Faith must be put under pressure. Sacrifice cannot be taught by syllogism. One cannot reason one's way to obedience in the Kingdom. To suggest otherwise is to suggest that the Cross is nothing more than a well-intentioned mistake.

Against this view, Isaiah speaks of a God who makes kings weep bitterly when they need to, and we need to recognize that God can and does heal physical suffering—but he is not obligated to do so, nor is it always in our best interest. This is not to discount the power of prayer, only to situate it within a biblical creation theology. Our prayers need to be careful to address the biblical God in theological, not anthropological categories. Whether God responds on our terms and in our categories cannot be a precondition to faith. The Great Physician is Sovereign Lord, not some deity easily controlled by exorcistic prayer or some bureaucratic HMO against which we have the "right" to complain.

Notes

1. In a letter to a young man struggling with sexual lust, Jerome calls this a "farcical story," and views Abishag as a metaphor for Lady Wisdom (*Letters* 52.2-4).

2. O. Loretz ("Ugaritisch *skn-sknt* und hebraisch *skn-sknt*," *ZAW* 94 [1982] 123-27), notes that both male and female "stewards" exist at Ugarit as well as Jerusalem, yet cautions that too little is known of the context in Kings to speculate further.

3. W. Brueggemann (*David's Truth in Israel's Imagination and Memory* [Philadelphia: Fortress, 1985] 121-28) emphasizes how persistent later tradents can be in their attempts to sanctify David's memory.

4. Bill Cosby, *Time Flies* (New York: Doubleday, 1987) 28, 48-49, 38-39.

5. Lissy Jarvik and Gary Small, *Parentcare: A Commonsense Guide for Adult Children* (New York: Crown, 1988) 2; James Halpern, *Helping Your Aging Parents* (New York: McGraw-Hill) 23.

6. Peter Drucker, *Managing the Non-Profit Organization* (New York: Harper Collins, 1990) 9.

7. A. Nanez, "The Transition from Anglo to Mexican American Leadership in the Rio Grande Conference," *Methodist History* 16 (1978) 67-74.

8. Richard Porter, "Following a Fallen Pastor: Recovering from Docetism," *Faith and Mission* 5 (1988) 45-57, describes the conflict he faces as a new pastor following a pastor who falls to sexual infidelity—a situation not all that dissimilar to David's (2 Sam 12:10).

9 Michael Blaine, "Succeeding a Patriarch," *Leadership* 14 (1993) 118-122.

10. On this see my essay, "Are Our Wounds Incurable?" in D. Shackleford, ed., *Today Hear His Voice: The Minor Prophets Speak,* 70th Annual Harding University Lectureship (Searcy, AR: Harding University, 1993) 313-24.

11. This verb, *habar,* repeats itself three times in 2 Chron 20:35, 36, & 37 in descriptions of Jehoshaphat's (illicit) alliance with Ahaziah. Often it has connotations of "alliance" with idols and idolatry in the OT (Deut 18:11; Isa 47:9, 12; Hos 4:17).

12. Opinions are divided over the status of Israel's queen mothers. G. Molin ("Die Stellung der *Gebîra* im Staate Juda," *TZ* 10 [1954] 161–75) thinks Judah was original-ly a matriarchal society in which (under Hittite influence) queen mothers worked hard to ensure the succession of their biological sons. H. Donner, however ("Art und Herkunft des Amtes der Königinmutter im Alten Testament," in *Festchrift Johannes Friedrich* [ed. R. von Kienle et al; Heidelberg: C. Winter, 1959] 105–45) rejects all the-ories of matriarchal hegemony.

13. *KTU* 1.2 i 38 (Prince Baal); iii 8 (Prince Yam). S. Gitin and M. Cogan ("A New Type of Dedicatory Inscription from Ekron," *IEJ* 49 [1999] 193-202) report that an inscription from ancient Ekron reads *lb`l wlpdy,* "for Baal and for Padi" (Padi is known from the annals of Sennacherib, *ANET* 287-88). This inscription "is the first evidence of this or any other male deity to be found in the excavations at Ekron" (p. 196).

14. L. Gaston, "Beelzebul," *TZ* 18 (1962) 247–55.

15. Baalshamayin is Yahweh's chief rival in imperial Aramaic texts (e.g., *KAI* 202.2, 3, 11, 12).

16. One would think that Jezebel's Tyrian gods would have the most influence on Ahaziah's decision, but for all we know Ahaziah may already have a relationship with Ekron and its gods.

17. Num 22-24; 2 Kings 5:3-5.

18. In *ARM* X.8, a local deity named Dagan-milik complains in a trance that King Zimri-Lim has "spurned me," but then this deity promises to "coax" him back.

19. E. W. Conrad, "The 'Fear Not' Oracles in Second Isaiah," *VT* 34 (1984) 129-52.

20. G. Fohrer (*Studien zu alttestamentlichen Texten und Themen* [Berlin: deGruyter, 1981] 172-87) defines even the Israelite view of illness in demonic cate-gories. B. Levine (*In the Presence of the Lord: A Study of Cult and Some Cultic Terms in Ancient Israel* [Leiden: Brill, 1974] 91) more carefully recognizes in the Hebrew Bible the presence of "anti-God forces...affecting the Israelite community at large."

21. See my *Balaam Traditions,* 20-65.

22. J. C. de Moor ("Rapiuma, Rephaim," *ZAW* 88 [1976] 323-45) points out that the West Semitic root *rp`,* "to heal," means "healer" or "savior" in Ugaritic. Often the term is a title for an Ugaritic king and can be a divine epithet for Baal in his role as healer and reviver of the "dead" ("savior-shades," *rapi`uma*).

23. Not his real name.

24. C. H. Spurgeon, "The Joy of the Lord," A Sermon Preached at the Metropolitan Tabernacle (Newington, England, Dec 31, 1871).

25. Aquinas, "Of Apostasy," *Summa Theologica* Part 2b, Question 12, Answer 1.

26. J. Wesley, *Journal* (Tuesday, Dec 2, 1735).

27. "Rimmon" ("thunderer?" v. 18), one of Naaman's gods (v. 18), is likely an epithet of Hadad, the Syrian equivalent of the storm-god Baal (W. Meier, "Hadadrimmon," *ABD* 3.13).

28. "Such was the fate of Elisha's servant in the story of Naaman; for though he took not by violence, yet he did a wrong. For to get money by deceit is wrong" (*Homilies of St. John Chrysostom on the Epistles of Paul to the Corinthians*: 2 Cor 11.1 [CD-Rom; Albany, OR: Ages Software, 1997] 845). "For the sake of Naaman the whole kingdom of Assyria (*sic*) was blessed of God" (Luther, *Table Talk* § 269). "And why did God choose that Naaman, a Syrian, should be healed by Elisha, but to put a disgrace on the nation of Israel?" (Calvin, *Commentary on Luke* 4.25). "The Syrians looked down with contempt on the Israelites, and yet this great man was willing to take the good news at the hands of this little maiden" (D. L. Moody, "Naaman the Syrian," in *Wondrous Love and Other Gospel Essays* [CD-Rom; Albany, OR: Ages Software, 1997] 65-75).

29. Not everyone sees a chiasm here. R. L. Cohn ("Form and Perspective in 2 Kings V," *VT* 33 [1983] 171-84), for example, sees the story of Naaman as a single continuous story independent of its context and comprised of three distinct units: unit 1 centers on Elisha in the healing of Naaman; unit 2 focuses on Naaman and his confession of faith in Yahweh; unit 3 narrates Gehazi's efforts to enrich himself at Naaman's expense. Note, however, that Cohn's "unit 2" looks very much like the chiasm proposed here.

30. M. L. Davies, "Levitical Leprosy: Uncleanness and the Psyche," *Expository Times* 99 (1988) 136-39.

31. D. Wright and R. Jones, "Leprosy," *ABD* 4.277-82.

32. See my "Miriam's Error," in *Reconciliation: A Study of Biblical Families in Conflict* (Joplin, MO: College Press, 1994) 61-72.

33. See my "Ruth the Moabite and the Blessing of Foreigners," *CBQ* 60 (1998) 203-17.

34. This is the tagline of the 1992 film *Leap of Faith* (written by Janus Cercone, directed by Richard Pearce, starring Steve Martin).

35. In Assyrian demonology, for example, the *labâsû* are the demons responsible for afflicting the extremities of the hands and the feet with leprosy (W. Farber, *labâsu, RLA* 6.409-10).

36. The verb *sâlah* ("to forgive") appears five times in Solomon's dedicatory prayer.

37. *Nisibene Hymns: Hymns for the Feast of the Epiphany* 5.6. See also Ambrose, *Concerning Repentance* 2.3.12, and Gregory of Nyssa, *On the Baptism of Christ*.

38. M. Volf, *Exclusion and Embrace: A Theological Exploration of Identity, Otherness, and Reconciliation* (Nashville: Abingdon, 1996).

39. E. Lehman, "Correlates of Lay Perceptions of Clergy Ministry Style," *RRR* 38 (1997) 211-230.

40. R. Salzmann, "A Strategy for Lay Ministry in the New Time," *Lutheran Quarterly* 24 (1972) 134-55.

41. L. Baumhover and C. Beall, eds., *Abuse, Neglect, and Exploitation of Older*

Persons (Baltimore: Health Professions Press, 1996).

42. T. Marotta, *Adolescent Male Prostitution, Pornography, and Other Forms of Sexual Exploitation* (San Francisco: Urban and Rural Systems Associates, 1982).

43. C. Moorehead, *Betrayal: Child Exploitation in Today's World* (London: Barrie and Jenkins, 1989).

44. J. Freie, *Counterfeit Community: The Exploitation of Our Longings for Connectedness* (Oxford: Rowman and Littlefield, 1998).

45. J. Gonsiorek, *Breach of Trust: Sexual Exploitation by Health Care Professionals and Clergy* (Thousand Oaks, CA: Sage, 1995).

46. H. Hart, "The Survival of Truth beyond Liberal Rationality," *Perspectives* 11 (1996) 17-20.

47. A. MacIntyre, *After Virtue* (Notre Dame, IN: University of Notre Dame, 1984) 6.

48. D. L. Jeffrey, "Knowing Truth in the Present Age," *Crux* 34 (1998) 19-28.

49. S. King, *The Green Mile* (New York: Plume, 1997).

50. A. Rofé, "The Classification of the Prophetical Stories," *JBL* 89 (1970) 427-40.

51. Ephraim the Syrian, *Nisibene Hymns* 41.10.

52. *b. Hul.* 7b; *b. Sanh.* 47a.

53. Josephus (*AJ* 9.8.6) claims Elisha receives a "magnificent funeral," but this is what Hellenistic audiences expect after the death of "great men."

54. H. Schulte thinks ("The End of the Omride Dynasty: Social-Ethical Observations on the Subject of Power and Violence," *Semeia* 66 [1995] 133-48) that Jehu's annihilation of the Omrides is responsible for Hazael's oppression, that the change of government in Samaria ushers in too much political change too fast—and Hazael takes advantage of it. This thesis fails to account, however, for (a) the likelihood that Hazael and Jehu in fact collaborate to destroy the Omrides (Tel Dan inscription), and (b) the impact the lack of a successor to Elisha has on the Jehu "dynasty."

55. Elisha says these words before Elijah's heavenly ascension (2 Kings 2:12).

56. T. Lewis discusses this passage at length alongside other biblical passages alluding to the unseen world of the dead (*Cults of the Dead in Ancient Israel and Ugarit* [HSM 39; Atlanta: Scholars, 1989] 99–127. I argue elsewhere that resurrection is a very old idea eventually picked up and adapted by Yahwistic prophets to focus attention on Yahweh as Living Sovereign ("Resurrection and Immortality," *TZ* 39 [1983] 18).

57. *Saving Private Ryan* (directed by S. Spielberg; written by Robert Rodat, 1998).

58. *The Patriot* (directed by Roland Emmerich, written by Robert Rodat, 2000).

59. F. G. Downing ("The Ambiguity of 'The Pharisee and the Toll-Collector' (Luke 18:9-14) in the Greco-Roman World of Late Antiquity," *CBQ* 54 [1992] 80-99) goes too far, however, when he attributes just as much self-absorption to the tax collector as the Pharisee.

60. L. Bundensen, *Goddependency: Finding Freedom from Codependency and Discovering Spiritual Self-Reliance* (New York: Crossroads, 1989) 3.

61. Aphrahat, *Demonstration* 6 (On Monks) §13.

62. Henry James, in a letter cited by Ralph Barton Perry, *Thought and Character of William James*, vol. 1 (Boston: Little, Brown, 1935) 158.

63. Previous "sick" kings include Jeroboam I, Asa, Ahab, Ahaziah, and Joram, though the reasons for each "sickness" are unique.

64. W. Hiemstra, "A History of Clinical Pastoral Education in the United States,"

Reformed Review 16 (1963) 30-47.

65. C. Seitz speculates ("Isaiah, book of [First Isaiah]," *ABD* 3.483) that "the whole point of the account of Hezekiah's sickness is to stress the ability of the royal house to divert a merited sentence of judgment. Hezekiah's sickness mirrors Jerusalem's sickness—his faithful prayer postpones a sentence of judgment spoken by the prophet Isaiah. The key verse in this regard (2 Kings 20:6) links Hezekiah's recovery to the recovery of the city."

66. I document many of these strange techniques in my dissertation, *The Balaam Traditions* (Atlanta: Scholars, 1990) esp. 20-65, "The Roles Enacted by Selected Ancient Near Eastern Magico-Religious Specialists."

67. M. Klunzinger and M. S. Moore, "Codependency and Pastoral Care: A Report from the Trenches," *RQ* 38 (1996) 172-3.

68. P. Brand, "And God Created Pain," *CT* 38 (1994) 18-23.

69. S. Kierkegaard, *Fear and Trembling* (trans. by W. Lowrie; Princeton, NJ: Princeton University Press, 1968) first published in 1843.

70. In S. Lasine's thinking (*Knowing Kings: Knowledge, Power and Narcissism in the Hebrew Bible* [SBLSS 40; Atlanta: Society of Biblical Literature, 2001] 239) Job is "a humiliated and obedient child who is forced to admit once again that he has no knowledge or rights in relation to his omnipotent and abusive father."

SIX

THE PRESSURE OF FOREIGNERS

MAKING PEACE (1 Kings 5:1-12)

Behind Solomon and Hiram stands a long historical trajectory. In the Amarna correspondence from Egypt, for example, a Phoenician king named Abimilku writes several letters to the Pharaoh addressing matters similar to the ones occupying Solomon and Hiram: food, security, and treaties.[1] When Hiram writes to congratulate Solomon, this looks like any other letter in the Amarna correspondence. Just as Abimilku writes to obtain food, so Solomon writes to secure wood (1 Kings 5:10-11; *EA* 154.5-19). Just as Hiram complains about the quality of Solomon's gifts, Abimilku complains about the quality of his neighborhood (1 Kings 9:12-14; *EA* 149.40-176). Diplomatic correspondence looks pretty much the same everywhere.

Yet this biblical episode introduces us to one of Israel's most complicated international relationships. Israel's treaty with Phoenicia, concluded here between "old friends" Solomon and Hiram, leads to more than just a new temple. Along with it comes a tremendous amount of baggage. Little is known about how this treaty affects Phoenicia, but Kings tells us a great deal about how it affects Israel. Architecturally, Hiram helps Solomon construct a religious sanctuary based on Canaanite/Phoenician prototypes.

Socioeconomically, Hiram partners with Solomon at a time when the entire Mediterranean world is one big Phoenician bazaar.[2] Religiously, it pushes Israel into an affair with Baalism with which it struggles violently and from which it never fully recovers.[3]

With regard to politics, opinions are divided over whether the Hebrew term *berît* ("treaty/covenant," v. 12) refers to a pre-exilic idea *rooted* in Israel's past or a post-exilic idea *reformulating* Israel's past.[4] Both positions harbor elements of truth, yet the repeated occurrence of the Akkadian word *mamitu* ("oath-treaty") in Abimilku's letters implies an entire history of covenant-making, long before the occurrence of *berît* here in the biblical texts.[5] Without treaties, obviously, neighbors are more likely to go to war. Without clearly established boundaries, neighbors will tend to live in suspicion of one other, not in "safety."[6] To imagine this process as having no history prior to the 5th century BC is to deny the witness of history itself, particularly as evidenced in the Amarna texts.

The Chronicler says that Solomon builds the temple because (a) Yahweh is superior to other gods, and (b) Israel needs a place to observe "the sabbaths and new moons and appointed festivals" (2 Chron 2:3-6). Kings, however, avoids such language, and though many see contradiction instead of complementation here,[7] it seems wiser to suggest that Kings simply has its own reasons for discussing this treaty: (a) war prohibits the Temple's construction under David; (b) Solomon builds the temple at a time of relative freedom from "adversary" (*satan*) and "disaster" (*pega`*); and (c) prophecy is the institution responsible for making it work.

First, though war is not David's only concern, war characterizes his reign more than it does Solomon's. Like the Roman emperor Augustus, David hates violence:

> War is like fishing with a golden net; the loss risked is always greater than the catch can be (Augustus).[8]

> Today, though I am the anointed king, I am weak. These sons of Zeruiah are too strong for me (David, 2 Sam 3:39).

Yet David's reign is so bloody and so violent that it becomes famous for little else but war. In fact, so famous is David's role as "warrior," centuries later the Syrians still characterize the "house of David" in bellicose language.[9] David spends the bulk of his reign making war, not institutions, and though it's difficult to tell how the narrator feels about it, it's not difficult to see his larger point. Solomon's institutional accomplishments are unthinkable apart from his father's military accomplishments.

Second, Solomon dismantles the military establishment to free up resources—resources he then uses to build the Temple. After David, Israel finds itself relatively unthreatened by enemies, and this gives Solomon an excuse to take on the military lobby. This does not mean that he will not, on occasion, fight:

> Who is this coming up from the desert
> like a column of smoke,
> perfumed with myrrh and incense
> made from all the spices of the merchant?
> Look! It is Solomon's carriage,
> escorted by sixty warriors,
> the noblest of Israel,
> all of them wearing the sword,
> all experienced in battle,
> each with his sword at his side,
> prepared for the terrors of the night (Song of Songs 3:6-8).

It simply means that as David is famous for waging war, so Solomon is famous for waging "peace" (*shalom*, v. 12). In fact, his very name means "peace" (1 Chron 22:9), and "peace" in the Bible is never merely the absence of war. In Hebrew, *shalom* denotes the (re)creation of wholeness out of brokenness.[10] *Shalom* is visionary leadership in the face of viral idiocy. Solomon can build the temple because David establishes enough *shalom* to make it possible, but to consolidate his authority he now has to purge his kingdom of its *satan*-adversaries.[11] His reign begins with a burst of violence, but it's only transitional violence, not institutional violence—and it's critical that we see the distinction.

Third, Kings insists on describing Solomon's temple-plans in overtly prophetic language. Unlike Chronicles, Solomon builds in Kings because it's his *destiny*—Nathan's oracle predicts it (2 Sam 7:12-16); this passage confirms it. This prophetic theology will heat up later as more prophets begin to challenge more kings, but already here the narrator wants to emphasize that Israelite life and culture cannot proceed or succeed without the involvement of the prophets. Where Chronicles reworks old mythological motifs into Zionistic rationales for the Temple,[12] Kings plainly sees the construction of the Temple as the fulfillment of prophecy.

Intratextual Reflection

This means that peacemaking is a major theme in the Solomon cycle (1 Kings 1-11), a theme which numbers the king's marriage to Pharaoh's daughter among its submotifs. With the Hiram treaty the narrator also reinforces this theme, situating it at the beginning of a long trajectory spanning the entire book of Kings. As any architect knows, no supporting pillars are needed under a bridge if the internal geometry is solid. So here we find no "pillars" in the *pressure of foreigners* trajectory because Israel's attitude toward foreigners has a unique internal geometry. Northern Israelite kings, for example, spend a great deal of time interacting with foreigners—sometimes positively, sometimes negatively, but always intensely. Jehu, Menahem, Pekahiah, Pekah and Hoshea all have places on this bridge/trajectory. In the south Ahaz, Hezekiah, Josiah, Jehoahaz, Jehoiakim, Jehoiachin and Zedekiah all spend time here too, often watching helplessly as Jerusalem gets sucked into one maelstrom of ancient Near Eastern politics after another.

Here the *pressure of foreigners* trajectory helps mold the shape of the Solomon cycle in three ways. First, international relationships often begin with peace-treaties, this narrator implies, but they can end in disaster. Compare, for example, the story of Solomon vs. the story of Hezekiah. In the beginning of the Solomon cycle, Solomon marries an Egyptian princess, covenants with a Phoenician king, and entertains an Arab queen. In the end, he finds himself surrounded by Edomite, Syrian, and Ephraimite enemies as he goes down by the head. The same pattern occurs when the Babylonian king Merodach-Baladan sends gifts to Hezekiah (2 Kings 20:12-20), and Hezekiah gives him a personal guided tour of Jerusalem's defenses. This enrages Isaiah, who promptly prophesies Hezekiah's doom. When this doom comes to pass a few chapters later, the clear implication of the trajectory as a whole is that international relations are at best problematic and at worst disastrous.

Yet second, peacemaking remains essential Kingdom business. Solomon practices peace not because he wants to outdo his father, and certainly not because he wants to accumulate more wives than his neighbors. Solomon wages peace because it's his destiny to do so. Though he may not be as focused on *shalom* as the One who says, "Blessed are the peacemakers, for they shall be called children of God" (Matt 5:9), he still stands head and shoulders above all his contemporaries—this treaty with Hiram "proves" it.

Third, peacemaking does not necessarily lead to apostasy. As one rabbi puts it, "If one sees a river in his dreams, he should rise early and say, 'Behold I will extend peace to her like a river'…before another verse occurs to him, 'for distress will come in like a river'" (*b. Ber.* 56b). In other words, there are good foreigners and there are bad foreigners, and each situation should be judged on its own merits. Israel has always wrestled with the problem of xenophobia ("fear of foreigners"), yet wiser Israelite heads have always argued that if Israel fails to make peace with its neighbors, the consequences might be—indeed, probably will be—disastrous. Thus the need for Solomonic wisdom when trying to navigate between peacemaking and isolationism.[13]

Theological Reflection

"Joggers Don't Budge, Cause Big Grudge."[14] So reads the headline of a story reporting that a jogger wants a court injunction against two of her neighbors because they will not yield to her the right of way. Instead, there's been an exchange of elbows and words and, according to one of the parties involved, saliva (!). Now the lawyers are involved, and the court is making these neighbors stay ten feet away from each other at all times. This story would be hilarious if it were not so tragic. Why are these neighbors turning to litigation instead of conversation? Why have they concluded that it's better to do business in a courtroom than a coffee shop?

Perhaps Jesus' words have never been more appropriate: "As he approached Jerusalem and saw the city, he wept over it and said, 'If you, even you, had only known on this day what would bring you peace—but now it is hidden from your eyes'" (Luke 19:41-42). Christ laments the stubbornness of his audience—the hardness of their hearts, the blindness dictating their judgments. If he feels this way about first-century Jerusalem, just imagine how he must feel about affluent Americans suing each other over jogging rights. Is there anything more pathetically illustrative of the phrase, "hidden from your eyes"? Selfish legalism is poisoning our culture and corroding our social fabric, but one particular aspect of the problem is hitting very close to home, at least to most readers of this book. Here's the question we're increasingly having to face: Who owns and controls the information ministers acquire in the normal course of their work? The answer is becoming increasingly unclear. Some courts are beginning to label as "fraud" and "false imprisonment" such fundamentally pastoral activities as conversion of new members and discipline of wayward members.[15] In short, the art of peacemaking has fallen on hard times, and the fallout is beginning to affect us in ways we could not have imagined a few years ago.

Personal peacemaking. What is marriage if not a "treaty" between "foreigners?"[16] Male and female, according to Paul, are essentially opposite, like God the Son *vis-à-vis* his human spouse, the Church (Eph 5:21-33). Failure to understand this truth is a primary reason why so many marriages fail. Much is said about this problem, but the gorilla in the middle of the room remains the ideological one. Are male and female different or the same? Successful marriages seem to be those in which both parties address this question honestly, and where each spouse abandons the role of "interested observer" for that of "proactive peacemaker." Just as Solomon's behavior toward Hiram is intentional and proactive, so ought mine to be toward *my* "neighbor."

Denominational peacemaking. Long ago I participated with a group of fellow seminarians in a youth retreat. Enthusiastic and excited, we started lining up speakers and putting together a schedule. Our local dentist could preach, so we asked him to be the keynote speaker, and the rest of us divided up the teaching responsibilities. Shortly before the event was to take place, however, a congregational leader took me aside and asked, "Do you ever want to preach in this county again?" Caught off-guard, I stammered, "Well, uh, yes....What's wrong?" He said, "Did you invite so-and-so to speak at our church?" (referring to our keynote speaker). "Yes," I replied, "Have you ever heard his sermon on...?" Cutting me off in mid-sentence, he clenched his teeth and spit out the words, "Are you crazy? You can't ask a *nig__* to preach in this church!" Never before had I heard such vileness from an elder in the church.

Our dentist was African-American, and this was my first experience with racism in my denomination. Apologizing to our dentist later, I'll never forget his response. "That's OK," he said. "We'll do it some other time." Again I was stunned. "What do you mean,'some other time?' Are you going to let them get away with this?" I wanted to go to this elder's house and confront him immediately, but my dentist wanted me to calm down and think it over. We both knew he had no plans to settle down in this community. He was only working in this poorest of southern counties to pay off a 3-year community-service commitment for his student loans. To this day I still get angry when I think about it—the "knowing wink" in the elder's eye, the cowardly silence of the congregation, the terrible message we sent to our teenagers. But I learned a lot about peacemaking from a humble dentist.[17]

SEARCHING IN SHEBA (1 Kings 10:1-13)

This story has inspired prophets,[18] mystics, poets,[19] novelists, theologians and artists.[20] Something about it simply captures the imagination, whether we focus on the mystery enshrouding this foreign queen, or ponder the wisdom informing this young king, or wonder at the elusiveness of Israel's God behind the scenes. Each of these characters is a well-traveled avenue into the story's theological core.

Most English translations have the Sabean queen visiting Solomon because of the fame of Solomon and his relation to the name of Yahweh (NIV). This reading, however, is less than certain. The earliest versions vary considerably (LXX, Syr, Vg), and few English translations adequately reflect the subtle connections linking the vocabulary here with the vocabulary animating preceding chapters, particularly the alliterative recurrence of the terms *shâma`* ("to hear/obey") and *shêm* ("name"; 1 Kings 5:22; 8:16, 29; 9:3). In addition, the root *shâma`* appears no less than six times in thirteen verses. Should this fact be given more weight, and more attention given to the use of the root in Yahweh's opening line, "I have heard" (*shâma`tî*, 1 Kings 9:3), the paragraph's introductory phrase might well be translated as follows: "When the Sabean queen heard of the obedience[21] of Solomon to the name of Yahweh...." At any rate, whether the spotlight focuses on Solomon's "fame" or Solomon's "obedience," it definitely shifts away from Solomon. Solomon's "fame" (Vg *fama*) and "listening heart" (*leb shôme`a*, 1 Kings 3:9), important as they are, are the object of this episode, not the subject. The Sabean is the one doing the "hearing" here, not Solomon. The primary action takes place in her, not him.

Like the Sabean, ancient Near Eastern leaders hear "reports" all the time, but seldom do such reports elicit long, dangerous journeys. Usually it's rumors of war or trade, not wisdom. Granted, we are dependent here on an Israelite narrator for all our information, but something still seems extraordinary about this particular report. Why does it so seize her attention? Does she see in Solomon a potential trading partner?[22] Does she see in him a military rival?[23] Does she see in him, as later legend so luridly speculates, a lover/mate?[24] Does the narrator think of her simply as another praise-mouthpiece to trumpet Solomon's achievements?[25]

Or does this queen, as the biblical narrator takes great pains to emphasize, come to Solomon because of an unquenchable "desire" (*hâpas*, v. 13) to "ask questions" (*shâ'al*, v. 13) about the "Name" (*shêm*,

1 Kings 9:3)? This question has largely been ignored. Whatever her motivations (and our interpretations sometimes "say more about us…than the story itself"),[26] we cannot afford to overlook this question. The education she receives from Solomon comes before us as a developmental process, and this process breaks down into three identifiable stages: *interrogation, perceptional shift,* and *affirmation.*

First, she "tests him." The use of this verb is unusual, and not necessarily because a woman is testing a man.[27] Primarily it's unusual because God is the exam-giver in Scripture, not human beings. God is the Divine Teacher who tests people (a) to see what kind of "healing" they want (Exod 15:25-26), (b) to see if they will follow his instructions (16:4), (c) to instill in them a healthy fear (20:20), (d) to distinguish Israel from other nations (Deut 4:34), (e) to humble and examine hearts (8:2), (f) to prepare believers for "the good" (*yâtab,* 8:16), and (g) to find out whether their love is genuine (13:3).

Only rarely do human beings test God. When Gideon lays out fleece to test Yahweh, the response is quiet patience mixed with unfettered grace (Judg 6:36-40). When the test comes from Israelites who abandon the covenant, however, we see a different response (Exod 17:7; Deut 6:16; Matt 16:1). The principle therefore appears clear. Spiritual motivation to a great extent determines the divine response (Gen 22:1; Psa 26:2; Heb 2:18). In light of the alternatives, mature Christians are generally thankful, as Forsyth puts it, to have a God who "cares enough…to be angry."[28] This is the only appropriate response to inappropriate tests of the divine.

But how does she test him? She does it by "hard questions" (lit., "riddles," *hîdôt*). No one knows exactly what kind of "hard questions" she asks, though one medieval commentator suggests the following as a possibility:

Sabean Queen: "What is an enclosure with ten doors—when one is open, nine are shut, and when nine are open, one is shut?"

Israelite King: "The enclosure is the womb, and the ten doors are the ten orifices of a person, namely the eyes, the ears, the nostrils, the mouth, the apertures for discharge of excreta and urine, and the navel. When the child is still in its mother's womb, the navel is open, but all the other apertures are shut. But when the child issues from the womb, the navel closes and the other orifices open up."[29]

What we do know is that riddle-telling serves several functions. Not only do riddles entertain guests at dinner-parties,[30] but good teachers constantly use them to provoke their students to think deeper than they might otherwise. Riddles—old or new, aural or visual—are an important educational tool, a pedagogical goad to challenge some students to take in more while their peers take in less. James Crenshaw unnecessarily moralizes this process when he argues that "riddles conceal valuable information from the unworthy while divulging important facts to those deserving them."[31] Sometimes this is true ("...unless you eat my flesh and drink my blood...," John 6:53), but more often than not riddles are simply pedagogical test balloons.

The story before us is a case in point. The Sabean queen tests Solomon not to examine his moral worthiness, but to find out (a) what kind of teacher he is, and (b) whether her questions will eventually lead to genuine "wisdom" (*hokmâ*, v. 8). What she discovers in this process forever changes her life, leading her to a sense of awe much like that which follows the two-prostitutes incident earlier (1 Kings 3:28). Here, as there, Solomon passes an important test, a test designed to validate his remarkable pedagogical gifts. But more than this, Solomon's God moves powerfully to the forefront of the Sabean's consciousness as soon as she realizes how difficult it is to conceal anything from her new teacher.[32]

Second, what happens next happens in every educational experience. Her perceptions begin to change—about Israel's king, about Israel's government, about Israel's God. In fact, the text is quite clear that she comes to "believe" (v. 7) because of what she *learns*. Not only does she discover the linkages between religion and politics, between economics and ethics, between art and spirit (this is the import of vv. 4-5), she also begins to ask deeper questions. Her summary response in v. 5 (lit., "and not is in her any more spirit/breath") looks very much like Job's summary response after the whirlwind speeches (Job 38:1-42:6). Even as Job falls on his face, stunned and shocked by the Power cyclonically exploding before his eyes, so the Sabean similarly gasps for breath. Responses like these are not uncommon among foreigners in the Old Testament.[33]

Yet someone who has never suffered the famine of knowledge will have difficulty "getting" this text. Those who have never suffered the bitter loneliness of spiritual exile will have difficulty identifying with this woman's experience—because what she experiences is the power of education. To have all of one's deepest questions no longer ignored, no longer ridiculed, no longer trivialized, but actually *answered*...well, this can be a "knock-the-wind-out-of-you" experience (*lô' rûah*, lit., "no wind"). Not

only does the heart fill with gratitude, but the mind roars with new energy, like a computer upgraded to a higher speed. True, there are sociological implications to this experience as well—the conflict between
"wanting to belong and yet not belong at one and the same time."[34] But
at root this text is about a wisdom-hungry student daring to make the
hardest of all educational moves—the move from the "comfort zone" to
the "faith zone."

Intratextual Reflection

Third, worship is the natural response to such an experience. Like the
many other "foreigners" who cross Israel's path—Melchizedek, Tamar,
Jethro, Balaam, Ruth, even Nebuchadnezzar (Dan 4:37)—this transformed
foreigner blesses Yahweh with a deep sense of gratitude (v. 9). Notice,
however, that the blessing she offers does not precede her educational
experience; it follows it. The Israelite narrator obviously has a vested
interest in highlighting the blessing instead of the process, but to ignore
the process is to focus too much on the icing and not enough on the
cake.

    If this story teaches anything, it's that worship naturally follows the
discovery of truth, and this immediately raises the question, "Can one
truly worship God apart from some kind of educational experience?"
Jesus' conversation with a Samaritan woman addresses this question
squarely. What the Father seeks, he says to another foreign woman, are
"true worshipers," i.e., believers who worship holistically in spirit and in
truth (John 4:21-24). Does this not encapsulate what the Sabean does? This
queen blesses Solomon's God because in the process of her education she
discovers "truth" ('emet, v. 6). Her desire for truth is what causes her to
begin her long search. Her desire for truth is what drives her away from
the safety of her homeland. Truth is what she most "desires" (ḥāpas, v.
13). As Polonius ironically puts it to Claudius,

> If circumstances lead me, I will find
> Where truth is hid, though it were hid indeed
> Within the centre.[35]

Because she finds truth in Solomon, she concludes from this experience that Yahweh "delights" in him (ḥāpas, v. 9, same verb), explicitly
connecting her experience with her teacher (Solomon) to her experience
with her teacher's God (Yahweh). She blesses both Solomon and Yahweh
because she understands that it is the synergy of the covenant partner-
ship between Solomon and Yahweh which causes Solomon's people to

be so "happy," and she not surprisingly wants to experience this happiness for herself. Should we be surprised by any of this? As the narrator puts it in his summary, this is how the whole world comes to know wisdom—by patiently, intentionally, and relentlessly searching for it (v. 24).

Worship, however—whether intricate or simple, exciting or jejune, uplifting or boring—is not education. These are not synonymous terms. The process of education is just that—a process. Education is fundamentally about training oneself to labor hard and labor well in the search for truth—wherever it is, however it looks, in whomever it might be found. Worship, however, is celebrating the joy of discovering truth. The goal of Christian education is not to segregate one from the other, but to find creative ways to complement and integrate one into the other. The Lord himself says that worship artificially segregated from the educational process is unacceptable to the Father, however well-meaning or well-packaged it might be (John 4:24). The temptation is great to short-circuit this process, but we need to recognize that truth in the Bible is never a static abstraction condescendingly lowered from Mt. Olympus for the benefit of an elite few. Truth is rather hard-won insight hammered out in the shadow of Mt. Zion for the benefit of all Creation.

Theological Reflection

Today a lady called the office to say that she was interested in taking a course at our school, but she was having difficulty making up her mind. Seems she had had a "bad experience" with a professor earlier, and was not sure whether she wanted to take another course with him. So I asked her a few questions. Had the professor been contemptuous in class? No. Had he been unfair in his assignments? Well, no. Had he been patronizing or condescending toward students? No. Had he been unprepared? No. Had he set an improper moral example? No ("of course not!"). "Well," I asked, "why was the class such a bad experience?" "Because he gave hard tests," she replied. "I can learn Hebrew without taking tests. After all," she added proudly, "I *am* a student of the Hebrew Scriptures."

Really? How can one be a student of the Hebrew Scriptures without learning Hebrew? How can one learn Hebrew (or anything else) without being tested? Would I allow a surgeon to operate on my son if she had never been tested, and tested with the "hard questions?" Why is Christian education any less important? How consistent are we in holding ourselves to the same high standards in theological education as we hold surgeons or attorneys? To ask it in the words of the prophet, "When you bring blind animals for sacrifice, is that not wrong? When you sacrifice crippled or diseased animals, is that not wrong? Try offering them to your governor! Would he be pleased with you? Would he accept you?" (Mal 1:8).

This episode addresses this question in two ways. First, it implicitly admits that theological education is not everyone's cup of tea, but for those who search, there's a process to follow. I can speak to this issue with some expertise because for several years my wife and I have been teaching in adult education programs in several local churches, and what we have discovered from this experience is that many churches take theological education seriously, but more than a few are willing to accept "crippled" curricula and "diseased" methodologies. Too many refuse to address the hard questions of ministry. Too many prefer the regurgitated sermon, the flashy website, and the worshiptainment experience in place of the "hard questions."

More need to follow the Sabean's example. Like her, many students have to fight against tremendous odds to "make the journey," just like she did. One of my students, for example, has to contend with a crippling illness of the hands and feet (using voice-technology to write his papers), a messy divorce, a Social Security system which hounds him mercilessly, a church which never encourages, and a family who thinks he's crazy for attending seminary. Another student has suffered the trauma of a double mastectomy, a husband who abandoned her, a teenage daughter who got hooked on drugs, and a denomination which wants to punish her for every mistake she's ever made. None of this prevents her from coming to class and wrestling with the hard questions. These people don't see themselves as victims. They see themselves as disciples.

Second, this story warns us about the dangers of a counterfeit education, or, to put it more positively, the benefits of a genuine one. Rather than relying on second-hand reports about Solomon's wisdom, the Sabean goes to Jerusalem to see with her own eyes. She refuses, in other words, to settle for secondary sources. Instead, she makes the extra effort to investigate the primary sources. Would that her example were more widely followed. Every professional knows that we have to take this principle seriously in the disciplines of medicine, business, or law, but why don't we apply it as consistently to the disciplines of theology, biblical studies, and church history—the very disciplines supplying the lifeblood of the Church?

Here's an example of what I mean. In 1990 two authors, a poet and an English professor, published *The Book of J*, a book which attempts to translate the oldest alleged pentateuchal source "document" into contemporary English.[36] Reviewers gushed over it when it came out, praising it as "a great book...a superb piece of translation," a work of "erudition," filled with "poetic leaps of the imagination."[37] Richard Friedman, however, was not impressed. In fact, he was outraged. This is not a book filled with "erudition," Friedman complained. Neither of these authors commands the ancient language of the text (Biblical Hebrew), nor do either of them make the effort to understand the text's historical, archaeological and/or literary contexts (not to mention its intertextual and intratextual contexts). *The Book of J* is little more than airport eye-candy, a blatant attempt to market a "spiritual" product to baby-boomer consumers who style themselves "students of the Hebrew Scriptures," but in fact are biblically illiterate.[38]

Fayette Breaux Veverka dares to ask the really hard question: "Do religious educators any longer play a role in American (church) culture?"[39] From her investigation, the answer is "no." This is because too many teachers and preachers today work only from the "safe" biblical passages, refusing even to raise the "hard questions," much less address them faithfully. To be sure, educators like Joe Marlow caution us not to despair over this, because much of the problem, in his opinion, is methodological instead of ideological.[40] But Scott Sunquist thinks we need to take our heads out of the sand. Contemporary preachers and teachers are deliberately, relentlessly, and dangerously dumbing down the Faith, and this is hurting the Church of Christ.[41]

The Sabean's story can be read on several levels. When Jesus reads it, he intertextually lays it alongside the story of Jonah and interprets these stories as indictments of his wicked generation (Luke 11:29-32). Amazed by the complacency of his contemporaries, Jesus invites them to re-read their history, goading their consciences with a series of analogies. If even Gentiles like the Ninevites and the Sabean queen, he asks, know where to look for truth, then why can't we? Why does this or any other generation choose to fritter away its opportunities and become complacent about truth? So deep is this blindness, he warns, we may soon find ourselves unable even to recognize the One in our midst who is greater than Solomon, much less worship him. A more pointed indictment of anti-educational conservatism would be hard to imagine—and note that it comes directly from Christ himself.

Charles Spurgeon uses this story to plead with the hearts of his generation: "I want you tonight to come to Him, just as the Queen of Sheba came to Solomon, only for weightier reasons. You do not want to learn anything concerning architecture or navigation, agriculture or anatomy. You want to know only how you shall be built up a spiritual house, and how you shall cross those dangerous seas which lie between this land and the celestial city."[42]

Spurgeon's age, like Christ's, is very different from ours. Nineteenth-century preachers could make a number of assumptions which, unfortunately, we can no longer make. Preachers to postmoderns face a slew of problems wholly different from theirs: biblical illiteracy, resurgent ethnic racism, the worship wars, stubborn paternalism, angry feminism, pagan spiritualities, rampant materialism—just to name a few. Our age looks very different from Spurgeon's. Yet God still provides. We can still learn how to practice the educational wisdom of Luther: *oratio, meditatio, temptatio*—"I pray, I reflect, I test."[43] With Spurgeon we can still plead, "You have heard the report; now, like the Queen of Sheba, go and see for yourself."[44]

THE EDIFICE COMPLEX (1 Kings 9:10-28; 10:14-29)

Foreign alliances are fragile, even when treaties are in place to protect them (1 Kings 5:1-12). When Solomon makes treaties with his neighbors, some of his interests lie southward, but his primary interests lie northward, and from the Amarna correspondence we can reconstruct something of the historical context. Acco, Shechem, and Megiddo, for example, are rival towns distinguished by little else than their penchant for bickering. Letter after Amarna letter shows them fighting with each other like children, constantly begging Pharaoh for troops and food and horses and soldiers.[45] Some of the Pharaohs of this period, particularly Amenhotep III (1386-1349 BC) and Amenhotep IV (Akhenaten, 1350-1334 BC) respond directly to these requests—but more often than not they just let them fight things out. The cities given to Hiram have a troubled history.

Where Kings focuses on Hiram's displeasure, however, Chronicles does not.[46] Kings mentions Solomon's rebuilding of Gezer, but Chronicles says nothing—the Gezer burning incident does not even appear in 2 Chron 8. Whereas Kings describes Solomon's alliances as *primus inter pares* ("first among equals"), Chronicles views Solomon as ruling "over all the kings from the Euphrates...to the border of Egypt" (2 Chron 9:26). On the surface, the paragraph in Kings looks like a patchwork of mini-episodes designed to transition from the achievements in chapters 3-9 to Solomon's "sudden" downfall in chapter 11.[47] Deeper inspection, however, reveals a textured composition skillfully woven together around a single verb: "to raise up." This is not immediately obvious from the translations, but several synonyms for "ascendancy" anchor these paragraphs around (a) the activity of Hiram, (b) the journey of Pharaoh's daughter, and (c) the activity of Solomon himself.

The first of these is the verb *nasa'* ("to support, lift up")—this word appears in the opening phrase, Hiram "lifted" him (up). Although NIV and several other translations move it to the end of v. 11, MT places it at the beginning—Solomon's gift of Galilean cities is a *response* to Hiram's earlier gifts.[48] Hiram begins the transaction by "lifting up" aromatic woods and precious metals, but Solomon responds by giving him twenty Galilean cities (apparently one city for every year of his contract). Hiram feels cheated, though, because these cities fall far short of his expectations. In fact, he pronounces them "Cabul" (*kabûl*), a word intended to communicate his disgust.[49]

The second verb is `alâ` ("to go/come up"), as in the phrase, "Pharaoh's daughter came up" (v. 24). To situate this queen in her own palace is to coordinate her fate with Solomon's decision to rebuild the *millô'* ("supporting terraces," NIV). Yet exactly what the *millô'* is we cannot say. Some think it refers to a "filling" of the space between the eastern and western ridges of the Tyropoeon Valley. Others suggest that it refers to the "supporting terraces" upon which David and Solomon build their administrative offices (2 Sam 5:9; 1 Kings 9:24).[50] The point is subtle, but clear: even as Hiram "lifts up" Solomon, so Solomon "lifts up" Pharaoh's daughter—something for which he later pays dearly.

The third verb is the same as the second, `alâ` ("to go/come up"), but here it takes on cultic overtones: Solomon sacrifices burnt offerings—lit., "Solomon brought up the 'brought-up' offerings" (*he`elâ… `olôt*). Here cultic behavior parallels political behavior, a connection even foreigners like the Sabean recognize (1 Kings 10:4-5), so by repeating this terminology over and over, the paragraph as a whole stretches a semantic field into a literary skeleton. In other words, Solomon causes *many* things to "go up"—whole burnt-offerings, the goodwill of a powerful neighbor, the profit margins of his business ventures—but soon it will become clear that not everything which goes "up" stays "up."[51] Put another way, not everything Solomon "builds" stays built.

Yet kings love to build, and Solomon is the quintessential builder. He builds Yahweh's temple and adorns it lavishly. He builds his own palace and alongside it, another for his foreign queen. He rebuilds Gezer after its destruction. He builds cities in the desert, cities for storage, cities for chariots. He builds two hundred golden shields and hangs them in the Forest of Lebanon—as ostentatious a sign of wealth as one will find in the Bible. He builds ships to navigate overseas markets. To impress his visitors he builds a gold and ivory throne six steps high and adorns it with golden lions.[52] He builds a chariot business in order to buy products in vast quantities, then sell them for a tidy profit. Money is no object for this king/entrepreneur.

Intratextual Reflection

The question, of course, is how to interpret all of this theologically. How does the narrator feel about all this wealth? How does he want us to feel about it? When we examine Solomon's "edifice complex" against the other stories on the *pressure of foreigners* trajectory, the initial spin looks positive. Solomon's building activity is portrayed as a success symbol. Having pulled Israel out of its backwater existence, Solomon can now do business with the nations. No longer a confederacy of warring tribes and bickering city-states (like those reflected in the Amarna letters), Solomonic Israel has become a major player on the international stage, attracting attention far and wide (example: the Sabean queen).

So why do the wheels come off in the next chapter? Why does this episode look so much like the calm before the storm? Is there another ideology at work here, an ideology at odds with Solomonic expansionism? Put bluntly, is there a downside to materialistic wealth? The answer, of course, is yes, and for a number of reasons.

First, the Cabul incident shows how unaccounted wealth can corrode covenant relationships. Why else preserve a story like this if not to show what can happen to old friends who only *say* they "love" each other? Hiram feels he deserves more for his services than a few scraggly villages in Galilee, and the fact that the Chronicler reverses the flow of their transaction is a significant editorial comment. The point is debatable. Is Solomon behaving like a "philosopher king"[53] or a "typical oriental despot?"[54] Are his riches an example of "free, unsolicited grace,"[55] or are they a "trap" designed to "unbalance" him?[56] The Cabul incident shows us a side of Solomon we would rather not see, what Winston Churchill calls "the curse of plenty."[57]

Second, much of Solomon's wealth comes from "forced labor," and this is more than embarrassing for a nation whose alleged mission is to "bless all the nations of the earth" (Gen 12:4). The narrator tries to delimit this "forced labor" to non-Israelites in this retelling of it (vv. 20-22), but this only heightens Israel's missiological hypocrisy. Making slaves of the nations is the exact opposite of being a light to the nations. Is "forced labor" an example of "the justice of Solomon's rule,"[58] or is it the fulfillment of the tyranny forecast by Samuel (1 Sam 8:10-18)?[59] Jeremiah's prophecy against the petty potentate Jehoiakim uncomfortably applies to Solomon as well: "Woe to him who builds his palace by unrighteousness, his upper rooms by injustice, making his countrymen work for nothing, not paying them for their forced labor" (Jer 22:13).

On the one hand, Israel's mandate to subdue the nations is a direct outgrowth of the biblical Divine Warrior traditions.[60] The holy war traditions are not peripheral to Israel's ancient faith, nor is the institution of "forced labor" (Heb *mas*) peripheral to the holy war traditions. Yet there is no escaping the narrator's uneasiness about all this. In the New Testament, Paul says little to condemn slavery directly, yet the institution itself is obviously unacceptable—compare the contrasting messages in Eph 6:5-8 and Gal 3:28. In the Old Testament, Moses reminds Israel of its Egyptian slavery experience in order to warn them against enslaving others (Deut 15:15; 16:12). Evidently this narrator wants to emphasize what can happen between friends when "the covenant politics of justice are replaced by the politics of power."[61]

On the other hand, Israel also roots itself in the Divine Kinsman traditions,[62] and international Yahwism operates on a missiological imperative to "enlarge" itself (*hirbîtâ*, Isa 9:3)—not necessarily at the expense of its neighbors, but not at its own expense either. Israel's mission is both centrifugal and centripetal, and, "at its best moments, recognizes signs of deep solidarity with the non-elect nations."[63] The distinction has to do with the theological difference between salvation and blessing in the Bible: "God's saving action is a special turning towards a particular group…. God's blessing, on the other hand…is different from saving insofar as it is…a gradual process, as in the process of growing, maturing, and fading….The saving God is also the blessing God."[64] Thus, if the Church is to bless the nations, we must learn how to follow Israel "at its best moments." Cross-cultural evangelism is about erecting bridges, not walls, about inviting, not excluding others from the messianic banquet (Matt 8:10-12).

Christian history, of course, bears witness to a long list of failures in this regard (the Crusades, the Inquisition, the "troubles" in northern Ireland, the Gulf War…), yet Christians are not unique in their failure to live up to their ideals. Nor is Israel, as the present episode painfully shows.

Theological Reflection

Dow hits 10,000! Just a few short years ago I remember asking a friend if the Dow Jones Industrial Average would hit 5,000. He assured me that it would, and I didn't believe him. Now, in spite of a few downturns in the market, I'm eating my words. America's post-Cold War economy is doing some pretty amazing things. Awash in this prosperity, some Americans have become far more interested in celebrating this material success than sharing it with others. What impact is this new wealth having? How is it affecting our priorities, our behaviors, our ethical decision-making?

Years ago Ron Sider asked whether it was right to spend 13.9 billion (in 1967 dollars) on church construction projects when 2.5 billion people had not yet heard the name of Jesus Christ.[65] His question still needs raising, because today we hear much different questions, rooted in much different priorities. Today, for example, we're asked to believe that worship is our "greatest spiritual challenge,"[66] that gender is our "deepest problem."[67] How things have changed. Doubtless there are several factors behind this obvious shift from the centrifugal to the centripetal, but affluence certainly stands at the top of the list. Unchecked and unchallenged, wealth can turn believers relentlessly inward, leading us to become more interested in buying toys than, say, donating scholarships to needy seminarians. This text stands as a warning against such self-centeredness, and in several pointed ways.

First, our theologies of stewardship must be intentional and balanced. Like Solomon, affluent Christians today stand at constant risk of succumbing to the powerful lure of the "edifice complex." Jesus constantly preaches about this, commanding his disciples to learn how to live together in the kind of community where the extremes of wealth and poverty are minimized, not maximized. Christology and ecclesiology should govern our economics—not the other way around. One practical application of this is that new church construction—when it's absolutely necessary to build—needs to reflect positively on the Gospel, not negatively. When we build buildings, the way we do it should never focus more attention on ourselves than the mission of the Kingdom.[68]

Second, if and when we do build, we need to stop using "forced labor." That is, we need to do more than just give lip service to the biblical principle of Jubilee and its implications within the New Testament— e.g., the community of Jesus' disciples, or the first Church in Jerusalem, or Paul's teachings about Christian sacrifice.[69] Over and over again the New Testament admonishes believers to work together in ways which minimize the extremes of wealth and poverty, and we need to get serious in the way we apply these principles. Class-oriented Christ-clubs are an affront to the life and teachings of Jesus Christ.

Third, whenever we build, we cannot do it apart from a life lived in covenant. If we have to build church buildings, we cannot afford to cut ethical corners with contractors or inspectors or government officials. We need to cut covenants with integrity and good will and in the spirit of Christ. We need to ask what it means to be the Church of Jesus Christ at precisely this moment—from the selection of an architect, to the review of floor plans, to the supervision of construction, to the final furnishings.[70] Granted, we need to be careful that we don't become as "gullible as sheep" instead of "wise as serpents." In April 1990, for example, the Supreme Court decided in *Oregon Employment Division vs. Smith* (a case involving the construction of buildings for religious purposes) that any reasonable law should prevail even in cases where such laws hinder freedom of religion. We need to be aware of such rulings because they may signal the coming of a new age of restrictions on church construction. Yet whatever we do, and however we do it, we need to do it in such a way that the Hirams among us never have an excuse to cry, "Cabul!"

LEAVE THE LIGHT ON (1 Kings 11:14-43)

Solomon's idolatrous behavior triggers a response in which Yahweh dramatically "humbles" him (v. 39). From the narrator's perspective, this is a theological signal of things to come—it's just a matter of time before the kingdom will implode and everything for which Solomon has worked will come crashing down. For all his "wisdom" (v. 41), Solomon's sins are just too egregious to ignore. After all, he willfully violates Torah and ignores not one, but two heavenly warnings (1 Kings 3:1-15; 9:1-9). Yahweh's judgment, however, as the text repeatedly points out, is longitudinal and measured in cases like these. Instead of taking away the kingdom from Solomon, he chooses instead to take it away from his son—and even then he allows a remnant to survive "so that David my servant may always have a lamp before me in Jerusalem, the city where I chose to put my Name" (Deut 12:5, 11). The judgment process begins when Yahweh starts "raising up adversaries" against David's rebellious son.

The first of these adversaries is Hadad the Edomite. Except for what we have here, almost nothing is known about this exiled leader, yet this is probably Hadad III, a man whose only known accomplishment is his successful disruption of the caravan route linking Ezion Geber to Jerusalem.[71] The reason for his hatred of Solomon is the fact that Solomon's father kills his father, and he wants revenge (2 Sam 8:13). In point of fact, David is responsible for the killing of a vast number of Edomites (18,000), the only survivor being this same Hadad, a "young boy" at the time *(na`ar qatan)*. This situation obviously reflects a significant measure of unresolved international conflict, and the Egyptians are quick to take advantage of it.

According to the Amarna correspondence, in fact, Egypt is a perennial sanctuary for exiled Palestinian leaders. Pharaohs are always eager to provide people like Hadad with help and support.[72]

Alongside this challenge from the south, a second adversary arises in the north. Rezon siphons off soldiers from Hadadezer's army in the hill country northwest of Damascus, a region called Zobah. The context behind this situation again goes back to the time of David, particularly his campaign against this same Hadadezer.[73] David marches all the way to the Euphrates to subdue the Syrians (2 Sam 8:3-6), then seeks redress soon after against the Ammonites for using Syrian mercenaries against Israel (10:6-19). Both campaigns involve Syrians from the region of Zobah, north of Damascus, and both involve this warlord Hadadezer. Rezon takes advantage of this situation to harass Solomon.

Third, Jeroboam's rebellion parallels both of these situations.[74] Like Hadad, Jeroboam goes into Egyptian exile to escape the wrath of a Hebrew king. And like Rezon, he begins his military career fighting against his own master. With Jeroboam, however, the narrator begins a complex narrative which continues on into the next several chapters. He describes Jeroboam, on the one hand, as a "man of standing" (*gibbôr hayil*). On the other hand, he describes him as one of Israel's most wicked kings, an assessment later emphasized by the rabbis: "Jeroboam (means) 'one who debases the nation' (*shyrb` `m*). Another meaning is 'one who foments strife in the nation' (*sh`sh mrybh b`m*). Another explanation is 'one who causes strife (*sh`sh mrybh*) between Israel and their heavenly father'" (*b. Sanh.* 101b). Faced with these diverging interpretations, Rabbi Johanan attempts the following harmonization: "Why did Jeroboam deserve to be king? Because he reproved Solomon. And why was he punished? Because he reproved him publicly (*brbym*, lit., 'among many,' *b. Sanh.* 101b)."

Recent scholars have imagined the prophet who confronts Jeroboam, Ahijah, as the representative of a priestly faction in Shiloh who supports Jeroboam against the Davidic monarchy—a later editor, one theory suggests, then de-emphasizes Jeroboam's positive attributes as the tradition is handed down.[75] Others see Ahijah as a typical northern prophet on the periphery of the Jerusalem regime. Thus Jeroboam comes to power not by God's will, but by this faction's desperation to find something better than Rehoboam.[76] Carl Evans more plausibly suggests that Jeroboam is a particular type of character, one common to many ancient Near Eastern traditions:

The Jeroboam of tradition is Israel's historiographical counterpart to the Naram-Sin of Mesopotamia's *Unheilsherrscher* ("condemned leader") traditions....In both cases the traditions emphasize the ruler's misfortune or condemnation and focus on a general calamity that overtakes the dynasty and nation, claiming that all is the result of certain religious offenses on the part of the king.[77]

Whatever the possibilities, the Jeroboam story is a fascinating amalgamation of divine will confronting human willfulness. It opens with Jeroboam and Ahijah "accidentally" bumping into one another outside the walls of Jerusalem. Urged by Yahweh, Ahijah takes off his cloak and starts tearing it to pieces, addressing Jeroboam via the prophetic message-formula, "Thus says Yahweh" (*kô 'amar yhwh*)—the first time this formula occurs in the Bible. When Ahijah invites Jeroboam to take ten of the twelve pieces of cloak, this ritual cements Jeroboam's leadership over the ten tribes of northern Israel. Thus, when the kingdom splits, it doesn't split down the middle. Instead, Jeroboam walks away with four-fifths of Israel in his calloused hands.

Intratextual Reflection

In light of the context, particularly the previous paragraph on Solomon's wives, this episode paints a horrid picture of Solomon's legacy. Like the floodwaters in Genesis, erupting from both above and below (Gen 7:11-12), Solomon's problems erupt from both within (wives and gods) and without (adversaries), and this leads us to the following insights.

First, this God will, if necessary, send adversaries. The word for "adversary" is *satan*, a word which later carries enormous freight in Judaism and Christianity. Here the word is not capitalized, however, because a *satan* is simply an "adversary," someone who accuses someone else of evil or malfeasance, usually in a judicial context.[78] Several times it appears in the Old Testament to refer to both celestial and terrestrial adversaries. When Yahweh gives another *satan* permission to harass another biblical leader (Job), the reasons given there are not nearly so clear as the reasons given here. Obviously this God sends adversaries to whomever he wants whenever he wants.

Second, Yahweh makes the same dynastic promises to Jeroboam that he makes to Solomon. Unlike most gods, Yahweh does not consider himself bound to the traditions and customs of Israel, and the readiness with which he is willing to start over can be a little startling, to say the least, particularly to readers unfamiliar with the biblical creation traditions. To Moses, for example, he says, "I have seen these people, and they are a stiff-necked people. Now leave me alone so that my anger may burn against them and that I may destroy them. Then I will make you into a great nation" (Exod 32:9-10). When Saul disobeys God in the Amalek affair, he immediately sends Samuel to anoint a replacement (1 Sam 15-16)—so here he responds in a similar way, rejecting Solomon's apostasies by offering his rival Jeroboam the kingdom. Yahweh is not bound by nationalistic desire, but by his creative will.

Third, this God always "leaves a light on," even when things look their bleakest. Paul reiterates this truth to the Corinthian church after he learns that a disciple is living immorally with his father's wife. Peeved that several believers have become proud of such behavior (Gk *pephusimenoi*, lit., "puffed up"), he demands that they "hand over this man to the Adversary" (Gk *tô satanâ*, 1 Cor 5:5—note the direct article). Yahweh is appalled at Solomon's behavior, yet he saves "one tribe so that David my servant may always have a lamp before me in Jerusalem." This lamp theology is significant because it shows (a) that this God keeps his promises, (b) that this God takes reverence for the Name seriously, yet (c) that God has more faith in his creation than do most of his creatures.[79]

Theological Reflection

How is it appropriate to apply this message about adversaries? Are there ever times when our idolatries provoke the same sort of response from God that Solomon's idolatries provoke? Putting the question another way, what is the difference between prophetic confrontation and adversarial judgment, and how can we tell the difference between the two?

Once I applied to a doctoral program at a prestigious graduate school, and had all but convinced myself that I would be accepted. I knew I could do the work. I knew I could learn the languages and master the mounds of material required. In my prayers I even had the audacity to thank the Lord in advance for smoothing the way with the administrators and other decision-makers handling my application. Yet when the days dragged by with no response I began to wonder whether God wanted me to do something else. Self-doubt and self-recrimination began buzzing around in the back of my mind. Like annoying gnats I couldn't seem to swat them away. I couldn't concentrate on my work. The children got on my nerves. My wife didn't dare ask me whether the mail had come that day or not.

Then the letter came. I pulled it from the mailbox and tore it open. Reading quickly, my heart jumped into my throat as my eyes fell to the formulaic words: 'unfortunately, we have far too many applicants for the limited number of candidates we can accept...." It was a rejection letter—the first one I'd ever received in my life. I couldn't believe it! For what seemed an eternity, I just stood there beside the mailbox reading and re-reading this letter as if somehow the very act of reading would change the words on the page.

That letter was an "adversary." I have difficulty accepting the possibility that this was not God's not-so-subtle way of reminding me that he was in control of the future, not me. There have been other adversaries since—often I've been too blind to see them as well—and over the course of a ministry I have seen God use them in rather ingenious ways to wrench out of my fisted hands the idols I think I need.

LIKE FATHERS, LIKE SONS (2 Kings 8:7-29)

Dynastic succession is a difficult thing. So disastrous is David's attempt at it, biblical historians devote several chapters to explaining why things turn out the way they do (2 Sam 9-1 Kings 2).[80] Solomon's problems with Jeroboam are not unique. In Anatolia, for example, a king named Awarku empowers one of his servants (a man named Azitiwada) who, like Joseph, fills the nation's granaries and preserves it from famine and pestilence, eventually becoming king in the process.[81] In Persia, the king Astyages cannot pass on his powers to his son because Cyrus, a hitherto loyal vassal, suddenly seizes the country in a well-orchestrated coup.[82] Similar intrigues occur in the annals of Greek and Roman history.

The story here, however, offers a new twist on an old theme—most remarkably, a prophet gets directly involved in the messy political process. Here a Syrian usurper named Hazael murders his master and seizes his master's throne, but only after becoming empowered by a Yahweh prophet.[83] Neither Solomon's nor Ahab's international intrigues go nearly this far, yet Elisha jumps headlong into internal Syrian politics. Why? What business does a Yahweh prophet have in such a world? On the surface Elisha's plan looks deceptively simple: (a) he prophesies Hazael's rise to power; (b) the Omrides quickly react; (c) the Omrides become mired down in a war they can't win; and (d) Jehu destroys the Omrides while they're preoccupied with Syria.

To use a sports metaphor, Elisha executes the "pick and roll." In basketball, this is when two offensive players work together to outmaneuver a single defensive player. One offensive player stands in the way of his opponent—he "sets the pick"—while the player with the ball uses him as a human shield. This forces the defensive player to make a decision, and when he does, the offensive player "setting the pick" "rolls" away toward the basket, receives the pass from his teammate, and scores. In other words, Elisha doesn't just sit the bench and watch the game while the Omrides pound the prophets into submission. He goes to Damascus and "sets the pick." He enlists Syria's aid because *this* is what it's going to take to finish the job begun at Mt. Carmel.

True, Hazael and Jehu are ambitious usurpers, yet Coach Yahweh knows how to handle cocky young men. Politically this means that he will do whatever it takes to defend his team (1 Kings 19:15). Theologically it means that Elisha's God can and will use any means at his disposal to accomplish his goals—even human ambition and ethnic hatred. The smell of rebellion is thick in this text. Hazael assassinates Ben-Hadad, his "father."[84] Jehoshaphat's son, Jehoram, "does evil in the eyes of Yahweh" (according to the Chronicler, he assassinates his siblings, 2 Chron 21:4), and from this chaos the narrator paints a dreary portrait of "sons" acting very much like their "fathers." Like Ahab, Joram tries once again to take Ramoth Gilead. Like Ben-Hadad, Hazael finds himself on the defensive before yet another Hebrew army. Because of these parallels, some propose collapsing these events into one single event,[85] but this is literarily myopic.[86] Repeating these themes over and over again not only cements their contours into forgetful minds, but also opens them up to ever-deeper interpretation. Having the "sons" mimic the "fathers" is a conscious narrative invitation to examine these themes and characters in depth and detail.

First, Ahab's ghost practically haunts this text. Both of these Judahite kings, Jehoram and Ahaziah, marry "daughters of Ahab," and the narrator is unflinching in his belief that these marriages are unholy. Like their "father" (Ahab), the "sons" (Joram, Ahaziah) choose wives who stand opposed to everything Mosaic, covenantal and Yahwistic. Just as Ahab marries Jezebel, so Joram and Ahaziah marry Omride idolaters.

Second, like the fathers, the sons underestimate the determination of their neighbors. Moab, Edom, and Aram are not going to go away, yet these adolescents have no real strategy for dealing with them—much less the Assyrian threat beginning to cloud the horizon. So they lurch from crisis to crisis, offering poorly-thought-out, *ad hoc* reactions to the challenges before them. Where Solomon at least dialogues with his neighbors about international affairs, these boy-kings turn quasi-isolationist. Instead of exporting Yahweh's salvation to the nations, these kings become a hypodermic needle for the Baal-virus.

Third, like *his* "father" (Elijah),[87] Elisha has to do something pretty distasteful. He has to hold his nose and go to the uncircumcised Syrians for help against his own people. This becomes clear in his conversation with Hazael, particularly at the moment when the prophet predicts Ben-Hadad's assassination. It's a revealing moment. Elisha finally and suddenly realizes the seriousness of Yahweh's intentions, and how much it's going to cost to put them into action. "What's the matter?," Hazael asks, and Elisha prophesies, "You will set fire to their fortified places, kill their young men with the sword, dash their little children to the ground, and rip open their pregnant women" (2 Kings 10:33).[88] In other words, the time for negotiation is over. From now on there will be no more warnings. No more miracles. No more mountain-top contests. The only way to save Israel now is radical surgery. Even as Naaman's leprosy forces him out of Damascus, so Israel's "leprosy" now forces Elisha into Damascus. Omride Baalism is threatening to snuff out the very spirit of Yahwism, and Yahweh will never allow this to happen.

Intratextual Reflection

This episode opens the door to a grisly chapter in Israel's history. On the *pressure of foreigners* trajectory it represents something of a turning point, because up to now Yahweh has refrained from using foreigners against his own people in the book of Kings (except for those who harass Solomon in 1 Kings 11). Assyria has not yet been allowed to make a move, for example, nor has Babylon or Egypt or the peoples of Anatolia. Now Yahweh removes his protection. He picks up these, his political instruments, and goes to work to save his people. This surgery will be painful, and will involve a large variety of medical tools—hammers, saws, scalpels, scissors (Syria, Assyria, Egypt, Babylon). Syria is going to play the role of "prep nurse." Assyria is going to play the role of "surgeon." Babylon is going to play the role of "post-op surgeon," carefully and competently addressing the problems caused by Jerusalem's lingering malignancies. Yet rather than fixate on the reasons behind Ben-Hadad's illness or the morality of Elisha's actions,[89] the intratextual context forces us to ask a different set of questions: "Why is it necessary for Yahweh to use foreign nations at all against Israel? Why is he abandoning the 'outpatient procedures' previously employed? How is Israel going to survive this radical theo-ectomy?

For these questions there are no easy answers, but when we try to examine them apart from their intratextual context, we get ourselves into a situation in which there are no answers. One reader, for example, ignoring the intratextual context altogether, wonders whether the gist of this history has only to do with Yahweh's "narcissism": "It's difficult being the son of a powerful, famous father like Yahweh. Call it the 'Frank Sinatra Jr. complex....Yahweh's demand for total love is an example of enforced idealization....Yahweh uses humiliation as a punishment tool....Yahweh is not a narcissist because he is absolute and self-sufficient; he is a narcissist precisely because he is *not* self-sufficient."[90] Such are the options to which students will turn when we willfully ignore or marginalize the intratextual context, or, to continue the metaphor, when we willfully focus only on the character of the surgeon to the exclusion of the reasons for the surgery.

Theological Reflection
Subject: Dead Horse[91]

When a Sioux discovers that his horse has died, he dismounts and walks away. Other "tribes" offer a variety of different responses:

1. Buy a stronger whip.
2. Change riders.
3. Threaten the horse with termination.
4. Appoint a committee to study the dead horse.
5. Arrange to visit other countries to see how others ride dead horses.
6. Lower the standards so that dead horses can be included.
7. Re-classify the dead horse as "living impaired."
8. Hire an outside contractor to teach on "How to Ride a Dead Horse."
9. Harness several dead horses together to increase their speed.
10. Provide additional funding and/or training to increase the dead horse's performance.
11. Do a productivity study to see if lighter riders would improve the dead horse's performance.
12. Declare that as the dead horse does not have to be fed, it is less costly, carries lower overhead, and therefore contributes substantially more to the economy than other horses.
13. Re-write the expected performance requirements for all horses.
14. Promote the dead horse to a supervisory position.

Who cannot relate to this silly illustration? We work as hard as we can "within the system" only to wake up one morning and discover, suddenly, that the horse upon which we've been riding all these years is as dead as a doornail. We discover one day that the system in which we've been investing our lives is complacent, or incompetent, or corrupt. Like Elisha, this makes us weep, but often it also makes us ask questions we would not otherwise ask. "Do I (a) stay within the system, (b) leave the system, or (c) try to create a new system?" Should I leave the denomination in which I've been raised, for example, just because I can find a few dead horses in it? Is God's Kingdom bigger than my denomination?

Thinking outside the system is sometimes necessary to fix the system. If complacent leaders continue to turn a blind eye to the legitimate problems facing Israel, Old or New (Gal 6:6), and continue to surrender its institutions to the loudest voice or biggest pocketbook, then maybe it's time to call in a new play. Maybe it's time for the "pick and roll." Why? Because the "sons" are not destined to repeat the mistakes of the "fathers"—and for several reasons.

First, it is indeed possible and sometimes necessary to go outside the system to fix the system. We may not have to go all the way to "Damascus"—we may just have to move to another state. We may not have to move geographically, just vocationally. We may decide to move from the pastorate to the classroom, or the classroom to the mission field. For those who can see it, "dead horses" are opportunities to begin a new writing ministry, or a ministry to senior adults, or a hospice chaplaincy, or a Young Life program. The point is that there's no need to leave "the system" just because a few "Omrides" have gotten themselves temporarily into positions of authority and control. Sometimes the best thing to do with a dead horse is to dismount and start looking for a live one.

Second, none of us is predestined to repeat the mistakes of our "fathers." Fatalism is not a biblical teaching. Certainly we can learn from our mentors' mistakes, but in no way are we predestined to repeat them. With a little practice, we too can learn how to execute the "pick and roll." Yet we need to be careful. Anne David urges pastors, especially, to be careful because there's a difference, in her mind, between "pastoral burnout" and "compassion fatigue."[92] Pastoral burnout is more vertical than horizontal. Compassion fatigue is more horizontal than vertical, and is more easily minimized by (a) identifying our gifts and resources, (b) matching these gifts and resources with the needs of other believers, (c) serving out of gratitude instead of compulsion, and (d) maintaining appropriate boundaries.[93]

Third, we can realize that God is always at work everywhere in the world. God doesn't just work through Israel—he works through *tâ ethnê* too (Gk "the nations"). When Elisha learns that he has to go to Damascus and anoint Hazael, he obeys without question. He may not like it, and he may not even understand it, but he obeys God. Whether Yahweh stops Baalism through an Israelite prophet or a Syrian king is relatively unimportant. What's more important is that Baalism be stopped. The Kingdom is more important than Joram's needs or Ahaziah's happiness or Elisha's job satisfaction or my puny human longings for power and prestige. Elisha goes to Damascus to obey Yahweh, not worship Rimmon (2 Kings 5:18).

TAKEOVER TARGET (2 Kings 14:23-29; 15:8-31; 17:1-6)

This section is tough reading because here Yahweh appears to abandon his people to a cruel fate. Whether this is the case or not, the books of Hosea, Amos, and Isaiah give us much more information about this period of history. Hosea, for example, focuses on Yahweh's agony over Ephraim's idolatries (Hos 11:7-9) and their incessant assassination plots (4:6). Amos focuses on God's anger at those who take bribes, steal grain, stack the courts, and humiliate the poor (Amos 5:12). Yahweh assures Ahaz (through Isaiah) that Pekah's attempts to partner with the Syrians is much ado about nothing (Isa 7:7). In many ways this part of Kings looks very much like the Gospel passion narrative. In many ways Christ's crucifixion profoundly parallels Samaria's destruction.[94]

Israel is prosperous under Jeroboam II, but it's a hollow prosperity, empty and shallow. Assyria will shortly arrive and throw Samaria into exile. Opinions are divided over exactly how long it takes Samaria's ship to sink, but that this ship *does* sink is not open to serious disagreement. Political pressure, taxation, invasion, siege, destruction, exile—all the strands of the international noose have wound their way around Israel's pampered neck, and Assyria is more than willing to pull the cord and watch her suffocate. The narrator theologically explains Israel's death in a way that looks like the way apostolic theologians try to explain the Cross. In short: "This is what sin can do. This is how much sin costs."[95]

Like the Titanic, Israel hits an iceberg, and Jeroboam, Zechariah, Shallum, Menahem, Pekahiah, Pekah, and Hoshea all make sure that the party stays lively on the upper decks, even as she goes down by the head. Some of these kings do more damage than others, yet all cope with life in the shadowlands. All have to cope with conspiracy, invasion, oppression—the fleeting shadow of promised foreign aid. Jeroboam II is well-known from the books of Amos and Hosea. Jonah the prophet we know from the book bearing his name, though this is the only place in Scripture where Jonah and Jeroboam historically connect.[96] Unlike the portrayal in the book of Jonah, here the prophet Jonah inspires his people. In fact, he inspires Jeroboam to expand his empire to borders reminiscent of the golden age of David. Yet Jeroboam's reign favors only the affluent. In contrast to the time of David, this is Israel's "gilded age," a time when comfortable Baalism too often substitutes for faithful Yahwism (Hos 2:1-8), when consumption becomes conspicuous (6:1-7), when the gap between rich and poor grows into a yawing canyon.

The kings in this period look much like broken chessmen—their paint chipped, their identities ambiguous, their once-proud offices worn down by wear. One of these kings reigns forty-one years (Jeroboam II), another a mere six months (Zechariah). Several conspire against their predecessors, and some are even assassinated. Instead of preparing for the future and building up their defenses, they allow Israel to grow fat. Instead of working hard and staying sober, they allow their people to lounge on ivory couches and guzzle wine in bowls (Amos 6:6). Israel hires herself out to any god who will have her, even paying them to fornicate with her (Hos 2:5-8). Unwilling to give up her addictions, Israel turns into a "silly dove," a "cake half turned," an "unfaithful wife," a "Baal-lipped whore," a "stubborn heifer," a "morning mist," a "band of marauders," a "burning oven," a "faulty bow," a "headless stalk," a "lost donkey," a "floating twig," a "wind-gulper," a "heel-grabber," a "calf-idol kisser."[97]

But Yahweh still cares for his people. Even though Baalism corrupts Israel to the core, to the point that foreign exile is the only way to save her, Yahweh still cares for his people. Even though Israel commits adultery with many lovers in the international marketplace, Yahweh still loves his people. He sees her bitter suffering, and he sees no shepherd to help her, so God himself picks up the mantle of leadership. By means of the prophet Jonah he encourages Jeroboam II to restore Israel's quasi-Davidic boundaries. He makes sure, in the middle of Israel's drunkenness, to find her a designated driver. He makes sure to keep a Jehu descendant on the throne of Israel to the fourth generation. Yahweh never completely abandons his people.

Yet alongside divine grace comes divine judgment. Menahem, for example, doesn't simply besiege the northern village of Tiphsah—he rips open the bellies of its pregnant women and viciously slaughters them. This foreshadows the even greater violence yet to come. Assyria pulls its armies up to the border of Ephraim, and Israel's landowners put up a tremendous amount of cash to buy them off. This foreshadows the economic violence yet to come. Tiglath-Pileser starts picking off the towns of Ijon, Abel Beth Maacah, Janoah, Kedesh, Hazor, Gilead and Galilee, and all Hoshea can do in response is plan more assassination plots. This foreshadows the "fiddling-while-Rome-burns" mentality yet to come (later painfully documented by the prophet Jeremiah). Shalmaneser hears that Hoshea has stopped paying tribute, but he doesn't schedule an arbitration hearing—he lays siege to the city. Three years later he captures Samaria and throws its king into prison. Forcibly he marches Samaria's inhabitants far away into foreign-sounding places like Gozan and Halah. Yahweh will use this violence to judge his people and cleanse his sanctuaries.

Intratextual Reflection
With this episode the *pressure of foreigners* trajectory shifts into high gear. Solomon's earlier treaty with Hiram may look innocent, but from this narrator's perspective it can only lead here. Israel's earlier political and religious alliances may look neutral (Baal-Melqart, Baal-Zebub, Ben-Hadad, Egyptian trade, Hazael), but from a prophetic perspective these relationships merely pave the way for Phoenician "fornication," Syrian "adultery," and Assyrian "rape." Israel has become a takeover target—too plump to ignore, too fat to resist, too ignorant to understand, too silly to care. What does the narrator want us to learn from this tragedy?

First, prosperous people do not readily change. Why should they? It doesn't matter whether the rest of the world is in distress—if my world is prosperous, why should I care about yours? Wealth insulates. Wealth promises more than it delivers. Wealth cuts people off from their neighbors. Jesus says it's hard for a rich man to enter the Kingdom (Matt 19:24), and this text helps to explain why, at a time when baby-boomers are inheriting more money than ever before in history, church members still give less than 3% of their income to the work of the Church.[98] It helps to explain why Christian leaders are leaning more and more on secular marketing techniques in order to compete for this paltry 3%. It explains why seminary presidents are having to abandon their roles as pastor-theologians to become professional beggars.[99] No, it may not be appropriate simply to compare America to the ancient city of Gomorrah,[100] but American believers have a lot to learn from texts like these.

Why do our missionaries have to beg for support when the wealth indices are shooting off the charts? Why do our pastors have to beg for volunteers when Western believers have more leisure time than ever before? Douglas John Hall has a response to these questions, and he dares to put it in explicitly theological language: "Stewardship, rightly conceived, constitutes a direct confrontation with the image of the human (*imago hominis*) by which we are enthralled."[101] Though we are the wealthiest nation on earth, we are also one of the most materialistic.

And this means, second, that God will allow us to reap what we sow. If we want to worship work, he'll let us become workaholics. If we want to worship sex, he'll let us become sex addicts. If we want to worship money, he'll let us become misers. If we want to worship leisure, he'll let us become dilettantes. If we want to worship denominational tradition, he'll let us worship that too—even as it goes down by the head. This God allows believers to reap what they sow, even if it means destruction and exile.

Third, Baalized believers make easy takeover targets. Whether we want to admit it or not, contemporary American culture is in the midst of urban gridlock, violent crime, breakdown of communal vision, loss of personal dignity, and even the loss of personal identity. In response to these problems, religious groups of all stripes are competing frantically for ways to reach "seekers," inventing newer and ever-more-creative spiritualities to jump-start their bureaucracies. Some of these methods are leading them to some embarrassingly pagan theological positions. Fundamentalism, liberalism, megachurch numerolatry, "worshiptainment," and several other counterfeit Christianities are competing for customers. Where are the prophets we need to warn us about these newer, subtler Baals?

Theological Reflection

Well, I work with some of them every day. Many of my colleagues and students are making tremendous sacrifices to teach and preach and write and serve the Lord in any way they can. "Samaria" may be falling to its doom somewhere, but not where I work. Instead I see believers daring to take a stand and swim if necessary against the "Assyrian tide." Mandy is one of them.[102] Unable to have children of her own, Mandy and her husband went to Eastern Europe to adopt two children, a brother and sister from Romania. On the flight home, both of these children tragically died in an airplane crash, and like Paul, this made Mandy "hard pressed on every side, but not crushed; perplexed, but not in despair; persecuted, but not abandoned; struck down, but not destroyed" (2 Cor 4:8). It took her a long time to get over it, but out of this tragedy came her decision to attend seminary, largely because she wants to help prepare others to face their own griefs by learning how to navigate around the Baals of codependence and independence.

Byung-Kim is another example.[103] The pride of his family, Byung-Kim came to the United States to attend graduate school, but while working on his PhD, a Christian friend invited him to a Bible study, and soon afterwards he became a Christian. The change in his life made him wonder whether to pursue a teaching career or full-time ministry, and he struggled with the decision for a long time. After graduation, teaching opportunities came pouring in after he became Dr. Byung-Kim. In fact, one university president offered him a tenure-track position in his homeland, but he turned it down. Instead of taking a teaching position in his country's most famous university, he enrolled in seminary and raised the support necessary to work in a parachurch organization devoted to helping college students find Christ.

Not every believer is a takeover target.

FROM THE FRYING PAN INTO THE FIRE
(2 Kings 15:1-6; 32-38; 16:1-20)

While Samaria dances on the decks of the Titanic, Judah prepares her sailboat for the water. Azariah (Uzziah), like Asa, begins his reign well, but soon he has to drop out of the race. Struck down by leprosy, he turns his throne over to his son, who comes to power at the relatively mature age of twenty-five (old by Judahite standards!). The place to which he retires is called a "house of freedom" (*bêt hahopshît*), but this reference may be a subtle antithetical parallel to Hoshea's "house of confinement" (*bêt kele*, 2 Kings 17:4). Both houses, in other words, are prisons. The Chronicler says that Azariah contracts leprosy because of his pride (2 Chron 26:16). That is, after he becomes successful in destroying armies and reclaiming seaports, he unwisely decides to offer incense in the Temple itself, attempting by this foolish act to "conquer" the priesthood just like he conquers the Philistines. Like Saul (1 Sam 13:9-15), this act alienates the priesthood, and this is how the Chronicler explains Yahweh's decision to strike him with leprosy.

Jotham is a transitional figure—in addition to doing what is right in the eyes of Yahweh, all we know about him is (a) that he rebuilds the Upper Gate of the temple of Yahweh, and (b) that he suffers from the development of yet another anti-Assyrian coalition, this one spearheaded by Rezin (of Damascus) and Pekah (of Samaria). Of course, this is not the first anti-Assyrian coalition to form in Syria-Palestine. From the annals of Shalmeneser III, we know of several other coalitions with whom Israel and Damascus partner in their attempts to fend off the Assyrians.[104]

Yet this biblical and extra-biblical evidence suggests that Judah and Israel are going through a confusing period in which they oscillate back-and-forth, especially in their attitudes toward foreigners. From Shalmeneser's famous "black obelisk," we know that Jehu pays tribute to Assyria as early as 840 BC (*ANET* 280), just after purging Israel of the remaining Omrides. We know from the Zakkur inscription that the Syrian Bir-Hadad leads a coalition comprised of Arpad and Sam'al (and several other Aramean cities) against Zakkur of Hamath (*ANET* 655–56). Zakkur escapes, barely, but the negative fate of his enemies—Arpad and Sam'al—suggests that Assyria is playing a behind-the-scenes role already. Further, the treaty between Ashur-nirari V (754-746 BC) and Mati'ilu of Arpad (*ANET* 532-33) suggests that Mati'ilu does what Ahaz does—solicit Assyrian aid out of fear of his neighbors. In short, by 800 BC Israel is partnering with Assyria against Damascus, and when exactly it shifts back to an anti-Assyrian stance is difficult to say (2 Kings 16:5).[105]

At any rate, Ahaz assumes power at the age of twenty, but participates in behavior so detestable it makes kings like Jeroboam son of Nebat and Ahab son of Omri look "righteous" by comparison. Ahaz does something even these kings won't—"pass his son through the fire," a ritual associated with Molech, a Transjordanian god of the netherworld (2 Kings 23:10).[106] Several theories try to explain Ahaz's attraction to this deity. Perhaps he wants to identify more closely with non-Yahwist Canaanites. Perhaps he wants to please the Syrians—in 2 Chron 28:23 Ahaz sacrifices to honor "the gods of Damascus."[107]

In the final analysis, we simply don't know why anybody would want to practice child sacrifice, much less a Hebrew king raised on the Mosaic Torah. What we do know is that this narrator is aghast by what he sees. Ahaz abandons the Davidic tradition of covenant loyalty for the way of the kings of Israel. Ahaz is a spiritual jellyfish, a leader who "shakes as the trees of the forest are shaken by the wind" (Isa 7:2). Calvin calls him a "wicked hypocrite."[108] Jerome accuses him of abandoning anything approximating real "faith,"[109] and Spurgeon refers to him as "the infidel king."[110]

In addition, Ahaz follows the "detestable ways of the nations" (*tô`abôt haggôyim*), and it's important to note that "child sacrifice" and "detestable" often appear together as a word-pair in the deuteronomic code: "You must not worship Yahweh your God in their way, because in worshiping their gods, they do all kinds of detestable things Yahweh hates. They even burn their sons and daughters in the fire as sacrifices to their gods" (Deut 12:31). Ahaz doesn't look as bad as Mesha (another king who practices child sacrifice; 2 Kings 3:27), but all Mesha does is offer a single holocaust-offering (`ôlâ`) in the midst of a crisis. Ahaz regularly sacrifices children as part of his religious devotion to Moloch.[111]

Third, he offers sacrifices and burns incense at the high places, a familiar condemnation to which the narrator adds, "on the hilltops and under every spreading tree." This language connects Ahaz's behavior to that of Rehoboam, another southern king with more money than sense. In northern Israel, the Elijah-Elisha traditions portray the Baal-Yahweh conflict as public contests, but Judah's idolatry is more private and secretive, and Judahite sources are far less forthcoming about the delicate matter of royal involvement. A hoary populism constantly bubbles beneath the surface of Judahite Yahwism, eventually becoming the conduit for old Canaanite beliefs which become officialized in the Jerusalem cult. Most scholars think (a) that populist religion is a constant irritant to priestly and prophetic Yahwism, and (b) that Ahaz is one of its earliest promoters.[112]

Fourth, Ahaz turns to Assyria not just for military aid, but for religious leadership. This is a very different picture from the one in Chronicles. In Chronicles, Syria and Israel don't just threaten, they ravage Judah. Pekah's rampage is so successful, in fact, fully 120,000 Judahite soldiers fall in a single day—all because Judah forsakes Yahweh, the God of their fathers (2 Chron 28:6). Pekah takes so many prisoners (200,000 wives, sons, and daughters) that a prophet named Oded has to tell him to send some of them back (28:7-11). Ahaz then responds to Pekah's attack by looting the Temple and locking its doors, thereby forcing the Judahites under his control to worship at the high places (28:24-25). Kings sidesteps all this, focusing instead on Ahaz's trip to Damascus, where he finds himself smitten by an altar he sees there. Whether this altar is Syrian or Assyrian is not known, but we do know (a) that he has an exact copy made for the Temple in Jerusalem; (b) that he incorporates it alongside the Solomonic bronze altar in a new "division of labor"; and (c) that he uses it to shift the balance of priestly power in Jerusalem.

Along with this foreign altar Ahaz changes a few other things in the Temple. He changes the look and position of the bronze altar (moved north), the bronze Sea (new pedestal), the Sabbath canopy (removed), and the royal entryway (removed in deference to the king of Assyria). The narrative quickly passes over these changes, but all of this is historically significant. How ironic it is that Chronicles has Yahweh striking Azariah down for committing "acts of impurity" (`ma`al`), while in Kings Azariah's son commits even greater priestly sins.

Intratextual Reflection

Ahaz wrestles with Assyria the way Ahab wrestles with Syria, the way Solomon wrestles with Phoenicia, the way Josiah wrestles with Egypt. Situating this conflict in its intratextual context makes it possible for us to examine it with greater precision and greater perspective, and when we do, one of the first things we notice is how power can shift, and shift quickly. It happens all the time. Pastors come and go. Presidents come and go. Whole civilizations come and go. Older institutions constantly mutate and evolve into newer ones. Like Ahaz, many bright, young believers are constantly looking for new altars upon which to seek guidance. Not all are as impressionable as Ahaz, of course, and certainly not all of the changes they suggest are unhealthy. But subtle are the pressures today to make us conform to the Dominant Reality instead of the Christian Faith.[113] As Screwtape puts it to Wormwood, the Devil does not want anyone to suspect "that [we] are now, however slowly, heading right away from the sun on a line which will carry [us] into the cold and dark of utmost space." No, he wants people to believe that "as long as [we] retain externally the habits of a Christian, [we] can still be made to think of [ourselves] as [people] who have adopted a few new friends and amusements, but whose spiritual state is much the same as it was."[114]

Second, some believers, like Ahaz, are trapped in a religious double-bind. Publicly, we do our jobs and go about our business—plumbing or preaching, teaching or painting, counseling or managing. Privately, though, there's often a gap between what we say and what we do. Not to sound too preachy, but are the detestable ways of the nations worming their way onto our television screens and our cinema screens and our computer monitors? Do we say one thing and do another? In some families, for example, abuse is rampant.[115] In some denominations, whole ministries are dedicated to dealing with the growing gap between the public and private spheres of the Church. One need only look at the long parade of leadership scandals now consuming our pastors to realize that Jesus' advice is more relevant than ever: "First clean the inside!" (Matt 23:26).

Third, when coalitions of enemies start putting us under pressure, where do we go for help? Do we go to Scripture? Do we go to wise counsel? Do we prostrate ourselves before the Lord in prayer and fasting? Do we, like Josiah, buckle down and return to Torah, even if it's been quite a while since we've looked there for help? Or do we, like Ahaz, run straight to the "Assyrians?" Do we look for the biggest and most powerful "tyrant" (biggest controversy, latest fad), throw ourselves on the ground and proclaim, "I am your vassal?"

Theological Reflection

Several areas of application come to mind as we reflect on these "Ahaz questions." Marriage, for example, is under attack from so many quarters today, we've simply grown numb to the onslaught. We've heard so many sermons about marriage from so many angles, we're just tired of hearing about it. We know the depressing statistics. We know what infidelity and divorce is doing to our kids. We know that children of divorce, in spite of vacuous populist arguments to the contrary, have a much harder life than children from two-parent families.[116] We know that the "Assyrians" are on our doorsteps, and we know what they want. Should we cave in to them? Should we copy their altars?

Or should we, as Isaiah counsels, "Be careful. Keep calm. Don't be afraid. Don't lose heart" (Isa 7:4). In spite of the statistics, in spite of the numbness, can we not still (a) strengthen the one-out-of-two marriages which don't end in divorce, and (b) find more effective ways to help divorced people find healing? The grief stages may appear in different people with varying degrees of intensity, but there is no mistaking what they generally are: the loss of the dream of marriage, the loss of intimacy, the loss of physical accessibility, the loss of being in a parental role, the loss of a certain legal standing, the loss of money and property, the loss of community, the loss of a sense of attachment.[117] Isaiah's advice therefore seems more than pertinent. When facing "the Assyrians" of divorce and abuse we need to listen carefully to the prophet's words: "Be careful. Keep calm. Don't be afraid. Don't lose heart."

Pastoral faithfulness is another subject we're tired of discussing. We hear nearly as much about it as we do about marriage, for pastoral abuse is dangerously on the rise, and its roots are easy to trace.[118] Those of us who pastor flocks and preach sermons and teach disciples and counsel the bereaved need to find new ways to put teeth into Isaiah's prophetic words. Daniel Louw points out that one of our biggest challenges today is simply to minister out of an adequate perception of who God is. This is why seminaries teach courses on systematic theology, by the way—to help ministers alter and expand their perceptions of God. Every believer has some understanding of God, but not all of these are transformative, and certainly not all of these are biblical. Some understandings are unhelpful, in fact, even toxic. Only by developing a healthy awareness of the biblical God can pastors and other leaders help believers grow in the Faith.[119]

Faithfulness in theological education is not even on the agenda of many believers. In fact, the idea that pastors and counselors and teachers and chaplains need to be trained—in spite of everything Scripture says about "training" (*paideuō*)—is as foreign to many believers as Greek and Hebrew. The practical result of this neglect is a noticeable rise in the number of "Ahaz-pastors" leading churches today. With denominational loyalty on the wane, we are now entering an age in which well-meaning, impressionable, yet dangerously untested leaders are telling us who God is—and they're not doing a very good job. Lest we forget, the imperative in Christ's Great Commission is not to "teach" or to "baptize"—as many would have us believe. No, the imperative verb in the Great Commission is *mathēteusate*—"make disciples" (Matt 28:19). Readers who ignore this tend either to cave in to the "Syrians" of hyper-pragmatism on the one hand or the "Ephraimites" of hyper-intellectualism on the other. Both options are biblically and theologically unacceptable. When will we decide to abandon the altars of pragmatism and intellectualism and rebuild the altars of discipleship, community, and the spiritual disciplines?[120]

IT'S NOT MY PROBLEM (2 Kings 20:12-20)

"Babylon" is hard to define. Nothing is said in the NT about the historical Babylonians, nor do we have any information about the huge city (225 square-miles, according to Herodotus) which ancient Mesopotamians call "The Gate of the Gods" (Akk *Bab-ilu*). On the contrary, the New Testament speaks of Babylon only in symbolic terms. The Great Harlot's secret name, for example, is "Babylon the Great" (Rev 17:5). The author of 1 Peter relays greetings to his readers from "Babylon," but this is likely a reference to Rome as *Babylon redivivus* ("Babylon revived").[121] Evidently the word "Babylon" is much like the contemporary word "gay"—later meanings have little or nothing to do with its original meaning. Readers familiar with "Babylon" from the Second Testament often find it difficult to comprehend its meaning in the First.

Even Hezekiah has a problem with it. Compared to Assyria, with whom he's more familiar, Babylon is a distant land to Hezekiah, a nondescript place populated by a nondescript people. Why else would he allow a cadre of Babylonians to inspect everything in his palace, even the treasury? Perhaps he has a reason for letting down his guard—after all, Babylon is relatively harmless at this point in history. The neo-Babylonian empire has not yet been ignited under Nabopolassar (626-605 BC), and his son Nebuchadnezzar (605-562 BC) has not yet begun terrorizing his neighbors.

Merodach-Baladan ("Marduk has given a son") is a Babylonian sheik best known for his ability to unite the Chaldeans and the Arameans against the Assyrians. From Assyria's perspective, he's nothing more than an annoying insect, a bothersome mosquito. At least twice he militarily embarrasses Assyria (722–710; 703 BC), even going so far as to secure aid and asylum from the hated Elamites in southern Persia.[122] Perhaps the reason for his Jerusalem trip is to invite Hezekiah to join yet another anti-Assyrian coalition.[123] Isaiah, however, takes a dim view of his intentions. In fact, Isaiah hates Babylon and things Babylonian. In Isa 14:4-23, for example, he launches a vicious attack against Babylon via a traditional "fall of the king" taunt-song, imagining Babylon's descent into hell as a satirical dirge.[124] Instead of comparing Babylon's world-view with Yahweh's (as in, say, 2 Kings 19:21-34), here he imagines Babylon as a freshly-scrubbed freshman walking onto a college campus. Wide-eyed and naïve, he trips over his own two feet as he makes his descent into hell, provoking a loud guffaw from his dead peers:

> Is this the man who shook the earth
>   and made kingdoms tremble,
> the man who made the world a desert,
>   who overthrew its cities
>   and would not let his captives go home?[125]

The conqueror who thought he could ascend into heaven now sits on a netherworld trash heap, covered with filth and maggots (14:13). Once victorious, now he's an outcast, a rejected branch, a corpse trampled underfoot (14:19), and the peoples struck down by his relentless aggression now sing, "How you are fallen!" (14:6). From Isaiah's perspective, Babylon more than deserves the coming judgment. That's why Isaiah responds so violently to Hezekiah's leniency. Hearing the news that Babylonian envoys have arrived in Jerusalem, he runs straight to the palace and demands,

> What did those men say?
> Where did they come from?
> What did they see in your palace?

Hezekiah's response, however, is both cagey and non-committal. In so many words, he says, "What's the matter? I'm just trying to be friendly. Lighten up, Isaiah!" Perhaps he sees this as just another state visit, like the Sabean queen's visit. Perhaps he sees the Babylonians as potential allies, an understandable position given what he's been through with the

Assyrians. At any rate, Isaiah seems genuinely amazed by Hezekiah's lackadaisical attitude.

Then he gets angry. Like his earlier oracle (2 Kings 20:1), he warns Hezekiah to prepare for the worst. He prophesies not just death, but the death of Hezekiah's descendants. Where the earlier oracle warns him to put his house in order, this one predicts that his descendants will become eunuchs in Babylonian palaces. Where Hezekiah's earlier response is to pray and weep bitterly, here he publicly commends Isaiah for his stance against Babylonian hegemony: "The word of Yahweh you have spoken is good." Privately, though, he celebrates his good fortune. Like a speeding motorist suddenly "let off the hook," he congratulates himself, "Will there not be peace and security in my lifetime?"

He has no idea what's coming next.

Intratextual Reflection

Once Bill Cosby tries to teach his son the importance of telling the truth.[126] His wife calls him at work, however, and tells him that his teaching strategy isn't working. So he decides to take his boy on a "trip to the woodshed." Smacking him on the bottom, the boy starts crying, and Cosby asks him, "Are you ever going to lie to me again?"

"Oh no, Dad. I'll never do it again. I've learned my lesson."

"OK then," he says gently, "you can go back into the house and wash up for dinner." Then, just as he's about to let him go—he smacks him again! Utterly surprised by this second swat, the boy cries out,

"Why did you do that, Dad?"

"Because that's what lying feels like, son."

Hezekiah too must be wondering why Isaiah hits him with a "second swat." After going through an Assyrian siege and his own personal brush with death, why is Isaiah now hitting him with this "woodshed" oracle? The answer is simple: because Isaiah knows what's coming next—a horror so unimaginable, so terrifying—no words will ever be able to convey it. Even if he were to show the future to Hezekiah, he probably wouldn't believe his own eyes: in a few short years Yahweh will bring these same Babylonians back to Jerusalem, and he will use them to destroy the Temple, the palace, and Jerusalem itself.

Theological Reflection

Hezekiah's attitude is understandable enough. Everyone wants peace and security in their lifetime, particularly if they've suffered like Hezekiah has suffered. The problem is that too many of us, like Hezekiah, have a tendency to worship peace and security, not just hope for it. "I haven't got time for the pain" isn't just an old advertising slogan. For many people it's a religious worldview.[127] Like Hezekiah, some choose to live in denial, and deal with the problem of pain in ineffective, irresponsible ways. For Hezekiah, this attitude exacts a high price—the decimation of his name and his inheritance. For Isaiah the price is high too. He knows that Hezekiah's attitude, left unchecked, will spread like wildfire and paralyze Judah. Procrastination and denial are perennial defense mechanisms against pain. John Maxwell calls them "the sly saboteurs."[128]

Hezekiah is a victim, and victims have a tendency to burrow into cocoons instead of turn to the Lord.[129] This is as true for Hezekiah as it is for any other sufferer. "Victims' rights" is the cry of our age. How often we hear cries of "Victim!" from children against their fathers, from employees against their employers. To be sure, the failure to do justice does breed class division and political instability, but revenge is a poor substitute for redemption. That I may have suffered abuse from my parents does not mean that I have the right to take vengeance against them. I have to decide what God wants. I have to decide whether God can handle my need for justice.

To refuse to deal with these issues in the present is a decision to bargain away the future. This is the thrust of Isaiah's oracle, and we can apply it to any number of areas, but one which cries out for immediate application is the embarrassingly narcissistic weight-loss industry. According to one poll, Western Christians fear gaining weight more than any other problem—more than financial ruin or divorce or nuclear war.[130] To respond to this "fear," entrepreneurial opportunists have launched a 2-billion-dollar-a-year "Christian dieting industry,"[131] and some of the methods they're using are as vacuous as they are heretical. Fasting and dieting are not the same thing, however difficult it is to find a distinction in the Christian diet literature. People diet in order to lose weight, improve appearance, and extend life—all perfectly noble pursuits. Believers fast, however, to open themselves up to God in a more intentional way. Jesus talks about fasting in the Sermon on the Mount, but not so disciples can nail down a better job or secure a prettier spouse.

The Straight Story is David Lynch's film about Alvin Straight.[132] As Lynch tells it, Alvin cares so much for his brother, he drives a 30-year-old lawnmower hundreds of miles just to be with him when he dies. Along the way, he faces a number of challenges—a mentally challenged daughter, his own failing health, and the challenge of reconnecting to a brother with whom he has not spoken in years. The point is that he doesn't wait to hear of his brother's death before he tries to make things right. He doesn't say, "it's not my problem." He gets out the John Deere and starts the engine.

Stories like this reflect the heart of the Gospel, whether they come from unbelievers or believers.[133] The Lord knows that there's absolutely no way we can get to him—our illness is too great, our debilitation too severe, our procrastination too culturally institutionalized. So he comes to us—not on a cloud or a whirlwind or a chariot. Like Alvin Straight, he comes to us in very unconventional ways, taking the hills one at a time, stopping along the way to help others.

Never does he think of saying, "You're not my problem."

Notes

1. N. Na'aman, "Amarna Letters," *ABD* 1.174-81. These 14th century BC letters are from various Syro-Palestinian vassals to various Egyptian pharaohs.

2. Phoenician kings have a long history of socioeconomic cooperation with other countries. For example, in *EA* 148.12-14; 151.15, 46, Abimilku of Tyre requests cattle fodder and security troops from the Egyptian crown, even listing his needs in measurable units, like 1 Kings 5:10-11.

3. L. E. Stager and S. R. Wolff, "Child Sacrifice at Carthage—Religious Rite or Population Control?" *BAR* 10 (1984) 30-51.

4. G. Mendenhall sees it as early ("Covenant Forms in Israelite Tradition," *BA* 17 [1954] 50-76); L. Perlitt sees it as late (*Bundestheologie im Alten Testament* [WMANT 36; Neukirchen: Neukirchen-Vluyn, 1969]). F. M. Cross anthropologically situates it in the "kinship ethos" of the West Semitic world (*From Epic to Canon* [Baltimore: Johns Hopkins, 1999] 10).

5. In *EA* 148.37, e.g., *mamitu* refers either to an "oath-treaty" between Tyre and Sidon or an "oath-treaty" between Sidon and Egypt (or both).

6. The word for "safety" in 1 Kings 4:25 (*betah*) is closely paralleled in *EA* 147.56, where Abimilku says of the Pharaoh, "because of my lord the king's mighty hand, I am calm, I am safe" (Akk *ba-ti-i-ti*).

7. F. M. Cross (*From Epic to Canon*, 94-95) sees a conflict between the presence of Davidic military activity in one place (1 Kings 5:17) vs. the absence of it in another (2 Sam 7:1). But underneath this *faux conflit* lies the unspoken presumption that David is either constantly at war or constantly at peace.

8. Cited in M. Luther, *A Treatise on Good Words* 4.15.

9. "[And I killed Jo]ram, son of [Ahab,] king of Israel, and [I] killed [Ahazi]yahu, son of [Joram, kin]g of the house of David" (translation by A. Biran and J. Naveh, "The Tel Dan Inscription: A New Fragment," *IEJ* 45 [1995] 12-13).

10. J. P. Healey, "Peace," *ABD* 5.206.

11. On *satan*, see the definitive study of P. Day, *An Adversary in Heaven: satan in the Hebrew Bible* (HSM 43; Atlanta: Scholars, 1988).

12. A. A. Da Silva, "A Comparison Between the Remains of Three Possible Mythological Motifs in the Old Testament Temple Building Narratives and their Counterparts in the Ugaritic Baal Cycle and the Keret-Epic" (M.A. Thesis, University of Pretoria, 1995).

13. For further analysis, see my "Ruth the Moabite and the Blessing of Foreigners," *CBQ* 60 (1998) 203-17; "America's Monocultural Heritage," *FH* 15 (Fall-Winter 1982) 39-53; and "Basic Attitudes Toward 'Foreigners' Among Selected Churches of Christ," *RQ* 24 (1981) 225-38.

14. C. Fiscus, "Joggers Don't Budge, Cause Big Grudge," *Arizona Republic* (May 14, 1999) A1.

15. B. A. Fisher, "Devotion, Damages and Deprogrammers: Strategies and Counterstrategies in the Cult Wars," *Journal of Law and Religion* 9 (1991) 151-177.

16. J. D. BeDuhn ("'Because of the Angels': Unveiling Paul's Anthropology in 1 Corinthians 11," *JBL* 118 [1999] 309) thinks Paul is arguing that "the creation of human beings as gendered and sexed is a rupture of unity to be overcome in Christ."

17. Eventually we held the youth retreat at the camp of a neighboring denomination.

18. In terms of world-wide impact, perhaps no other text has done more to color the popular imagination than Sura 27.15-44 in the Qur'an. According to the prophet Muhammad (assuming Muhammad is the author of this Sura), the purpose of her visit is to give Solomon an opportunity to bring her "into submission" (Arab *mslmyn*); i.e., convert her to Islam. In spite of the fact that she sits on a "powerful throne" where the chiefs in her country respect the "command" invested in her, Solomon does not entertain her questions because she is never allowed to ask any. Indeed, we are never allowed to wonder whether she even has any. Instead Solomon tests her to see whether he can "divert her (*wsdh'*, lit., 'block her way') from the worship of others besides Allah" (27.42-43). Not a word is said about this woman's intellectual curiosity, one of the biblical story's main themes.

19. N. Ganjavi and J. C. Bürgel (*Chosrou und Schirin* [Zürich: Manesse, 1980]) point out a number of parallels between the Arab "romance" of Solomon and Bilqis (the queen's name in the Arabic legends) and the romance of Chosrou and Schirin in ancient Persian poetry. Maya Angelou works with the theme in contemporary poetry (*Now Sheba Sings the Song* [New York: Dutton/Dial Books, 1987), as does John Freeman (*Solomon and Balkis* [London: MacMillan, 1926]).

20. Handel's oratorio *Solomon* is one of the more famous musical renditions (Germany: Philips, 1985), but comparably evocative is the work of Randall Thompson, *Solomon and Balkis* (Boston: E. C. Schirmer Music Co., 1942).

21. Revocalizing MT *shêma`* to *shemâ`*.

22. Gray, 241.

23. Shalmaneser III (858-824) reports having to face in war a cavalry of one thousand camels from Arabia (*ANET* 279). Tiglath-Pileser III (744-727) reports receiving tribute from a queen of Arabia named Zabibe (*ANET* 283).

24. LXX, for example, changes the phrase "Happy are your men" in v. 8 to "Happy are your wives" (Gk *gunaikes*), yet later Jewish, Arab and Ethiopian traditions

go wild, portraying her as everything from "seductive temptress" to "hairy (Lilith) demon." Alice Ogden Bellis surveys the variants in her article, "The Queen of Sheba: A Gender-Sensitive Reading," *Journal of Religious Thought* 51 (1996) 17-28.

25. DeVries, 138, thinks "the story as told has as its aim to exemplify Solomon's paradigmatic virtues of wisdom and wealth." Nelson, 65-67, emphasizes this even more strongly.

26. Bellis, "Queen of Sheba," 28.

27. Rabbi Samuel ben Nahmani tries to steer his students away from the sexual dynamics of this encounter through a bit of philological acrobatics: "Whoever says that the *mlkt* (queen) of Sheba was a woman is in error; the word *mlkt* here means the 'kingdom' of Sheba" (*b. B. Mets.* 59a)

28. H. Escott, ed., *The Cure of Souls: An Anthology of P. T. Forsyth's Practical Writings* (Grand Rapids: Eerdmans, 1971) 113.

29. *Midrash Hachefez*, cited in A. S. Rappoport, *Myth and Legend in Ancient Israel*, vol. 3 (New York: KTAV, 1966) 128.

30. Greek and Roman guests who fail to solve after-dinner riddles are sometimes "punished" by being "forced" to drink salted wine (J. Crenshaw, "Riddles," *ABD* 5.723).

31. Crenshaw, "Riddles," 721.

32. NIV translates *n`lm* as "too hard," but this is not what the word means. This word refers to "hidden" things (like "wisdom," Job 28:21).

33. See my "Ruth the Moabite and the Blessing of Foreigners," *CBQ* 60 (1998) 203-17.

34. M. Warner, "In and Out of the Fold: Wisdom, Danger, and Glamour in the Tale of the Queen of Sheba," in C. Büchmann and C. Spiegel, eds., *Out of the Garden: Women Writers on the Bible* (New York: Fawcett Columbine, 1994) 163.

35. Shakespeare, *Hamlet*, Act 2, Scene 2, line 157.

36. *The Book of J*, translated by David Rosenberg and interpreted by Harold Bloom (New York: Grove Weidenfeld, 1990). The problem, of course, is that no two scholars on earth can agree over which verses are to be included in this hypothetical "document," a cold fact which these authors never address or even admit.

37. These comments, from the *Village Voice Literary Supplement* and the *Washington Post Book World*, are printed on the book's back cover.

38. R. E. Friedman, "Is Everybody a Bible Expert? Not the Authors of the Book of J," *Bible Review* 7 (1991) 16-18, 50-51.

39. Fayette Breaux Veverka, "Congregational Education: Shaping the Culture of the Local Church," *Religious Education* 92 (1997) 77-90.

40. J. Marlow, "Effective Bible Study with Oral Adults," *Christian Education Journal* 16 (1995) 80-98.

41. W. Scott Sunquist, "A Prolegomenon to a Theology of Christian Education," *Christian Education* 7 (1987) 59-74.

42. C. H. Spurgeon, "A Greater Than Solomon," *The Spurgeon Sermon Collection*, vol. 3 (Portland, OR: Ages Software, 1997) 248 (sermon preached on Feb 6, 1881).

43. Cited in G. Ebeling, *Word and Faith* (London: SCM, 1963) 306 (changing the nouns to verbs).

44. Spurgeon, "A Greater Than Solomon."

45. In *EA* 85, e.g., the ruler of Byblos, Rib-Addi, asks Pharaoh for food, troops

and horses, and becomes upset when they don't arrive on time. Similarly Hiram of Tyre complains to Solomon that the merchandise for which he has paid 120 talents of gold is substandard.

46. In fact, in the later account, Solomon rebuilds the cities which Huram gives him, and settles Israelites in them (2 Chron 8:2).

47. For a more detailed analysis, see D. Jobling, "'Forced Labor': Solomon's Golden Age and the Question of Literary Representation," *Semeia* 54 (1992) 57-76.

48. MT's order is reflected in LXX, Syr, Vg, Luther, NEB, RSV, NRSV and NJPS. In Chronicles, the transaction is reversed: Solomon rebuilds the villages that Hiram has given him (2 Chron 8:2).

49. Josephus argues that "Cabul" means "unpleasant" in Phoenician (*AJ* 8.5.3). In Talmud (*b. Shab.* 54a), *kbwl* is interpreted as meaning "unproductive" (*l' `byd pyry*, lit., "not making fruit").

50. W. H. Mare, "Millo," *ABD* 4.835.

51. This "ascendancy" motif continues in 1 Kings 11:14 when Yahweh ironically "raises up" something himself ("Yahweh raised up an adversary") to punish Solomon for turning his heart toward other gods.

52. Lions are the premier symbol of power in Mesopotamia, particularly in Assyria; see P. Albenda, "Ashurnasirpal II Lion Hunt Relief BM124534," *JNES* 31 (1972) 167-78.

53. K. I. Parker, "Solomon as Philosopher King? The Nexus of Law and Wisdom in 1 Kings 1-11," *JSOT* 53 (1992) 76.

54. R. E. Clements, "The Deuteronomistic Interpretation of the Founding of the Monarchy in I Sam VIII," *VT* 24 (1974) 403.

55. De Vries (*Kings* 53).

56. L. Eslinger, *Into the Hands of the Living God* (Sheffield: Almond, 1989) 137.

57. Winston Churchill, cited in *CT* 43, 9 (Aug 9, 1999) 66, from a lecture given on Feb 3, 1932.

58. Parker, "Solomon as Philosopher King," 80-81.

59. B. Grillet and M. Lestienne (*Premier livre des Règnes* [Paris: Cerf, 1997] 71, 196) argue that the prophecy in 1 Sam 8:10-18 intends to warn Israel against the dangers of (a) a permanent army, and (b) the centralization of power.

60. *CMHE* 91-111.

61. B. C. Birch, *Let Justice Roll Down: The Old Testament, Ethics, and Christian Life* (Louisville: Westminster/John Knox, 1991) 223.

62. F. M. Cross, *From Epic to Canon* (Baltimore: Johns Hopkins, 1998) 3-21.

63. D. Senior & C. Stuhlmueller, *The Biblical Foundations for Mission* (Maryknoll, NY: Orbis, 1983) 315.

64. C. Westermann, *Elements of Old Testament Theology* (Atlanta: John Knox, 1982) 102-03.

65. R. J. Sider, "Cautions Against Ecclesiastical Elegance," *CT* 23, 20 (1979) 1090-95. W. L. Hendricks ("Where Do We Worship?" *Baptist History and Heritage* 31 [1996] 26-37) cites statistics which place the 1994 value of Southern Baptist church buildings alone at $25,832,040,545.

66. M. S. Hamilton, "The Triumph of the Praise Songs," *CT* 43, 8 (1999) 28-35.

67. For a response, see G. Hugenberger, "Women in Church Office: Hermeneutics or Exegesis? A Survey of Approaches to 1 Tim 2:8-15," *JETS* 35 (1992) 341-60.

68. R. Johnson and G. Martin, "Facilities for New Church Development," *Brethren Life and Thought* 36 (1991) 226-38.

69. J. Bassler, *God and Mammon: Asking for Money in the New Testament* (Nashville: Abingdon, 1991).

70. P. L. Ferguson, "So You Are Going to Build ... ," *Reformed Liturgy and Music* 31 (1997) 190-94.

71. J. R. Bartlett, "An Adversary Against Solomon: Hadad the Edomite," *ZAW* 88 (1976) 205-26.

72. E. F. Campbell, "The Amarna Letters and the Amarna Period," *BA* 2 (1960) 32-22.

73. W. T. Pitard, *Ancient Damascus: A Historical Study of the Syrian City-State from Earliest Times until Its Fall to the Assyrians in 732 B.C.E.* (Winona Lake, IN: Eisenbrauns, 1987).

74. Extra-biblical proof of Jeroboam's existence comes from the mention of his name on a 9th century seal (*GEH* 6.2.20.2.). Formerly thought to be from the time of Jeroboam II (8th century), many now date this famous seal to the time of Jeroboam I (see, e.g., G. W. Ahlström, "The Seal of Shema," *SJOT* 7 [1993] 208-15).

75. M. A. Cohen, "The Role of the Shilonite Priesthood in the United Monarchy of Ancient Israel," *HUCA* 36 (1971) 59-98.

76. R. R. Wilson, *Prophecy and Society in Ancient Israel* (Philadelphia: Fortress, 1980) 184-87.

77. C. D. Evans, "Naram-Sin and Jeroboam: The Archetypal *Unheilsherrscher* in Mesopotamian and Biblical Historiography," *Scripture in Context II: More Essays on the Comparative Method* (W. W. Hallo, J. C. Moyer, and L. G. Perdue, eds.; Winona Lake, IN: Eisenbrauns, 1983) 114, 124.

78. P. L. Day, *An Adversary in Heaven: satan in the Hebrew Bible* (HSM 43; Atlanta: Scholars, 1988). For a review, see *JBL* 109 (1990) 508-10,

79. Yahweh's "lamp-promise" to David repeats itself in 1 Kings 15:4 and 2 Kings 8:19.

80. L. Rost, *The Succession to the Throne of David* (Sheffield: Almond Press, 1982; trans. of 1926 German ed.).

81. Gibson (*SSI* 3.47).

82. Since the Behistun Inscription is the only primary source, and since Darius wrote it, this "history" may not be reliable (P. Briant, "Persian Empire," *ABD* 5.236-40).

83. The Assyrian Shalmeneser III calls Hazael "son of nobody" (*ANET* 280) but there is strong evidence in the Tel Dan inscription that he thinks of Ben-Hadad as "my father" (see W. Schniedewind, "Tel Dan Stele: New Light on Aramaic and Jehu's Revolt," *BASOR* 302 [1996] 75-90).

84. Addressing Elisha, Hazael calls Ben-Hadad "your son" (*binkâ*, v. 9), and Ben-Hadad is Hazael's "master" (*'âdôn*, v. 14).

85. Marsha White's attempt to get at the "original" story is typical ("Naboth's Vineyard and the Legitimation of a Dynastic Extermination," *VT* 44 [1994] 66-76).

86. R. Alter, "The Techniques of Repetition," in *The Art of Biblical Narrative* (New York: Basic, 1981) 88-113.

87. "My father! My father! The chariots of Israel!" (2 Kings 2:12).

88. J. Naveh and I. Eph`al ("Hazael's Booty Inscriptions," *IEJ* 39 [1989] 192-200)

document the extent of Hazael's success in a 9th century BC Aramaic inscription from Samos. Under a depiction of four naked goddesses the writing on this plaque reads: "That which Hadad gave our lord Hazael from `Umqi in the year that our lord crossed the river" (probably a reference to Hazael's crossing of the Euphrates).

89. David Howard (*Joshua* [New American Commentary 5; Nashville: Broadman, 1998] 106-112) offers a thoughtful critique of Rahab's deception (Josh 2:4-6), but few commentators address the ethics of Elisha's deceptive behavior.

90. Stuart Lasine, *Knowing Kings: Knowledge, Power and Narcissism in the Hebrew Bible* (SBLSS 40; Atlanta: Society of Biblical Literature, 2001) 220, 224, 234, 261, 263.

91. I got this from a student via e-mail.

92. C. Anne David, "Avoiding Compassion Fatigue," *Journal of the American Academy of Ministry* 1 (1992) 29-39.

93. On the growing problem of clergy depression, see my "Jeremiah's Identity Crisis," *RQ* 34 (1992) 135-49.

94. D. G. Buttrick, "Preaching and the Passion Narratives," *Reformed Liturgy and Music* 24 (1990) 6-10.

95. K. L. Younger, "The Deportations of the Israelites," *JBL* 117 (1998) 201-27); G. Galil, "The Last Years of the Kingdom of Israel and the Fall of Samaria," *CBQ* 57 (1995) 52-65.

96. J. N. Lawrence ("Assyrian Nobles and the Book of Jonah," *Tyndale Bulletin* 37 [1986] 121-32) holds the consensus view that Jonah is a post-exilic composition (5th or 4th century BC). A minority view, however, challenges this position, based on this single biblical reference. B. Carradine (*Bible Characters* [Chicago: Christian Witness, 1907] 61) imagines that Jonah is the prophet who anoints Jehu (!).

97. Hosea's metaphors bring this era dramatically to life; see N. Stienstra, *Yhwh is the Husband of His People: Analysis of a Biblical Metaphor with Special Reference to Translation* (Kampen: Kok Pharos, 1993).

98. M. Hamilton, "We're In the Money," *CT* 44, 7 (June 12, 2000) 41.

99. E. Clarke, "Presidents and Finances," *Theological Education* 32 (1995) 21-32.

100. Robert Bork (*Slouching Towards Gomorrah: Modern Liberalism and American Decline* [San Francisco: HarperCollins, 1997]) criticizes practically everything about contemporary American culture in this bitter memoir—an increasingly obscene pop culture, rising illegitimacy, long-term welfare dependency, dangerous leniency with violent criminals, abortion, euthanasia, feminist aggression, legalized racial discrimination (affirmative action), dumbed-down education, antireligious media bias, and socially disintegrative multiculturalism.

101. D. J. Hall, *The Steward: A Biblical Symbol Comes of Age* (Grand Rapids: Eerdmans, 1990) 95.

102. Not her real name.

103. Not his real name.

104. H. Cazelles, "Syro-Ephraimite War," *ABD* 6.282-85.

105. The key problem is how to interpret *yhwdh* in 2 Kings 14:28. Is it a reference to "Judah," or is it a reference to the north-Syrian district of "Yaudi"/"Sam'al"? Also problematic is the syntax of this verse, to which a variety of English versions testify.

106. The origin of this cult is unknown, though M. Weinfeld has plausibly suggested that child sacrifice to Baal (or El, or Hadad, or any other divine "monarch") is

simply the logical outgrowth of divinized monarchicalism ("The Worship of Molech and of the Queen of Heaven and its Background," *UF* 4 [1972] 133–54). Molech appears sixteen times in the OT, five of these in the book of Kings (1 Kings 11:5, 7, 33; 2 Kings 23:10, 13).

107. M. Cogan (*Imperialism and Religion: Assyria, Judah and Israel in the Eighth and Seventh Centuries B.C.E.* [Missoula, MT: Scholars, 1974] 72-88) denies that Ahaz imports anything Assyrian into the Jerusalem cult, though this is difficult to accept in light of the astral deities found there during Josiah's reign (2 Kings 23:4, 11).

108. Calvin, *Commentary on Matthew* 1:22.

109. Jerome, *Letter to Pammachius* 57.8.

110. C. Spurgeon, "Israel and Britain: A Note of Warning," (Albany, OR: Ages Software, 1994; original sermon preached on June 7, 1844).

111. LXX implies this by translating MT hip`il *he`ebîr* with *diêgen*, an imperfect indicative active of *diagô*, "to pass through."

112. S. Ackerman, *Under Every Green Tree: Popular Religion in Sixth-Century Judah* (HSM 46; Atlanta: Scholars, 1989).

113. W. Brueggemann, *Deep Memory, Exuberant Hope* (Minneapolis: Fortress, 2000) 6.

114. C. S. Lewis, *The Screwtape Letters*, Letter # 12 (New York: MacMillan, 1961) 54 (first pub. in 1943).

115. I know this from my experience as a pastoral counselor; see also my *Reconciliation: A Study of Biblical Families in Conflict* (Joplin, MO: College, 1994) 123-37.

116. J. Wallerstein & S. Blakeslee, *Second Chances: Men, Women, and Children a Decade After Divorce* (New York: Ticknor and Fields, 1989).

117. S. Hagemeyer, "Making Sense of Divorce Grief," *Pastoral Psychology* 34 (1986) 237-50.

118. S. Grenz & R. Bell, *Betrayal of Trust: Sexual Misconduct in the Pastorate* (Downers Grove, IL: InterVarsity, 1995); P. Rutter, *Sex in the Forbidden Zone* (New York: St. Martin's, 1989); J. Gonsiorek, ed., *Breach of Trust: Sexual Exploitation by Health Care Professionals and Clergy* (Thousand Oaks, CA: Sage Publications, 1995); M. Fortune, *Nothing Sacred? When Sex Invades the Pastoral Relationship* (San Francisco: Harper and Row, 1989). This is not an exhaustive bibliography.

119. D. Louw, "God as Friend: Metaphoric Theology in Pastoral Care," *Pastoral Psychology* 46 (1998) 233-42.

120. G. Hope, "Revisioning Seminary as Ministry-Centered," *CC* 106 (1989) 107-11.

121. Opinions are divided. C. Thiede thinks 1 Pet 5:13 refers to Rome ("Babylon, der andere Ort: Anmerkungen zu 1 Petr 5,13 und Apg 12,17," *Bib* 67 [1986] 532-38), while J. Applegate ("The Co-Elect Woman of 1 Peter," *NTS* 38 [1992] 587-604) questions this interpretation.

122. J. Brinkman, "Sennacherib's Babylonian Problem," *JCS* 25 (1973) 89–95.

123. J. Brinkman, "Elamite Military Aid to Merodach-Baladan," *JNES* 24 (1965) 161-66.

124. H. Jensen ("The Fall of the King," *SJOT* 5 [1991] 121-47) traces the "fall of the king" theme back to Indo-Iranian, Greek, and Roman culture, as well as Sumerian and North Semitic cultures. The poems in Isa 2, 10, and 14 all stand as Hebraic contributions to this trajectory.

125. Mark Shipp (*Of Dead Kings and Dirges: Myth and Meaning in Isaiah 14:4b-21* [SBL Academia Biblica 11; Leiden: Brill, 2002]) argues convincingly that this poem is a satire of a royal dirge.

126. B. Cosby, *Fatherhood* (Garden City, NY: Doubleday, 1986) 91-95.

127. P. Brand, "And God Created Pain," *CT* 38 (1994) 21.

128. J. Maxwell, "The Sly Saboteur," *Leadership* 14 (1993) 52-7.

129. M. Klunzinger and M. S. Moore, "Codependency and Pastoral Care: A Report from the Trenches," *RQ* 38 (1996) 171.

130. Cited in D. Okholm, "Rx for Gluttony," *CT* 44, 10 (Sept 4, 2000) 63.

131. D. Meinz, cited in L. Winner, "The Weigh and the Truth," *CT* 44, 10 (Sept 4, 2000) 52.

132 Disney, 1999.

133 R. Mouw, *He Shines in All that's Fair: Culture and Common Grace* (Grand Rapids: Eerdmans, 2001).

SEVEN

THE PRESSURE OF REFORM

DEDICATED TO REFORM (1 Kings 8:1-66)

After a long journey, including "prison time" in Dagon's temple (1 Sam 5:2) and twenty years in the home of Abinidab (7:1), the Ark eventually comes to rest in the Temple of Yahweh. It's hard to overemphasize the significance of this event. According to priestly tradition, Yahweh "dwells" among his people in several ways—a pillar of fire by night, an iridescent cloud by day (Exod 13:21). In fact, one of his titles is "the cloud-rider" (Psa 68:5), an epithet deeply rooted in old Canaanite traditions (*UNP* 103). Much of the Temple's strange iconography is similarly indebted to Canaanite sources: "Go in and take down the shielding curtain and cover the ark of the Testimony with it. Then...cover this with dolphin hides, spread a cloth of solid blue over that, and put the poles in place" (Num 4:5-6).[1] Here, at the dedication of the Temple, another Yahweh cloud appears (v. 10) and its appearance is designed to connect events in Solomon's time with the Exodus event.

According to tradition, the only artifacts in the Ark are the Torah tablets (v. 9), yet Christian writers also mention Aaron's rod and a jar of manna (Heb 9:4). These latter go inside the Ark, while the torah scroll goes alongside it (Deut 31:26). No one knows exactly how this all goes together, but this takes nothing away from the fact that the Ark is Israel's most powerful sacred icon, more sacred even than the Tent of Meeting.[2] In wartime it channels the power of Yahweh, both offensively (Josh 6:4-13) and defensively (7:6).[3] In peacetime it replicates the power and presence of Moses by splitting open the Jordan like Moses splits open the Sea (Josh 3:3-4:18; Exod 14:21). Mysterious and unpredictable, it can bless as well as curse, as the inhabitants of Bethel (Judg 20:27), Shiloh (1 Sam 3:3), Ebenezer (4:5), Ashdod (5:1), Gath (5:8), Ekron (5:10), and Beth Shemesh (6:13) all find out. After David succeeds in uniting the tribes it moves into its permanent home in Jerusalem (2 Sam 6:17).[4]

Mobile tent-shrines are not uncommon in the ancient Near East,[5] and the comparative evidence is too abundant to argue against the authenticity of a pre-exilic Hebrew tent-shrine.[6] Sociologically, the Ark functions in different ways among different Hebrew groups. To priests, it's Yahweh's primary instrument for expiating sin, the tool for separating holy things from profane things. In fact, its lid (*kapporet*, Lev 16:2) is the only pure place in the entire cosmos.[7] To politicians, it's the generator and focal point of Israelite power, Israel's political "logo," so to speak.[8] To prophets (Hos 8:12), it's a depository for Torah (Deut 10:1-9; 31:26), a transmitter for sending out the Word to the nations (2 Kings 23:25).

To celebrate its new home, Solomon prepares a magnificent dedication speech,[9] and while scholars like J. Levenson and B. Halpern continue to argue over matters of structure and detail,[10] G. Knoppers convincingly demonstrates that 1 Kings 8 is chiastically symmetrical:

> Assembly (8:1-3)
>   Sacrifice (8:5)
>   Blessing (8:14-21)
>   Solomon's Stance (8:22)
>   Invocation (8:27-30)
>   Three Petitions (8:31-36)
>   Generalizing Petition (8:37-40)
>   Three Petitions (8:41-51)
>   Invocation (8:52-53)
>   Solomon's Stance (8:54)
>   Blessing (8:55-61)
>   Sacrifice (8:62-64)
> Dismissal (8:66)[11]

Theologically, the prayer at the center of this chiastic speech is a seven-fold petition designed to emphasize a number of priestly themes (vv. 27-

53). Each petition focuses on a different kind of conflict. Conflicts between neighbors need resolution (vv. 31-32). Wartime atrocities need healing (vv. 33-34). Droughts and depression need lifting (vv. 35-36). Attacks on the land—animal, viral, human—all need removing (vv. 37-40). Homesick warriors need encouraging (vv. 44-45). Prisoners of war need grace (vv. 46-51). That there are seven of these petitions is an indication that Solomon petitions Yahweh "completely" in this prayer.[12] Not coincidentally, it indicates that Yahweh's forgiveness comes only to those worshipers who know (*yada*) the Name and turn (*shub*) from their sins (vv. 34, 36).

This is a fixed pattern in biblical reform theology: prayer, confession, repentance, forgiveness. Rooted in kinship language, the covenant works best when Israel commits itself to the spiritual disciplines necessary to keep it alive and healthy. What sets this speech apart from the other programmatic speeches in Deuteronomy-Kings, however, is the centrality of two themes: (a) *foreigners* and (b) *forgiveness*. These themes bond together, epoxy-like, to give this prayer its distinctive character. "Foreigner" (*nokri*) appears twice in the fourth petition (vv. 41-43), while *salah* ("to forgive") sprinkles itself five times throughout the speech (vv. 30, 34, 36, 39, and 50).

Intratextual Reflection

This is the first of several important interludes in Kings. Like prodigals coming to themselves (Luke 15:17), Israel's leaders occasionally look up from what they're doing and ask, "What are we doing—and why are we doing it?" We see this clearly in Josiah's reforms (2 Kings 22:1-23:25), because once he realizes how far Jerusalem has drifted away from the covenant, he determines to cleanse the covenant people of their suffocating idolatries. We see it also in the incident where two prophets spar with one another over what obedience really means (1 Kings 13:1-34)—not to mention the half-hearted attempts of Ahaz and Jehoiakim to effect reform in the midst of chaos and uncertainty (2 Kings 15:32-16:20; 23:36-24:7). Some of these reforms might be called reform "movements," and some may be more spiritually motivated than others, yet all contribute to the *pressure of reform* trajectory.

Intertextually, Solomon understands (with Steven) that no physical building can contain the Almighty (Acts 7:48). But he also knows that worshipers need a "place" (Heb *maqom* appears six times in this chapter, vv. 6, 7, 21, 29, 30, 35). Like all peoples, Israel needs a place to experience cosmic stability in a chaotic world. Israel needs a place upon which to focus its religious aspirations. Solomon therefore prays that the Temple might become such a place.

Theological Reflection

What a special day! Bob and Wanda[13] are standing in my living room, dressed in their finest, their five children gathered around them like pliant sunflowers. The purpose of this occasion is to renew their wedding vows, but the mood now is much different than it was just a few short weeks ago. Bob had showed up in my office disheveled and depressed after living in the backseat of his car for a couple of weeks. Afraid to go home, he knew that Wanda had found out about the four-year affair he'd been having behind her back. His out-of-state mistress had actually called the house and told her everything. Shame-filled and guilt-ridden, Bob suffered the fear of every adulterous father—that he might lose his children and never see them again. Watching him gag on this fear, I finally asked him the dreaded question: "Let's call Wanda, OK?" Recoiling in terror, he arched his back like a wounded animal. "No! I can't!" "Yes, you can. You have to."

Finally he picked up the phone, and Wanda immediately came over. Arriving out-of-breath, she looked like a war-weary nurse arriving for work, a frightened child trying to screw up the courage to get on the bus for the first day of school. Sitting beside him, she took his hand and asked her husband, "Where have you been?" Shame covered his face like a mask as he coughed out the words, "I don't know ...." Then quietly, firmly, after a few minutes of quiet conversation, she said, "Let's go home, honey." And that was it. They went home and went on with their lives, picking up the pieces and starting over. Rarely have I witnessed such unmerited favor. Rarely have I seen such grace. Her words freed him from prison. They purified his spirit and filled him with hope. Ministers rarely get to see what I saw that night. I saw a man fall to his knees before the wife of his youth and I saw the spirit of Christ channel its way through her surrendered spirit and forgive him of his sins. Reflection on this text and this event leads me to the following theological opinions.

First, confession and repentance are essential for spiritual growth. In spite of scholastic attempts to over-explain them,[14] or fundamentalist attempts to dumb them down,[15] or "enlightened" attempts to dumb them up,[16] we desperately need to recover these spiritual disciplines.[17] Yes, we can always use more sermons and seminars about forgiveness, but what we really need are more Bobs confessing their sins, and more Wandas forgiving them when they do.

Second, forgiving "foreigners" is always going to be harder than forgiving "friends." "Love your enemies" is what separates Christ's teaching from all other religious teachings because what Christ demands goes completely against the grain of human nature. We can speculate and theorize about it all we want, but the truth remains that people refuse to forgive their enemies because they don't really think it's necessary to forgive their enemies. They think it's too costly—and they're half right. Forgiveness is costly, often bringing with it a "whiteness to the hair, lines to the face, a cutting anguish, and a long, dull ache."[18] Forgiving "foreigners," however, is especially costly because by definition these are people who do not share our Kingdom Dream. Examples: Jonah refuses to forgive the Assyrians even in light of Yahweh's desire to do so (Jon 4:1-2). Peter refuses to eat with Gentiles for fear of the circumcision faction (Gal 2:12). Calvin executes Michael Servetus largely because Servetus speaks out against Calvin's strict socio-religious policies in Geneva.[19]

Forgiveness like Wanda's is hard to find.

THE CHALLENGE OF PROPHECY (1 Kings 13:1-34)

Sandwiched between the Solomon and Elijah cycles, this episode ushers us into a whole new world. While it tells us much about the character of Jeroboam, it tells us much more about the character of prophecy, particularly the thorny problem of true-vs.-false prophecy. Yet when we look at the story as a whole, another theme comes clearly into focus—the challenge of prophecy itself. Nowhere else in Scripture do we see the prophetic vocation so seriously examined and so unflinchingly critiqued: "What did you go out into the desert to see? A reed swayed by the wind? If not, what did you go out to see? A man dressed in fine clothes? No, those who wear fine clothes are in kings' palaces. Then what did you go out to see? A prophet...?" (Matt 11:7-9). What this story emphasizes is that courage and single-mindedness aren't just admirable traits—they're essential to prophetic ministry because Israel's God has high expectations of his prophets. Unlike other gods, this God refuses to work through creaky intellectuals or politicized priests. Yahweh's prophets have to say what they're told to say, or Yahweh won't use them at all.

Bethel is a well-known cultic center, but its predominant characteristic here is its proximity to Jerusalem. Jeroboam's southernmost calf-shrine is just ten miles north of Jerusalem. The protagonist of the story is an anonymous "man-of-God" from Judah (*'îsh 'elôhîm*), a man who, like Amos, is a southern preacher sent to rebuke a northern king (Amos 7:10-17). For the story's antagonist, however, we might choose from a whole slate of candidates. Is it Jeroboam, the idolatrous king? Is it the old Bethel prophet who deceives his colleague? Is it the southern prophet himself?

Like Jeremiah's laments, is this narrative designed to "inscape" the prophetic vocation for all the world to see?[20] Or is it designed to highlight the sociological challenges prophets regularly face?[21] Whatever the interpretive possibilities, the story itself divides into two complementary sections: a public encounter between a prophet and a king, followed by a private encounter between two prophetic colleagues.

The public confrontation is acrimonious and bitter. Called to preach by the word of Yahweh (*debar yhwh*), a southern prophet travels north. Curiously, he says nothing to Jeroboam himself when he arrives, but goes straight to the furniture and starts preaching: "O altar, altar! This is what Yahweh says."[22] What this altar hears is no happyfaith sermon, but a brutal prediction of a terrifying future: (a) a Davidic king (not an Ephraimite one) is going to arise and purify all Israel; (b) the judgment he executes will be extremely violent; and (c) Yahweh will give Jeroboam a sign (*môpet*) to prove the veracity of his prediction. This is Kings' first instance of predictive prophecy.[23]

What happens next happens fast. Jeroboam raises his hand, points at the prophet, and commands his servants: "Seize him!" Before they can respond, however, the royal hand turns to beef jerky. Then, as if on cue, the altar splits down the middle and vomits the charred remains of Jeroboam's idolatrous calf-sacrifices onto the sanctuary floor, defiling it instantly. Terrified, the king suddenly "converts" to Yahwism, and cries out, "Intercede with Yahweh your God and pray for me that my hand may be restored!" Amazingly, Yahweh responds to this prayer and returns the royal fingers to their original shape. All of this happens in a matter of seconds: the prophecy, the king's response, Yahweh's strike, the king's request, the prophet's prayer, and Yahweh's restoration.

Instead of thanking the prophet for saving him, however, Jeroboam tries to reward his new, powerful friend. Like Israel after the sea-miracle (Exod 16-18), Jeroboam develops an acute case of theological myopia, and for a moment it looks like the prophet is going to allow it. He hesitates and wonders, perhaps, whether he should accept this king's dinner invitation—until he realizes what Jeroboam really wants: "Even if you were to give me half your possessions, I would not go with you, nor would I eat bread or drink water here. For I was commanded by the word of Yahweh: 'You must not eat bread or drink water or return by the way you came'" (1 Kings 13:1-9).[24] In this way he passes an important test. He decides to obey Yahweh and say no to royal power and prestige. Only by refusing Jeroboam's gifts will he be able to maintain his integrity and the integrity of his mission.

It's the private encounter which proves his undoing. An older colleague from Bethel hears what's happened and rushes to intercept his southern colleague with yet another dinner invitation. The question, of course, is why? What motivates him to do this? Is it admiration? Jealousy? Loneliness? Curiosity? The text doesn't say, only intimates that unlike the king's invitation, this one does not appear to come from a recognizably hostile source. This one comes from a colleague, not an enemy. Anticipating resistance, this colleague even comes prepared with a number of reassurances. He too is a prophet (*nabî*) and moreover, an angel has told him to lift Yahweh's noxious ban against food and drink.

Finally, the southerner gives in, and Yahweh again responds. A message comes not to the southerner but to the northerner, and the language it contains is stronger than the language of the Jeroboam oracle. This second oracle has blistering phrases like, "You have defied the word of Yahweh" and "You have not kept the command of Yahweh your God." As in the previous encounter, Yahweh again sends a prophet to pronounce judgment against sin, but this time the messenger himself is the target of judgment. For the sin of idolatry Jeroboam temporarily loses the use of a hand. For the sin of disobedience the southern prophet is immediately put to death.

Having delivered a true oracle, the northern prophet suddenly sees the bigger picture and realizes the depth of his sin. He realizes immediately that Yahweh's word is an unstoppable force, an irresistible power. Sooner or later it will have its way, publicly or privately. Yet because he realizes this after the fact, all he can do now is mourn his colleague's death. We have no reason to doubt his sincerity, but perhaps he's less concerned with the loss of a colleague than the fact that he lives in a cowardly culture led by a cowardly king. After all, why should Yahweh have to send a southern prophet to confront a northern king? Are there no northern prophets to speak out against idolatry? Are there no northern prophets to challenge injustice?

Intratextual Reflection

"Prophecy" can mean many things to many people, and one of the purposes of this story is to define Yahwistic prophecy. Soon this narrator will introduce his readers to the powerful figures of Elijah and Elisha, but before he does he wants to define his terms. Prophecy is a diverse, hoary phenomenon in the ancient Near East. Old Amorite prophets from Hammurabi's era, Transjordanian prophets from Moses' era, Assyrian prophets from Elijah's era—some of these predate the Hebrew prophets by several centuries. To the average Syro-Palestinian, prophecy can include anything from divinational "science" to shamanistic clairvoyance.[25] But to the narrator of Kings prophecy has only one function: to elicit obedience to the word of Yahweh. This passage underlines this emphasis because it so clearly demarcates prophecy's boundaries within a distinctively Yahwistic grid. The warp and woof of this grid includes both predictive and declarative words because both are essential components in Yahwistic prophecy.

Not every instance of Yahweh's word (*debar yhwh*) is predictive in Kings: e.g., Shemaiah's warning (12:24); the man-of-God's commissioning (13:1); the man-of-God's warning from Yahweh (13:9); the Bethel prophet's warning (13:17); Yahweh's use of a prophet to condemn another prophet (13:20); Yahweh's various commands to Elijah (17:2, go to Kerith; 17:8, go to Zarephath; 18:1; 21:17, go to Ahab); the *debar yhwh* questioning Elijah (19:2; 21:28); Jacob's name changing to Israel according to the *debar yhwh* (18:31); *debar yhwh* as something Jehoshaphat wants to seek (22:5); the *debar yhwh* as the catalyst of Micaiah's vision (22:19); Jehoshaphat recognizing that Elisha indeed has the *debar yhwh* (2 Kings 3:12).

But the *debar yhwh* often is predictive, regardless of all (post)modern attempts to explain it away.[26] Over and over this narrator points out that contemporary events are fulfillments of earlier prophecies: e.g., the man of God's prophecy to Eli (1 Kings 2:27); Nathan's prophecy to David (5:19; 8:20); Ahijah's prophecy to Jeroboam (12:15); the fulfilling of the "sign" of the man-of-God regarding the altar at Bethel (13:5); the warning to the man-of-God from Judah (13:26); Ahijah's prophecy about Jeroboam's son (14:18); Ahijah's prophecy about the destruction of Jeroboam's house (15:29); the prophet Jehu's prophecy against Baasha about the destruction of his house (16:12); the fulfillment of Joshua's ancient curse (16:34); the fulfillment of Elijah's promise to the Zarephath widow (17:16); Micaiah's prediction about Ahab (22:28); Elijah's prophecy about Jezebel's death (21:23 ... 22:38); Ahaziah's death according to the *debar yhwh* through Elijah (2 Kings 1:17); the miraculous feeding of a hundred (4:44); the prediction of economic downturn according to the *debar yhwh* (7:1, 16).

This narrative deliberately, unashamedly, and overtly champions the word of Yahweh, and because it does, its importance to biblical theology is crucial. In Kings, the word of Yahweh is what drives the dedication of the Temple (1 Kings 8:1-66), Jeroboam's judgment (14:1-20), Joash's temple repairs (2 Kings 12:1-21), Hezekiah's stand against Assyria (18:1-16), and Josiah's reformation (22:1-23:25). By mentioning Josiah's name so overtly here (v. 2), this prophecy foreshadows the all-encompassing reform attempt at the conclusion of Kings. In spite of its petty subversions and political shenanigans, in spite of its terrible famines and foreign invasions, in spite of its weak prophets and idolatrous kings, Israel's Yahwists are committed to the principle of *semper reformanda.* How might a text like this be communicated most effectively to contemporary believers?

Theological Reflection

First, we might emphasize that the word of Yahweh must indeed come from Yahweh. This applies to worship, preaching, teaching, counseling, stewardship, administration—every aspect of the Kingdom. If this story teaches anything, it's that theocentric words will be challenged, but will eventually take priority over anthropocentric words. This is often hard for us to envision, much less champion, when so much of what we hear on a given Sunday morning sounds more like Sesame Street than this oracle to Jeroboam. How theocentric is contemporary preaching? How clearly and consistently do we hear a word from Yahweh? Over four decades ago, John Reumann predicted that the desire for shorter, tamer sermons would eventually take over the pulpit, and further, that this would lead to liturgical experimentation in lieu of justice-drenched preaching.[27] Has his prediction come true?

And when someone dares to speak a word from God, does this word have the courage to confront the idolatries which harrass our people? Are we training "reliable people" (2 Tim 2:2) to minister without possessiveness and serve without imposition? Idolatries of all sorts beckon us constantly, tantalizing us with their promises, deceiving us with their lies. Golden calves of all sorts are demanding our allegiance: the idolization of psychology,[28] the idolization of technology,[29] the idolization of worship,[30] the idolization of possessions,[31] the idolization of sexuality,[32] the idolization of parentolatry[33]—just to name a few. Where are the prophets we need to warn us about these idolatries?

Second, obedience to the Word cannot be "conditional." It cannot depend on our likes and dislikes. Certainly obedience should never be selective—failure to recognize this is why divine judgment falls so swiftly in this text on a hitherto successful preacher. But if we expect our leaders to govern justly, we should choose people who are more interested in being faithful than being brilliant. If we expect managers to stop dehumanizing their employees, perhaps these employees need to stop denigrating their managers. If we expect teachers to teach our children well, perhaps we need to teach our children to value learning as a lifelong discipline.

However we spell it—formation, development, integration, congruence, authenticity—if we're to model the word of Yahweh before others, then "faith" cannot be something based simply on our likes and our dislikes.

Radical as it sounds, we're going to have to learn to trust one another. Even as the southern man-of-God serves all Israel by obeying Yahweh's word, so pastors need to learn how to serve their congregations as congregations—even those who are difficult and cantankerous, even those whose altars need splitting every now and then. Moral leadership cannot work if it's anchored only to style and technique. We need look no further than the current epidemic of pastoral failures to realize that ministry doesn't work this way. Regardless of what we hear constantly, obedience is not a bad word, but an essential word in the prophet's lexicon.[34]

Third, the price for turning back (*heshîbô*, v. 23) the genuine prophets in our midst from doing their jobs must be higher—much higher. The prophet from Ephraim discovers how God feels about collegial obstructionism in a rather unforgettable way. What price should pastor-bashers today have to pay for such obstructionism? What price should power-hungry lay leaders have to pay for harrassing and persecuting God's faithful preachers? So few of my best students are willing to take up the mantle of preaching anyway, it really angers me when I see them shot to pieces within the first year of their first pastorate. Too often we stand by quietly while biblically-ignorant folk theologians beat up our students.[35] It's disgraceful. Granted, many pastors need to renounce their idolatries, too, especially those which lead to self-indulgence—this is the lesson of vv. 11-34.[36] Yet all believers need to obey the Word when it's faithfully preached—this is the lesson of vv. 1-10.

PROPHECY'S HORRIFIC POWER (1 Kings 14:1-20)

If the Bethel encounter has sound and fury ("Seize him!"), this one has camouflage and deceit. On the surface this looks like any other meeting between a prophet and a king. But technically there's no meeting here between Jeroboam and Ahijah at all. Jeroboam never speaks directly to Ahijah, nor Ahijah to him. All communication goes through an intermediary, Jeroboam's wife. Just as Nathan earlier uses Bathsheba to mediate with David (1 Kings 1:11-14), so Jeroboam uses his wife to send messages to Ahijah. Where Bathsheba is a mother worried about the fate of her son, Jeroboam's wife worries about the fate of her son, Abijah.

That this strategy fails is like saying that Kennedy's 1961 decision to invade the Bay of Pigs "failed." Not only does it fail—it fails miserably.

Jeroboam's disguise-scheme so infuriates Ahijah, the response he sends back is so horrific, it dwarfs the altar-oracle of the previous chapter. Not only does he predict the death of Jeroboam's son, he prophesies the annihilation of every last male in Jeroboam's house. Ostensibly the motivation for approaching Ahijah in the first place is Abijah's ill health, but behind this stands a much deeper longing. Like every king, Jeroboam wants to create his own dynasty, a living depository to store all his accomplishments for future generations. Since dynasties are impossible without healthy sons, Abijah's ill health is Jeroboam's first dynastic crisis, much like the one David faces in 2 Sam 11-19, though on a much smaller scale. Looking for a way out of it, Jeroboam decides to approach the prophet from Shiloh, but where their first meeting had been positive (1 Kings 11:29-39), this one blows up in his face, in spite of several efforts to guarantee its success. These include: (a) the decision to use a "safe" mediator, (b) the decision to deceive Yahweh's prophet, and (c) the decision to send a gift (ten loaves of bread…some cakes and a jar of honey) as advance payment for services rendered. Doesn't the king know that Ahijah is blind (rendering this deception strategy meaningless)? Doesn't he know from his encounter with the southern prophet that payment strategies don't work with Yahweh's prophets?

When the queen arrives, Ahijah begins the onslaught straight away: "Come in, wife of Jeroboam…You have not been sent to me. I have been sent to you!" At the core of his message stands a single Hebrew word, *qashâ*, and defining it clearly is crucial to understanding this episode. The NIV reads *qashâ* as part of the phrase preceding it ("I have been sent to you…with bad news," *qashâ*). But in light of its usage elsewhere (Exod 1:14; 7:3; 1 Kings 12:4), it's more likely that we should read it here with what follows: "I have been sent to you…(and) harsh (is the news)!" In other words, Ahijah's message is not just bad news—it's incredibly harsh news. What are the implications of this?

First, Ahijah rebukes Jeroboam for abusing God's grace. Yahweh has "torn" the kingdom away from the house of David,[37] and given four-fifths of it to Jeroboam. He has made him the leader of his own nation, yet Jeroboam's response has been to presume on God's grace—worse, to do evil (*tara*) by making idols (Asherah poles as well as idols made of metal).[38] Thus the king backs Yahweh into a covenant corner, from which Yahweh is obligated to respond as his covenant partner.

Second, Yahweh dispenses punishment in measured stages. Abijah will surely die, says Yahweh, but he will not die disgracefully. His body will not fall victim to scavengers. God will permit it a decent burial, and all Israel will mourn for him. Still, his death will become a precursor of many violent things to come—it will be the first in a long line of truly disgraceful deaths. Although the word "sign" does not appear here as it does in the southern prophet's oracle (*môpet*, 13:3), the message is the same: immediate disaster, bad as it is, is only the beginning of judgment. Because of Jeroboam's sin, his son's death will inaugurate a hellish spiral. Even as the southern prophet predicts the coming of a righteous son (13:2), so Ahijah predicts the coming of a righteous king to save them from these things (14:14).

Stunned by these *qashâ*-words, the queen has nothing to say in response. All she can do is take the oracle back to her husband and prepare for the worst. All the way home she knows that "the greater haste she makes, the sooner she will see her son dead."[39]

Intratextual Reflection

What a horribly disquieting scene! Can we even imagine the heaviness weighing down this mother's heart as she makes the trek home to Tirzah? Having gone to Shiloh in hope, why does she have to come back in despair? Having obeyed her husband, why does she have to pay such a terrible price for it? It doesn't seem fair. Yes, she's made a mistake, but why punish her for something her husband has done? Why aim so horrific a message at her instead of Jeroboam? Does she really deserve to be confronted by *qashâ*-words about bobbing reeds and rotting corpses? One could more easily accept this for a Jezebel or an Athaliah—but why this poor lady?

Well, why does the southern prophet have to die in the previous chapter? Why have him die for something so "simple" as having lunch with a colleague? Each of these characters seems an innocent bystander because the questions they face—whether to break bread or seek help for a sick child—do not in themselves look very crucial. Yet appearances can be deceiving. This is why Yahweh sends prophets in the first place: to point out the subtle differences between "appearance" and "truth." Jeroboam is interested only in appearances, apparently. He thinks he can redefine words like "truth" and "justice" to meet his own needs. He thinks he can use his wife's legitimate suffering to force this prophet to knuckle under and do his bidding. He thinks he can project a noble image to the world while remaining duplicitous behind-the-scenes.

Theological Reflection

The knock on my door is soft, barely distinguishable.

"Can I come in?" she asks.

"Sure," I reply.

Slinking into a corner chair, she fidgets with her hair while I take a seat across from her, the coffee table standing between us like an electrified fence. Neither of us is surprised by this meeting, and neither of us particularly wants it. We both saw it coming months ago.

"Pastor, can you help me?" she asks. "You know what I'm going through. You know how much I love the Lord. And you, of all people, know what my husband's really like. He's a good man. It's just that he can't...help himself. He has such strong natural urges. The Bible tells me I have to submit to him, right? He doesn't want to hurt the baby...." (The "baby" to which she is referring is her 14-year-old daughter by a previous marriage—a young woman being sexually abused by her present husband).

"Tell me what to do, pastor. I don't want to go through another divorce. I don't want to lose him!" At the mention of "lose," her voice cracks and she breaks down—and for a moment I feel genuine compassion for her—until I realize what she's doing to her daughter. This mother doesn't want to make a decision. She doesn't want to render "judgment" of any kind against her husband, even when her daughter is being abused.

Many of us know people like this. Perhaps it's someone in our family. Perhaps it's someone in our church, or at work. Duplicity and deception are in no way limited to dead Hebrews, and they are in no way limited to duplicitous kings like Jeroboam. What do we say to such people? How can we help them do what's right? More to the point, how can a text like this help them deal honestly and faithfully with the evil they're trying so hard to ignore and cover up? How can it help them trust more completely in the Word when, frankly, it looks a little harsh sometimes? Here are a few suggestions.

First, deception is evil. No matter how cleverly it's presented or how skillfully it's spun, a lie is still a lie, and no believer can afford to be confused about this. When tempted, no one should say, "God is tempting me. For God cannot be tempted by evil, nor is he tempting anyone" (James 1:13). Deception sears the conscience and brings pain. Truth, on the other hand, is not always clear, especially when many "suppress" the truth (Gk *katechô*, Rom 1:18), "exchange" the truth (*metalassô*, 1:25), and "reject" the truth (*apeithô*, 2:8). Against such behavior we need to learn how to "speak" the truth (*legô*, 9:1) and "rejoice" in the truth (*sugchairô*, 1 Cor 13:6). For Paul, there's no middle ground: "We have renounced secret and shameful ways. We do not use deception, nor do we distort the word of God. On the contrary, by setting forth the truth plainly we commend ourselves to every man's conscience in the sight of God" (2 Cor 4:2).

Deception corrupts the Body and outrages the Spirit. Who wants to be part of a church known more for its propaganda than its passion? Who wants to worship in an assembly known more for its showmanship than its spiritual depth? Failure to distinguish between propaganda and prophecy can make any church vulnerable to the Jeroboams of this world. Henrik Ibsen (1828-1906) populates many of his plays with reprehensible "Christian" characters like Strawman (the stupid pastor), and Bishop Nicholas (the political schemer) because the religious culture in which they live breeds such hypocritical behavior. Whether or not we agree with his characterizations (Ibsen was an atheist), the critiques themselves are strikingly correct. Christians who make a habit of cutting moral corners deserve to be parodied.[40]

Second, true prophets cannot be bought—this is what makes them true. True prophets do not hide behind academic, political, or ecclesiastical disguises. Integrity is the clothing they wear and transparency is the image they want to project. For example, though pressured by the priest Amaziah, Amos refuses to knuckle under and give in to his demands (Amos 7:1-10). Instead, he exposes Israelite society for what it is—a moral swamp. He boldly champions God's sovereignty over the world. He pleads on behalf of the powerless. He challenges the king's arrogance. Amos knows that truth is always the first casualty when believers refuse to imagine the world from a theocentric perspective.

Third, the judgment of God can be, well, terrifying. In my opinion, this is one of the story's core themes. Apart from divine judgment, there can be no divine justice, because sin is real and evil is persistent. The more we resist this truth, the less we understand the nature and character of the biblical God. Resistance to Yahweh's righteous judgment pushes us not only closer to Jeroboam, but further away from the Cross, because the Cross is where God's penultimate judgment strikes the cosmos like a hammer. If Christ does not have to die, then God the Father is demonic—thus, how tragic it is that so many believers misunderstand the Atonement as "undeserved suffering" at the hands of a "vindictive God." Better to see it as divine judgment against sin. Better to view it as sacramental extension of Yahweh's divine holiness. The suffering of Christ and the death of Abijah demonstrate Yahweh's commitment to authentic justice, and authentic justice cannot exist apart from authentic judgment.[41] God's wrath is a horrific thing no human being wants to face, and false prophets will always tell us that it's not a problem because it "doesn't exist." But it does exist:

> When Ananias heard this, he fell down and died, and great fear seized all…great fear seized the whole church (Acts 5:5).

> When this became known to the Jews and Greeks living in Ephesus, they were all seized with fear (19:17).

> Knowing therefore the terror of the Lord, we persuade men (2 Cor 5:11, KJV).

> Submit to one another out of fear of the Christ (Eph 5:21).

> Work out your salvation with fear and trembling (Phil 2:12).

> Those who sin are to be rebuked publicly, so that the others may fear (1 Tim 5:20).

> There is no fear in love, but perfect love drives out fear, because fear has to do with punishment (1 John 4:18).

In *The Green Mile*, Stephen King tells a fable about the terrifying reality and inevitability of judgment.[42] The protagonist in the story is a prison guard named Paul Edgecomb, a good man who finds himself caught in a horrifying dilemma from which he cannot escape. One of his prisoners is a man named John Coffey, and when Edgecomb learns that Coffey has been unjustly accused, this throws him into a moral crisis. In one gut-wrenching scene he confesses to his wife his growing fear that one day he will stand before God in the Judgment, and answer to God for "putting to death one of his miracles." The State of Alabama says that he has to push 10,000 volts of electric current through the six-foot-eight-inch body of a man he knows is being unjustly accused—and it's tearing him up inside. The book's final scene brings this conflict to a boiling point as Edgecomb wrestles with how to do his job without abandoning his conscience—and leaves us wondering whether he ever finds a way out of his dilemma.

Both of these stories—one from real-life ministry and one from popular fiction—show us how difficult it is to make moral decisions in the face of persistent evil. However much we suffer, however much we seek to run from the responsibility of making decisions in the midst of such pain, however much we cry out to God for help, eventually we have to face such decisions. Eventually Jeroboam has to answer for the way he's treated his wife. Eventually Paul Edgecomb will have to answer for the way he's treated John Coffey. Eventually the mother in my office will have to tell God (and the police) why she has allowed her husband to abuse her daughter.

Prophetic faith is always about The Judgment.

TAXES AND TRUST (2 Kings 12:1-21)

Years of hiding out in the Temple have apparently convinced Joash that it needs a facelift. Over a hundred years have gone by since its original construction, so when Joash becomes king he makes what he doubtless thinks is a simple proposal: "Let's restore the Temple." The priesthood's response, however, is less than enthusiastic. From their perspective, it's one thing to rescue a prince from the "Red Queen" (Athaliah); it's another to have to obey him, particularly when he sticks his nose into decisions involving money. So here's what they decide: "Let's let the fundraising plan go ahead, but let's filibuster on the details." They decide to turn Joash's construction project into a sixteen-year boondoggle, and this drives a deep wedge between the crown and the priesthood. That they eventually assassinate him at the end of this filibuster is strong evidence that the solution they reach is problematic. What's behind this conflict? Is this dispute about an older generation refusing a younger generation's natural desire for power? Or is there more underneath the surface?

The Chronicler thinks so. In fact, in Chronicles, Joash does not become the victim of an assassination plot—he becomes a devotee of Asherah (2 Chron 24:17–19). Kings says nothing about this, of course, but when Jehoiada's son (Zechariah) confronts him publicly about his idolatrous behavior, Joash has him assassinated (24:20–22). Then the priests retaliate and this explains their assassination of the king; i.e., they murder him for murdering one of their own. Granted, the Chronicler assigns blame to several sources in this incident: (a) the Levites fail to restore the Temple (not the priests); (b) the funds raised are the tax imposed by Moses the servant of Yahweh and by the assembly of Israel for the Tent of the Testimony; and (c) Hazael actually invades Jerusalem (24:23–25—in Kings he only threatens to invade). But in Kings Joash doesn't die because of idolatry. He dies because he oversteps his bounds with the priesthood about Temple funds. It's the money which kills him—how to collect it, how to spend it, how to manage it, how to control it. Where the Chronicler focuses on exonerating the priesthood, Kings focuses on the conflict between the crown and the priesthood. Where the Chronicler vilifies Joash as an idolater, Kings focuses on sensitive questions about taxes and trust.

In Kings, Joash seeks to restore the Temple by inquiring into three separate funding sources: (a) the money collected in the census, (b) the money received from personal vows, and (c) the money brought voluntarily. Each of these sources contributes to the greater Temple treasury, i.e., the money brought as sacred offerings to the temple of Yahweh. We might call these the "general funds." Next to these are the more tightly-guarded "priestly funds"—monies earned from the guilt offerings and sin offerings combined with other monies specifically belonging to the priests.[43] Whether the king wants access to these funds, too, is not immediately clear,[44] but if he does, this would explain the priests' violent reaction. Perhaps they're worried that he might go after their 401K accounts![45] Whatever the case, fundraising is a sensitive issue long after the death of Joash: "May vessels of ministry be procured with the offerings consecrated to Temple repair? Are these [a part of] the equipment of the altar and, therefore, purchasable via the offerings consecrated to Temple repair, or are they rather among the requirements of the sacrifices, and therefore purchasable by Temple funds?" (*b. Ket.* 106b)

This is an age-old problem. "Taxation without representation is tyranny," goes the old American Revolutionary War cry. George Harrison's song, "Taxman," ends with the words: "Now my advice for those who die: Declare the pennies on your eyes."[46] Jesus has strong opinions about taxation (Matt 18:17; Luke 18:10-14), and the Qumran sectarians who precede him do as well: "Into the hands of the slothful do not place an affair, for he will not follow your orders (*ml'ktk*). And do not send him to collect something, for he will not watch over all your provisions (*l' ypls kl 'rhwtyk*). Do not trust in the collector of taxes (*'ysh tlwnh*) to collect money for your 'necessities' (*hwn lmhswrk*)" (4Q424 1.6-8).

Nobody likes to be taxed. The Hebrew word in this Qumran text (*'rk*) primarily means "to assess, line up," but secondarily it can mean "to tax" (i.e., assessment precedes taxation, Luke 2:1). In the Bible, Jehoiakim evaluates the value of Judah's land before taxing it to pay tribute to Pharaoh Neco (2 Kings 23:35). Menahem does the same thing to get the Assyrians off his back (15:20). Joash's mistake may simply be that he goes to the treasury twice—once to fund a domestic project (temple restoration), then once again to fund a defense project (the Syrian war). To the first request the priesthood shows passive-aggressive resistance. To the second they draw up assassination plots, in spite of Jehoiada's attempt to broker a solution.

Redactoral interpreters will always suggest easy ways out of texts like this,[47] but the wiser course is to imagine how recent events may have looked to these priests: (a) Hazael (probably) conspires with Jehu to eliminate Joram and Ahaziah;[48] (b) Athaliah retaliates, then loses power to Yahwist loyalists; (c) Joash intends well, but oversteps his fundraising authority; (d) Hazael takes advantage of the ensuing chaos; and (e) Joash tries to buy him off with gold found in the treasuries of the temple of Yahweh and the royal palace. From a purely priestly perspective, one can easily make the argument that Joash is well-meaning, but naïve. Even without the more-detailed portrait in 2 Chron 24, Joash looks something like a Connecticut Yankee in King Arthur's Court—well-intentioned, but out of his element.[49]

Intratextual Reflection

From the monarchy's perspective, this interpretation is unacceptable. From the monarchy's perspective the story fits best on a *pressure of reform* trajectory. Joash, in fact, is the first monarch to pull Judah away from the yawning abyss which later swallows her whole—and for this he deserves some credit. He also deserves credit for restoring Yahwism after six years of Athaliah, so we need to be careful we don't make him appear more naïve than he actually is. Joash doesn't just wake up one day and order a reconstruction project. Apparently he wants to use this project to energize Judah against the "Baalist Project" of his predecessor, Athaliah. Like all the other stories on this trajectory, this one has a lot to say about corrupt leaders and corrupt institutions and the need to reform both.

Solomonic Jerusalem, as we know, encounters relatively little resistance to its construction projects—until Rehoboam tries to tax the populace beyond its capacities. As soon as Solomon dies, several northern Israelites murder his tax-collector (Adoniram, 1 Kings 12:18). As soon as Jehoiada dies, his priestly colleagues turn against the boy-king he rescues, Joash. The tenderness of age combines with the intransigence of bureaucracy to turn this into a disaster. The Temple desperately needs repair—both physically and spiritually—but Joash (unlike Solomon) has to work with an entrenched bureaucracy unwilling to surrender an inch of its turf. The proverb therefore seems true: "presidents come and go, but bureaucracies last forever." Eventually the Temple does get a facelift, and the crown and the priesthood do hammer out some sort of compromise. But while they fight it out, Hazael of Damascus prepares his invasion plans. Syria knows what it wants, whether Jerusalem does or not.

Bureaucracies simply don't like change. In a famous speech to the

Continental Congress, Patrick Henry urges his fellow colonists to consider the alternative: "If we wish to be free…we must fight! I repeat it, sir, we must fight! An appeal to arms and to the God of hosts is all that is left us!…the battle is not to the strong alone; it is to the vigilant, the active, the brave. Gentlemen may cry, 'Peace, Peace'—but there is no peace…. I know not what course others may take; but as for me, give me liberty or give me death!"[50] Henry delivers this speech because he wants to break through the genteel ideals of his neighbors and force them to face the uncomfortable truth: the alternative to freedom is slavery—whether it's the slavery of ignorance or the slavery of paying taxes to a government which cares nothing about colonial politics. Americans can only wonder what life would be like had this speech not had its desired effect. Contemporary believers might also wonder what life might be like should we surrender the Church to bureaucratic politics instead of messianic faith. What does this text have to say to us?

First, we need to change our thinking about change. Religious people don't often want to hear this, but change is not a suggestion in the Bible—it's a command. "Repent and believe the good news." "Repent and be baptized." "Unless you repent, you will all likewise perish."[51] Reform is impossible without change, and genuine reform cannot happen as long as powerful bureaucracies are allowed the power to stop it. Sometimes bureaucracies are passive-aggressive; sometimes they hide behind a flurry of good ideas. Sometimes they exercise power through budgets and committees and ordination requirements.[52] Are budgets important? Are ordination requirements necessary? Of course they are, but not at the expense of messianic faith. Christ is Lord—not my denomination, not my government, not my family, and certainly not the shogun-like bureaucracies lording themselves over many local churches.

Second, we need to redefine what "priests" are supposed to do. Priestly faith is not simply about order and stability and maintenance. These are components of priestly ministry, of course, but primarily priestly ministry is about repairing boundaries and healing relationships.[53] That so many bureaucracies still define "priest" in medieval instead of biblical categories is directly tied, in my opinion, to our contemporary leadership crisis. The apostle Peter envisions the Church as a kingdom of priests, each priest responsible for the other, all built up into a holy priesthood (1 Pet 2:5). Priestly ritual is supposed to make it easier to repair wounds, not harder. Priestly ritual is supposed to aim at inclusivity, not exclusivity. Too many contemporary priests spend too much time identifying boundaries, and too little time repairing them.

Does holiness need to be preserved? Of course—but not because priests say so. We need to live holy lives because Messiah is holy. Do sinful people need to be challenged? Yes—but not because priests say so. Sinners like you and me need to renegotiate the boundaries between sin and holiness in light of what the Great High Priest has done to the Curtain (Heb 10:20). Is the Bible the standard for the pursuit of this holiness? Yes—but not because priests say so. The Bible is our standard because it leads us to the Word become flesh, the Apostle and High Priest of our confession. Holiness is not about saying whatever we want, then bathing it in soggy ritual. Holiness is about surrendering to the Holy One and serving one another as His royal priesthood.

Semper reformanda ("always reforming") is one of our most precious slogans. Luther, Calvin, Zwingli, Knox, Campbell, Wesley, Ignatius, Zinzendorf, Wyclif, Hus, Bonhoeffer—all the Reformers champion this biblical principle. "A mind is not born again merely by having some portion of it reformed; it must be totally renewed."[54] "The first duty of a preacher of the Gospel is…to rebuke everything in life that does not have… Christ as its base. Thereby he will lead people to a recognition of their miserable condition, and thus they will become humble and yearn for help."[55] "Repentance consists in sorrow for one's sins, and a firm purpose not to commit them or any others."[56]

Theological Reflection

Driving to work today, the lead story on the radio is the President's growing feud with Congress over a projected 250 billion dollar surplus. Predictably, everybody wants a piece of the financial pie. Military folk want to spend it on newer and better defense systems. Educators think it's high time we give serious attention to paying teachers what they deserve. Businesspeople are demanding tax relief. There's nothing like a budget surplus to start an argument.

As a pastor I've sat through countless budget meetings. Usually it's possible to reach a consensus without too much difficulty, but only when everybody realizes that nobody gets everything. Teachers want more money for materials; maintenance deacons want more money for air conditioners; youth ministers want more money for camp scholarships; senior pastors want more money for their staffs. What's amazing to me, as I read through this story, is how often the conflict between Joash and his priesthood mirrors the conflicts I've personally witnessed. To be specific, I've seen many naïve, young staff people walk into budget meetings with no idea of how the process works—only to collide head-on with "the priesthood." Older lay leaders resent being told what to do when it comes to money, and it's not always easy to read their signals. Renegotiating the church budget may not be the most exciting thing about ministry, but it's certainly one of the most important. What can we learn about it from this text?

First, no one should ever assume personal access to the church's general funds. To presume this kind of power only encourages the kind of response we see in this episode. Yes, sometimes preachers need to be a voice for change, but we need to be as "wise as serpents." I remember preaching in a small church to which no budget report had been presented in years, and suspicions were beginning to rise. I could have preached on this problem publicly, but instead I decided to take our treasurer out to lunch (a lovely lady who'd been serving in this capacity for several years). When I discovered that she was only doing her job because no one else had volunteered, I asked her if she wanted any help. She practically jumped over her green beans—"Yes! Do you think we could find somebody to write checks for a few weeks so I can take a vacation next month?" This sister had not taken a vacation in years because she didn't want to leave her post, and when we found somebody to help her out, the "crisis" evaporated. Not all budget problems are so easily resolved, of course, but good process is still good process.

Second, we need to realize that lay volunteers don't have to volunteer. They want to volunteer, and wise leaders will recognize their devotion. We need to commend them publicly for their work. We need to create an atmosphere of trust and solidarity not easily corrupted by gossip and whispering. We need to spend much time in prayer with and for our lay leaders. We need to thank God for the privilege of working with people who love Christ so much. Where money is concerned, we need to appeal to the wisdom of those most gifted in managing it, even as we hold them theologically accountable.

Third, all money-related issues need to come (and stay) before the Lord in prayer. Once I attended a budget meeting in which the conversation heated up over whether to buy land. Some at the table thought we should go into debt to buy this land. Others strenuously objected to this proposal, arguing that we should live by faith and challenge the congregation to step up and give. Would that a Jehoiada could have bored a hole in a box and solved our dilemma! Eventually, we reached a compromise between the debt-free purists and the pro-debt realists and bought the land in chunks—one chunk with church funds, the other through church bonds (another form of giving). What I have learned from such experiences is that the most important thing to remember whenever believers get together to spend the Lord's money is (a) it's the Lord's money, and (b) God will help us disburse it properly if we stay close to his Word in the process.

WHO DO YOU TRUST? (2 Kings 18:1-37)

This chapter narrates the first two episodes of the Hezekiah cycle, a cycle which includes the following components: (a) Hezekiah's commitment to reform, (b) Assyria's threatening challenge, (c) Hezekiah's prayer, (d) Isaiah's indictment of Assyria, and (e) Hezekiah's deliverance (2 Kings 18:1-20:21). Even though Samaria has fallen victim to Assyria, Jerusalem remains free—at least temporarily—and Hezekiah's uprightness (yâshâr) appears to be the primary reason why. Unlike Ahaz, Hezekiah is a reformer who does what is right (yâshâr) in the eyes of Yahweh. From the narrator's perspective, only David (1 Kings 9:4), Jehoshaphat (22:43), Jehu (2 Kings 10:30), Joash (12:2), Amaziah (14:3), Azariah (15:3), Jotham (15:34), Hezekiah (18:3), and Josiah (22:2) even try to "do what is right" (yâshâr).

But except for Josiah, no Hebrew king is more "upright" than Hezekiah. He doesn't cave in to populists. He reforms Judah by destroying its most visible Baalist symbols—the high places, the Asherah poles, the ubiquitous sacred stones (matsebôt) standing sentinel-like over the tombs of the dead.[57] Unlike Ahaz, Hezekiah turns immediately to Yahweh in the struggle against Assyria—not to Baal or Asshur or Nergal or Molech. Politically he turns at one point to Egypt for help, even "confessing wrong" before the Assyrian emperor Sennacherib.[58] But the clear implication is that this narrator respects his integrity and admires his courage.

In Chronicles Hezekiah's first official act is to break the locks on the Temple and reopen Yahweh's house. To reinstate Yahweh worship he purifies the Temple of its defilements, making it possible to observe Passover again. To pay for it all he initiates a successful fundraising campaign in which all Israel brings a great amount, a tithe of everything (2 Chron 29:1-31:21). Like Azariah, though, Hezekiah has a major character flaw—the Chronicler calls it pride of heart (32:26)—yet both Chronicles and Kings portray him as a powerful reformer, a king who "trusts" in Yahweh (bâtah, v. 5).

Sennacherib's plan is to test this trust. Ripping through Judah like a chainsaw, he pauses at Lachish long enough to dispatch a delegation to Jerusalem of three Assyrian lieutenants, who face off against three Hebrew lieutenants (Eliakim, Shebna, and Joah). The taunt-speech they deliver raises a single piercing question: "On what are you basing this confidence of yours?" Playing off the king's main character trait (*bâtaḥ*, "trust," v. 5), this question goes not only to the heart of his character, but also the heart of this speech.[59]

Sennacherib, first, conceptualizes Hezekiah's "rebellion" in a rather generic way: "On what are you basing this confidence of yours?" (lit., "What is this trust you are trusting?" *mâ habbitâḥôn hazzeh 'asher bâtâḥetâ*). "On whom are you depending?" (*bâtaḥtâ*). Good questions. Upon whom is Hezekiah depending? Himself? Egypt? His Davidic lineage? Doubtless Sennacherib raises this question in all his stump speeches, yet it remains provocative and pointed and disturbing. From Sennacherib's perspective, Jerusalem looks like just another conquest on the road to glory. Assyria's military machine has proven itself practically unstoppable. Hamath has fallen. Samaria has fallen. Before Sennacherib finishes with Lachish, he will leave a burn-layer so thick, 20th-century archaeologists will gape at it in astonishment.[60] What can Hezekiah do before such raw power?

Second, this speech is not afraid to deal with political specifics. Sennacherib accuses Hezekiah, for example, of depending on Egypt for chariots and horsemen. Vindictively he labels Pharaoh a splintered reed of a staff, an ally who pierces and wounds his allies because he has no power of his own.[61] Echoing this taunt, Isaiah chastises Judah in similar-sounding language: "Woe to those who go down to Egypt for help, who rely on horses, who trust in the multitude of their chariots and in the great strength of their horsemen" (Isa 31:1). Where Sennacherib wants to intimidate, however, Isaiah wants to warn. He especially wants to warn this young king about the danger of depending too much on chariots instead of God, of relying too much on horses instead of prayer. Sennacherib's desire is not just to conquer Jerusalem, but to bring glory to his war-god, Assur. Armies need rest and provision, and this tactician knows that not having to build siege-ramps is a better strategy than having to build them. He cares nothing about Judah's religious peculiarities, but he does understand the power of specific language to intimidate others.

Third, Sennacherib mocks Hezekiah for trusting in Yahweh: "And if you say to me, 'We are depending on Yahweh our God'—isn't he the one whose high places and altars Hezekiah removed? Do not let the god you depend on deceive you when he says, 'Jerusalem will not be handed over to the king of Assyria.'" Here we come to the nub of it. Sennacherib knows enough about Hezekiah's sputtering reform movement to know that many—perhaps a great many—of the residents of Jerusalem don't like it very much. Thus he appeals to their anger. He offers them "mercy" and "compassion" and joins with them in mocking their king and his old-fashioned reforms. He stirs up their anger over the destruction of their beloved high places. Does this strategy work? Do Hezekiah's people begin to wonder whether the king is on the right track with these reforms?

Sennacherib's speech ends with two parting shots: (a) "Don't blame me; I'm only the messenger," and (b) "Hey—we can still make a deal!" The first of these is as pretentious as it is blasphemous. Before the siege of Sepharvaim he probably claims the authority of their god, too (Adrammelech). Before the siege of Hamath he probably claims the authority of their god (Ashima; 2 Kings 17:30-31; ANET 284-87). Still, his question is a haunting one, particularly when we lay it alongside the words of Yahweh—"I send him [Assyria] against a godless nation, I dispatch him against a people who anger me" (Isa 10:6). Interestingly, both Sennacherib and Isaiah credit Yahweh with this siege, not Assur, though the differences in motivation should be obvious: Sennacherib invokes the Name to intimidate; Isaiah invokes it to pastor and shepherd. The fact that both prophet and pagan invoke the Name is as ideologically revealing as it is literarily ironic.

Finally, the Assyrians challenge Judah to "make a bargain with my master." The bargain they suggest, of course, has nothing to do with "covenant," because "covenant" (berît) is not their goal. Intimidation and assimilation are the goals of this "deal" (hit`ârab).[62] Sennacherib wants to deceive Hezekiah, not covenant with him. To preserve men and matériel, he thinks, "Why not offer every Judahite his own vine and his own cistern? I've got nothing to lose by making such promises."[63]

Intratextual Reflection
Corporations often care little about ethics until the lawyers start calling. Married couples often ignore their marriages until one spouse has an affair. Churches often postpone reform until the membership drops and the budget evaporates. Crisis, in other words, tends to generate reform. Sometimes reform is proactive; sometimes it's reactive. Corporate managers might "suddenly" decide to hire an ethics officer, for example, or write a new vision statement.[64] Church leaders might "suddenly" decide to hire a new pastor, or start a children's ministry, or build a daycare facility (a popular fund-generator). What does Hezekiah do? Hezekiah is an "upright" leader (yâshâr), and we certainly don't want to make light of his reform attempts, but it's not accidental that he responds the way he does to this particular crisis. Each episode on the *pressure of reform* trajectory has a slightly different character. Solomon, for example, builds the

Temple and dedicates it to Yahweh—after he survives a challenge to his kingship. Jeroboam's golden calves occasion two chapters about the power and terror of the prophetic Word (13:1-14:20). Josiah's reform comes in response to fifty years of idolatry under Manasseh (2 Kings 22:1-23:35).

On June 8, 1978, Alexander Solzhenitsyn raised a rather Sennacherib-ish question to the graduating class of Harvard University: "The forces of Evil have begun their decisive offensive, you can feel their pressure, and yet your screens and publications are full of prescribed smiles and raised glasses. What is the joy about?"[65] In fact, when we examine their speeches side-by-side, Sennacherib and Solzhenitsyn have a lot in common. Both are outsiders. Both are blunt. Both are formidable critics who come from cultures vastly different from the ones they criticize. Both are unafraid to talk in specifics and aim at a specific audience ("Speak to us in Aramaic, not Hebrew!"). More to the point, the contents of their speeches are very similar. In fact, three of the themes in Solzhenitsyn's speech pose an uncanny resemblance to the themes in Sennacherib's speech.

First, both Sennacherib and Solzhenitsyn operate on the premise that every nation trusts in Something or Someone. Trust is the operative word when Sennacherib puts a knife to Judah's jugular and asks, "In whom do you trust?," and though Solzhenitsyn avoids the personal pronoun, the blade he uses is still sharp:

> The blindness of (Western) superiority…upholds the belief that vast regions everywhere on our planet should develop and mature to the level of present-day Western systems, which in theory are the best and in practice the most attractive. There is this belief that all those other worlds are only being temporarily prevented by wicked governments or by heavy crises or by their own barbari-ty or incomprehension from taking the way of Western pluralistic democracy and adopting the Western way of life. Countries are judged on the merit of their progress in this direction.[66]

To him, this is pure arrogance: "However, this is a conception which develops out of Western incomprehension of the essence of other worlds, out of the mistake of measuring them all with a Western yardstick. The real picture of our planet's development is quite different." Solzhenitsyn sees a specific reason for this blind belief. With Alasdair MacIntyre, he thinks that the European "Enlightenment Project" has neutralized the foundations of Western morality by imposing upon it an artificial para-digm: "We are now experiencing the consequences of mistakes which had not been noticed at the beginning of the journey. On the way from the Renaissance to our days we have enriched our experience, but we have lost the concept of a Supreme Complete Entity which used to restrain our passions and our irresponsibility."[67] The consequences of this shift have been disastrous: "We have placed too much hope in political and social reforms, only to find out that we were being deprived of our most precious possession: our spiritual life."[68]

Second, both Sennacherib and Solzhenitsyn agree that every nation battles within itself to define the essence of its trust, especially during times of crisis. Sennacherib, for example, argues that Jerusalem is woefully unprepared to deal with the realities of the Assyrian military machine. He thinks Hezekiah's response is based largely on shaky (Egyptian) promises.[69] He sees Jerusalem's ambivalence as something he can turn to his own advantage.

Similarly, Solzhenitsyn argues that "despiritualized materialism" lies at the core of the West's ambivalence. For him, the West's problem is not "secularization," but "despiritualization," i.e., the systematic removal of something once foundational to Western culture. This ambivalence is having a profound impact on international politics, he thinks, but it also impacts other areas of life. Having survived the Gulag prisons, for example, Solzhenitsyn is amazed at how easily Americans sue each other over the pettiest of matters. American "legalism" (his word) is rapidly replacing voluntary self-restraint because too many Westerners have bought into the deception that the law alone can solve our conflicts. "If one is right from a legal point of view, nothing more is required, nobody may mention that one could still not be entirely right, and urge self-restraint, a willingness to renounce such legal rights, sacrifice and selfless risk: it would sound simply absurd."

Third, both Sennacherib and Solzhenitsyn see the core human dilemma as spiritual in nature. Sennacherib lists all the gods who abandon the cities he's conquered for Assur. He does this because he wants to show that Assur's power is superior to all other gods—including the minor grotto-deity he thinks is hiding out in Jerusalem in a lightless cube. Solzhenitsyn similarly denigrates the false gods of the West: "We turned our backs upon the Spirit and embraced all that is material with excessive and unwarranted zeal. This new way of thinking, which had imposed on us its guidance, did not admit the existence of intrinsic evil."

Theological Reflection

Years ago I accepted a call to a mid-sized church hemorrhaging badly from a declining membership. The members complained about everything: the cost of the new buildings, the former pastor's leadership style, the "bad location," the fraying carpet, the "overpaid" staff, the absence of a promised youth program. One of the most embarrassing incidents of my life came when I had to field phone calls from several angry bondholders. The church had financed its physical plant by selling bonds, but when it began missing its payments, the bond company simply forwarded their angry clients to us. The first month of my new job I had to listen to some very angry bondholders demanding their money. It's difficult to explain a congregation's budget woes to an angry bond-holder when (a) you're still unpacking your books, and (b) you have no idea about the true budget situation because (c) it was withheld from you at the interview. Getting through this crisis taught me several lessons.

First, when interviewing for a position on a church staff, it's essential to talk to the treasurer and look at the books because what we might be hearing are empty words instead of coherent strategy. This is no reflection on the congregation, just wise policy (I learned this the hard way!). Many congregations simply haven't thought much about stewardship and finances. Others have, but may or may not have a clear biblical vision about it. Of course, it goes without saying that it's a good idea to make sure that one's working relationship with a church is clearly laid out in a written covenant explaining the expectations of each party. Written covenants can go a long way toward limiting misunderstandings down the road.

Second, when the crisis hits it's important to remember that God is still God. Our God saves because our God is able (Dan 3:17). When the temptation comes to start sending out résumés—and come it will—it's usually better not to listen to the rhetoric of the loudest "Rabshakeh" (2 Kings 18:17, KJV) yelling on the phone or whining to the secretary outside the office door. Better to stay focused on the Mission. Better to empower the disciples, cast the vision, visit the sick, comfort the bereaved, and preach the Word.

Third, desperate church leaders sometimes "fudge the truth." It does no good to get bitter over it. It just happens. In fact, we should expect it to happen, sooner or later. Solzhenitsyn is right. We really do live in a time when people are more enamored of technology than ethics. Yet God sees. God knows. God understands. God saves.

THE POWER OF THE SCROLL (2 Kings 22:1-23:30)

Josiah's reform takes place in the vacuum created by Assyria's withdrawal from Syria-Palestine. This withdrawal occurs, in part, because two Assyrian upstarts, Sin-shar-ishkun and Sin-shum-lishir, revolt against the weak Assyrian king Assur-etel-ilani in 627 BC, and the Babylonian king Nabopolassar is quick to take advantage of it.[70] Suddenly on the defensive, the once-invincible Assyrians have to reposition their troops to engage this new threat from the south. Josiah is quick to take advantage of this too, asserting his independence.[71] Doubtless he allies himself with Egypt to support Assyria against the Babylonians, though this explanation fails to explain why the Egyptians eventually kill him.[72]

The prophet Huldah takes Josiah's reform to another level by confirming the disaster about to be unleashed. Everything written in the book—the book just discovered in the Temple basement—is about to come true, she prophesies. This word, "book" (*seper*) appears about seventy-two times in Kings—thirteen times in this episode alone—because the Josianic reformation proceeds on the assumption that everything has to happen "by the book." When Huldah confirms what Isaiah earlier says to Hezekiah,[73] what these prophets say challenges the tenets of populist Zionism and exposes it for what it is—a terribly skewed interpretation of the book. Judah has egregiously broken the covenants in the book, thus Yahweh's anger will burn against this place and not be quenched—though Josiah will be spared by humbling himself (see 1 Kings 21:29).

Armed with Huldah's confirmation-oracle, Josiah leads Judah into the most sweeping reform movement in its history. Like Jehu, he attacks everything "foreign" in Judah, marking off three areas for immediate cleansing: (a) the Temple and its precincts, (b) the high places in Judah, and (c) the sanctuaries of the old northern kingdom. Taking the laws in Deut 12-26 seriously, he launches a campaign to centralize all of Yahwism around the Temple, believing with all his heart that this is the only place where Yahweh causes his Name to dwell (2 Kings 23:27; see Deut 12:5).[74]

Intratextual Reflection

Intratextually, the lives of Josiah and Joash have a lot in common (2 Kings 11-12). Each king comes to power as a boy. Each comes to power in the wake of a royal assassination (Athaliah/Amon). Each comes to power on the wave of strong Yahwistic reaction to foreign religious pressure. Each works with a Yahwist priest behind the scenes (Jehoiada/Hilkiah). Each king, under the influence of his patron-priest, focuses his attention on cleansing the Temple. And each makes a covenant "by the pillar" in order to revive the Davidic kingdom dream (2 Kings 11:14; 23:3).

Each boy-king grows up, moreover, in an atmosphere of resistance, and each dies a premature death under suspicious circumstances. With so many parallels, the question of whether one story copies from the other is literarily imaginable,[75] but of greater theological significance is the fact that the *faith seeking reform* trajectory begins with stories about prophetic power (1 Kings 13:1-14:20), then illustrates this power through a series of "good" kings struggling to obey it (2 Kings 12; 22:1-23:35), before it ends with a story about a "bad" king's failure (Jehoiakim, 23:36-24:20).

Where these parallels differ is the way they variously portray "the book." First, the greatest difference, though it may seem obvious, is that Josiah's discovery of a Torah scroll (*seper ḥattôrâ*, "book of the Law") fuels his reform's success, whereas Joash makes no such discovery and experiences no such success. The reason that Josiah escapes criticism in Kings is largely his devotion to "the book." Second, when Joash tries to broaden his reforms beyond conventional priestly boundaries, he encounters stiff resistance. Why? Intratextually, the most likely answer is that he possesses no written authority upon which to validate his reform proposals. Joash's good intentions never really translate into Josiah-like action. Third, when Jehoiada makes a covenant on Joash's behalf, he constructs a document designed to ring the wagons around Joash, and his intentions seem obvious: to establish a covenant between the king and the people (2 Kings 11:17). Josiah's covenant, however, is not so much priestly charter as prophetic preamble. Josiah's covenant promises to follow Yahweh and keep his commands, regulations and decrees with all his heart and all his soul, thus confirming the words of the covenant "written in this book" (2 Kings 23:3). To Joash's covenant, the people say nothing—not a word—while to Josiah's covenant all the people pledge themselves.[76]

This brief intratextual analysis therefore suggests that the narrator sequences these stories the way he does because he wants to emphasize the power of the written Word. Josiah's reforms go deeper and farther than Joash's because he bases them on something deeper than tradition or custom. The written Word has power, persistence, and authority. With it, a reformer can spark and sustain a long-lasting reform. Without it, reform movements seem to have difficulty getting off the ground and maintaining momentum. Without it, would-be reformers must rely on good intentions in the face of persistent resistance, whether from internal sources (priests at high-place cult-shrines) or from external sources (foreign invaders bringing foreign religions).

Theological Reflection

This episode stands at the pinnacle of Kings' reformation trajectory and sums up many of its most important themes. Reformation requires faith, determination and absolute commitment to the written Word. When we look at the life of any major reformer—John Hus, Martin Luther, John Calvin, Menno Simmons, John Knox, Alexander Campbell, Ignatius Loyola—these same common denominators keep popping up in their reforms as well. After fifty-five years of Manasseh, Josiah knows he will have to mobilize an entire network of delegate-leaders if his reforms are to make headway, and the process he adopts is worth summarizing carefully: (a) serious Bible study leads to (b) personal conviction ("he tore his robes"), which leads to (c) a deeper seeking of the divine will, which leads to (d) a greater willingness to receive counsel (in this case, from a female prophet), which leads to (e) a greater desire to empower disciple-leaders, which leads to (f) a renewal of corporate conviction (via covenant), which leads to (g) decisive corporate action.

No reform movement can survive without the power of the Scroll.

Notes

1. F. M. Cross suggests (*From Epic to Canon*, 89) that Israel uses dolphin hides because there is an organic connection between the tabernacle and the Tent of El in Canaanite myth—the latter, like later Phoenician cults, doubtless incorporating sea motifs in its iconography.

2. R. J. Clifford ("The Tent of El and the Israelite Tent of Meeting," *CBQ* 33 [1971] 221-27) convincingly argues that El's abode on Mt. Zaphon is a "domed tent," based on careful reading of the paralleled synonyms in *KTU* 1.19.211-14 and *KTU* 1.4.iii.23-24. Whether the inhabitants of Ugarit actually used such tents as movable shrines remains unproven.

3. J. Morgenstern, "The Ark, The Ephod, and the 'Tent of Meeting'," *HUCA* 17 (1942/43) 153-226.

4. F. M. Cross (*From Epic to Canon*, 93) thinks that the Tent of David is "transitional between the tribal shrine of Shiloh and the dynastic chapel of Solomon." Whether the polarity between "tent" and "temple" arises out of a polarity between the "house of Baal" and the "tent of El" in Canaanite myth is more possible than probable.

5. H-J. Zobel, "'*arôn*," *TDOT* 1.367-68.

6. Though M. Dibelius (*Die Lade Jahves* [FRLANT 98; Göttingen: Vandenhoeck und Ruprecht, 1906] 112-13) is one of the first in a long line of scholars to deny the Ark's premonarchical existence.

7. J. Gutmann ("The History of the Ark," *ZAW* 83 [1971] 22-30) lists the Ark's variegated sociological functions.

8. Psa 132 explicitly links the Ark's priestly and political roles (T. Fretheim, "Psalm 132: A Form-Critical Study," *JBL* 86 [1967] 289-300).

9. Other programmatic speeches include Deut 1:1-4:40; 31:1-29; Josh 1:1-18; 23:2-16; Judg 2:1-5; 1 Sam 12:1-25; 2 Sam 7:8-16; 2 Kings 17:7-23; and 21:2-16.

10. J. Levenson ("From Temple to Synagogue: 1 Kings 8," *Traditions in Transformation: Turning Points in Biblical Faith* [ed. B. Halpern and J. Levenson; Winona Lake, IN: Eisenbrauns, 1981] 143-66) thinks 8:22-53 is basically exilic; B. Halpern (*The First Historians: The Hebrew Bible and History* [San Francisco: Harper & Row, 1988] 168-69) thinks it is basically preexilic.

11. G. Knoppers, "Prayer and Propaganda: Solomon's Dedication of the Temple and the Deuteronomist's Program," *CBQ* 57 (1995) 234.

12. E. Talstra (*Solomon's Prayer* [Kampen: Kok Pharos, 1993] 108-26) offers an exhaustive literary analysis.

13. These are not their real names.

14. T. Aquinas (*Supplement to the Third Part of the Summa Theologica* [Portland, OR: Sages, 1997] Part 4, Question 1, Answer 1, Objection 3), for example, tries to segregate "contrition" from "confession," so that "it is not always necessary for the contrite person to have the purpose of confessing and of making satisfaction."

15. D. A. Moody ("Theology in the Renewal of Baptist Life," *Perspectives in Religious Studies* 23 [1996] 5-23) emphasizes how difficult it is to be evangelical and non-sectarian.

16. H. Sasse ("Sin and Forgiveness in the Modern World," *CT* 11 [1967] 539-41) argues that because of the Renaissance and the Enlightenment many people have no sense of sin, and thus feel no need to practice forgiveness.

17. Richard Foster's Renovaré seminars, based on his book, *Celebration of Discipline* (San Francisco: Harper, 1988), are trying to call the Church back to the fundamental spiritual disciplines.

18. W. Barclay, *The Letter to the Hebrews* (Daily Study Bible; Louisville: Westminster/John Knox, 1976) s.v. Heb 9:15-22.

19. T. J. Davis, "Images of Intolerance: John Calvin in Nineteenth-Century History Textbooks," *Church History* 65 (1996) 234-48.

20. S. Hopper ("The 'Terrible Sonnets' of Gerard Manley Hopkins and the 'Confessions' of Jeremiah," *Semeia* 13 [1978] 63) uses the term "inscape" to describe Jeremiah's inner sufferings in Jer 11:18-12:6; 15:10-21; 17:14-18; 18:18-23; 20:7-18 (the "laments").

21. On the basis of evidence from Emar, D. Fleming argues ("The Etymological Origins of the Hebrew *nabî*: The One Who Invokes God," *CBQ* 55 (1993) 217-24) that the *nabî* is not so much "the one called" by God (the position of W. F. Albright) as "the one who calls/invokes" God. This definition finds support in the newer evidence coming to light from Mari. *ARM* 26.216, for example, expressly mentions Hanaean "prophets" (H. B. Huffmon, "The Expansion of Prophecy in the Mari Archives," in *Prophecy and Prophets* [ed. Y. Gitay; Atlanta: Scholars, 1997] 14).

22. Perhaps the prophet uses an indirect technique like those used by prophetic figures elsewhere. Yahweh can and does use the subconscious (Dan 2), mediums (1 Sam 28), and even talking donkeys to communicate his word (Num 22). Preaching to an altar looks tame by comparison.

23. H. Bullock (*An Introduction to the Old Testament Prophetic Books* [Chicago:

Moody, 1986] 136) sees here the combination of two predictive prophecies—one distant (Josiah's restoration), the other immediate (the splitting altar). Like the combinations in Isa 8:1-4 and Jer 28:1-17, the second is designed to build faith in the as-yet-unfulfilled first.

24. Note the similar refusals of financial remuneration in the traditions about Balaam (Num 24:13) and Daniel (Dan 5:17).

25. Huffmon, "Expansion"; M. Nissinen, *References to Prophecy in Neo-Assyrian Sources* (Winona Lake, IN: Eisenbrauns, 1998).

26. J. J. M. Roberts refuses to surrender prophecy's predictive element in his article, "A Christian Perspective on Christian Prediction," *Int* 33 (1979) 240-53.

27. J. Reumann, "Retreat From the Word or Return To It?" *Lutheran Quarterly* 13 (1961) 308-21.

28. O. Guinness, "America's Last Men and Their Magnificent Talking Cure," *Journal of Biblical Counseling* 15 (1997) 22-33.

29. L. Basney, "Technolatry Unmasked," *The Other Side* 33 (1997) 8-11.

30. P. Westermeyer, "From Idolatry to Freedom," *Perspectives* 11 (1996) 10-12.

31. C. J. H. Wright, "God or Mammon: Biblical Perspectives on Economics in Conflict," *Mission Studies* 12 (1995) 145-56.

32. L. Melina ("Homosexual Inclination as an Objective Disorder: Reflections of Theological Anthropology," *Communio: International Catholic Review* 25 [1998] 57-68) sees homosexuality not only as a deliberately chosen lifestyle, but as a spiritual attitude intent on denying the created order.

33. See my *Reconciliation: A Study of Biblical Families in Conflict* (Joplin, MO: College Press, 1994) 45.

34. D. Beekmann, "Leadership for Pastoral Development," *Word & World* 13 (1993) 42-50.

35. K. C. Haugk and R. S. Perry, *Antagonists in the Church* (Minneapolis: Augsburg, 1988).

36. T. W. Hall, "The Personal Functioning of Pastors: A Review of Empirical Research with Implications for the Care of Pastors," *Journal of Psychology and Theology* 25 (1997) 240-53.

37. This same word describes the "tearing open" of the altar in 13:3.

38. *Massekâ* is often translated "molten image" (NIV idols made of metal). This word is one of the primary links between narratives about Jeroboam's cult and the story of Aaron's golden calf.

39. Josephus, *AJ* 8.273.

40. M. C. Allen, "The Clergy in Ibsen's Plays," *Religion in Life* 31 (1962) 279-93. Ibsen is generally acknowledged as the founder of modern prose drama.

41. W. C. Placher, "Christ Takes Our Place: Rethinking Atonement," *Int* 53 (1999) 5-20.

42. S. King, *The Green Mile* (New York: Pocket, 1996).

43. L. Wright ("*Mkr* in 2 Kings XII 5-17 and Deuteronomy XVIII 8," *VT* 39 [1989] 438-48) thinks the Temple's funds fall into two categories: (a) the money freely given by the people, and (b) the money procured by the "selling" (*makkar*) of sin and guilt offerings.

44. The crux of the problem lies in how to interpret the ambiguous term *mkrw* in v. 5. MT vocalizes as *makkârô*, which, if derived from the verb *nâkar*, could mean

"his acquaintance" (lit. "recognized one," *BDB* 648). LXX, however, reads *praseôs autôn* ("their selling"), evidently a translation of the Heb verb *mâkar*, "to sell." MT and LXX are both singular, but this does not stop many of the versions from reading *mkrw* as a plural noun (NIV" treasurers"; NRSV "donors"; NJPS "benefactors"). KJV and ASV, however, read "his acquaintance" (sg.).

45. A modern-day parallel might be, say, the Enron schandal or a university president spending endowment funds for new classrooms. R. Kessler ("Gott und König, Grundeigentum und Fruchtbarkeit," *ZAW* 108 [1996] 214-32) seriously doubts whether Israel's pre-exilic kings could appropriate land for themselves without opposition (1 Kings 21), but he does think that they go after other sources, like temple taxes, to fund various projects "under the table."

46. George Harrison, "Taxman" (The Beatles, *Revolver*, 1972). This is a reference to the old British custom of placing pennies in the eye-sockets of corpses.

47. C. Levin ("Die Instandsetzung des Tempels unter Joasch ben Ahasja," *VT* 40 [1990] 51-88), for example, sees the verse about tribute (v 18) as the text's oldest reliable verse, around which a later redactor inserts the story of the temple repairs by Joash (simply because both paragraphs use the word *qodâshîm*, "sacred offerings/ objects").

48. Confronted by the biblical witness (Jehu kills "seventy kings," 2 Kings 10:1) and the Tel Dan inscription (where the author—probably Hazael—claims to kill "seventy kings") Biran and Naveh ask, "Is it possible that Hazael sees Jehu as his military agent?" (A. Biran & J. Naveh, "The Tel Dan Inscription: A New Fragment," *IEJ* 45 [1995] 18).

49. Mark Twain, *A Connecticut Yankee in King Arthur's Court* (New York: Charles L. Webster & Co., 1889).

50. The University of Oklahoma has posted this speech at www.law.ou.edu/ hist/henry.html.

51. Mark 1:5; Luke 3:13; Acts 2:38. The Greek word for "repent" is *metanoeô*, "Change your mind!"

52. As a seminary professor, it is very frustrating to invest large amounts of time and energy into potential pastors only to see them abused by denominational ordination committees, most of which are populated by people who have never pastored a church.

53. Anthropologically this is what priests do in all religious systems; see my "Role Pre-Emption in the Israelite Priesthood," *VT* 46 (1996) 316-29.

54. Calvin, *Institutes* 2.3.1.

55. Luther, *Preface to Romans* (trans. by A. Thornton from H. Volz and H. Blanke, eds; *Martin Luther: Die ganze heilige Schrift deutsch* [Munich: Roger & Bernard] 1972) 2263. Originally written in 1545.

56. S. B. Varenne, ed., *The Spiritual Exercises of St. Ignatius of Loyola* (New York: Vintage, 2000) 30.

57. C. Graesser argues ("Standing Stones in Ancient Palestine," *BA* 35, 2 [1972] 34-63) that *matsebôt* function (a) as memorials for dead persons, (b) as legal markers, (c) as markers to commemorate important events, and (d) as markers of sacred cult-sites. D. Manor ("Masseba," *ABD* 4.602) points out that the Bible uses the Heb word *matsebôt* to refer to "standing" objects (*nâtsab*, "to stand") which are both condoned and condemned in the OT.

58. Isa 30:1-5; 31:1-3 (confirmed by Sennacherib's annals, scattered over several

stelae, *ANET* 287-88).

59. This verb (*bâtah*) appears in 2 Kings 18:5, 19, 20, 21, 22, 24, 30; 19:10 (eight times in the Hezekiah cycle).

60. R. Barnett, "The Siege of Lachish," *IEJ* 8 (1958) 161–64.

61. Sennacherib probably refers here to Tirhakah, a Pharaoh of Sudanese origin and the third member of the 25th Dynasty (690–664 BC; 2 Kgs 19:9; Isa 37:9).

62. The hitpa`el of `*ârab* means "to exchange pledges/to mingle together." This rare verb occurs in Psa 106:35, where the psalmist bewails the tragedy of Israel's mingling (*yit`ârab*) with the nations and adopting their customs.

63. R. Hyman, "The Rabshakeh's Speech: A Study of Rhetorical Intimidation," *JBQ* 23 (1995) 213-20.

64. In the Salomon Brothers scandal, the board of Salomon fired top-level management and hired the millionaire investor Warren Buffet to clean things up (M. Mayer, *Nightmare on Wall Street* [New York: Simon and Schuster, 1993]).

65. All citations are from http://www.hno.harvard.edu/hno.sibpages/speeches/solzhenitsyn.html.

66. This criticism is not unique to Solzhenitsyn—missiologists have been saying the same thing for years (e.g., G. Pixley, "Missions in Central America Today under the Pressure of Imperialism," *American Baptist Quarterly* 11 [1992] 133-41; H. Grunder, "Christian Mission and Colonial Expansion: Historical and Structural Connections," *Mission Studies* 12 [1995] 18-29).

67. "Enlightenment Project" is MacIntyre's phrase (*After Virtue: A Study in Moral Theory*, 2nd ed. [Notre Dame, IN: University of Notre Dame Press, 1984; first published in 1981] 11-12).

68. Solzhenitsyn goes on to illustrate the results of this loss in several areas, focusing on geopolitics, economics, ethics, law, philosophy, and the work of the press.

69. The idiom underneath the NIV's translation "empty words" is *debar shepatayim `etsâ* (lit., "word of lips counsel").

70. D. Wiseman, *Chronicles of Chaldaean Kings (626–556 B.C.) in the British Museum* (London: Trustees of the British Museum, 1956) 55-62.

71. The Chronicler extends Josiah's conquest north of Samaria into Galilee, but so far the archaeological evidence supports only the Kings account (see J. Naveh, "The Excavations at Mesad Hashavyahu," *IEJ* 12 [1962] 89-113).

72. Most assume that Josiah goes out to stop Egypt from supporting Assyria, but in 2 Chron 35:11 the Chronicler argues that Josiah dies because he disobeys God (thus "explaining" the problem of Huldah's prophecy of a peaceful death in 2 Kings 22:20). R. Nelson attractively suggests ("Realpolitik in Judah [687–609 BCE]," in *Scripture in Context II* [eds. W. W. Hallo, J. C. Moyer, and L. C. Perdue; Winona Lake, IN: Eisenbrauns, 1983] 177-89) that Pharaoh Neco kills Josiah by treachery in order to take over Megiddo for himself as a fallback fortress—in case the Babylonians push him that far south.

73. 2 Kings 20:17; 21:12-14. Many see these prophecies as inserted by a later hand, but such views imply that no pre-exilic prophet ever warns Judah about the consequences of her idolatry—and this is too ridiculous an argument to take seriously.

74. Since the time of Wellhausen the scholarly consensus has seen it the other way around—that Deuteronomy is the product, not the inspiration, of the restoration. This theory is under siege today (e.g., E. Kragelund Holt, "The Chicken and the Egg

- Or: Was Jeremiah a Member of the Deuteronomist Party?" *JSOT* 44 [1989] 109-22).

75. C. Levin argues ("Die Instandsetzung des Tempels unter Joasch ben Ahasja," *VT* 40 [1990] 51-88) that Jehoida is patterned after Hilkiah, but there is no reason not to see it the other way around, or that both priests follow a conventional stereotype.

76. Lit., "all the people stood in the covenant." That is, even as Josiah "stands" by the "standing pillar" (`âmad `ammûd), so the people respond by "standing" (`âmad) in the covenant.

EIGHT

THE PRESSURE OF YAHWEH

I HAVE A DREAM (1 Kings 3:1-15)

Having successfully defended his kingdom against both internal and external adversaries, Solomon finally turns to the business of government. Before getting down to work, though, he has an intense religious experience at Gibeon. He doesn't see visions of heavenly ladders (Jacob), or hear voices in the desert (Moses), but what he does experience sets the tone for his entire administration. Dream theophanies follow conventional patterns in ancient literature. The pattern "sacrificial offering—dream—celebratory banquet" is one of the most common as Canaanite, Anatolian, Mesopotamian, and Egyptian sources all show kings experiencing dreams at the beginnings of their reigns.[1] Solomon's dream is hardly unique.[2]

Oneiromancy (lit., "dream-magic"), however, is a delicate matter in the Hebrew Bible. Sometimes, as with Jacob's dream at Bethel (Gen 28:12-16), the symbolism is obvious. At other times, however, dreams can be quite incomprehensible apart from some sort of "professional" interpretation (Gen 40:5-19; 41:1-36; Judg 7:13-15; Dan 2:1-45, 4:1-24). As time goes by (and the problem of abuse grows acute), priestly attitudes toward dream-interpretation slowly harden, particularly in later biblical (Isa 29:8;

Job 20:8, Qoh 5:6) and post-biblical literature (Sir 34.1-7; 40:1-11; Wis 17-18; 1 Enoch 83-90).[3] Eventually a whole set of criteria develops to distinguish "true" dreams from "false" dreams (Deut 13:1-5; Jer 23:25-32; 11Q19, col. 54 [the Temple scroll]).

Kings stands near the beginning of this biblical trajectory, and tips its hand by the way it juxtaposes Solomon's dream with his unsavory marriage to an Egyptian foreigner. Comparing this narrative to its parallel in Chronicles, no foreign princess appears in 2 Chron 1:1-13,[4] and Kings says nothing about why Solomon weds a woman from Egypt instead of Israel (whatever happened to Abishag?). We know little about the Egyptian-Israelite politics standing behind this tradition,[5] but we do know that she appears several times in Kings, and each time she does the narrator makes unsavory comments about her relationship to Solomon: (a) Solomon builds her a palace (1 Kings 7:8); (b) her father, the Pharaoh, gives her the village of Gezer as a wedding gift (9:16); and (c) Solomon moves her entire retinue to Jerusalem (9:24).[6]

Similar concerns condition his remarks about the "high places." This is an oft-repeated worry in Kings, and the present episode conveys this worry through the ingenious placement of a single word—"however" (Heb *raq*). Yahweh's Temple has yet to be built...*however*, the people are sacrificing at the high places. Solomon loves Yahweh and walks according to the statutes of David...*however*, he continues to sacrifice at the high places. Chronicles registers no such discomfort with the high places. Instead, the Chronicler practically legitimizes Gibeon, noting that two Mosaic cult-items are preserved there: the tent of meeting and the bronze altar. Neither of these items appears in the parallel Kings account because the prophetic narrator wants to emphasize that "even kings such as David and Solomon are meant to be subordinate to the priests."[7] In short, the Kings narrator feels that what goes on at the high places is dangerous and irresponsible—therefore the fact that the famous story of Solomon's dream occurs at a "high place" is a problem for him, a problem he needs to handle with integrity within the boundaries of his prophetic theology.

First, in Kings Yahweh says, "Ask for whatever you want me to give you." Only rarely in ancient theophanies do deities speak first, and when they do, only rarely do they begin their messages with imperative commands. More often than not the conversation starts with a question, like El's question to Kirta: "What ails Kirta, that he weeps...? Does he wish for the kingship of the bull, his father?"[8] Sometimes one god addresses another god while the human dreamer "listens in"; for example, "Anu said to Enlil, 'Why did they kill the Bull of Heaven?'"[9] At other times the opening line is an introductory word of identification; e.g., "I am your father, Harmakhis-Khepri-Re-Atum."[10]

Yahweh's style is different. Yahweh is the one who starts the conversation, and even if we assume this dream to be solicited,[11] it's hard to imagine a more abrupt declaration of grace than "Ask for whatever you want me to give you." After everything this king has been through—the intrigues, the challenges, the tough decisions—how can this not be an exhilarating experience?

Second, Solomon responds. Instinctively he acknowledges his awareness of Yahweh's "great kindness" (*hesed gadôl*). Carefully he recognizes that Yahweh both "creates" (`*asîta*) and "preserves" (*tishmar*). Judiciously he notes that Yahweh (not Nathan or Bathsheba or David) is the reason why the monarchy has survived its first power transfer. To the deity's inquiry he blurts out what so many say when confronted with the Presence of God: "I am but a young child." Elsewhere Jeremiah utters these same words (Jer 1:7), but Solomon acknowledges his youth not to evade God's call, only to acknowledge his inexperience.

Careful readers will recognize that Solomon never asks for wisdom in this text, though this is undoubtedly a wisdom text. He does not ask for God to send down divine wisdom from above, nor does he ask for a philosophical understanding of wisdom as an ideal. Instead he asks for a "listening heart" (*leb shome`a*). He does not ask for the world to change around him; he asks for the world to change inside him. He does not ask God to balance the royal budget, or destroy his enemies, or guarantee his health.[12] He asks instead for a teachable heart, a heart willing to "listen"/"obey" (*shama`*) the Word of God, even when that Word leads to difficult paths and pressures. Some rabbis argue that Solomon does not ask for wisdom because he suspects that this is what Yahweh secretly wants him to request (*Eccl. Rab.* 2). But to such cynicism it seems wiser to argue that Solomon's primary intention is to learn how to live by faith instead of fear.

Intratextual Reflection

This is the first of several theophanies in Kings. Theophanies occur at the beginning of the Solomon cycle and then again very near the end (1 Kings 9:1-9). The third theophany in Kings occurs when Yahweh speaks patiently and directly to the prophet Elijah (19:1-18). The remaining two are less intimate, yet no less dramatic. In 2 Kings 2 Yahweh lowers a fiery chariot to take Elijah up into heaven, and in 2 Kings 17 he summarizes his rationale for sending Samaria into exile. That this trajectory begins so promisingly and ends so disappointingly is no accident. Instead it reflects the structure of the book as a whole. Israel's apostasy increases in direct proportion to its distance from Yahweh, and this means that even the most amazing acts of grace ("Ask for whatever you want me to give you") eventually deteriorate into terrifying acts of judgment ("So Yahweh was very angry with Israel and removed them from his presence," 2 Kings 17:18).

This becomes clearer when we compare the theophany to Solomon (1 Kings 3) with the theophany to Elijah (1 Kings 19). Yahweh initiates both encounters, and both occur at night. Both occur in relatively private places—a high place in Gibeon, a cave in Horeb—and both occur after violent incidents in which the recipient barely escapes with his life (Solomon's survival of his adversaries; Elijah's survival of Jezebel). Both show us strong leaders struggling to regain their confidence, and in both we see a divine-human dialogue designed to minister to each leader. The dissimilarities come in (a) the way in which Yahweh initiates each dialogue, (b) the response of each leader, and (c) the response of Yahweh to each leader's response.

First, to Solomon God issues a simple invitation ("Ask for whatever you want me to give you"), but this is not what he says to Elijah. To Elijah he asks, "What are you doing here, Elijah?" Perhaps his approach to Elijah is different because prophets and politicians are differently "wired." Perhaps Yahweh prefers to begin God-prophet dialogues with questions and God-king dialogues with commands.[13] Whatever the reasons, each leader's response reveals something about his character. Solomon's recognition of his inexperience stands in stark contrast to Elijah's defensiveness. One man seems ready to listen to God. The other seems too wounded to listen. Fresh from Carmel with the blood of 850 prophets on his hands, Elijah responds immediately and intensely, begging for help as he runs from Jezebel. Solomon, however, says nothing about himself until he first thanks God for what he's already been given. One leader stands at the beginning of his ministry; the other stands near the end.

Second, because each leader stands at a different point, Yahweh's responses are differently tailored. To Elijah, he responds by testing him to see whether, in the midst of his fearfulness, he can still distinguish Yahweh's voice from the louder, but less significant sounds of tornado, earthquake, and fire. As he does with Jeremiah, he approaches his wounded prophet in stages.[14] Only when Elijah has calmed down long enough to listen (*shama*) does he allow him to hear his still, small voice. Were we to compare Yahweh's style with, say, Paul's, the comments here look much like Paul's comments to Corinth—a church he loves, but one with which he has to be very patient and very intentional. Solomon, on the other hand, looks more like the Philippian church—equally beloved, yet more mature in Christ.

Theological Reflection

Herodotus relates a legend in which Cyrus' adversary, Astyages, has a disturbing dream.[15] Alarmed by this dream, he calls in the Magi, who warn him that a child will be born to Astyages' daughter, and that this child (Cyrus) will eventually replace him as king. Believing this oracle, Astyages immediately dispatches a servant to kill the child, but the servant cannot bring himself to do it. Instead, he switches Cyrus with another, stillborn child, and the story comes to a climax when the child's true identity is revealed.

Of interest to us here is what happens next. Defeated and despondent, Astyages goes back to the mysterious guild of the Magi and asks them if there is anything they can do to help him, seeing that their advice has back-fired terribly. The response of the Magi gives us a rare glimpse into the world of ancient Near Eastern prophecy: "Even in our prophecies, it is often but a small thing that has been foretold…(sometimes) the consequences of dreams come to nothing in the end."[16] In other words, "Oops! Sorry! Sometimes we get it right, sometimes we don't! In the final analysis, you're the one who has to deal with the consequences. Good luck!"

The Bible never portrays prophecy like this, nor is Yahweh ever portrayed as some kind of wind-up doll who performs on cue. God appears to Solomon not because he has nothing else to do, and certainly not because he's obligated to. He comes to Solomon because he wants to give him a mission. Solomon's response is positive, but whether he responds positively or negatively is irrelevant. Neither response changes the character of the Divine Commissioner—as Jesus puts it later, "I tell you that out of these stones God can raise up children for Abraham" (Luke 3:8). Yet the fact that Solomon does respond the way he does leads to the following reflections about his leadership style.

First, wise leaders put their trust in a Kingdom Dream. After years of research Robert Dale has discovered that the difference between a healthy church and an unhealthy church is the fact that "dreaming churches plan… (while) doubting churches solve problems."[17] Yet even among those who dream, not every church has a Kingdom Dream. In the Gospels, Jesus speaks over eighty times about the Kingdom Dream, and his disciples are those who lead people to emulate his Dream instead of, say, the American Dream or the Corporate Dream. All churches move through cycles of birth, growth, maturity, and sometimes decline, but the healthy ones are those who serve out of their dreams, not their doubts.

Second, effective leaders are those who teach others how to distinguish the Kingdom Dream from all other dreams. This truth came home to me when I co-preached a funeral for a 35-year-old man whose mother was Anglo-Christian and father was Iranian Muslim. Knowing that half the audience would be Muslim, and knowing that the deceased's only sister, a Christian, wanted me to speak clearly and faithfully about the resurrection hope, I chose John 11 as my text—the story of two sisters grieving the loss of their brother. Following my remarks, a Muslim friend of the family spoke about the deceased's many fine characteristics, yet said nothing about his faith. Afterwards a Christian friend came up and said, "You know, this is the first time I've been to a funeral like this, and I've got to tell you, I've never appreciated being a Christian any more than I do today." Why? The Kingdom Dream is different from other dreams.

Third, effective leaders are joyful. They enjoy life. They laugh at themselves. That this needs to be underlined should be obvious to anyone working in ministry today. In a recent 20-year survey conducted by *Leadership* magazine, for example, only 24% of the pastors surveyed said they remained "very positive" about the ministry.[18] Equally revealing were the responses of their spouses. When asked whether they wanted to stay in the ministry or not, only 56% of them gave an unqualified "yes." Fully 25% of these pastors have suffered the painful experience of forced resignation, and of this number, 43% felt they were forced out their churches by factions of "ten people or less." A large number, 62%, said that their congregations were never told the truth about the reasons for their departure.

What this means, of course, is that there will always be good reasons to complain about the ministry. Ministry is hard, thankless work, and discovering the price for doing it faithfully can be a bone-jarring experience.[19] Yet Solomon's God is delighted when his servants renounce complaining to embrace listening. Having served several congregations as a senior pastor, I can personally testify not only to the authenticity of this survey, but to the need for joy in the lives of my colleagues. Once a church board promised me, upon hearing of our youth minister's resignation, that they would find a replacement. Decades later they have still not hired a youth minister. Once a wealthy board member took me out to lunch to warn me that unless I stopped preaching about social justice he would take the church's wealthiest members and leave. Well, he's left—and the church is thriving like never before. Another time an elder warned me that unless I disinvited the keynote speaker to our upcoming youth rally, an African-American, he would "see to it that you never preach in this county again."

In each of these situations God has given joy in the midst of pain, grace in the midst of sorrow. When I feared being abandoned to the ecclesiastical wolves, he raised up prayer warriors to shield my family from harm. When I worried about dwindling finances, he raised up faithful stewards to sustain and help. When I became emotionally depressed, he drained the bitterness from my soul and gave me back my joy, so that I might fully rejoice with the psalmist: "He is my loving God and my fortress, my stronghold and my deliverer, my shield, in whom I take refuge" (Psa 144:2).

WARNING: KEEP LISTENING! (1 Kings 9:1-9)

At Gibeon, Yahweh promises Solomon long life and riches—if he remains faithful. He warns him to pull back and regroup. He warns him not to stray from the Mission. What looks secondary at Gibeon now turns primary. Watching the temple grow, brick by brick, plank by plank, Yahweh warns Solomon that any move toward covenant violation, regardless of the violator's status, will inevitably lead to judgment. In many ways, therefore, the end of the Solomon cycle looks much like the end of Deuteronomy. Yahweh's warning here echoes the blessing-curse formulae at the end of Moses' farewell speech in Deut 28, and three verbs especially stand out: "I have heard," "I have consecrated," and "I have put."[20]

First, "I have heard" (*shama`ti*) most often refers to human creatures "listening to" and/or "obeying" their Creator (the semantic range of *shama`* includes both meanings). Israel's most famous liturgy, for example, the Shema (Deut 6:4), focuses Israel's attention on its most important responsibility—listening to God. Jews and Christians unanimously agree on this point.[21] Only rarely does *shama`* refer to the deity's desire to participate in the listening process, yet four times in Kings *shama`* appears in the mouths of Yahwistic emissaries. Near the end, for example, Yahweh responds to Hezekiah's agony about Assyria with the words, "I have heard" (2 Kings 19:20). Then he responds again—"I have heard"—to Hezekiah's pleas for healing (20:5). After Josiah's inquiry to Huldah, he says, "Because your heart was responsive and you humbled yourself before Yahweh when you heard what I have spoken against this place and its people, that they would become accursed and laid waste, and because you tore your robes and wept in my presence, I have listened" (*shama`tî*)" (2 Kings 22:19). Thus, to Solomon's rote recitation of the promise ("let your word that you promised your servant David my father come true," 1 Kings 8:26), Yahweh responds with words clothed in "garments of torah."[22]

Second, "I have consecrated" (*hiqdashtî*) is the validation for which Solomon seeks. To live before Yahweh in holiness (*qadash*) is the "impossible dream" of every believer. However neglected in contemporary theology, holiness is a predominant theme in the Old Testament, particularly in the priestly literature. Though much Protestant theology regards Hebrew cultic traditions as "primitive, magical, and manipulative,"[23] it's not difficult to make a case for their centrality in Scripture, nor is it difficult to trace their impact on early Judaism. In the Qumran War Scroll, for example, a priestly Jew exults: "We shall direct our contempt at kings, derision and disdain at mighty men. For the Lord is holy (*qdwsh*) and the King of Glory is with us, together with the holy ones" (1QM 12.7-8). Drawing from the biblical holiness tradition, these ideas about God's holiness can and do mutate into rather baroque forms and formulae. Candidates for acceptance into the *yahad* ("covenant community"), for example, must submit daily to "holy counsel" (1QS 2.25). They must affirm sectarian, extremist views about the "holy spirit" (1QS 4.21). They must surrender all their possessions in order to join "the Holy Congregation" (1QS 5.20). Some Qumranian Jews (who may or may not have been Essenes),[24] are obsessed by what they perceive to be a defiled Jerusalem temple, and try to replace the Temple with themselves as Israel's "Holy of Holies" (*qdwsh qdwshym*, 1QS 8.5-6).

Paul similarly reworks these holiness themes, but instead of crafting them into ever-more-baroque permutations, he Christologizes them, arguing that the Church—both Jew and Gentile—is the Holy Spirit's true temple (1 Cor 3:16-17; 6:19).[25] Members of Christ's Church are to be governed by ethical integrity, not ethnic purity (Eph 5:5),[26] and should think of themselves as offerings of living sacrifices, "holy" (Gk *hagios*) and pleasing to God (Rom 12:1).[27] Christian interpretation of *qdsh* takes an entirely different tack from the interpretations proposed at Qumran.

The third verb, "to put," syntactically anchors the key phrase, "(I have) put my Name there forever." To put the Name in a specific place (*mâqôm*) is a very ancient idea, appearing not just in the Hebrew Bible (Deut 12:5, 11, 21), but also in other ancient literature. In the Amarna correspondence, for example, a chieftain named Abdihiba refuses to abandon Jerusalem because "the king (Pharaoh) has put his name in the land of Jerusalem."[28] In Israel, the Name of Yahweh not only challenges the claims of other gods (like Pharaoh), but it "takes the place which in other cults is occupied by the cultic image."[29] Solomon's primary reason for constructing the Temple is therefore to protect the divine Name, and this leads inevitably to the exclusion of all other (Name-less) temples and sanctuaries. Solomon wants to make sure that the Temple in Jerusalem becomes Yahweh's official and only residence.

Intratextual Reflection

Locating the Name in the Temple is Israel's attempt to answer the question, "How can God be in one place and all places simultaneously?" To put it in more contemporary theological language, "How can God be both immanent and transcendent at the same time?"[30] Too much should not be made of Solomon's ingenious solution, however—the narrator of Kings is not a disciple of Plato, nor is his theology cut from the same cloth as even the New Testament Letter to the Hebrews. Our concern is intratextual. How, for example, does this warning interface with other theophanic warnings, like the one in 2 Kings 17? In 1 Kings 9 God warns Solomon not to serve other gods. In 2 Kings 17 the narrator shows us just how large the iceberg under the phrase "other gods" can be. Lurking underneath this phrase lie the customs of the nations (2 Kings 17:8), the high places (17:9), and unacceptably high levels of sociopolitical "secrecy" (*hapa'*, 17:9). In 1 Kings 9 Yahweh warns that even though the Temple looks "imposing" (*`elyôn*), Solomon's failure to keep covenant can and will lead to his becoming an international "joke" (*mashal*). In 2 Kings 17, however, no one is laughing. Instead, the writer spends an inordinate amount of time condemning Israel's addictions—addiction to idolatry, addiction to divination/magic, addiction to the blood-lust of human sacrifice, addiction to the "selling" of human beings.

Solomon therefore opens a door in Israel which can never again be shut. In lieu of a listening heart, Israel develops into a stubborn people, despising "his statutes, and his covenant that he made with their ancestors, and the warnings that he gave them" (2 Kings 17:15). All this lies behind the opening words of 17:14: "they...would...not...listen."

Theological Reflection

Pastors know only too well what it's like to work with people who won't listen. Most often we see this problem in those believers we might call, for lack of a better term, peripheral. Yet the problem becomes agonizingly complex when such behavior takes root in the heart of congregational leaders (v. 9). Once I had the privilege of pastoring a medium-sized church with great potential. About the third year of my ministry, a professional engineer moved into our area and onto our elder-board. I really enjoyed this brother's company because, besides being a dedicated Christian, he was just a lot of fun to be with. Since both of us were musicians, we often performed together at local retirement villages and church potlucks. We prayed together at countless elder meetings. We encouraged struggling church members together. We visited hospitals. I saw him give unselfishly (and anonymously) to a host of good causes.

As the years went by, however, I watched him slowly change. Driven by a corporate business model—and lacking the exegetical tools to realize what it was doing to him—I watched him try to change the congregation into his own professional image, pushing us hard on a number of fronts. I began to see that unless he was in control of a conversation or discussion, he didn't really listen to what anyone else was trying to say. I began to notice how relentlessly he tried to micromanage people. In short, I began to realize that his gifts were well suited for some aspects of ministry, but not for pastoral leadership.

Things came to a head when we began congregational discussions about a sensitive matter affecting our church—gender justice. Convinced that silencing women in public worship at all times was exegetically indefensible, theologically imbalanced, and fundamentally unjust, a few of our leaders began raising the issue privately. The elder-board, including my friend, knew that unless we addressed the matter responsibly, our plans for growth would never materialize. God would not bless our prayers for growth and too many visitors to our assemblies would continue to be offended by the all-male ethos of our assemblies and policies. We all therefore agreed, after much prayer and study, that the best way to address this problem was to be proactive from the Word, not reactive from our tradition.

This strategy immediately came under attack as the more conservative members of the church began going to this elder to complain—and he caved in like a house of cards. One Sunday morning he would greet me with a hearty "good sermon today!" The next Sunday, after talking to the conservatives, he would scowl at me from a seat in the rear and refuse to make eye contact. This went on for months. Finally, he asked for a meeting, and we tried to talk it out. It was not a pleasant conversation. At one point I asked him to point out where I had departed in my preaching from the "game plan" upon which we had all agreed as a leadership team. I asked him if he was still committed to our plan and our vision for the future, and I'll never forget his response. Taking a long sip of iced tea, he gingerly put down his glass and pushed away from the table. "If you don't stop preaching about this issue," he said in a quavering voice, "I may have to take a few families with me and start another church."

Now, the purpose for telling this story is not to debate gender justice, but to illustrate the process of listening. Whether or not everyone on a leadership team can agree at all times about every issue is not germane to the point I'm making—of course we can't. Gender or race or worship or evangelism or missions or hermeneutics will always be on the table. But these issues can never be addressed seriously as long as we continue to ignore the integrity of the listening process—this is the point of Yahweh's warning. Instead of planning proactively from the Vision he received at Gibeon, Solomon begins responding reactively to his pagan environment. Instead of viewing this conflict as an opportunity to get serious about studying Scripture in its historical and literary context, my friend chose the path of least resistance—reactionary traditionalism. Instead of listening to the Word, he chose the path of political manipulation.

Growth is impossible when leaders stop listening.

A STILL, SMALL VOICE (1 Kings 19:1-18)

After the incident at Carmel, Elijah receives two diametrically opposed messages from two diametrically opposed messengers (Heb *mal'ak* can mean either "messenger" or "angel"). Jezebel's messenger arrives first. Incensed at the slaughter of her protégées, she pledges in the name of her gods to make Elijah's "soul" (*nepesh*, NIV "life") like their now-deceased souls. Seizing on this word, *nepesh*, the narrator weaves it in and out of this episode like a scarlet thread. Elijah runs away to save his *nepesh* (v. 3). Panting and tired, he speaks to his *nepesh* (v. 4). Discouraged, he asks Yahweh to take away his *nepesh* (v. 4). Dejected, he reminds Yahweh that his enemies want to destroy his *nepesh* (vv. 10, 14). Like Jonah, he takes a hard look at his "failed ministry" and despairs. In fact, the death-wish he utters looks almost exactly like Jonah's. In 1 Kings 19:4, Elijah compares "my soul" (*napshî*) to "my ancestors"; in Jon 4:3, Jonah compares "my death" with "my life." Apparently Jezebel's power is so frightening, simply hearing about her intentions is enough to freeze a prophet in his tracks.

Yahweh's angel (*mal'ak*) brings a much different message. This messenger comes to comfort Elijah, not threaten him. Like Jonah, Elijah goes through an incredibly emotional experience, followed by a tense period of wait-and-see. Jonah struggles with a prejudiced heart; Elijah struggles with a fearful heart. Jonah hides and sulks under a "vine" (*qîqayôn*); Elijah collapses from exhaustion under a broom tree (*rôtem*). Jonah witnesses the grace of Yahweh's salvation; Elijah experiences fire from heaven. Most noticeably, both prophets ask Yahweh to take their *nepesh*, so deep are their feelings of rejection. Elijah's questions haunt him like a demon: "Why has the Carmel showdown done so little to change the hearts of the people? Why have they not rejected Baal *en masse* and rallied behind Yahweh? What can I possibly do to top this?"

While Elijah broods, Yahweh acts, sending his angel to feed him with miraculous food, slowly guiding him away from Mt. Carmel toward Mt. Horeb (Exod 19-20). Once he arrives, he asks a single penetrating question: "What are you doing here, Elijah?" Shortly he will ask it again, after parading a number of spectacles before Elijah's eyes—a stone-crunching wind, an earthquake, a devouring fire. Each of these phenomena figures prominently, of course, in Moses' wilderness-wandering experience (Num 16:31-35), yet here, unlike there, Yahweh is not in the wind, not in the earthquake, not in the fire. So where is God in this prophet's hour of need? This is not an unimportant question to ask when someone is going through a faith-crisis.

Eliphaz's vision offers a striking intertextual parallel to this one (Job 4:12-17). Both Elijah and Eliphaz face extraordinary experiences: Elijah has a theophany; Eliphaz has a hair-raising vision. Immediately afterwards both hear the same thing, a "quiet sound" (*qôl demamâ*; NIV "gentle whisper").[31] Yet the emphasis in each text is on the message which follows, not the experience itself, and the message which follows does not try to replace the numinous experience. Instead it carefully clothes the experience in words consistent with previous divine encounters (e.g., the Sinai theophany). In short, Yahweh wants to teach Elijah that the Word is capable of transmitting rational information as well as numinous experience.[32] Instead of an earthquake, Elijah feels something "quiet." Instead of a tornado, his ears strain to the sounds of a gentle whisper. After re-establishing contact God then re-issues his earlier question: "What are you doing here, Elijah?" Perhaps he repeats it again because he wants to teach Elijah something about prophecy's limitations (1 Kings 13). Perhaps he does it to emphasize that nothing more need be added to the Sinai covenant. Perhaps he wants Elijah to realize that a prophet's job is not to legislate new laws, but communicate old ones faithfully.[33]

At least two additional factors need to be considered, however, before we can leave this text: (a) the immediate context, with its strong contrast between Jezebel's rebuke and Yahweh's nurturing; and (b) the immediate foreground in Judaeo-Christian tradition where Moses and

Elijah become venerable icons—one a representative of the Law (Moses), the other a representative of the Prophets (Elijah). Elijah is not just a "new Moses," and prophecy is not just a rehashing of the Law. Much more is at stake in this encounter: "I have been very zealous for Yahweh God Almighty. The Israelites have rejected your covenant, broken down your altars, and put your prophets to death with the sword. I am the only one left, and now they are trying to kill me too" (1 Kings 19:10). Structurally, Elijah's response to God consists of three critical arguments which, when analyzed carefully, introduce us to some of prophecy's deepest core values—and it's important that we recognize them for what they are.

First, Elijah is concerned about Israel's lack of covenant knowledge. From the prophetic point of view, covenant rejection is Israel's central problem—everything else is symptomatic of this core problem.[34] Constantly the prophets complain about covenant ignorance, from Hosea in the north to Micah in the south (Hos 4:6; Mic 6:5), from Moses at the beginning to Malachi at the end (Deut 29:4; Isa 32:4; Jer 10:14; Mal 2:7). Jesus complains about it as well, rebuking his audience on more than one occasion for ignoring and dismissing and marginalizing their covenant heritage (Matt 21:42; 22:29; Luke 24:27; John 10:31-38). Granted, the "knowledge of God" is much more than mere intellectual information, yet the fact remains that vibrant faith cannot grow and flourish in educational quicksand. No one rejects covenant who has not first rejected the discipline of learning about covenant.

Second, Elijah laments the devastating impact this ignorance has on worship. Unlike Baal's altars, Yahweh's altars lay broken down in ruins, and this says volumes about the genetic connection between education and worship. Like Elijah, Hosea also preaches to northern Israelites enmeshed in Baalism. Like Elijah, he understands that Israel's covenant-abandonment is the result of a process: (a) first Yahweh's priests and prophets abandon their educational posts (Hos 4:4-6); (b) then Israel begins to "play the harlot" with Baal and Asherah (4:7-10). When Elijah rebuilds the altar on Carmel, this is what worship renewal is supposed to look like—not the song-and-dance of the Baal prophets. The impulse to take something broken and "heal" it (*râpâ*) is not anything like the decision to reject one's heritage.

Third, Elijah laments what covenant ignorance and vacuous worship have done to Israelite morality. Murdering prophets goes far beyond "agreeing to disagree" over matters of religion. Paul makes a similar argument in the Letter to the Romans when he argues that moral depravity (Rom 1:24-32) is predicated on theological ignorance (1:18-23). The narrator of Kings sees but a short step from corrupt theology to corrupt worship, and an even shorter step from corrupt worship to corrupt ethics.

All three of these criticisms stand behind Elijah's contention that he is zealous for Yahweh. What exactly he means by "zealous" is difficult to say. This term (*qanâ*) can mean both "jealous" and "zealous," but basically it denotes strong religious conviction, sometimes commendable (Num 25:13; Ezek 39:25), and sometimes not (Deut 32:16, 21; 2 Sam 21:2; Ezek 8:3). When Moses complains about the burden of ministry, for example, Yahweh responds by "withdrawing" (*'atsal*) some of Moses' "spirit" (*rûah*) and delegating it to seventy hand-picked helpers. Then, after they begin "prophesying" (*yitnabbe'û*), Joshua demands that Moses delimit their power, and Moses' response is revealing: "I wish that all Yahweh's people were prophets and that Yahweh would put his Spirit on them!" (Num 11:29).

Where Moses is thankful, however, Elijah laments what he hastily imagines to be divine abandonment. He thinks he's the only one left in Israel remaining faithful to Yahweh. He fails to realize that a full seven thousand believers have not yet bowed down to Baal—one hundred times the seventy elders given to Moses. Where Moses decides to serve, Elijah asks to die. Whatever his reasons, in other words—fear, pride, brokenness—Elijah has reached his limit,[35] and Yahweh acknowledges this by commanding him to anoint a successor: Elisha.

Intratextual Reflection

"Theophany" is a combination of two Greek words: *theos* + *phanos*, lit., "god-appearance," and since theophanies are rare, it's not insignificant that four of them appear in Kings: "Solomon's Dream" (1 Kings 3:1-15), "Solomon's Warning" (9:1-9), "A Still, Small Voice" (19:1-18), and "Passing the Mantle" (2 Kings 2:1-25). In each of these encounters God suddenly appears without warning, and the experience of facing him is uniformly terrifying. Solomon is supposed to learn from his encounters about the seriousness of the Law. Presumably Elijah is supposed to learn something about the "quietness" of the Word. It may be that this "quietness" (*demamâ*) refers to a kind of non-verbal "murmuring" where God reveals his deeper intentions,[36] but interpretations like this do not take into account the intertextual parallels with Eliphaz's vision (Job 4:12-17), nor do they seriously examine the intratextual context within Kings itself.

Elijah's concern with covenant, worship, and ethics in Israel is only half the conversation. The other half is the divine imperative—irresistible, mysterious, and unyielding in its power. In effect, Yahweh says, "I hear what you're saying, Elijah, and you do make some excellent points.

Ministry is hard. But what are you going to do? Are you going to serve me or not?" This sounds like the same divine response to Jeremiah after that prophet's first lament: "If you have raced with men on foot, and they have worn you out, how will you compete with horses?" (Jer 12:6). Intratextually the showdown on Carmel (chapter 18) continues on Horeb (chapter 19), only now the "hot war" between Yahweh and Baal in chapter 18 turns into a "cold war" between Yahweh and Elijah in chapter 19. Like Jeremiah, Elijah faces a "progressive paradox," and Yahweh wants him to figure out a faithful response.[37]

Theological Reflection
Once I asked a colleague to speak at a graduation ceremony for our high school seniors, and he did an exceptional job. From opening illustration to final application, he never lost our attention. He inspired and convicted us. He encouraged us. He challenged us. He did what all good preachers do: he brought us nearer to the Holy One. Only about twenty or so had turned out to hear him than night, but it didn't seem to matter, not to him. To us, it was just another graduation banquet, but to him it was another chance to preach. His sermon that evening was a sparkling jewel, as deeply biblical as it was socially relevant. For a man so young he had already mastered that most difficult of homiletical disciplines: how to stand before God and wait. Imagine my surprise when he told me afterwards he was planning to leave the ministry. When I asked him why, all he could say was, "I just don't have another Sunday left in me."

Clergy depression is not new—in fact, it's as old as the Call itself. What is new is the degree to which non-biblical explanations for it are taking over the contemporary conversation. Ministers are quitting, some argue, because of professional unfulfillment, economic disadvantage, emotional vulnerability, and/or administrative overload. No one doubts that these are troubling issues, yet we need to question seriously whether these are the primary factors.[38] To Jeremiah's laments, Yahweh (a) assures his prophet that the threats against his life will fail (Jer 11:21-23), (b) warns him not to overanalyze his problems from a human perspective (12:5-6), (c) reminds him that the divine patience has limits (15:19), and (d) reminds him of his covenant promise (15:20-21).[39] To Elijah's lament, he repeatedly asks, "What are you doing here, Elijah?," and read together, these texts suggest the following possibilities for interpretation:

First, the burden of preaching is heavy. It's okay to admit it, as long as we remain open to receiving help. Sensing a burdened heart in his audience, Spurgeon once remarked, "You, my dear brother, have been working for God in a neighborhood where you have met with little but opposition and disappointment, and you have almost resolved that you will go away from the place. 'The soil is hard,' you say, 'and breaks the ploughshare. Shall oxen plough upon a rock?' 'Tis in vain for you to continue your labor there, you think." Then he responds to this need, like Yahweh responds to Elijah: "Hear the word of the Lord this night. He speaks to you not by any earthquake of judgment…, neither by any fiery word of severe rebuke; but perhaps through me this evening he may speak with a still, small voice that shall just meet your case and send you back to your labor."[40]

Preaching is an unbearable burden apart from the Lord's help.

Second, changing contexts usually changes little, because when we move we take our baggage with us. Moving from a "Mt. Carmel Church" to a "Mt. Horeb Church"—in and of itself—does little to address the core question, "What are you doing here?" Whether God calls me to serve in Maryland or California, Viet Nam or Brazil, large church or small, I still need to address seriously the "Elijah question." It matters little where I do it, or how I do it. What matters is whether I do it. Luther grasped this clearly: "Our Lord God had to ask Moses as many as six times. He also led me into the office in the same way. Had I known about it beforehand, he would have had to take more pains to get me in. Be that as it may, now that I have begun, I intend to perform the duties of the office with his help."[41] Pat Miller is blunt about the burden to which we're called: "I wish I could tell you that I thought Amos felt satisfied at the end of the day, or that Isaiah went home to play catch with little Shear-yashub with a sense of a job well done.…No, there are no fringe benefits to the prophetic ministry—except one: the promise of God's presence along the way."[42]

Third, Yahweh remains gracious in the midst of our burdens. He knows our limitations. He knows when and how to send us the help we need. He knows when Elijah needs to retire, and he certainly knows when you and I need to step out or step back. Preachers who think they're indispensable are a sorry lot. Nobody owes me this job. I've simply been given an opportunity to serve the King for a while. Some will listen to my message. Some will not. The issue is not whether I please everyone, or even whether I please myself. The issue is whether I'm willing to listen to that still, small voice when it whispers to me in the darkness.

PASSING THE MANTLE (1 Kings 19:19-21; 2 Kings 2:1-25)

This is Kings' only example of prophetic succession. Presumably, this is an important phenomenon, so it's a little puzzling that we don't have more examples of it. Political succession is by far the focus of the book of Kings—whether peaceful (Asa succeeds Abijah) or violent (Solomon exterminates his rivals, Zimri assassinates Elah and his family), whether planned (Rehoboam succeeds Solomon) or unplanned (Jehoram succeeds Ahaziah). But prophetic succession appears to operate within a different set of parameters, and much of what we know about it comes from elsewhere in Scripture, particularly Moses' farewell speech in Deut 18:14-22. This speech is a manifesto about Hebrew prophecy. In it, Yahweh warns Israel not to listen to sorcerers (*me'onenîm*) and diviners (*qosemîm*). Instead, Israel is to listen only to *nabî'*-prophets, and then only of a certain kind—"a prophet like me from among your own brothers" (Deut 18:15). In other words, Moses puts prophecy on a rather short leash. The only kind of prophet Yahweh finds acceptable is (a) a *nabî'*, (b) "like Moses," and (c) indigenously Hebrew.[43] That this "prophet-like-Moses" tradition develops a life of its own testifies to its centrality in the biblical tradition,[44] and the fact that the entire Elijah-Elisha cycle is a not-so-subtle reprise of the Moses-Joshua tradition is significant.[45]

Elijah is therefore a *nabî'*-prophet out of this strict Mosaic mold. Like Janus, the two-faced Roman deity from which we get the word "January," prophetic succession has two "faces"—one looking back (Elijah), and one looking forward (Elisha). To use another metaphor, prophetic succession is like the "passing of the baton," that critical moment in a race when one tired runner (Elijah) passes the baton to a new, fresh runner (Elisha). Perhaps the best metaphor, though, is the one embedded in the text itself—"mantle" (*'adderet*). Repeated no less than five times, the mantle metaphor gives this text a character and depth it would not otherwise have. Here's how:

First, Elijah throws his mantle onto the back of a young farmer, Elisha (1 Kings 19:19-21). Like Samuel the prophet (*nabî'*, 1 Sam 9:9), Elijah takes something common and consecrates it for a holy purpose. Homespun cloth may not look "sacred," but by throwing it onto the back of Elisha, Elijah makes it so. Whether Elisha will accept what it represents is another question entirely. Just as David goes through a lengthy transition before succeeding Saul, so Elisha decides to count the cost and consider whether he wants to accept this new position.

Second, Elijah uses something common to accomplish something uncommon. Where Moses uses a shepherd's staff to divide the Sea, Elijah uses a shepherd's mantle to divide the River. That the Jordan needs to be divided, much less crossed, may not seem immediately obvious from the text's historical context, but from its intertextual context it's clear that if Elijah is to become a prophet like Moses he will have to demonstrate the ability to "cross the uncrossable." Just as Moses leads Joshua to the edge of the promised land, so Elijah leads Elisha to the edge of prophetic ministry. Prior to this he seems to lead Elisha on a wild goose chase—from Gilgal to Bethel to Jericho to the Jordan. Discerning readers know, however, that most biblical leaders have to go through wilderness journeys. Moses goes through one. So does Jesus. So does Elijah. Thus, at each point on his final journey, Elijah tests the conviction of his new disciple. Whether he fully prepares him for ministry is impossible to say, but like Moses at the Sea and Joshua at the River (Josh 3:9-17), Elisha is not someone who can graduate from Elijah's mentor ministry until he learns something about how to "cross the uncrossable."[46]

Once across, he asks Elisha what he can do for him, and Elisha's response is immediate: "Let me inherit a double portion of your spirit" (lit., "two mouth[ful]s of your spirit"). The only other mention of this curious phrase is Deut 21:17, "He must acknowledge the son of his unloved wife as the firstborn by giving him a double portion of all he has," and this has caused a few rabbis to wonder how it might be tied to Elisha's ministry. Commenting on the passage where the corpse touches Elisha's bones (2 Kings 13:21), one rabbi suggests, "Perhaps [this miracle] was to fulfill Elijah's blessing, as it is written, 'Let a double portion of your spirit be upon me'" (b. Hull. 7b). Another rabbi takes a different tack, however, suggesting that "double portion" refers not to one, but to two resurrections, each somehow "performed" by Elisha: (a) in addition to the miraculous resurrection of the dead corpse, Elisha also (b) "heals the leprosy of Naaman, which weighs the same as death" (b. Sanh. 47a). Paul Watson rejects these interpretations and argues that this phrase is simply a metaphor for Elisha's desire to please his mentor.[47]

Whatever the possibilities, the third mention of mantle occurs at Elijah's ascension into heaven, one of the most dramatic scenes in the Bible. Heavenly ascents are common in the mystical literature, if not in Scripture. In Jewish mystical literature, for example, prophetic seers go on heavenly journeys of various types for various reasons.[48] Among less Hellenized Jews, the reason can be to "invade heaven" or receive a divine revelation. Among more Hellenized Jews, the motive may be to become immortal, or to obtain a foretaste of the next world.[49] Little of this can be projected back onto Elijah, of course, but it's important to recognize that Elijah's heavenly ascent stands at the base of a long trajectory. Scholars call this trajectory "merkabah" (from the Hebrew word *merkabâ*, "chariot"),[50] and the fact remains that faint echos of merkabah motifs occur in Old Testament tradition (e.g., Jacob's "ladder," Gen 28:10-17, and the *bêt harekabîm*, lit., "house of the charioteers," Jer 35:2).[51]

The point is that Elisha has to make a decision. Will he pick up his mentor's mantle? Will he accept the challenge to become a "prophet like Moses?" Elisha's decision is the episode's crucial, pivotal center. When he dares to follow his mentor into ministry, he too becomes a "prophet like Moses." To underline this, the narrator has him ask the most important question of his life, "Where now is Yahweh, the God of Elijah?"[52]—then quickly rattles off two miracle-stories to confirm Elisha's prophetic power. However strange they may seem to us, the narrator's intention is to show the lengths to which Yahweh will go to confirm Elisha's new prophetic ministry. The first is a miracle of blessing (lit., "healing" [*rapa*]), and the second is a miracle of cursing (*qalal*—because if Elisha is to be a prophet like Moses (Deut 28), he too must be able to "bless" as well as "curse."

Intratextual Reflection

Where Yahweh comes to Solomon and says, "Ask for whatever you want me to give you" (1 Kings 3:5), here he comes to Elisha (through Elijah) and asks, "What can I do for you?" (2 Kings 2:9). At Horeb, he tests Elijah with fire and earthquake and a great wind (*rûah gedôlâ*, 1 Kings 19:11). Here he uses "wind" to yank his prophet off the face of the earth and bring him home (*se`arâ*, v. 11). Where Elijah demands that Elisha "abandon" (*`azab*) his livelihood (1 Kings 19:20), Elisha swears never to "abandon" Elijah (*`azab*, vv. 2, 4, 6). These are just a few of the intratextual parallels.

But passing the mantle is not easy—in fact, it can be downright "difficult" (*qashâ*, v. 10) because established leaders often find it hard to let go of the reins. This is true for all leaders, from presidents to presbyters. Instead of preparing ourselves for the inevitable task of passing the mantle, too many of us choose to circle the wagons and defend our turf. Instead of proactively mentoring replacements, we become defensive and reactionary. In fact, some of us have to be clubbed over the head before we'll let a younger person wear "our" mantle, though the commandment is clear: "You shall anoint Elisha son of Shaphat of Abel-Meholah as prophet in your place" (1 Kings 19:16).[53] How can we illustrate and apply this principle to contemporary ministry situations?

Once I took a position as the preaching minister of a relatively young church. Arriving with great expectations, I soon discovered that the associate minister in the next office resented my coming. Having been passed over for senior pastor, he simply bristled whenever I tried to talk with him. Whenever I tried to schedule a staff meeting, for example, he called to say he was "unavailable," often scheduling a hospital visit or some other good work at the same time. When I tried to sit down and talk with him about my vision for the church, he glowered and scowled like an angry child. When I asked him what role he wanted to play in implementing this vision, he once blurted out, "You know, this thing doesn't seem to be working. Ever think you've made a mistake in coming here?"

Leadership transitions can be very difficult.

But God is gracious to pull us through them.

Theological Reflection

In the apostolic period different churches approach ministry in different ways. Where the tension in the Old Testament is between "prophet" and "priest,"[54] the tension in the New Testament is often between apostle/prophet/teacher vs. bishop/presbyter/deacon.[55] This tension comes to a head in the medieval period. Luther's indictment of rampant clerical corruption,[56] for example, echoes Calvin's belief that "the purity of the ministry...(has) degenerated."[57] Pastors trained by Zwingli could be terribly unprincipled,[58] and those trained by Wesley could be accused of being "unconverted."[59]

As any Bible teacher can attest, though, the majority of our students more often look like Elisha than Elijah. Every day we get the opportunity to spend time with believers who ache for a "double portion of the Spirit," disciples who need and want to be taught and mentored. In fact, mentoring is an idea whose time has again come. As Theophan the Recluse puts it, "For the avoidance of error, have someone to advise you—a spiritual father or confessor, a brother of like mind—and make known to him all that happens to you in the work of prayer."[60]

Disciples need mentors to come alongside them and help them grow, and mentors need to echo the practice of the Christian Church when they mentor these students. As educators we need to do much more than just pass on the material in our lecture notes. We need to commit seriously to the process of pastoral formation. The Elijah-Elisha relationship shows us a clear example of this long before disciples began seeking out mentors in the deserts of Egypt or the mountains of Europe. Most scholars agree that the *benê hannebî'îm* ("sons of the prophets") are groups of students who gather around Elijah and Elisha for this very purpose. And most are agreed that Isaiah refers directly to this process when he talks of "my disciples" (*limmudây*, Isa 8:16).

Among Hellenistic Jews, rabbis are expected to mentor students, so the fact that early Christians continue this educational tradition should come as no surprise. Jesus handpicks twelve students for a special mentor/student relationship in what believers universally recognize as the most important school ever established (Mark 1:16-20). Paul begins his education as a disciple of Rabbi Gamaliel (Acts 22:3), and later he follows the example of his mentor by mentoring others in the Faith—Timothy, Titus, Silas, Priscilla. Priscilla and Aquila continue the tradition by taking Apollos under their wing (Acts 18:24-26), and this mentoring tradition continues on into the ministries of Clement, Origen, Ambrose and many other educators.[61]

The Elijah-Elisha mentorship thus stands at the beginning of a long trajectory and resistance to mentoring as a "new idea" may be explained by the story of the "rat in the statue." The story goes that the emperor of China summons a sage and asks, "What is our most vexing problem?" The sage replies, "The rat in the statue." The emperor thinks he's joking. "The rat in the statue? What does this mean?" The sage replies, "Most houses keep wooden statues to honor their ancestors, but rats frequently gnaw into them and build nests, forcing worshipers into a quandary. Should we save the statues and put up with the rats, or should we burn the statues and get rid of the rats?" Applying this story to mentoring, "Should we go on training pastors in ways which are proving to be more and more ineffective? Or should we take more seriously 'newer' ideas (like mentoring) which challenge us to change significantly the way we teach?"[62] Our answer to this question will go a long way toward forming the next generation of pastors and other Church leaders.

The chariots are coming. Proactive theologies of prophetic succession may or may not replace reactive ideologies of clerical powerbroking, but whether we decide to celebrate the dynamic tensions within the Church or lament the virus of clerical sclerosis paralyzing it here and there, the chariots are still coming. The questions remain just as urgent whether we choose to address them or not: Are we going to pass the mantle to the next generation, or are we going to hold on to ecclesiastical power for as long as we possibly can? Do we want to train pastors or clone protégées? Do we imagine the Church as a global force expanding into every family, tribe and nation, or do we have a different vision in mind for the Church of Christ?

WHY EXILE? (2 Kings 17:7-40)

The first thing we need to see in this final programmatic summary is that Yahweh doesn't simply allow exile. Yahweh causes exile. Yahweh sends people into exile, and for some very specific reasons. Exile is Israel's "time-out." Exile is Yahweh's response to Israel's stubbornness. Like any longsuffering parent, Yahweh decides to send Israel into another room to think things over. To support this interpretation of the Exile against other, competing interpretations, the narrator builds his case like a skilled prosecutor, leaving no stone unturned, no behavior unexamined. Basically, his thesis is this: exile is the result of Israel's determination to abandon its covenant with Yahweh. From Kings' perspective, Assyria is not the cause, only the means for (re)establishing this covenant, and the purpose of this final diatribe is (a) to explain Samaria's fall in terms of this covenant paradigm, and (b) to warn Judah about the same thing possibly happening to them. Structurally it breaks down into four parts.

Part One is Yahweh's testimony. Like other prophetic lawsuits, Yahweh "bears witness" (`ûd, v. 13) to the truth, even though it means testifying against his own people. Unbelievably, Yahweh argues, Israel has turned to other gods in spite of the fact that Yahweh is the one who "brought them up" from Egypt (`âlâ), who drove out the nations before them (lit., "disinherited," yârash), who "sent into exile" (gâlâ) the nations who lived in Canaan prior to Joshua, who "testified" against Israel (weyyâ`ad), and who "spoke" to Israel (`âmar) at Mt. Sinai. Even now, he argues, Yahweh continues to speak through his prophets and seers (lovingly called "my servants"), imploring Israel to turn away from evil and "observe" covenant (shâmar). Like many other prophetic lawsuits (Isa 1:2-3; 1:18-20; Jer 2:4-13; Micah 6:1-8; Hos 4:1-3), this suit lays out the facts before a jaded audience which has decided to reject historical covenant for mythological fantasy.

Part Two narrates this history in some detail. Exile happens because Israel "sins" against Yahweh (hâtâ`), fears other gods, follows the practices of the nations, secretly does things (lit., "covers up," hâpâ`), builds high places, "sets up" sacred stones and Asherah poles (nâtsab),[63] "burns incense" (qâtar), "provokes" Yahweh to anger (kâ`as), and "serves" idols (`âbad). Exile is the result of Israel's refusal to take seriously what Jesus calls the "first commandment"—"listening" (shâma`, Matt 22:38). Instead, Israel stiffens its corporate neck, refuses to trust Yahweh, "rejects" (mâ`as) and "forsakes" (`âzab) Yahweh's commands.[64] Israel chooses to imitate the nations, makes idols of popular images (calves, sacred stones), bows down to the astral deities of their conquerors, and worships Asherah and Baal.[65] Adding insult to injury, Israel has even gone to the horrid extreme of sacrificing its sons and daughters in the fire and practicing divination/sorcery (*qâsam/ nâhash*).[66] Borrowing a word made famous by Qoheleth, the narrator labels all this activity "worthless" (*hebel*, lit., "filled with air").[67] Dusting off a term from the Ahab stories, he sums up Israel's behavior as *mâkar*—Israel has "sold itself" into evil.

Part Three is Yahweh's judicial decision, after weighing the historical evidence, and the narrator conveys it through four active verbs. Earlier God "tore" them away from the house of David through Jeroboam I (*qâra`*). Now he "removes" (*tsûr*) them from his presence, "rejects" (*mâ'as*) them, "afflicts" (*`ânâ*) them, and "sends" them away (*shâlak*). Whether Yahweh's case is justifiable or not, no covenant can exist without enforcement, and because Israel's behavior is so inexcusable, enforcement must be swift and clear. Otherwise there can be no covenant at all.

Part Four is aftermath. To replace the Israelites the Assyrians import captives from Babylon, Cuthah,[68] Avva, Hamath, and Sepharvaim.[69] Of the gods listed here Nergal is probably the best known; the rest are merely localized versions of mostly chthonic deities from the Sumero-Akkadian pantheon.[70] What Assyria does is simply replace polytheistic Israelites with polytheistic Mesopotamians. Yahweh deports Israel while the Assyrians import foreigners into the land to take their place. Instead of following the Israelites into Assyria, however, the narrator keeps his focus on the land. On the one hand, Israel's new inhabitants are alarmingly pagan. If Israel's idolatry is bad, he seems to be saying, the idolatry of these people is far worse. This is the legacy of covenant violation: disobedience, disrespect, and polytheistic pluralism where Yahwistic faith once stood.

Intratextual Reflection

This diatribe is the final episode on the *pressure of Yahweh* trajectory, and this alone makes it a very important passage. In first-person speech Yahweh soberly defends his actions and warns Judah not to make the same mistakes Samaria has made. After this speech there will be no more warnings from God—no more explanations, no more admonitions, no more rationales, no more oracles. Granted, Isaiah will convey a word or two to Hezekiah, and Josiah will solicit a response from Huldah about the Temple scroll. But this is really Yahweh's last major speech, and Kings' best example of pure Yahwism. Here are the main points:

First, Yahweh wants his people to remember that exile is not a new idea. Exile is rather an old solution to an old problem. Had God not sent the nations into exile, for example, Israel would never have been able to settle Canaan in the first place.[71] In spite of the Baalist fantasies propagated by Jezebel's prophets, Israel does not own the land—in fact, no one "owns" this or any other part of the Creation. Should Israel have been more interested in keeping covenant than in drinking wine from bowls (Amos 6:6), she might have understood this. Ownership is a presumption, never a promise. Yahweh owns the land, and it is because of the nations' poor stewardship that he sends them into exile. Where earlier he uses Israelites to displace Canaanites, here he uses Assyrians to displace Israelites.

Failure to understand this facet of God's character has unfortunately led many a theologian to presume that Yahweh is an "angry God" or worse, a god inferior to the Father of Jesus Christ. This miserably uninformed conclusion can only be reached by ignoring the first three-quarters of the Bible. Those determined to propagate it today either link the Jews eternally to Syria-Palestine via a flimsy eschatological framework, or they dare to pick-and-choose theologies of liberation (Exodus) over theologies of suffering (Exile) to suit their own whims. For those who link the Jews eternally to Palestine, the Exile is simply unexplainable—thus, we rarely hear anything about it in their preaching. For those who argue that "justice" equals "liberation," we need to remind them that had it not been for the Exile, the Bible might never have been written at all, and Judaism might never have survived the transition from temple to synagogue. "One of the most remarkable features of the faith of the Old Testament is that the exile, the experience of historical disruption, displacement, and failure, produced not despair, but hope."[72]

Second, Yahweh of Hosts demands acceptable worship. The narrator defines "worship" here in an interesting way: "They neither worship Yahweh (lit., "fear," *yare*) nor adhere to (lit., "do," *`asâ*) the decrees and ordinances, the laws and commands that Yahweh gave the descendants of Jacob, whom he named Israel" (v. 34). Worship is not something based on (what Alasdair MacIntyre calls) "emotivism."[73] No, worship has a concrete goal, a *telos*, and to those who would argue that monotheism replaces henotheism only after the Exile, this text is a problem:

Verse 33 — "They worshiped Yahweh, but they also served their own gods in accordance with the customs of the nations from which they had been brought."

To this indictment, the narrator parallels a second:

> Verse 34 – "To this day they persist in their former practices. They neither worship Yahweh nor adhere to the decrees and ordinances, the laws and commands that Yahweh gave the descendants of Jacob, whom he named Israel."

See the parallel? "Worship Yahweh, but also their own gods" parallels "not worship Yahweh." Henotheism, in other words, is just as unacceptable to this narrator as polytheism.[74] For him, monotheism is the only appropriate stance of a true Yahwist, however un-Enlightened it might appear to the culture at large.[75]

Third, the testimony of Torah is authoritatively equivalent to the testimony of prophets and seers. Yahwism is based on something "written" (*katab*, v. 37), on statutes and ordinances and torah and commands. But so are the practices of the nations. They too operate by a system of statutes (*huqqôt*, v. 8). Social injustice, therefore, is not the root cause of the exile. Israel rather goes into exile because of the poisonous way idolatry undermines the words of the prophets. This view not only challenges the Samaritan/Sadducean propensity to trust in Torah alone; it also elevates dynamic conceptualizations of Scripture over those which are static. In Christian theology, the Word (a) becomes flesh in Christ, (b) becomes flesh in Scripture, and (c) becomes re-enfleshed through faithful proclamation.[76] This means that contemporary preaching—to the extent that it's anchored in the biblical Word—ought to be accorded serious authority, much more than it presently receives. In 2 Kings 17, the commandments and statutes of Moses are parallel to the testimony of the prophets and seers, and Samaria's failure to realize this is what leads to her destruction.[77]

Theological Reflection

Jonathan Magonet suggests two helpful ways to look at the problem of exile, macroscopic and microscopic.[78] On a macroscopic level, we can view exile as the result of autonomous national existence vs. perpetual emigration. The Palestinian refugee camps of Gaza, for example, well illustrate this perpetual macro-tension, as do the problems involved with foreign immigration into, say, the American Southwest. Both situations have to do with vastly different people-groups trying to occupy the same land at the same time.[79] "Lions" can always be depended upon to attack these immigrants (the "lions" of bureaucracy, the "lions" of exploitative employers, the "lions" of unfair tax laws, etc.). Further, kings may send "priests" as temporary solutions (the INS, UN peacekeepers), but solutions like these can fail when they are based on inadequate stewardship ideologies.[80]

On a microscopic level, people can exile themselves in a number of ways. Believers daily walk away from God, from Christ, from the Church, from anything remotely connected to "home."[81] We live in a culture scarred by dislocation and cocooned in seclusion.[82] Living in a Connecticut boarding house during one of my own exiles, I remember a next-door neighbor who spent every evening in his room with a TV dinner in one hand and a beer in the other. Each night when I came home from work he would be there, the flickering television images casting his slumping shadow against the dreary walls of a darkened hallway. No one ever came to visit him, nor did he ever go out with friends for a drink. Paul McCartney writes about such people in one of his early songs:

> All the lonely people...
> where do they all come from?
> All the lonely people...
> where do they all belong?[83]

Exile in this sense is painfully familiar to many Westeners, and one of the best strategies for dealing with it comes, in all places, from a letter written to earlier exiles (Jer 29:4-7). Hearing of their pain and sorrow, Jeremiah encourages the Babylonian exiles (a) to accept this exile as punishment for their sins, (b) to trust that it has a higher moral purpose, (c) to determine not merely to survive, but to grow from the experience, and (d) to pray for the welfare of their hosts.

Advice like this still seems appropriate.

Notes

1. C. L. Seow, "The Syro-Palestinian Context of Solomon's Dream," *HTR* 77 (1984) 146.

2. A. L. Oppenheim, *The Interpretation of Dreams in the Ancient Near East* (Philadelphia: American Philosophical Society, 1956) 245-55.

3. Rabbinic sources are conflicted over the significance of dreams. On the one hand, dreams are believed to have no effect (*b. Git.* 52a; *b. Hor.* 13b), or to reflect

only the dreamer's own thoughts (*b. Ber.* 55b), or to be nonsense (*b. Ber.* 55a). Other rabbis believe that "a dream uninterpreted is like an unread letter" (*b. Ber.* 55a).

4. "While in 1 Kings 3 Solomon's receipt of wisdom is connected with the theme of his good government, in 2 Chronicles 1 the donation occurs in close conjunction with the...transfer of cultic interest from...Gibeon to Jerusalem" (W. J. Dumbrell, *The Faith of Israel: Its Expression in the Books of the Old Testament* [Grand Rapids: Baker, 1988] 276).

5. S. Herrmann ("Die Königsnovelle in Ägypten und Israel," *Wissenschaftliche Zeitschrift der Karl-Marx-Universität,* Leipzig Gesellschafts- und Sprachwissenschaftliche Reihe 1 [1953/54] 51-62) emphasizes Egyptian influence, arguing that the narrative of Solomon's dream belongs to a class of royal literature called Königsnovelle ("king-stories," like the stories of Amen-hotep II and Thut-mose IV, *ANET* 246, 449).

6. Walsh, *Kings* 70.

7. L. Grabbe, *Priests, Prophets, Diviners, Sages: A Socio-Historical Study of Religious Specialists in Ancient Israel* (Valley Forge, PA: Trinity Press International, 1995) 39.

8. This is the Canaanite deity El's question to the Canaanite king Kirta (*UNP* 13). Note also the goddess Ishtar's question to the Hittite king Hattushili III, "Shall I abandon you to a (hostile) deity?" (cited in Oppenheim, *Dreambook,* 254).

9. This is Enkidu's dream about the heavenly council, recounted to his friend Gilgamesh (*ANET* 85-86, Hittite version).

10. This is the famous dream of Thutmose IV inscribed between the paws of the Sphinx (Oppenheim, *Dreambook,* 251).

11. "Incubation" is the word anthropologists use to describe dream solicitation (Oppenheim, *Dreambook,* 188).

12. See the examples in Oppenheim (*Dreambook,* 245-55).

13. J. Goldingay ("Modes of Theological Reflection in the Bible," *Theology* 94 [1991] 181-88) argues that biblical theological reflection assumes a variety of forms.

14. A. R. Diamond points out that Yahweh responds directly and forcefully to Jeremiah at first, then eventually stops responding (*The Confessions of Jeremiah in Context: Scenes of Prophetic Drama* [JSOTSup 45; Sheffield: JSOT Press, 1987] 144).

15. Well-known to Bible readers as another of Yahweh's "messiahs" (Isa 45:1), Cyrus is the king who, in 538 BC, releases the Jews from Persian captivity (Ezra 1:1-4).

16. Herodotus, *Histories* 1.120.3.

17. Robert D. Dale, *To Dream Again: How To Help Your Church Come Alive* (Nashville: Broadman, 1981) 1-12.

18. Go to http://www.christianity.net/leadership/study/page5.html.

19. See my "Jeremiah's Identity Crisis," *RQ* 34 (1992) 148.

20. Not all of these verbs appear in the first-person.

21. H. Horowitz ("The Sh'ma Reconsidered," *Judaism* 24 [1975] 476-81) argues that the Shema (Deut 6:4) is a text best understood in an ancient Near Eastern covenantal context; i.e., that this central tenet of Judaism really aims to establish and renew, periodically, a powerful and all-pervading covenant bond between Israel and God. A.-C. Arvil ("Ecoute, Israel," *Nouvelle Revue Theologique* 118 [1996] 709-26) thinks that Jesus' eagerness to cite it aloud only underlines this theology of covenant.

22. "If a man looks upon the Torah as merely a book presenting narratives and everyday matters, alas for him....The tales related in Torah are simply her outer gar-

ments, and woe to the man who regards that outer garb as the Torah itself" (*Zohar* III.152, a medieval Jewish mystical work cited in M. Fishbane, *The Garments of Torah: Essays in Biblical Hermeneutics* [Bloomington, IN: Indiana University, 1989] 34).

23. See the critique of Protestantism in W. Brueggemann, *Theology of the Old Testament* (Minneapolis: Augsburg Fortress, 1997) 651-52.

24. N. Golb, *Who Wrote the Dead Sea Scrolls?* (New York: Simon & Schuster, 1995) 95-116.

25. "Don't you know that you yourselves are God's temple and that God's Spirit lives in you? If anyone destroys God's temple, God will destroy him; for God's temple is holy (Gk *hagios*), and you (pl.) are that temple" (1 Cor 3:16-17). "Do you not know that your (sg.) body is a temple of the Holy Spirit?" (1 Cor 6:19).

26. "No immoral, impure (Gk *akathartos*)...person...has any inheritance in the kingdom of Christ" (Eph 5:5).

27. Contrary to the views of E. Käsemann, Paul in no way desacralizes this tradition in order to segregate holiness from ethics (cited in M. Black, *Romans*, 2nd ed. [NCBC; Grand Rapids: Eerdmans, 1989] 167).

28. *EA* 287.60.

29. G. von Rad, *Old Testament Theology,* vol. 1 (New York: Harper & Row, 1962; trans. from 1957 German ed.) 183.

30. J. G. McConville, "God's 'Name' and God's 'Glory'," *TB* 30 (1979) 149-63.

31. In Job 4:16 Eliphaz hears a "hushed voice" (NIV). In Kings Elijah hears a sound both "quiet" (*demamâ*) and "refined" (*daqqâ*), but the root of *dqq* means "to pulverize." Doubtless this is how Elijah feels at this point in his life: "pulverized."

32. R. R. Wilson, *Prophecy and Society in Ancient Israel* (Philadelphia: Fortress, 1980) 135-296.

33. W. J. Dumbrell, "What Are You Doing Here? Elijah at Horeb," *Crux* 22 (1996) 12-19.

34. D. Gowan, *Theology of the Prophetic Books: The Death and Resurrection of Israel* (Louisville: Westminster/John Knox, 1998) 3.

35. B. Robinson ("Elijah at Horeb, 1 Kings 19:1-18: A Coherent Narrative?" *RB* 98 [1991] 513-36) thinks Elijah's problem is pride and self-centeredness, not fear. R. B. Allen ("Elijah the Broken Prophet," *JETS* 22 [1979] 193-202) thinks that Elijah is not terrified, simply broken by Jezebel's persecution.

36. N. Waldman, "South and Silence," *JQR* 22 (1994) 228-36.

37. See my "Jeremiah's Progressive Paradox," *RB* 93 (1986) 386-414.

38. C. W. Gaddy, *A Soul Under Siege: Surviving Clergy Depression* (Louisville: Westminster/John Knox, 1991); S. Hauerwas and W. Willimon, "Ministry as More than a Helping Profession," *CC* 106 (1989) 282-84.

39. A. R. Diamond (*The Confessions of Jeremiah in Context: Scenes of Prophetic Drama* [JSOTSup 45; Sheffield: JSOT, 1987]) sees two cycles in Jeremiah's laments. To the first, God responds, but to the second God does not respond. Similarly, to Elijah's first complaint about ignorance, worship, and immorality, Yahweh responds. To his verbatim response, however, Yahweh simply relieves him of duty.

40. C. Spurgeon, "God's Gentle Power," (Portland, OR: Ages Software CD-Rom, 1992); Sermon # 3498, first preached on Sept 10, 1871.

41. Luther, *Table Talk* # 113 (Fall, 1531).

42. P. Miller, "The Prophets' Sons and Daughters," *Princeton Seminary Bulletin*

22 (2001) 284.

43. J. Blenkinsopp (*A History of Prophecy in Israel* [Philadelphia: Westminster, 1983] 59) admits that the "prophet like Moses" in Deut 18:15 later comes to be applied to individual figures like Jesus of Nazareth, but insists on interpreting this text historically instead of typologically; i.e., as "referring to the prophetic succession as a whole."

44. See, e.g., 4Q175 (4QTestimonia, a collection of quotations and commentary on Deut 18:18-19). R. R. Hutton ("Moses on the Mount of Transfiguration," *Hebrew Annual Review* 14 [1994] 99-120) traces the "prophet like Moses" tradition's evolution in the NT, and T. L. Brodie ("The Departure for Jerusalem [Luke 9:51-56] as a Rhetorical Imitation of Elijah's Departure for the Jordan [2 Kings 1:1-2, 6]," *Bib* 70 [1989] 96-109) sees Luke's Gospel as highly indebted to the Elijah-Elisha tradition.

45. Dumbrell ("What Are You Doing Here?" 12-19) is cautious about making comparisons between Moses and Elijah, but P. Satterthwaite's arguments are persuasive ("The Elisha Narratives and Coherence of 2 Kings 2-8," *TB* 49 [1998] 1-28).

46. T. Dozeman points out ("The *yam-sûp* in the Exodus and the Crossing of the Jordan River," *CBQ* 58 [1996] 407-16) that even as Yahweh challenges the Egyptian gods via the plagues, so the crossing of "uncrossable" water barriers challenges the Canaanite deities Yam ("sea") and Nahar ("river").

47. P. Watson, "A Note on the 'Double Portion' of Deuteronomy 21:47 and 2 Kings 2:9," *Hartford Quarterly* 8 (1965) 70-75.

48. J. D. Tabor, *Things Unutterable: Paul's Ascent to Paradise in its Greco-Roman, Judaic, and Early Christian Contexts* (Lanham, MD: University Press, 1986).

49. C. Begg, "Josephus' Portrayal of the Disappearances of Enoch, Elijah, and Moses: Some Observations," *JBL* 109 (1990) 691-93.

50. The book of 3 Enoch is a good example of merkabah, because in it a seer (Rabbi Ishmael) ascends to heaven through six "palaces" before viewing God's heavenly chariot (see P. Alexander, "3 [Hebrew Apocalypse of] Enoch," *The Old Testament Pseudepigrapha* [J. Charlesworth, ed.; New York: Doubleday, 1983] 223-315).

51. C. Knights ("Who Were the Rechabites?" *Expository Times* 107 [1996] 137-40) sees the Rechabites (Jer 35) as "prophets" who follow a strict religious order. F. S. Frick ("The Rechabites Reconsidered," *JBL* 90 [1971] 279-87) sees them merely as a guild of chariot-makers (wheelwrights).

52. MT has a phrase rarely picked up by the translations, but which sheds additional light on Elisha's question. It is the phrase *'ap hû'* immediately following the line, "Where (now) is Yahweh, the God of Elijah?" LXX reads *aphpho*, but this is a transliteration, not a translation. Apparently NIV inserts "now" as an attempt to translate the phrase, but it is unclear why we should insert a temporal adverb. Talmud frequently uses the phrase to mean "the same" (*b. Keth.* 6b and *passim*), suggesting the possible translation, "Where is Yahweh, the same God of Elijah?"

53. The last word in this line is the critical one (*tahtekâ*, "instead of you"). Yahweh wants Elijah to find a replacement, not a partner.

54. M. Weber's analysis (*The Sociology of Religion* [Boston: Beacon, 1964] 46) has been particularly influential.

55. C. A. Volz, "The Office of the Ministry in the Early Church," *Word and World* 9 (1989) 359-66.

56. "We read everywhere in the prophets how they rebuke the kings (and) priests…for always inventing new ways and not remaining on the one and only path"

(*Luther's Works*, vol. 41, p. 214).

57. Calvin, *Institutes* 1.1.13.

58. R. Henrich ("Konrad Hermann, genannt Schlupfindheck," *Zwingliana* 18 [1989] 20-35) reviews the controversial preaching career of Konrad Herrmann, for example.

59. E. H. Nygren, "John Wesley's Changing Concept of the Ministry," *Religion in Life* 31 (1962) 264-74.

60. Theophan the Recluse, cited in Kenneth Leech, *Soul Friend* (San Francisco: Harper, 1980) 34.

61. M. Charles-Murray, "They Speak to Us Across the Centuries. 6. Ambrose," *Expository Times* 109 (1998) 228-31.

62. L. Spence, "The Case Against Teaching," *Change* 33 (Nov-Dec) 11-19.

63. This verb, in contrast to the more common ʿāmad, often denotes the "standing up" of images and icons. E. T. Mullen (*The Assembly of the Gods: The Divine Council in Canaanite and Early Hebrew Literature* [HSM 24; Chico, CA; Scholars, 1980] 231) sees it as "a technical term for participating in the (divine) assembly" in Job 2:1.

64. Note the symmetry: Israel rejects Yahweh (2 Kings 17:14), therefore Yahweh rejects Israel (17:20).

65. According to Deut 16:22 an A/asherah is "planted" (*nâtaʿ*), but a sacred stone is "erected" (*qûm*). Baal has a sacred stone (2 Kings 3:2) erected in his temple (10:27). A. Biran has unearthed several examples of these sacred stones ("Sacred Spaces: Of Standing Stones, High Places and Cult Objects at Tel Dan," *BAR* 24 [1998] 38-45, 70).

66. This word-pair is prophetic shorthand for the occult world (see my *Balaam Traditions*, 61).

67. Qoh 1:2, 14; 2:1; 2:11, 15, 17, 19, 21; 3:19; 4:4, 7.

68. Modern Tel Ibrahim, 20 miles northeast of Babylon, seems the most likely location for Cuthah, an ancient site famous for venerating Nergal, god of the underworld (2 Kgs 17:30). Josephus later calls the Samaritans "the Cutheans" (*AJ* 11.4.4).

69. S. Kaufman ("The Enigmatic Adad-Milki," *JNES* 37 [1978] 101-9) argues from both literary and linguistic considerations that Sepharvaim was a city in Phoenicia, not Syria, Babylonia, or Elam (as many presume).

70. The most important thing to note about Nergal is his association with Molech. Both are chthonic netherworld deities (G. Heider, *The Cult of Molek: A Reassessment* [JSOTSup 43; Sheffield: JSOT, 1985]).

71. The verb for "exile" (*gâlâ*) appears six times in this paragraph (17:11, 23, 26, 27, 28, 33).

72. B. Birch, W. Brueggemann, T. Fretheim, & D. Petersen, *A Theological Introduction to the Old Testament* (Nashville: Abingdon, 1999) 350.

73. A. MacIntyre, *After Virtue: A Study in Moral Theory*, 2nd ed. (Notre Dame, IN: University of Notre Dame Press, 1984; first published in 1981) 11-12.

74. Monotheism is the belief in one God to the point of denying the existence of all other "gods." Henotheism is the belief in the superiority of one God over all other gods. Polytheism is the belief in many gods (M. Beck, *Elia und die Monolatrie* [BZAW 281; Berlin: DeGruyter, 1999] 5-6).

75. R. Gnuse, for example, asserts that "monotheism is unnatural...(while) polytheism makes far better moral sense" (*No Other Gods* [Sheffield: Academic Press, 1997], 214). S. Lasine (*Knowing Kings: Knowledge, Power and Narcissism in the Hebrew Bible* [SBLSS 40; Atlanta: Society of Biblical Literature, 2001] 263) argues that

"polytheism removes a burden—the burden of being used as human mirrors for the one and only biblical God, the jealous and demanding father."

76. "The Christ message is, let me repeat, not one truth among others; it is the truth" (K. Barth, *Dogmatics in Outline* [New York: Harper and Row, 1959, trans. from 1949 German ed.] 70).

77. Textually v. 13 bears directly on how we interpret the warning to Judah. MT reads *kl nby'w kl ḥzh* (ketib reading). Since *nby'w* is morphologically awkward ("by all his prophet," [sg.]), the Masoretes pluralize to "prophets" (*nby'y*, qere reading). This, however, creates a nomen regens for which there is no following nomen rectum, creating an incomplete construct clause ("by all the prophets of..."). LXX reads *pantôn tôn prophêtôn autou pantos horôntos*, "all his prophets, every seer," a solution which pluralizes "prophets" but keeps the 3rd masc. sg. suffix (i.e., no construct clause). Syr reads *klḥwn tḥdwḥy nby' wkl ḥzy'* ("by all [pl.] his servants, prophets and every [sg.] seer"), a solution which seems to follow LXX, but inserts "servants" from the latter part of the verse. I suggest that the easiest solution is simply to shift the *waw* in the original MT from the end of *nby'* to the beginning of *kl*, reading "every prophet and every seer." Syntactically this makes better sense and it preserves the parallel between Israel and Judah. Yahweh's strategy, in other words, includes both Israel (whose primary intermediary is the *nby'*) and Judah (whose primary intermediary is the *ḥzh*). For a discussion, see R. Wilson, *Prophecy and Society in Israel* (Philadelphia: Fortress, 1980) 136, 254.

78. J. Magonet, "Guests and Hosts," *Heythrop Journal* 36 (1995) 409-21.

79. W. Brueggemann, *The Land,* Overtures to Biblical Theology (Philadelphia: Fortress, 1977) 1-14.

80. Jean-Pierre Ruiz, "Among the Exiles by the River Chebar: A U.S. Hispanic American Reading of Prophetic Cosmology in Ezekiel 1:1-3," *Journal of Hispanic/Latino Theology* 6 (1998) 43-68.

81. W. Brueggemann, *Cadences of Home: Preaching Among Exiles* (Louisville: Westminster/John Knox, 1997).

82. See my *Ruth* commentary, NIBCOT 5 (Peabody, MA: Hendrickson, 2000) 300-06.

83. P. McCartney, "Eleanor Rigby" (recorded on April 28-29, 1966 at Abbey Road Studios, London, England).

NINE

THE PRESSURE OF VIOLENCE

MAKING TOUGH DECISIONS (1 Kings 1:28-2:12)

At the beginning of the book of Kings, David takes a long look at his country's leadership dilemma, swallows hard, and makes a tough decision. Exactly what he means to accomplish by this decision, of course, is open to debate. Genetic dynastic succession has never proven itself successful in Israel, so this is *terra incognita* for David. Jonathan has not successfully replaced Saul and neither Amnon nor Absalom have successfully replaced David. So it's no wonder that he approaches this decision as cautiously as he does. Not only does he have to choose one of his sons over the others, but from bitter experience he knows that the fate of the unchosen son will not be a pleasant one.[1]

Fatherly warnings are not unexpected at times like these. Worked into motifs, these warnings become themes, and worked into stories, these themes give shape and structure to the identities of whole cultures. The Canaanite deity El, for example, warns Yam (one of his sons) that unless he drives Baal (another of his sons) out of his "dominion," Baal's power might well revive, and Yam may have to face him all over again, renewed and revived.[2] In one of Aristophanes' satires, a conversation ensues between two characters over the relative strengths of Zeus' sons.

One asks: "Which of Zeus' sons do you think is the greatest man?" to which his friend answers, "I judge no man superior to Heracles the mighty!"[3] Debates like these doubtless animate Solomon's supporters as they extol his achievements.

The narrator shapes this episode by means of the simple verb "to call" (*qir'û*, vv. 28, 32). First, David calls for Bathsheba, his favorite wife, and tells her that Solomon's future will be secure (and, by implication, her own). Then, second, he calls for Zadok the priest, Nathan the prophet, and Benaiah the commander. Having called these supporters to his side, he then orders that Solomon be anointed as king, delineating the details of the inauguration ceremony so carefully, the conclusion seems obvious that this is formalized political ritual, scrupulously exact and legally precise.

To cement this important power transition, Solomon's supporters perform two important rituals: (a) they transport the king-elect to Gihon on the king's mule, and (b) they "anoint" (*mashab*) him "king" (*melek*). What the ceremonial mule represents exactly is hard to say, other than the fact that it's David's ceremonial mule.[4] Anointing, however, is a ritual well-attested in the ancient Near East,[5] though only six kings are anointed in Israel: Saul, David, Solomon, Jehu, Joash, and Jehoahaz. Each of these particular anointings represents a special confirmatory function of some kind, and Solomon's anointing is designed to neutralize Adonijah's claim to the throne (see *Lev. Rab.* 10.8).

In other words, David moves swiftly to stabilize his (son's) government. With one swift stroke he charts the future of the nation. This is one of the great turning-points of Israelite history. Just as the adoption of the alphabet transforms writing, so the adoption of dynasty transforms Israel. Yet literarily, this decision comes down to us only as one of several death-bed decisions on David's part, and we need to investigate the structure in which it's housed. We could conclude that David no longer sees Adonijah as a problem, but this does not explain (a) the horrible fate Adonijah soon experiences, nor (b) the mercy David recommends for Barzillai's sons. Should we ask whether there is a common denominator in these decisions, the most likely candidate seems to be their literary and historical connection to Absalom. Joab is David's nephew (2 Sam 17:25), but he's also Absalom's murderer. Joab is David's loyal "hit-man" (11:17) and "enforcer" (20:14-22), and Solomon says he executes him for the murders of Abner and Amasa. Yet this passage makes clear that David has never forgiven him for killing Absalom. Shimei is the Benjamite who curses David after Absalom's conquest of Jerusalem (2 Sam 16:5-14), and Solomon executes him to eliminate the last vestiges of Saul's family.[6]

Yet while the decisions about Joab and Shimei force Solomon to "show yourself a man" against David's enemies, the Barzillai decision encourages him to use moderation while doing so. David wants Solomon to show mercy to a particular family, but the larger lesson here is the necessity to practice mercy as a matter of principle when making decisions. Just as Moses admonishes Joshua to "keep Yahweh's charge" (*shamar mishmeret,* Deut 11:1; Josh 22:3), so David admonishes Solomon in exactly the same language (*shamar mishmeret,* v. 3). Yahweh's "ways" (*bidrakaw*), "decrees" (*huqqôtaw*), "commands" (*mitswôtaw*), "laws" (*mishpataw*) and "requirements" (*`edewôtaw*) all pile up in an intertextual heap here as David's language defaults to the language of Torah.[7] Torah is the only way to insure that David's line "will never fail to have a man on the throne of Israel" (2 Sam 7:8-29). Thus Barzillai is "political ballast" in this text, a "rose between two thorns"—Joab and Shimei.

Intratextual Reflection

At first glance, the episodes about "Making Tough Decisions" (1 Kings 1:28-2:12), "Mothers Needing Miracles" (2 Kings 4:8-37), and "Final Four" (25:27-30) seem equally unrelated, yet underlying them all runs an ugly intratextual thread. Each of these texts deals in some way with the *pressure of violence* in Israel. David's problem is not just dynastic succession. His problem is the dilemma of survival against very determined enemies. We need only look at the lament Psalms to see this. Joab, for example, could easily be the "betraying companion" in Psalm 55:

> My companion attacks his friends; he violates his covenant.
> His speech is smooth as butter, yet war is in his heart.
> His words are more soothing than oil, yet they are drawn swords
> (Psa 55:20-21).

Shimei, on the other hand, represents the unquenched anger of Saul's family toward the Davidic house (1 Sam 20:31; 2 Sam 16:8). Thus, where Joab represents those who think they can serve Yahweh through acts of violence, Shimei represents those who think they can hide behind clan violence while they plot against the Lord's anointed.

The intratextual context highlights this theme. The crisis facing the Shunammite, for example, is violence against her family, while the crisis facing Jehoiachin is violence against Judah as the surviving remnant of God's people. Learning of her son's death, the Shunammite runs to Elisha expecting salvation, and when we compare her story with 1 Kings 1:28-

2:12, the following parallels jump out: (a) both stories have parents agonizing over the fates of children; (b) both stories involve parents losing
sons to death; and (c) both stories show us characters having leadership
roles thrust upon them in the midst of these horrors. Looking ahead to the
end of the trajectory, Jehoiachin's release from prison will look very much
like David's "release" here (see the Introduction). Where the Babylonian
king Evil-Merodach speaks "kindly" (*tobôt*) to Jehoiachin, David has
Solomon speak "kindly" (*hesed*) to Barzillai's sons. Where Evil-Merodach
teaches his successor (Neriglissar) about clemency, David also teaches his
successor (Solomon) about clemency. Where Jehoiachin receives permission to eat at Evil-Merodach's table, Barzillai's sons receive permission to
eat at Solomon's table. These stories deal with the problem of violence in
a number of ways.

Theological Reflection

In 1939 Albert Einstein wrote a famous letter to Franklin Roosevelt about
the potential dangers of atomic power. Shortly afterwards, the President
appointed a young physicist named Robert Oppenheimer to direct the
Manhattan Project, a top-secret military project designed to respond to the
threat of German nuclear technology. Seeing his first mushroom cloud in
1945, Oppenheimer is said to have quoted a line from the *Bhagavad Gita*,
"If the radiance of a thousand suns were to be burst at once into the sky,
that would be like the splendor of the Mighty One.... I am become death,
the shatterer of worlds."[8]

Well, just as that first mushroom cloud immobilizes Oppenheimer,
something very similar is responsible for immobilizing David. David, we
remember, has seen more violence than any king should ever have to
see. Like the United States in 1943, his enemies refuse to stop pressuring
him. Adonijah's coup is the latest in a string of political crises, and the
decision he makes in response to it impacts not only the nation, but his
family on at least two levels.

First, David apparently figures out what successful fathers already
know: it's better to fight for our families than with them. Sometimes it's
necessary to make tough decisions—to weigh options and decide what's
best for our families because they rely on us for leadership and guidance.
Sometimes it means taking a pay cut so the family doesn't have to move
again. Sometimes it means missing a promotion. Sometimes it means making a move. Whatever the cost, every parent has to make such decisions,
and the cost can sometimes be high.

This came home to me one night on a New Year's Eve flight from

Cincinnati to Phoenix. Packed with loud, boisterous travelers, our plane was winging its way home from Christmas break with every seat filled, as I recall, except the one next to mine. Thinking I was going to have the aisle to myself, I was about to stretch out and claim my space when I spotted him—this little blonde head of hair bobbing up and down the center aisle. Arriving at my row, the flight attendant looked down and asked, "Sir? Can Mikie sit next to you today?"

"Sure," I said. Then, putting on a smile, I threw out my cheeriest "Hi, Mikie."

Silence.

Seat-belts clicked and overhead compartments slammed shut. Speakers blared instructions and tray-tables snapped into place. His stubby legs hovering over the floor, Mikie cinched up his seatbelt and waited patiently for take-off. It was only when my eye found the courage to wander sideways that I saw the tears beginning to trickle down his little face. After we lifted off—and I could successfully fight down the baseball-sized lump getting stuck in my throat—I asked him to show me his backpack, and out of it came his most precious treasure, a photo album. Gingerly, warily, like a holocaust survivor, he began leafing through its pictures—pictures of his cousins, pictures of his Daddy, pictures of "my new Mommie," pictures of "my real Mommie"—precious mementos of his once-a-year, once-upon-a-time life. Not once did he smile or laugh or respond in any way to my questions. It was like he couldn't hear anything, so immobilized was he in his own little world. The look on this 6-year-old's face was like…well, like the "shatterer of worlds."

Regardless of the reasons, and regardless of how explainable they may be, entirely too many Mikies are going up in mushroom clouds today, the innocent victims of nuclear family war. David learns that it's better to fight for our families than with them.

Second, wise leaders know the importance of showing mercy in the midst of judgment. David's instructions about Barzillai represent much more than intuitive savvy. They're reminders of how important it is to maintain our theological balance in the midst of turbulent situations. Reactionary overkill is always easier than balanced judgment, especially when we're under pressure. Wise leaders know how to tell the difference—even so angry a leader as Job knows how to tell the difference.[9] Solomon will have to deal with this kind of pressure the rest of his life, and David does not want him to be eaten alive his first week in office. On the contrary, he wants him to become an effective leader, and he knows that this will take more than just good intentions. It will take determination and faith. Servant leadership is not about saber-rattling or legal maneuvering, nor is it genetically transferrable. To teach these truths to his son, David leaves him with a powerful visual aid—and Solomon remembers it every time he sits down to eat.

SAVIOR YAHWEH (2 Kings 3:1-27)

Joram is less wicked than his father (Ahab) or mother (Jezebel), though he struggles with their legacy. Sometimes he makes courageous decisions—like his decision, for example, to remove the sacred stone of Baal (*matsebat habba`al*) that his father had made. The narrator wishes that he might also have dismantled the Baal temple as well (1 Kings 16:32), but Joram is not Josiah. Joram is not a great reformer. This episode tells us that the major irritant in his life is Mesha, king of Moab, and from this episode we can conclude that one reason for his conflict with Mesha is his brother's (Ahaziah's) failure to neutralize him (probably because of his [Ahaziah's] wounds, 2 Kings 1:1). The name Mesha means "savior" (from the verb *yasha`*, "to save"), and this story is very much a story about salvation.

Evidently Mesha rebels against Israel because (a) Ahab's death produces a leadership vacuum, and (b) Mesha gambles that Ahab's sons will be too weak to challenge him. The Moabite Stone informs us that Mesha freely admits to a history of vassalage under Israel, but this does nothing to quell his anger at the Omrides.[10] In a list of his "adversaries," for example, Mesha mentions "Omri king of Israel" (`mry mlk ysr'l, lines 4-5), as well as Omri's "son" (line 8): "The king of Israel had fortified Ataroth for himself, but I fought against the town and took it, and I killed all the inhabitants of the town, a spectacle for Chemosh" (lines 10-12). Like most public memorials, the purpose of this one is to give glory to the writer's national god.[11]

But there's a broader context. Although the Bible and the Moabite Stone give us much pertinent information about the history of this conflict, neither of these sources mentions the recent defeat of the Syro-Palestinian coalition at Qarqar (853 BC), the famous battle where the Assyrians under Shalmeneser III successfully turn back the armies led by Hadadezer the Syrian and Ahab the Israelite (Joram's father). This battle is important for many reasons, but not least because it signals the beginning of the end for Israel and her neighbors. After Qarqar, it's just a matter of time before the Assyrians will conquer the entirety of Syria-Palestine and subject it to brutal rule.

But this is not a story about Assyria, nor is it really a story about Moabite aggression or Israelite nationalism. The focus of this story is the prophet Elisha and his ministry of healing. Fresh from his ordination at the Jordan, Elisha stands on the cusp of an amazing ministry, and to introduce him properly the narrator narrates his story as an echo of the story of Micaiah ben Imlah (1 Kings 22). Both episodes show us Yahweh prophets prophesying before Omride battles. Both critique these battles as poorly planned and miserably executed. Both portray Jehoshaphat as "the righteous Yahwist." Both show a Yahweh prophet ridiculing the king's prophets. And before both battles, Jehoshaphat recites the same verbatim promise: "I am as you are, my people as your people, my horses as your horses."[12]

These are remarkable similarities, yet the differences are just as striking. First, Joram does not act like his father Ahab. Where Ahab cavalierly dismisses Micaiah, publicly humiliating him and throwing him into prison, Joram adopts a very different attitude toward the prophet Elisha. After all, Micaiah does not prophesy to a desperate king wandering in the desert, nor does Joram find himself surrounded by hundreds of groveling prophets. Joram's situation is quite different from Ahab's. Joram, unlike Ahab, worries that Yahweh will abandon him to his enemies: "Has Yahweh called us three kings together only to hand us over to Moab?" So, where Micaiah verbally attacks Ahab, Elisha's rhetoric is less aggressive. Where Micaiah condemns Ahab, Elisha eventually blesses Joram and helps him get the things he needs to survive: water for his army and deliverance from his enemies.

Second, the battles for Ramoth-Gilead (Ahab) and Kir-Hareseth (Joram) have very different outcomes. Where Micaiah delivers an oracle of doom to Ahab, Elisha delivers to Joram an oracle of hope. Where Ahab dies from a "stray" arrow at Ramoth-Gilead, Joram walks away from Kir-Hareseth a saved man. From a literary perspective Joram's story is a typical "Edom-story," because the word *'edôm* means "red," and biblical narrators love to play on this word when describing the Edomites. Where Esau ("Edom") says to Jacob, "Quick, let me have some of that red stuff" (Gen 25:30), for example, here the Moabites mistake water for blood in the land of "redness." The narrator's strategy is therefore more linguistic than hydraulic:

> Who is this coming from Edom,
>> from Bozrah, with his garments stained crimson ...?
> Why are your garments red (*'adôm*),

like those of one treading the winepress ...?

Their blood spattered my garments,
I trampled the nations in my anger;
in my wrath I made them drunk
and poured their blood on the ground.[13]

In other words, Moabite confusion over the "redness" of the water is an intentional play-on-words, a narrative injection of color into an otherwise drab battle-report. This does not explain everything going on in the story, of course, but it does explain the "redness" of the language, and it certainly seems preferable to the "naturalistic" explanations of later historians.

Ignoring the pun altogether, for example, Josephus notes that "God had caused it to rain very plentifully at the distance of three days' journey into Edom."[14] His explanation of Mesha is just as wooden—more than this, it shamelessly plays to his patrons' prejudices against the Jews and all things semitic. Josephus argues that Mesha's sacrifice is not out of devotion to Chemosh—the very theme of the Moabite Stone—but out of "despair and the utmost distress."

> For he took his oldest son, who was to reign after him, and lifting him up upon the wall, that he might be visible to all the enemies, he offered him as a whole burnt-offering to God, whom, when the kings saw, they commiserated the distress that was the occasion of it, and were so affected, in way of humanity and pity, that they raised the siege, and every one returned to his own house.[15]

Doubtless these emotions are present in Mesha, but explanations like these completely miss the theological point. Israel's retreat from Kir-Hareseth does not occur out of "pity," nor is it due to Chemosh's anger[16] or Israel's fear[17] or Mesha's success in using Canaanite ritual to good effect.[18] Israel's retreat occurs because of Yahweh's ability to do what Chemosh cannot do—"save."

From an intratextual perspective, this confrontation clearly echoes the terrible confrontation on Mt. Carmel. What we really have here, in other words, is another showdown between competing deities. On Mt. Carmel, Elijah demands that Israel choose between Yahweh and Baal. Here at Kir-Hareseth, the choice is between Yahweh and Chemosh, and the question driving both episodes is the same: "When the chips are down, who has the power to save?" On Mt. Carmel, the question is whether this or that sacrifice is going to effect salvation. Here the choice is between a deity who makes water in the desert and a deity who drinks the blood of children via public sacrifice. The deeper issue here is whether human life is worth saving at all. To Yahweh, human life—even Omride human life—is worth filling a ditch or two with water. To Chemosh and his descendants, humans are simply "meat" for the gods.[19]

Human sacrifice, to be blunt, is an abominable practice perpetuated by misguided people who refuse to recognize the true "Mesha," the true Savior. One application of this theme should be immediately obvious today because the line between child abuse and paternal discipline is becoming rather blurry among those who've decided to worship the wrong Mesha (see Deut 21:18-21). The biblical exceptions only prove the rule. Jephthah sacrifices his daughter to fulfill a vow (Judg 11:39), for example, but nowhere does Yahweh show the slightest inkling of approval for this decision. Abraham prepares to sacrifice his son Isaac, yet Yahweh rescues the child before he goes through with it, and this clearly shows Yahwistic abhorrence to human sacrifice (Gen 22:1-18).[20] Later on, the Talmud condemns all three of these examples—Jephthah's daughter, Abraham's son, and Mesha's son (*b. Taan.* 4a)—yet the first two are not really comparable to the third because neither Jephthah nor Abraham routinely practice child sacrifice as part of a religious cult.[21]

At first, Israel's response to Mesha's abhorrent act looks ambivalent. Instead of closing in for the victory, Joram and his army back away and leave the battlefield. Like the conflict between Balak and Moses in Num 22-24, it's not easy to tell how, exactly, this conflict ends.[22] Yet Joram has good reason to run away. The text makes it very clear: the fury (*qetsep*) against Israel is great. What does this mean? Hebrew has several words for "fury," but this one, *qetsep*, denotes the deity's automatic response to cultic violation (Deut 9:19), vow-breaking (Josh 9:20), violation of the *herem*-ban (22:20), and child sacrifice (2 Kings 3:27). In other words, this is a special kind of fury, and Joram runs away from Kir-Hareseth for the same reason the Assyrians run away from Jerusalem (2 Kings 19:36). Something unthinkably terrifying has happened. Joram runs away from Kir-Hareseth for the same reason you or I would run away from a nuclear explosion.

Intratextual Reflection

Intratextually this episode resonates well with "Making Tough Decisions" (1 Kings 1:28-2:12), "Mothers Needing Miracles" (2 Kings 4:1-37), "Pick and Roll" (9:1-10:36), and "Final Four" (25:27-30). Not only does it demonstrate Yahweh's role as Savior, but it subtly contrasts Yahweh's salvific claims with those of other savior-figures in Israel's immediate environment (Chemosh, Mesha, Molech, Baal). Each episode on this trajectory features a ("miraculous") turnaround: David saves Solomon from a violent death; Jehu saves Israel from the Baal virus; Jehoiachin survives the Jerusalem holocaust and saves the messianic line from extinction. Each of these texts highlights Yahweh's determination to rescue his people from violence and abuse.

To illustrate, take the episode in the very next chapter, "Mothers Needing Miracles" (2 Kings 4:1-6). At first glance, there seems to be no organic connection between Joram's dilemma and the dilemma facing this mother. Yet each of these characters is profoundly "lost"—Joram in the wastelands of Edom; this widow in the bowels of a bloated bureaucracy. That a creditor would have the gall to threaten an Israelite widow and push her into even deeper poverty only proves how far Israel has drifted from its moral moorings. The Law demands that widows be protected, not harassed (Deut 25:5-10), that unscrupulous creditors be punished, not rewarded (24:10-13). Thus the fact that each of these characters turns to Yahweh—instead of another "savior"—is significant, and for several reasons.

Theological Reflection

First, Yahweh is the only proven Savior. Yahweh is the one who saves, not Chemosh. This character trait is fundamental to God's very being. Yahweh is a Savior-God. Just as Mesha's name extols his god as "savior," so Elisha's name extols his God ("my God saves"). Max Lucado captures this well in the title of one of his early books, *No Wonder They Call Him the Savior*,[23] and the prophet of Babylon proclaims it with boldness and power:

> Before me no god was formed,
> nor will there be one after me.
> I, even I, am Yahweh,
> and apart from me there is no savior (*môshî`a*)
> I have revealed and saved and proclaimed—
> I, and not some foreign god among you (Isa 43:10-12).

The Christian faith emerges out of a similarly competitive environment.[24] Asclepius, for example, is a Greek savior-god whose cult holds sway over much of the Mediterranean world before and after the time of Christ. Dozens of votive inscriptions still stand at Asclepeia-sanctuaries throughout Turkey and Greece—in fact, I have personally placed my fingers in the Greek words for *kurios* ("lord") and *soter* ("savior") etched into these granite columns.[25] Such memorials stand as mute witness to the fact that our spiritual ancestors had to compete head-to-head with dozens of foreign cults, all built around savior-deities of every conceivable stripe. No wonder Christian claims about Jesus have such a polemic edge. For our ancestors Jesus alone deserves the title "Savior of the world" (John 4:42). For them God does not exalt Asclepius, he exalts Jesus as Savior (Acts 5:31).

Second, miracles happen. Sometimes water appears in the desert. Sometimes fire falls from heaven. Sometimes oil flows from empty jars. As I write these words, one of my students has just gone through painful cancer surgery to remove a lump on her neck. Yesterday her husband e-mailed a note to those of us standing watch on the prayer chain:

> Hi everybody,
>
> We are dealing with some difficulties today, for which I would greatly appreciate your prayers. She is struggling to get enough food to sustain her, due to sensitivities to the tube feeding formula, and she is having some breathing difficulty. On the good side, we have just received some new medicine which is doing a better job with the pain and we pray that it is effective for the whole period between doses. Thanks for your prayers. Also due to this situation, prayers are preferred over calls and visits right now.
>
> Thanks.

This morning, after a night of prayer, the following message lit up my computer screen:

> Thanks for your prayers! The breathing difficulties have pretty much subsided. The power of prayer really works! This morning she had 4 oz. of food—a great start! What a blessing, compared to what we were dealing with not so many hours ago.
>
> Again, thanks for the prayer coverage.
>
> Bless all of you!

Not all prayers are answered so positively or so immediately, of course, but just try to convince this husband that prayer doesn't work! Miracles still happen—not necessarily because we pray for them, but because the Savior is able to do far more than we can ask or imagine (Eph 3:20).

Third, human violence never saves. The impulse driving Mesha is still driving many of us. Of course, we don't usually label the violence we see today as "human sacrifice." We prefer to euphemize such horrible ideas with innocuous-sounding phrases like "child abuse," "parent abuse," or "underprivileged." No amount of euphemism, however, can cover up such senseless, horrid violence. I live in a state where the license plates—*the license plates*—proclaim, "It shouldn't hurt to be a child."[26] I live in a city where elderly parents routinely suffer neglect and abuse at the hands of their own children.[27] One can well understand why non-believers turn to atheism or polytheism when they see "Christians" acting this way, routinely sacrificing their loved ones to the gods of "I'm-Too-Busy," or "I-Don't-Want-The-Responsibility," or the very popular god of "It's-My-Body." God has a special fury reserved for such behavior.

In *Saving Private Ryan*, Capt. Miller's squad wanders around for days behind enemy lines on a deceptively simple mission: find Pvt. James Ryan and bring him home.[28] Pvt. Ryan's only qualification for salvation is the fact that three of his brothers have already died in battle, and the U. S. Army does not want to be responsible for snuffing out the last remaining Ryan. Some of his rescuers find this terribly unfair. They argue and complain that the mission is too costly, especially when their comrades start paying the ultimate price for his salvation. They doubt whether a single soldier's life is worth endangering the entire squad. They doubt whether the Army knows what it's doing. They doubt whether Capt. Miller's leadership is just.

The Church is often just like this squad of soldiers. Wandering around behind enemy lines, we bicker and fight. We argue and debate. We gripe and groan. We look for easy ways out of our Commission. We see the violence all around us and we argue over how to "count the dogtags" of the victims. We drink miraculous water from rivers of grace and we complain about the taste.

But every now and then we see the look on the face of the "Pvt. Ryans" among us.

And we feel the Presence of the Savior.

MOTHERS NEEDING MIRACLES (2 Kings 4:1-37)

Kings delights in working and reworking a number of motifs, molding and remolding them into a variety of intratextual shapes. Parallel accounts in the Gospel narratives do the same thing, sometimes expanding, sometimes contracting the events in Jesus' life. In Mark, for example, Jesus casts demons out of a man whose name is Legion (Mark 5:1-20), but in Matthew he casts demons out of two demoniacs, not one (Matt 8:28-34). Literary doublets like this have led to whole schools of thought positing the "priority" of Mark over Matthew, but Old Testament scholarship is less interested in hypothetical schools than the fascinating ways in which narrators mold and re-mold ancient Near Eastern motifs to suit their own purposes.[29]

The present text is a good example. In 1 Kings 17, Elijah saves a Zarephath widow with miraculous food, then resurrects her son from death. Here, Elisha saves a family with miraculous food, then resurrects the son of an entirely different person—the Shunammite woman. One story has both miracles benefiting a single character, the other parcels them out to two separate characters. Historians wonder whether we have one or two events here, or whether one of these stories is older than the other, or whether there might be a prophetic resurrection tradition underlying both traditions (a "Q"-type source). But these are not the only or even the best questions to ask. Why do we have two versions of these particular miracles? Why does the narrator repeat stories about "oil-replenishment" and "resurrection?" What is the theological point he is trying to make by emphasizing these themes?

Intratextual Reflection

In 1 Kings 17 Elijah makes two demands of the Zarephath widow: "Bring me a little water" and "Bring me a morsel of bread." In the Elisha cycle, it's the widow who begins the conversation, however, not the prophet. In the Elijah narrative, the prophet issues a command, "Don't be afraid!" In the Elisha narrative, we hear a question, "What can I do for you?" In the first story, death is the widow's greatest fear. In the second, the primary fear is the loss of "my two boys" (*yeladay*). In the first story Elijah tests the widow to see if she will feed Yahweh's prophet before she feeds her family. In the second Elisha makes himself available to save, apparently with no strings attached.

The intratextual density between these texts is remarkable, and highlights the theological intentions within each. The narrator's purpose in the Elijah narrative is to show how important it is for all Israel—kings, palace stewards, widows—to revere Yahweh and respect his prophets. Rampant Baalism has pushed the question of Yahweh-loyalty to a crisis point, yet despite this, Elisha does not ask his disciples to demonstrate their Yahwism by deciding, say, whom to feed first in a famine. In fact, famine is not even the driving issue. Elisha's goal is rather to demonstrate the power of Yahweh to save anyone, whether poverty-stricken or well-to-do. Where the Elijah story is tough and gritty, the Elisha story is tender and poignant.

This distinction becomes clear when we analyze the resurrection theme highlighted in both texts. The context of Elijah's resurrection is decidedly hostile: "What do you have against me, man of God? Did you come to remind me of my sin and kill my son?" Only when her son returns to her alive does the Zarephath widow put down her guard and proclaim her faith. In the Shunammite story, however, Elisha's matron goes to a lot of "trouble" (*harad*) on his behalf. With her husband's consent she constructs and furnishes a room for the prophet, and Elisha seems touched by her kindness and concern. With the birth of her son, however, the narrator takes us deeper into this character than he does with the Zarephath widow. Elisha offers her his political connections as a reward for her "trouble," but she respectfully declines the offer, and this leads to a trialogue between Elisha, Gehazi, and the Shunammite over what to do next. Finally Elisha turns to Gehazi and asks, "What can be done for her?" and Gehazi suggests, "Well, she has no son and her husband is old." Immediately Elisha seizes on this "need" and predicts the birth of a son. The Shunammite, however, like the Sidonian before her, responds with fear and trepidation before the prophetic Word.

Where the Sidonian attacks Elijah for bringing sin and death, however, the Shunammite calmly saddles her donkey and assures her husband that everything is "all right" (*shalôm*, v. 23). In v. 27 she also assures Gehazi that everything is "all right" (*shalôm*), but in fact everything is not all right, and this becomes painfully obvious when she finally reaches Elisha. Gehazi tries to push her away, but Elisha intervenes, wondering to himself why Yahweh has not revealed the reason for her pain. All of this takes place on Mt. Carmel, the epicenter of Israel's prophetic struggle. Previously at Mt. Carmel, no one dared to touch Elisha's mentor (Elijah), but here the narrator uses the Carmel connection to rework his theology of resurrection into another key.

Theological Reflection

Once I was invited to preach to a rather large church. Not having had many opportunities to preach to such a large audience, I was rather taken aback by the size of everything until a lady in the third service brought me back down to earth. Grabbing my hand after the sermon, she asked, "What do you do when the Lord never seems to answer your prayers? Should I stop asking him for help?" Not knowing what she meant, I asked, "What are you praying for?," and with tears welling up, she blurted out, "For my children's salvation!" What makes the Bible so relevant to questions like this is the fact that the God of the Bible cares as much for desperate mothers as he does for beleaguered politicians. Two dimensions of this truth deserve closer scrutiny.

First, Yahweh is a merciful Savior. Can we ever overemphasize this? "A wonderful Savior is Jesus my Lord, a wonderful Savior to me!"[30] One of the reasons why the same types of stories keep popping up in Scripture is because this narrator doesn't want his readers simply to become acquainted with these themes—he wants them to memorize them. Frequent repetition helps to anchor these themes into forgetful minds. Yahweh is not simply a God who opposes false prophets and challenges false gods. He also responds to desperate people in desperate situations. Today, as I write these words, a student has just walked into my office, embarrassed and angry and hurt and humiliated. Married to a man who spends money irresponsibly, she feels the joy ebbing out of their marriage and she doesn't know how to stop it. She loves her husband, but his adolescent selfishness is crushing the life out of her. Unless something changes soon she fears for the future of her marriage and her children.

Her plight is a not an uncommon one. I see it all the time. When financial correspondent Ray Brady retired from CBS News, the piece he chose for his final broadcast was a story about credit card companies. Here's what he discovered.[31] *Fact:* Many banks and other lending institutions frequently target college freshmen in the same way tobacco companies used to target teenage smokers in the U. S. (and still do in the Third World). *Fact:* Hundreds of universities across America habitually cut sweetheart deals with credit card companies, selling them the addresses of their students in order to balance their budgets. *Fact:* The University of Tennessee (to cite one example) has charged as much as 16 million dollars for selling the telephone numbers of its students to these companies.

I can personally testify to this problem because my own college-age sons used to receive approximately one letter per week from banks and other lenders promising low interest rates and several-thousand-dollar spending limits. These companies are shamelessly trying to seduce young people into debt, and it's a disgrace. In Brady's piece, he reported that one Georgetown University student lapsed so deeply into debt she had to drop out of school to start paying it back. Eleven years later, she still hasn't been able to graduate. It's going to take more than a few jars full of oil to free our kids from this kind of slavery. For some of our children it may take years to dig out—if they ever do. We need to stand against such rampant consumerism and teach our kids how to fill up the "empty jars" in their lives in more appropriate ways. We need to help them distinguish between Baal-inspired propaganda and Christ-centered stewardship.[32]

Second, Yahweh cares for the rich as well as the poor. In my opinion, this is one of the reasons why we have two stories focusing on this theme, each with its own socio-economic context. Loss is loss, regardless of who experiences it, and Yahweh's grace extends as much to rich mothers facing heartbreak as poor mothers facing bankruptcy. Yahweh does not target his grace to particular ethnic, religious, or socio-economic groups. Perhaps this is why Jesus re-emphasizes this theme for his audience: "I assure you that there were many widows in Israel in Elijah's time, when the sky was shut for three and a half years and there was a severe famine throughout the land. Yet Elijah was not sent to any of them, but to a widow in Zarephath in the region of Sidon" (Luke 4:24-26). Perhaps this is why he so overtly links it to another story about a rich foreigner: "And there were many in Israel with leprosy in the time of Elisha the prophet, yet not one of them was cleansed—only Naaman the Syrian" (Luke 4:27).

Jesus uses these stories to warn us about the consequences of refusing the Son of God, regardless of the position of those doing the rejecting ("If even a starving Sidonian can understand the need to pursue truth over tradition—then what's *your* problem?"). The narrator of Kings emphasizes the global reach of the Savior's grace. To those who believe that money can save—or religion, or ethnicity, or any other idol—stories like these are disturbing because they teach that God's grace cannot be determined by the size of one's bank account or the country of one's origin or the language of one's ancestors. Scott Rodin believes that Christians who balk at this message are missing the point of the Gospel: "Without knowing the one who created us, we are left to ourselves to define what is noble, what is worthwhile, what is meaningful, what constitutes success, what defines fulfillment, and what can bestow genuine purpose on our existence....And we can only do so according to our fallenness, which inevitably results in a distorted way of measuring success."[33]

As a parent, I pray every day for my children's salvation—not just that they won't die in an auto accident or marry cruel people, but that they will escape the slavery of such life-draining idolatry. I pray that they will grow deeper in their love for the Savior. I pray that they will experience the energizing power of the resurrected life. I pray that they will develop the spiritual depth necessary to weather whatever life might throw at them. But I also know that they're growing up in a culture that slavishly follows such idols to the detriment of the Kingdom.

Sociologists know that the loss of a child is one of the worst traumas a family can face, and I discovered this truth when two close friends lost their son to a rare liver disease. Told by their doctor that the genetic chances of producing another child with the same disease were one-in-four, they prayed fervently for wisdom. The funeral for their son was barely over when they found themselves pregnant, and this scared all of us. Although their daughter arrived healthy and disease-free, the wounds from their son's death had not healed. In spite of the joy of their daughter's birth, mom especially underwent a massive change in personality—gaining weight, burying herself in work, slowly twisting the anger inside of her into a lariat of bitterness. Dad, for his part, tried to deal with the pain in his heart and the dramatic change in his wife, but lacking the appropriate spiritual disciplines, he floundered terribly. Painfully I watched my friend turn into "a detached biblicist," a man for whom the Bible became little more than "a spiritual first-aid book."[34] Every time I tried to talk to him about it he changed the subject to something more "appropriately theological." "So... have you read so-and-so's book on the Holy Spirit? What do you think about that article on Christology I sent you last month?" Eventually he had an affair with a co-worker and divorced his wife.

What have I learned from this and other, similar experiences? I have learned that unrepented anger is like a nuclear bomb—eventually it's going to go off and people are going to get hurt. I've also learned that resurrection is much easier to accept when it's not my child lying dead in that tiny coffin. I have learned that broken people often resist help from those who love them most, and I have learned that suffering causes some people to put their trust in the Savior, and some to put their trust in themselves.

WAS BLIND, BUT NOW I SEE (2 Kings 6:1-23)

True to form, the narrator again lays out a pair of miracle-stories: (a) a man with a borrowed ax-head reaches out and saves it from sinking into the Jordan (sparing him the cost of replacement); then (b) a frightened servant has his eyes miraculously opened (saving him from anxiety and possible injury). Subtle catchwords link these two vignettes together. Just as Elisha converses with the "sons of the prophets," so the Syrian king converses with his servants, and each of these conversations orbits around the same catchword *mâqôm* ("place"). The "sons of the prophets" want to build their own "place" (*mâqôm*). The Syrian king flits from "place" to "place" searching for vantage points from which to attack. Elisha miraculously finds the "place" (*mâqôm*) of the fallen ax-head. So too he ascertains the hidden "place" (*mâqôm*) of the hostile Syrian king (vv. 2, 6, 8, 9, 10).

The second catchword is the exclamation, *'a'hâ 'adônî*, "Oh, my lord!" (vv. 5, 15). In the first story, the worker losing his ax-head exclaims *'ahâ* 'adônî ("Oh, my lord!"). In the second story Elisha's servant wakes up one morning to Syrian chariotry at his front door, causing him to cry out, 'ahâ 'adônî ("Oh, my lord!"). Both stories have to do with the reality of the "unexpected," and both raise the question, "What should people of faith do when they're caught off-guard?"

The shorter of these vignettes functions as a porch into the second, a hilarious farce designed to poke fun at the powerlessness of human beings before Yahweh's unseen power.[35] "Unseen" is the key word here. To the "unseeing," Yahweh's power and being are mysterious, veiled, "unseeable." To the "seeing," Yahweh's power is real and vital and reliable—"seeable." These are not just king-vs.-prophet cartoons, nor are they political manifestos designed to highlight social conflicts between Israelite classes of elites and peasants.[36] These are stories about the importance of "seeing" one's salvation and, as such, are interpretable on several levels.

First, Elisha prays that his servant might "see." Frustrated by Elisha's ability to predict his whereabouts, the Syrian king desperately tries to track him down. Hearing he might be at Dothan, he sends a crack squadron of his best troops to bivouac overnight and ambush him at dawn. The next morning, as it turns out, Elisha's servant is the first to walk outside...and "see" a phalanx of chariots lined up in attack formation. Paralyzed with fear, he cries out 'ahâ 'adônî, "Oh, my lord!" He has no idea what to do when confronted by "the unseeable."

But Elisha does. Seeing the same chariots and the same soldiers he does not cry out, nor does he launch an attack against Syria on his own initiative. Instead, he speaks an oracle of assurance to his servant: "Don't be afraid,"[37] then he does something very rare in the book of Kings—he prays.[38] The focus of his prayer is itself unexpected because he does not pray for personal salvation or his enemies' destruction or heavenly rapture. Instead, he prays that his servant might "see" the salvation already present.

Second, he prays that the Arameans might be struck blind. Like Odysseus with Polyphemus (the Cyclops), Elisha decides to have some fun with his enemies.[39] Where Odysseus blinds Polyphemus, Elisha blinds the Arameans. Where Odysseus calls himself "No Man"—so that, when asked his attacker's name, can only say what he's been programmed to say[40]—so also Elisha programs his attackers: "This is not the road and this is not the city. Follow me, and I will lead you to the man for whom you are looking." Technically Elisha is lying to these soldiers, just as he lies to Ben-Hadad later (2 Kings 8:10). But to read this story from a wooden legal perspective is to miss the point. This is farce—in fact, one of the best examples of farce in the Bible. Storytellers who perform farce are expected to make it hilarious by using slapstick humor and outrageous characters to raise ridiculous questions: "How does Elisha do it? Does he line up everybody in single file? Does he make them wander in a circle? In a square? In a trapezoid? How do they know where to camp for the night? How does he get this Syrian squadron past the Samarian sentries? Does he put a finger to his lips and whisper, 'Shhhhh!?' What do the Samarians do when they look up to see Elisha, like some pied piper, leading a bunch of blind Syrian soldiers into the streets of downtown Samaria?" Both Homer and this writer understand the power of humor to make a point.

Third, once he has taken them where he wants them Elisha prays, "Yahweh, open the eyes of these men so they can see." These are the very same words he prays earlier before his "blind" servant; now he recites them again to pull off one of the funniest practical jokes in the Bible. Unfortunately, though, like many contemporary commentators, the Israelite king doesn't get the joke. Playing the role of the "dumb Omride," he blurts out, "Shall I kill them, my father? Shall I kill them?" This carica-ture is not unlike the Israelite king in the Naaman story, another editorial cartoon from this brilliant satirist. In short, there's just no way these Israelite kings are not going to look clueless in the book of Kings. But there's a message here behind the humor, and it's important that we high-light it. The problem with this king is that he is too fearful to have faith, and because he lacks a saving faith, he chooses instead to live a life enslaved by tired arguments and boring legalities.

Responding to his king, Elisha tries to explain the joke—"Do not kill them....Would you kill men you have captured with your own sword?" In so many words he asks, "Well, when you go to war and take prisoners, you show them leniency, right? So...how is this any different?" "Set food and water before them so that they may eat and drink and then go back to their master." Like Gehazi—another humorless Israelite—this king is just too fearful to live by faith.

Intratextual Reflection

Patterning itself after the Elisha cycle, Mark's Gospel portrays Jesus' min-istry as a dynamic study in "salvation" and "sight."[41] In Mark 8:22–10:52, the Marcan evangelist sandwiches Jesus' passion predictions—the core of Marcan theology—between two healings of two blind men, intentionally contrasting their "sight" with the disciples' "blindness":

· Jesus heals blind eyes (8:22–26).
· First passion prediction and attendant events (8:27–9:29).

· Second passion prediction and attendant events (9:30–10:31).
· Third passion prediction and attendant events (10:32–45).
· Jesus heals blind eyes (10:46–52).[42]

By means of this technique Mark retreads these old prophetic motifs and repackages them for a newer audience. In fact, this "faith"-vs.-"sight" polarity finds its way into a number of later traditions, though various writers work the polarity in various ways. In Mark's case the evangelist wants to show that Jesus is able to cure physical blindness, but that miracles alone cannot guarantee spiritual "sightedness." Only faith in the Atonement of the Son of God can heal humanity's deepest "blindness."[43] In Kings this episode serves as one of several *pressure of violence* stories, and interpreting it in its intratextual context leads us to recognize the following themes.

First, whether it's the death of a baby or the loss of one's freedom, all of us live in a world of the unexpected. The question is not whether unexpected things might happen, but how we will respond to them when they do. Will we fight? Will we flee? Will we fear? Will we have faith? If the Elisha tradition teaches anything it's that God habitually allows the unexpected to happen, and further, the reason he does is so that believers might learn how to develop eyes to "see" and ears to "hear." Wolfhart Pannenberg acknowledges that this is a difficult truth to grasp, especially for those who try to read these stories through a hyper-rationalistic lens promising complete scientific control of the text. Truly Christian faith cannot occur when we do this. Faith occurs only when the Bible's Hebraic theology is contextualized, not perverted or dismissed or replaced.[44] In the Bible the Incarnate Word of God is never a "principle" one "constructs," but a Savior one trusts in the midst of unexpected invitations.[45]

Second, Yahweh has a sense of humor. I mention this not to overemphasize the obvious, but to complain against humorless religionists who habitually and painfully misinterpret the Bible. Unless one is brain dead it's impossible to read a story like this and come to the conclusion that God did not create humor. Of course there's no need to go to the extreme and make the Bible into some sort of shallow jokebook, but this isn't our problem today. Farce, satire, irony, parody—all these and many other literary techniques appear often in biblical narrative to accomplish distinct theological purposes, but much biblical scholarship is unable to "see" it. Readers who cannot "see" this dimension of God's grace need to take another look because C. S. Lewis is right: Satan is just too dull-witted to be funny.[46]

Third, God wants his children to live by faith, not fear. It's not enough simply to realize that God is powerful, or even All-Powerful. I must decide whether I want to surrender my life to Him. It's not enough to realize that God is All-Knowing. I must decide what I believe when I can't "see" what he's doing. It's not enough to ponder forever my response to this God. I must actively respond. When Augustine realizes the inevitability of this choice, he knows immediately what he has to do:

> Continence...smiled on me with a persuasive mockery, as if to say, "Can you not do what these youths, what these maidens can do...? Cast yourself upon Him. Fear not. He will not withdraw Himself and make you fall. Cast yourself fearlessly upon Him. He will receive, and will heal you." When I blushed exceedingly... she again seemed to say, "Stop your ears against your unclean members...that they may be mortified. They tell you of delights, but not like the law of the Lord your God."[47]

Theological Reflection

Faith can do some pretty remarkable things. When the Los Angeles Lakers went into Madison Square Garden for game seven of the 1970 NBA Championship, for example, they underestimated the faith of the New York Knicks.[48] Two games prior, they'd succeeded in knocking the Knicks' inspirational leader, Willis Reed, out of contention with a knee injury—or so they thought. Laker Wilt Chamberlain had been banging away at Reed for the entire season, but when the championship series came around, he almost ended his career, so violent was his attack on Reed. The sight of Reed hobbling off the court in game six sent dejected Knicks fans to the exits in despair. With Reed out of the game, everyone expected the remaining game to be a mop-up.

No one expected to "see" anything different.

But ten minutes before the game, while players were taking their warm-up shots, while Chamberlain and the rest of the Lakers were gloating over their "victory," while the commentators were pronouncing the Knicks "dead"—Willis Reed started taping up his pain-filled knee. He forced himself to get out of his chair and he hobbled out of the safety of the locker room. No one expected him to play. The doctors told him not to play. When he started running down the tunnel at Madison Square Garden he was halfway to the court before the cameras even knew he was coming to play. The moment when he ran on to the court is one of Knicks fans' most hallowed memories. The Garden just went crazy. Knicks fans—even

Laker fans—around the country jumped to their feet in amazement as Willis Reed led his team to victory and became the series MVP.

Faith is always full of surprises.

PICK AND ROLL (2 Kings 9:1-10:36)

When reading the Jehu tradition, many interpreters accept the text's editorial perspective and view him as a loyal Yahwist committed to "Yahweh's continuing mastery over Baal and the political machine promoting Baal worship."[49] From the narrator's point of view, he looks to be merely and only a purgation tool in the hands of Yahweh. Others, however, view him in less favorable terms. When Jehu slaughters the royal families of both Judah and Israel, for example, this signifies to some readers that a Yahwistic minority has become desperate enough to use terrorism as a weapon. They question Jehu's use of violence and deception, in some cases ignoring the tradition's theological characteristics for a hypothetical reconstruction of its politics.[50]

Others read the Jehu story against the Ahab story, isolating and comparing the language-forms in both accounts and rejecting the possibility that any ancient annal could have lain beneath this text.[51] Support for such a view, however, often relies more strongly on the redactoral possibilities above the text than the theological conflicts within the text. Even among those who accept the story as historically true, many doubt whether everything Jehu does in Yahweh's name has Yahweh's approval. Hosea's negative appraisal, for example, is quite serious (Hos 1:4), as is the negative appraisal in the text itself (2 Kings 10:31). Thus, the conclusion seems obvious that the biblical tradition is ambivalent. Jehu receives the same negative reprimand as every other northern king, but he also receives high praise: "Because you have done well in carrying out what I consider right, and in accordance with all that was in my heart have dealt with the house of Ahab, your sons of the fourth generation shall sit on the throne of Israel" (2 Kings 10:30).

This may well be "the strongest endorsement given to any northern monarch,"[52] yet the problem remains. Most interpretations fail to address the narrator's most pressing goal: to articulate a prophetic theology of reform against a violent, highly Canaanized religious environment. Many important questions still wait to be addressed. Why does the Yahwist prophet Hosea, for example, excoriate the Yahwist king Jehu for doing what the Yahwist prophet Elisha (by proxy) commissions him to do: exterminate the house of Omri (Hos 1:4)? Why does Jehu so fervently attack

Canaanite religion, only to submit so quickly to Assyrian hegemony?[53] Why does this narrator include this text at all in his history of Israel? Whether Jehu's submission is religious or political is, again, debatable, yet the famous Black Obelisk does show him kneeling before Shalmaneser III,[54] and this fits poorly with the biblical tradition's portrayal of this king. Incongruities like these are provoking a number of explanations from a variety of perspectives today.[55]

At the beginning of the Jehu cycle Elisha and Hazael stand waiting for the fulfillment of Elijah's commission (1 Kings 19:16). Nudged by Elisha, Hazael successfully drags the Omrides into a costly border war, thereby destroying the anti-Assyrian coalition formally binding Israel to Syria. The Arameans wound Joram in battle and the king has to retreat to Jezreel to lick his wounds. Elisha sends an emissary to Ramoth-Gilead to anoint Jehu "king over Israel," but this proves to be a very risky move because Joram is still very much Israel's king.

Paralleling this risky political move, however, the narrator makes an equally daring literary move. He steps up the satirical attack begun in the Mt. Carmel narrative (1 Kings 18:26-29), then revisited in the farce of the blind Syrians (2 Kings 6:8-23), then revisited again in the Samarian siege narrative (6:24-7:20). In this last episode, for example, a king's official complains that Samaria is doomed and voices grave doubts whether salvation is even possible, not even if a heavenly "window" were to open up and rain down divine blessings on their heads (2 Kings 7:2). Robert LaBarbera has convincingly shown that this response parodies the debate between Kothar-wa-Hasis and Baal over whether or not to put a window in Baal's palace (for the Ugaritic text, see *KTU* 1.4 v 58-vii 29). In fact, he makes a convincing case for reading all of 2 Kings 6:8-7:20 as "cleverly constructed satire" aimed at "the ruling elite of the day…, whether they come from Samaria or Damascus."[56]

On this matter of satire biblical scholars have for some time been emphasizing its ubiquity and importance in the prophetic literature. Theodor Gaster, for example, once spoke of Hosea as a "sustained satire on pagan seasonal festivals."[57] David Marcus identifies no less than fourteen examples of satire in the Hebrew Bible,[58] and Gale Yee has shown that parody tends to replicate, like a virus, the anatomies of the literary forms it subverts.[59] Thomas Jemielity, however, addresses the ideological reasons why prophets (and prophetic narrators) so often gravitate to satire.[60] Like the Roman satirists Horace and Juvenal, he argues, Hebrew prophets use satire because it has the power to "deny and subvert the acceptable moral form which complacency imposes on human action."[61] Prophets use satire to challenge the elitist powerbrokers of their day, attacking both the character of their enemies and the literary traditions they most revere. Sometimes these attacks can be vulgar (one thinks of Ezekiel's preoccupations with excreta and genitalia), and sometimes they can degenerate into little more than "controlled rhetorical chaos."[62] Yet underneath satire's "generic instability,"[63] it can generate an amazingly wide range of "technique, theme, and victim."[64]

The coronation of Jehu is a case in point because, first, the liturgist at this coronation is a nameless "son of the prophets." This is not Samuel, the great prophet, or Zadok, the great high priest. We have no idea who this person is, and this is precisely the point. His anonymity is deliberate, and this increases our surprise when we hear an entire oracle come out of him. Elisha gives him one scripted line—"This is what Yahweh says: 'I anoint you king over Israel'"—but this rookie turns it into a sermon. He commands Jehu to "destroy the house of Ahab and avenge the blood of my servants the prophets." He compares the house of Ahab to the house of Jeroboam son of Nebat and defames him by association with Israel's most famous "evil leader."[65] He predicts that the dogs will devour Jezebel, and though we could read these lines as redactoral embellishment, the more likely possibility is that they form part of a deliberate literary strategy.[66]

Second, most kings are commissioned to build things (temples, armies, palaces, economies). This king, however, is commissioned to destroy and avenge and devour, and the objects of this destruction are not Israel's enemies, but Israel's leaders. Like a surgeon, Jehu is commanded to go into Israel's body politic and cut out all the cancer he can find, even to the point of taking out some of the pink tissue around the edges. Whether or not (post)moderns understand or accept or approve of this mission, Jehu does what he's commissioned to do—exterminate the house of Omri, not engage it in ecumenical dialogue.

Third, the narrator goes on to parody the community's reaction to all this. At first, this liturgist receives no respect from the community, only ridicule. Jehu's men even label him a "madman" (*meshuggâ`*, 2 Kings 9:11). After Jehu's coronation, however, their opinions quickly change as ridicule turns to fear and the robes start piling up at Jehu's feet. What follows next is even more fascinating, however, and requires a bit of background explanation.

Students of Canaanite religion are very aware that ever since the Ugaritic texts came to light in the 1930s the goddess Anat has been a great puzzle.[67] In one text, for example (*KTU* 1.3), she defends her brother Baal by destroying his enemies, but she does so with a level of glee found nowhere else in these texts. Some have tried to tie this bloodbath myth to a seasonal calendar, supposing it to be a primitive attempt to revive the so-called "vegetative spirit."[68] Others hypothesize that her devotees may have engaged in some sort of homeopathic ritual for which this purgation ritual is a blueprint—perhaps a "ritual combat" of some sort designed to provoke Baal into ending the sterility of summer and sending down the autumn rains.[69]

Intratextual Reflection

Others draw parallels between this myth and various sections of the Hebrew Bible.[70] Philip Stern, for example, applies Mark Smith's[71] trenchant suggestions about the Anat myth to Psa 23, pointing out common references to "tables among enemies," the destruction of both "house and valley," and the "house of the deity."[72] Peter Craigie proposes that the Song of Deborah parallels the Anat myth in at least five ways: (1) Deborah, like Anat, has a male warrior assistant; (2) Deborah, like Anat, is a leader of warriors; (3) Deborah "dominates" (*tdrky*) her enemies on the battlefield (Anat is called a mistress of "dominion," *drkt*); (4) Anat is a "maiden" (*rhm*), so too Deborah is a "maiden" (*rhm*); and (5) Deborah, like Anat, commands a military host of stars.[73] Craigie argues that the biblical authors are quite aware of this tradition, whether or not it ever finds a home in an alleged Anat cult.[74]

Jeffrey Lloyd suggests that Anat engages in two separate battles because at the root of her story lies the primordial desire of conquerors to perfect their conquests. Citing evidence from Moab, Egypt, and Ugarit, Lloyd argues that ancient conquerors cannot declare total victory until some of their prisoners are brought before (the statue of) their deity and ritually sacrificed.[75] Should this be the case, the narrator of 2 Kings 9-10 looks to be parodying the Canaanite tradition. Just as Anat purges the earth, so Jehu purges Israel. Just as Anat purges both "field" and "house," so Jehu purges both "field" and "house." Just as Anat adorns herself and puts on paint, so Jezebel adorns herself and puts on paint. The following chart breaks down these parallels into subcategories of characterization, plot, and theme.

Jehu's Purge (2 Kings 9:14-10:36)	Anat's Purge (*KTU* 1.3 i-iii)

Characterization

One purging tool: Jehu	One purging tool: Anat
Two enemies (Joram & Ahaziah)	Two "enemies" (Gapnu & Ugar)
Jehu stacks 70 "heads" (*rô'shîm*)	Anat kicks "heads" (*rísh*) around like "balls"
Jehu "fills his hand" with the bow (*qeshet*)	Anat's signature weapon is her "bow" (*qsh*t)[76]
Jezebel adorns herself	Anat adorns herself
Jezebel uses *pûk* on her eyes ("antinomy")	Anat uses *ánhb* on her eyes ("snail dye")
Jezebel looks out a window	Anat closes "the gates"
Jezebel's "palms" (*kap*) are barely visible	Anat proudly wears the "palms" of warriors on her belt
Jezebel's "skull," "feet" and "hands" are her only remains	Anat's "liver," "heart," "knees" and "fingers" participate in her victory

Plot

Two battles: one in the field, one in Baal's "house" (*bêt*)	Two battles: one in the field, one in the "palace" (*bht*) of Anat
Jehu "meets" (*qârâ'*) several officials before final battle	Anat "meets" (*qry*) "pages" (*'glm*) before final battle
Jehu meets Joram at Naboth's "field"	Anat meets enemies at the "foot of the rock" (*bsht 'gr*)
Jehu shoots an arrow (*hetsî*) through sickly Joram's heart	Anat shoots "old men" (*shbm*) with "shafts" (*mt*)
House of Baal has a "city" in it (*'îr*)	Anat fights "between two cities"
Jezebel mocks her enemies	Anat mocks her enemies
Jezebel's "blood" (*dâm*) spatters	Anat plunges her knees into "blood" (*dm*)

Theme

Justice	Purgation
Prophetic covenant	Priestly power
"House"	"House"
Reward for obedience	Celebration of enemies' defeat

Keeping in mind satire's "generic instability," we need to re-emphasize that no intertextual comparison can ever be "certain," especially when informed scholars cannot agree on matters as basic as tablet placement and narrative sequence. Some of these parallels will seem more convincing than others. Still, the main characters in these traditions are amazingly similar because both enact flat roles as purifying agents. Anat purges both valley and town on behalf of Baal, her master and lord. Jehu likewise purges Israel on behalf of Yahweh, his master and lord. In the Canaanite myth Anat "raises her voice" against two low-level deities, Gapnu and Ugar, in order to defend her brother Baal against further divine attack. In the Hebrew story Jehu does not even bother to engage, he simply exterminates the kings of Israel and Judah (Joram and Ahaziah)— that is, the narrator summarily deflates these kings' exaggerated self-images by paralleling them, however subtly, with two deities at "the lowest level of the divine assembly."[77]

Further, each agent focuses on "perfecting" (Lloyd's term) their respective purges. Each purges something "outside" (field/wilderness) as well as something "inside" (city/temple). In the Canaanite text Anat does this by kicking her enemies' heads around like soccer balls, then wearing their palms into battle. In the Hebrew text Jehu stacks up his enemies' heads before Samaria's gate, then forces his foes to look at them while he makes a speech. Since myths are by definition fluid and repetitious, several of these parallels shift back and forth between similarly "flat" characters. Sometimes the parallel is between Anat-Jehu; sometimes between Anat-Jezebel. Just as Anat mocks her enemies so Jezebel mocks hers, calling Jehu "Zimri," the infamous assassin-king who precedes the Omrides (1 Kings 16:15-20). And while we might speculate why Anat adorns herself Jezebel's motives seem a bit more obvious. Jezebel paints her eyes because Anat paints her eyes. Jezebel puts on antimony (*pûk*) because Anat puts on murex (*ánhb*). Whether this is warpaint or mascara is never stated in either tradition, yet the biblical narrator seizes on it to satirize this Phoenician queen, right down to the details of her *toilette*.

Beyond characterization, however, each plot-line structures itself around two battles: one in the "valley" and one in the "town." In the Canaanite myth Anat becomes dissatisfied with "fighting in the valley" and "takes herself to her palace." Once inside, she starts rearranging the chairs and tables and starts slaughtering her enemies, until "sated with fighting in the house, with battling between the tables" (*UNP* 83). The same plot-sequence occurs in the Jehu narrative—*in the same order.* Jehu begins his attack in the plain outside Jezreel, but quickly moves the battle inside to massacre his enemies in the temple of Baal. Outside on the plain, he purges Israel's military establishment. Inside Baal's temple, he purges Israel's religious establishment.

Further, if Kings is playing off this well-known myth, this helps explain why the biblical text uses historical flashbacks and other suspense-building features in this fascinating story. In the Canaanite cycle Anat "meets youths" (*wtqry ʿglmm*) before going into battle. In Kings, however, Jehu "meets" (*qârâ*) a whole slew of people—a "horseman," a "second horseman," Jezreel's "officials, elders, guardians, and palace administrator," the "city governor," and a traditionalist named "Jehonadab son of Recab." In each of these "meetings," a different messenger asks Jehu, "Is it peace?...Is it peace?"[78] Jehu responds by "turning" (*sâbab*) each messenger into an ally and descending on Joram like a "madman" (a clear allusion to the "madman" prophet mentioned earlier, 2 Kings 9:11). Finally, the two enemies square off in a climactic battle. In the Canaanite myth Anat engages her enemies at "the foot of the rock" (*bsht ´gr*, perhaps a reference to her own mountain-top sanctuary).[79] In the Hebrew narrative the parties meet at the moral epicenter of the biblical tradition—Naboth's vineyard. Intensifying the suspense, Kings even inserts an historical flashback to explain why Joram has to die here. This is brilliant writing—a powerful mixture of irony, history, satire, and theology. Just as Anat picks up her bow, so Jehu "fills his hand with the bow." Just as Anat drives out "old men" with her "shafts" (*mt*), so Jehu shoots a final "shaft" (*hetsî*) into the king's heart. How fitting it is, from a Hebrew perspective, that Joram not only dies at the site of his mother's most heinous crime, but that the story preserving it parodies his mother's most sacred religious tradition.

Theological Reflection

Like all ancient Near Eastern myths the Anat cycle is a ritual reflection of a powerful political institution: priestly power. Ritualized purgation is the mother's milk of priestly politics. To see this one need only look at the bitter rivalries between the priests of Amon and Akhenaton in Egypt,[80] or the priests of Marduk and Nabonidus in Babylon,[81] or even the struggle between the Teacher of Righteousness and his fellow Jerusalem priests 150 years before Christ.[82] Not to see the political realities behind these narratives is to segregate story from history, and not only is this unnecessary, it horribly misconstrues the meanings of these ancient texts. As Eckart Otto reminds us, "the mythical world of the gods is not a peaceful place," and this is because the priesthoods responsible for creating these texts are constantly at war with each other.[83]

Whether the narrator of Kings fully focuses on this reality or not, what we find in lieu of priestly purgation in the Bible is the prophetic theme of prophetic justice. Yahweh establishes the contours of this justice at Sinai and Solomon re-establishes its implications in his Temple dedication speech (1 Kings 8:21). Jezebel utterly challenges this prophetic theology when she murders Naboth and steals away his inheritance. Whatever else this text may be saying, murder and theft are universally recognized crimes. Whether Jehu goes too far in administering Yahweh's justice is another, more difficult question—even the prophets cannot agree on how to answer it.[84] But that justice has to be meted out in a just way is a conclusion upon which everyone can agree—otherwise Israel's deity is a pious fraud.

Further, each tradition focuses on its respective ideological fundamentals. From a Canaanite perspective the Anat myth serves "to bind together two originally independent myths about the king-god Baal's struggle against Chaos by means of a common skeletal theme focused on the construction of Baal's palace."[85] From a Yahwistic perspective, however, behavior like Anat's raises a much more serious question, a question challenging the heart of the prophetic theological agenda. Where is prophetic justice even articulated in the Canaanite religious tradition, much less championed? Could it not be that Kings parodies Israel's enemies' traditions so harshly because this narrator wants his audience to learn something about the nature of violence? Could it be that he wants his audience to learn how to distinguish between the context driving Anat's violence vs. the context driving Jehu's violence?

Context is never so critical as when interpreting violence. Where Baal seems desperate to secure a house for himself, Yahweh also wants to build a "house" (2 Sam 7:11)—only a "house" of a different kind. Yahweh's house is a place of covenant justice, a place where widows and prostitutes and mothers and lepers and slave girls can experience real "justice" (*tsedâqâ*) and authentic "peace" (*shâlôm*). Characters like these are conspicuously missing from the Canaanite myths and Kings' narrator wants his readers to wonder why. By parodying the Canaanite tradition he challenges his audience to learn how to distinguish between competing religious ideologies.

The problem for many contemporary interpreters is either (a) a total indifference to the text's literary-historical context, or worse, (b) the imposition over it of a foreign context. Jehu acts violently, yes, *but so does Anat.* Simply blanching at the violence itself will do little to interpret the meaning of either ancient text. Should not the behavior of each violent character be interpreted in his/her own context first before attempts are made to translate its implications?[86] Too many (post)modern interpreters have little appreciation for the fact that prophetic parody is a "savage, frequently unsettling laughter that God and his prophets enjoy" at the expense of their enemies.[87] Thus, whether or not we view this text as a parody, or whether this particular definition of parody is universally acceptable, some explanation of this "unsettling laughter" is preferable to no explanation. Rolf Knierim reminds us that "the conceptual distinction between just and unjust violence rests on preconceptions which determine what is just and unjust."[88]

Finally, each tradition epitomizes its main themes through poetic summaries. In the Baal cycle, a newly-coiffed Anat picks up her harp and sings of her devotion to Baal, focusing her attention on two traditional themes: (1) the preservation of Baal's family and (2) the elimination of Baal's enemies:

> She sings the love of Mightiest Baal,
>> the passion of Pidray, Daughter of Light,
>> the desire of Tallay, Daughter of Showers,
>> the love of Arsay, Daughter of the Wide World.
> "What enemy rises against Baal?
> What foe against the Cloudrider?
>> Surely I fought Yam, the Beloved of El,
>> Surely I finished off River, the Great God,
>> Surely I bound Tunnan and destroyed (?) him.
>> I fought the Twisty Serpent,
>> The Potentate with seven heads." (*UNP* 109, 111)

By contrast, the prophetic oracles in Kings focus on (1) Yahweh's decision to keep his promise, and (2) Yahweh's desire to reward Jehu's faithful obedience:

> "Yesterday I saw the blood of Naboth and the blood of his sons, declares Yahweh, and I will surely make you pay for it on this plot of ground, declares Yahweh" (2 Kings 9:26).

> "Because you have done well in accomplishing what is right in my eyes and have done to the house of Ahab all I had in mind to do, your descendants will sit on the throne of Israel to the fourth generation" (2 Kings 10:30).

The Jehu tradition is therefore a satirical parody designed to champion a clear theological agenda to a culture raised on and fascinated by violence. Much like the episodes preceding it, this one tells the story of Israel's history not as dry chronicle, but as powerful satire aimed squarely at the religious traditions of Israel's enemies. As Gale Yee points out, only two things are necessary for parody to work: (1) the literary work being parodied has to be at least nominally familiar to the audience; and (2) they must be able to "make the connections" and "get the joke."[89] Assuming this is true, Jehu's coronation and purge may well be one of the most sophisticated "jokes" in the entire Bible.

MESSIANIC FAITH (2 Kings 11:1-21)

With this episode the narrator completes his history of the house of Omri, tying up several loose ends. Again he organizes his material around a simple chiasm:

> Jehu's coronation
>> Jehu's purge
>>> Yahweh's Victory Over Baal
>> Athaliah's purge
> Joash's coronation

Athaliah is Joram's wife—Jehoshaphat's daughter-in-law, Ahab's sister— and this text portrays her as an angry Omride bent on violent vengeance.[90] Like Saul, she leads her people into the sin of genocide and in the process almost succeeds in snuffing out the house of David. That she is unsuccessful in exterminating David's "seed" (*zera*'; NIV "family"), however, is testimony to both the courage of her opponents and the faithfulness of Yahweh. Athaliah's purge is about as close to extermination as David's family ever comes (with the possible exception of Elimelech's death in Ruth 1:1-5), yet violence like this, so offensive and so heinous, is distressingly common in the ancient world. Amnon rapes his sister. Absalom murders his brother. Solomon executes his brother. Amenhemhet I dies at the hands of an assassin.[91] Adrammelech and Sharezer murder their father (2 Kings 19:37). Nero executes his mother: "He thought of poisoning her, but she guarded against this by the habitual use of antidotes. He tried to have her drowned, but she swam to safety from the shipwreck he had arranged. His men pursued her to her villa.... It took many blows to kill her."[92]

Against Athaliah's violence, however, determined resistance arises from a quarter we might not ordinarily expect. No military champion or political rival rises up to challenge her, nor does Yahweh send a prophet. Instead, her opponents are a determined aunt and uncle—another example of minor characters triumphing over major characters. Aunt Jehosheba saves Joash from death, and six years later Uncle Jehoiada anoints him as king.

Intratextual Reflection

This episode reprises several motifs from previous episodes. First, like the story of Jehu, this is a purgation story. Like the goddesses they worship, both Jezebel and Athaliah have clear religious agendas and neither are afraid to use terror as a weapon. Jezebel rules behind the scenes in Samaria. Athaliah rules behind the scenes in Judah until her son dies and she takes over the kingdom of Judah. Obviously these are powerful women, shrewd politicians, devoted Baalists, formidable queen-mothers.[93] Yet to praise the "leadership qualities" of these queens is to ignore the whole intratextual context. This story does not appear in Kings to raise admiration for these women. This story is preserved to show how possible it is to survive even the most horrific kinds of religious abuse. Messianic faith can prevail over the direst of circumstances.

Second, like the crisis-coronations of Solomon and Jehu again a faithful Yahwist secretly anoints a savior. Where the northern tradition describes its secret coronation via a parody (Jehu), the southern tradition describes its secret coronation in cryptic priestly language. In the north a prophet anoints Jehu after a long series of preparatory events stretching all the way back to Horeb (1 Kings 19). In the south a priest anoints Joash after another long series of preparatory events: the decision to "steal away" (*gânab*) one of the doomed Davidic heirs; the decision to hide this child at the temple of Yahweh for six years; the decision to form a praetorian guard to protect him from harm (complete with loyalty oath); the decision to arm them with the spears and shields that belonged to King David, stored in the temple of Yahweh; the decision to place a crown on the son of David; the decision to present him with a copy of the covenant; and finally the decision to anoint him king.

This priestly language intensifies into a crescendo as Jehoiada prepares his people for Joash's coronation. When Athaliah (like Adonijah after his "coronation") hears a distant ruckus, she soon discovers Joash standing by the pillar (`ammûd)—the narrator adding, significantly, "as was the custom."[94] Then she cries out (like Joram before Jehu) "Treason! Treason!" (2 Kings 9:23). To avoid defiling the temple Jehoiada takes Athaliah away from the temple's holy precincts and has her executed, like Jezebel, in a place frequented by horses. Most importantly—and this is where the priestly tradition is very intentional—Jehoiada cuts covenants and keeps records of these events. Jehoiada's intention is not just to save a baby. His goal is to save Mosaic Yahwism. Having removed Athaliah from power, he now leads the people of the land against the Baal temple and they tear down its altars and idols (lit. "images," *tselem*). Only after all these carefully planned events take place—anointing, assassination, purgation, coronation—does Jehoiada bring out and introduce Joash to the inhabitants of Judah.

Third, like Jehu's purge, this violent story maintains a clear theological focus in the midst of terrible events. Political revolution is an important sub-theme, yes, but it's not the text's primary theme. Compared to other coronation stories in Kings this one introduces us to a new theme we have not yet previously seen—*messianic faith*. This is the first time we see believers put their faith so determinedly in a future deliverer. Yes, Nathan engineers Solomon's coronation at the beginning of Kings, but Solomon is already prepared to lead. Elisha sends a messenger to anoint Jehu, yes, but Jehu is already a commander in the field. Here Jehoiada works from the presupposition that if he can save just one of these Davidic heirs the people of Judah will rally around him after he comes to the maturity of manhood. This is the Bible's first mention of messianic faith in a "coming one."[95]

In truth, none of Jehoiada's actions can be explained apart from this faith—the great care with which he establishes a phalanx of protection around the child, the great care with which he extricates Athaliah from power, the great care with which he attacks the Baal temple and its priesthood, the great care with which he writes everything down for posterity—covenants of loyalty, covenants between Yahweh and Joash, covenants between Joash and the people, covenants between Yahweh and the people. Where Jehu relies on charismatic anointing, Jehoiada relies on a Coming One. Where Jehu relies on the loyalty of fellow Israelites, Jehosheba trusts that the baby trembling in her arms will someday rescue his people from their enemies.

Theological Reflection

"Give me your right hands to kiss, my children, give them to me. Oh hands and lips so dear to me, Oh noble face and bearing of my children, I wish you happiness—but in that other place. What is here your father has taken away. Oh, how sweet is the touch, how tender the skin, how fragrant the breath of these children! Go in, go in. I can no longer look at you, but am overwhelmed by my pain."[96]

Medea pours out her heart to her children in this famous soliloquy because she is furious at her husband. To punish him for his infidelities she decides to kill his (and her) children. She decides that killing his children is preferable to raising them as his heirs. Like all tragic heroines, she faces an incredibly difficult choice—eternal shame vs. eternal revenge—and she makes this choice under extreme duress.

Greek tragedy almost voyeuristically revels in such conflicted heroes, putting them under tremendous pressure to see what they will do. Sophocles, for example, puts his protagonist through the wringer in his famous play Oedipus Tyrannus. Euripides explores the netherworld's ever-increasing levels of pain through the eyes of his hero Herakles. Aristophanes satirizes his culture's obsession with death in his play *Frogs*.[97] Contemporary films only retread these hoary themes. M. Night Shyamalan's *The Sixth Sense* probes death's psychological and spiritual boundaries through the eyes of a child ("I see dead people"). Martin Scorsese's *Bringing Out the Dead* parodies death's dreariness through the eyes of a lonely paramedic. Jerry Zucker's *Ghost* dismisses death's finality via a sappy love story bathed in adolescent myth.[98]

Messianic faith is different. Messianic faith is an adult response to the problem of death. Messianic faith doesn't satirize or obsess about death. It attacks death at its most vulnerable level, its "Achilles heel." It strips death of all power and pretense. Messianic faith has produced the most convincing, most persuasive, and most powerful anti-death literature in existence. It is the deepest kind of faith and the present episode displays several of its most enduring qualities.

First, messianic faith is constant. For six years Jehoiada and Jehosheba stay focused on their mission. They don't just trust Yahweh on weekends and do what they like the rest of the week. Rescuing the Davidic line from Athaliah's spies takes messianic faith, not "happyfaith." Dietrich Bonhoeffer, stunned by Germany's decision to exterminate the Jews, and even more stunned by the Church's lackadaisical response to this evil, agonizes over it like a modern-day Jehoiada before a modern-day Athaliah. Like Jehoiada, he decides not to play the role of Jehosheba; that is, he does not become the first to plot Hitler's death. He has to be persuaded that "faith without works is dead, being alone" (James 2:17). But when he does get involved he doesn't look back. He remains constant and determined and steadfast in his faith. He surprises all his colleagues by leaving a promising career in New York to return to Germany and establish Finkenwalde, a seminary-in-exile designed to provide real theological education to students, not the spineless drivel they hear from the state church. He faces agonizing decisions about life and death and comes to the conclusion that "it is worse for a liar to tell the truth than for a lover of truth to lie."[99]

Second, messianic faith is active, not passive. Jehoiada does not have to lift a finger to help Joash, nor does Jehosheba. Jehosheba does not have to get involved in this plot. She could decide to accept things the way they are. Why not just hide out in the palace and let Athaliah do what she wants? Why not just treat her like the Red Queen in *Alice in Wonderland*, the preening monarch who's always screaming, "Off with their heads!"?[100] Somebody else can take the responsibility for rescuing the house of David, right? Of course, there is a time for waiting on the Lord, for putting blood on the lintel and waiting for the death-angel to pass over. But Jehosheba believes this is not that time. Faced by this crisis, she believes that the appropriate response is to act, and act quickly. Jehosheba therefore stands in a long line of faith warriors. Solomon has to deal with Adonijah. Elijah has to confront Ahab. Elisha has to go to Damascus. Jehu has to go to Jezreel. Jehosheba has to save this baby.

Third, messianic faith is hope-filled, not pain-filled. Messianic faith is the only antidote strong enough to address and neutralize the present (post)modern culture of victimization. Biblical faith is not about guessing the will of a conflicted king (Oedipus), nor is it about hoping against hope for a mythical superhero to save the day (Herakles, Superman, the President, the CEO of one's company). Messianic faith is not about pain endurance (Stoicism) or pain management (aspirin, heroin, "soma," tradition).[101] Messianic faith is about trusting in the Coming One, the One who will show the way out of darkness. Baal's priests talk a lot about overcoming death. Messiah overcomes death. Baal's priests talk a lot about salvation. Messiah saves. "Nobody else but God would ever have thought of justifying those who are guilty....How can they be forgiven and justified? Their fellowmen, despairing of them, say, 'They are hopeless cases.' Even Christians look upon them with sorrow rather than with hope. But not so their God."[102]

One summer afternoon my pregnant wife and I pulled up to our first parsonage in a yellow Ryder truck and already things weren't going well. I wouldn't go so far as to say that the congregation lied to us. They'd just grossly underestimated the amount of time it would take to finish the construction of the parsonage. I will never forget the look on my wife's face as she looked at our "new home." Only the first floor even looked finished. No dry wall. No electrical wiring. No insulation. No vinyl siding. No plumbing. No roof. Tired from our three-day trip, we tried as hard as we could to put a smile on our face as our new elder board enthusiastically shared with us their vision of the future. No one called to tell us that we didn't have a house yet, and to make matters worse, instead of showing us to the apartment we expected to occupy in the interim, the elders shared with us their plan to save money. They wanted us to move in with various members of the church for two weeks at a time until the parsonage was completed.

Hearing this, we just looked at each other in disbelief. No one, of course, had any idea how long it was going to take to finish the parsonage (the contractor was working only in his spare time). Nor did anyone think to ask us what we wanted. So, from June 10 to Nov 15 we moved in and out of several members' houses as my pregnant wife frantically searched for a place to nest. Everyone told us how bad they felt about our situation, but no one did anything about it. Instead, people exhorted us to see the positive side ("after all, you're getting to know the congregation a lot quicker than you would otherwise!"). Months went by as life began to blur together into one long *Saturday Night Live* skit. There were some genuinely funny moments—like the time when one of the deacons, upset that my wife kept vomiting at the smell of his sauerkraut, actually said to her, "Could you please let me know in advance the next time you're going to get sick—we don't want to waste any more food."

But most of it wasn't funny. This situation tested our faith like nothing else we had ever experienced.

Yet all this was nothing compared to the "moving day" incident.

Having hung the last door and nailed down the last piece of carpet, I drove "home" to my weary wife one wintry afternoon and helped gather up our things. Excited and hopeful, we drove over to the now-completed parsonage. Cold and tired, we waddled up the stairs to her new bedroom—she was so great with child I thought she would burst! But just as I put my hand to the door-handle, one of the elder's wives swung it open from the other side. "Oh, you can't move in today," she said matter-of-factly, holding the business end of a vacuum cleaner between us. "I haven't finished cleaning yet. It's going to be another couple of days before you can move in. I'll call you when I'm ready." Then she closed the door in our face and went back to work.

Well, that was the last straw. We went back to the car and started unpacking our things. Concerned that she had not made herself clear she came over to us and repeated herself, "I'm sorry, but I'm not ready for you yet"—to which I responded, "I'm sorry too, but we're moving in today." For what seemed an eternity we just stared at each other, eyeball to eyeball, until she packed up her vacuum cleaner and left. At first, I thought she would go home and pray and finally realize how insensitive and rude she'd been. I presumed that elders wives were by definition mature enough to see through such circumstances to the larger picture. But I was deeply mistaken. This woman had started this church in her basement (as she constantly reminded us), so I guess she figured that this gave her the right to tell us (and everyone else) what to do—right down to where we ought to hang our family pictures (I'm not kidding!).

That's when "Jehosheba" showed up ("blessed be his name!"). Had it not been for another one of our elders—a wise, holy man—we might never have resolved this conflict. Realizing that this lady was not going to budge he came to us right away and apologized for her behavior. Would we be willing to attend a meeting with her in her home? Of course, we said. Eventually we straightened everything out, but not because the parties to this dispute necessarily were wise or mature. God brought us back together because one of his "Jehoshebas" had messianic faith.

Notes

1. Tomoo Ishida sees the longing for a "King Gideon" (Judg 8:22) as an "isolated event" in premonarchic Israel (*The Royal Dynasties in Ancient Israel* [Berlin: de Gruyter, 1977] 1), but the Amarna letters clearly show the existence of royal estates in Palestine centuries before Saul and David (N. Na'aman, "Royal Estates in the Jezreel Valley in the Late Bronze Age and Under the Israelite Monarchy," *EI* 15 [1981] 140-44).

2. *UNP* 87. Several Canaanite myths focus on sibling rivalry between deities, particularly Yam vs. Baal and Baal vs. Mot.

3. Aristophanes, *Clouds,* lines 1048-50.

4. Anything associated with the king's person is believed to have special significance. That this significance can be religious is clear from 2 Sam 8:18, where David's sons are explicitly called "priests" (*kohanîm*; NIV softens to "royal advisers").

5. At 13th century Ugarit *mshh* describes Baal's "anointing" of Anat's "horns" (*UNP* 183). At 13th century Emar, Baal's high priestess has her head shaved and "anointed" at her ordination (lit., "poured over," *tabaku, Emar* 369.9). In the Old Testament no less than 11 individuals appear as "anointed" (or potentially anointed) royal figures: Saul, Eliab, David, Absalom, Solomon, Jehu, Hazael (?), Joash, Jehoahaz, Zedekiah, and Cyrus.

6. W. Brueggemann ("On Coping With Curse: A Study of 2 Sam 16:5-14," *CBQ* 36 [1974] 175-92) sees in Shimei a champion of faith/dissent—a far different view from the one presented here.

7. Deut 6:2; 8:11; 10:13; 11:1, 28:15, 45; 30:10, 16; 1 Kings 3:14; 2 Kings 23:3.

8. H. Gardner, *Leading Minds: An Anatomy of Leadership* (New York: Basic, 1995) 99.

9. See my "Job's Texts of Terror," *CBQ* 55 (1993) 662-75.

10. The Moabite Stone is written by this same Mesha, probably erected in c. 830 BC. For a translation, see *ANET* 320-21.

11. Chemosh is the national deity of the Moabites, who, like Baal, has his own temple cult (restored from an inscription found in 1958 [*SSI* 1.83, cited in G. R. Mattingly, "Chemosh," *ABD* 1.897]).

12. 1 Kings 22:4 // 2 Kings 3:7. Whether or not the narrative of the battle of Kir-Hareseth is a doublet of the earlier battle at Ramoth Gilead is an interesting, but hypothetical question (*pace* P. Satterthwaite, "The Elisha Narratives and Coherence of 2 Kings 2-8," *Tyndale Bulletin* 49 [1998] 25-28).

13. Isa 63:1-6 (emphasis added). The character and the geographic region of Edom are both "red," and one need only descend into the necropolis at Petra to realize just how red. Note that the three letters *'-d-m* can spell "human" ("Adam") "Edom," "red," and even in one text, "blood" (*KAI* 43.11, prosthetic aleph).

14. Josephus, *AJ* 9.37. Josephus proposes that the Moabites believe the Israelites and Judahites "slay one another out of thirst" (*AJ* 9.38-39).

15. Josephus, *AJ* 9.43-44.

16. J. B. Burns, "Why Did the Besieging Army Withdraw? (2 Kings 3:27)," *ZAW* 102 (1990) 187-94.

17. G. M. Harton, "The Meaning of 2 Kings 3:27," *Grace Journal* 11 (1970) 34-40.

18. B. Margalit, "Why King Mesha of Moab Sacrificed His Oldest Son," *BAR* 12 (1986) 62-63.

19. In the Phoenician/Punic texts the child-victim is called "meat" (*bsh'r, KAI* 162.2), "righteous sprout" (*tsmh tsdq, KAI* 43.11) and, simply "my blood" (*'dmy, KAI* 43.11).

20. I am aware that many follow Kant's rejection of this divine act as ethically reprehensible, but see the brilliant response to Kant in J. Levenson, "Abusing Abraham: Traditions, Religions, Histories, and Modern Misinterpretations," *Judaism* 47 (1998) 259-77.

21. Contra Klaas A. D. Smelik, "Moloch, Molekh or Molk- Sacrifice? A Reassessment of the Evidence Concerning the Hebrew Term *Molekh*," *SJOT* 9 (1995) 133-42.

22. S. Mowinckel marvels ("Der Ursprung der Bil`amsage," *ZAW* 48 [1930] 238) that the conflict between Moses and Balak "has no conclusion...no war...no result."

23. M. Lucado, *No Wonder They Call Him the Savior* (Portland, OR: Multnomah, 1987).

24. J. Neusner, ed., *Christianity, Judaism, and other Greco-Roman Cults* (Leiden: Brill, 1975).

25. H. C. Kee, "Self-Definition in the Asclepius Cult," in *Jewish and Christian Self-Definition, Vol. 3: Self-Definition in the Greco-Roman World*, eds. B. F. Meyer and E. P. Sanders (Philadelphia: Fortress, 1982) 118-36.

26. This slogan covers billboards and some license plates in Arizona because child abuse is a major problem in this state (S. G. Ornelas, "A Cross-Cultural and Intra-Cultural Comparison of Child Abuse Potential Scores and Reliability Estimates," PhD dissertation, Arizona State University, Tempe, 2000).

27. J. Pritchard, *The Abuse of Elderly People: A Handbook for Professionals* (Philadelphia: Jessica Kingsley, 1992).

28. Written by Robert Rodat and directed by Steven Spielberg (1998).

29. M. Fishbane, *Biblical Interpretation in Ancient Israel* (New York: Oxford,

1985) 381-440.

30. Fanny Crosby, "A Wonderful Savior" (New York: Hope Publishing Company, 1918; written in 1890).

31. Ray Brady, "College Credit," CBS Evening News (May 3, 2000).

32. Scott Rodin's *Stewards in the Kingdom: A Theology of Life in All Its Fullness* (Downers Grove, IL: InterVarsity, 2000) is a good place to start.

33 S. Rodin, *Stewards in the Kingdom*, 59-60. See also G. Ritzer, *Explorations in the Sociology of Consumption: Fast Food, Credit Cards, and Casinos* (Thousand Oaks, CA: SAGE, 2001) and R. D. Manning, *Credit Card Nation: The Consequences of America's Addiction to Credit* (New York, Basic, 2000).

34 Rodin, *Stewards*, 60.

35. Aristophanes is the acknowledged master of Greek farce (e.g., *The Flies*), but the Hebrew Bible has its share, too. In Esther, for example, Queen Esther exposes Haman's plot, Ahasuerus the king storms out in a rage, and upon his return sees Haman falling upon his wife on her couch. Although we know that Haman is begging for mercy the king assumes his intentions are sexual (Esther 7:7–8). We get the joke because we know that farce relies on "mistaken identity" and "mistaken motive." T. R. Hobbs sees farcical elements in the story of Naaman, too ("Naaman," *ABD* 4.968).

36. R. LaBarbera, "The Man of War and the Man of God: Social Satire in 2 Kings 6:8-7:20," *CBQ* 45 (1984) 637-51.

37. E. W. Conrad points out (*Fear Not Warrior: A Study of the 'al tîrâ Passages in the Hebrew Scriptures* [Chico, CA: Scholars, 1985]) that in addition to its usage forty times in the OT, "Fear not!" oracles occur approx. thirty times in the NT. Jesus uses the phrase to assure his disciples both before (Matt 10:26, 28) and after his resurrection (28:10).

38. Each miracle here is preceded by prayer. The only other time Elisha prays in Kings is over the dead son of the Shunammite (2 Kings 4:30).

39. Homer, *Odyssey* 9.400-415.

40. "My friends, it is 'No man' who is slaying me by guile!" (*Odyssey* 9.408).

41. M. Goulder ("The Pre-Marcan Gospel," *SJT* 47 [1994] 453-71) sees the pre-Marcan tradition portraying Jesus as a second Elisha.

42. P. J. Achtemeier, "Mark, Gospel of," *ABD* 4.546-47.

43. J. B. Tyson, "The Blindness of the Disciples in Mark," *JBL* 80 (1961) 261-68.

44. W. Pannenberg, "Die Kontingenz der geschöpflichen Wirklichkeit," *Theologische Literaturzeitung* 119 (1994) 1049-58.

45. T. Hart, "The Word, the Words and the Witness: Proclamation as Divine and Human Reality in the Theology of Karl Barth," *Tyndale Bulletin* 46 (1995) 81-101.

46. One humorless clergyman cancels his subscription to *The Guardian* (first publisher of the *The Screwtape Letters*) because "much of the advice given in these letters…(is) not only erroneous but positively diabolical" (*The Screwtape Letters and Screwtape Proposes a Toast* [New York: MacMillan, 1968] v). This man looks much like this Israelite king.

47. Augustine, *Confessions* 8.11.

48. Willis Reed & Phil Pepe, *A View from the Rim* (Philadelphia: Lippincott, 1971).

49. W. S. LaSor, D. A. Hubbard, and F. W. Bush, *Old Testament Survey*, 2nd ed. (Grand Rapids: Eerdmans, 1996) 207.

50. G. W. Ahlström, "King Jehu—A Prophet's Mistake," in *Scripture and History*

in Theology: Essays in Honor of J. Coert Rylaarsdam, eds. A. L. Merrill and T. W. Overholt (PTMS 17; Pittsburgh: Pickwick Press, 1977) 47-69.

51. H. D. Hoffman, *Reform und Reformen: Untersuchungen zu einem Grundthema der deuteronomistischen Geschichtsschreibung* (ATANT 66; Zurich: Theologischer Verlag, 1980) 99-101. P. Hanson (*The People Called: The Growth of Community in the Bible* [San Francisco: Harper and Row, 1986] 147) takes a sociological tack, arguing that Jehu perverts the whole "Yahwistic notion of community."

52. E. T. Mullen, "The Royal Dynastic Grant to Jehu and the Structure of the Books of Kings," *JBL* 107 (1988) 196, 197.

53. While evidence is lacking for Assyrian religious hegemony, the famous Black Obelisk of Shalmaneser III clearly shows "Jehu son of Omri" (*ia-ú-a mâr hu-um-ri*) kneeling and paying homage (*ANET* 281).

54. That *Ia-ú-a mâr Humri* does in fact refer to Jehu is the conclusion of M. Weippert, "Jau(a) mar Humri: Joram oder Jehu von Israel?" *VT* 28 (1978) 113-18.

55. Is he a biological (but objectionable) "son of Omri?" (T. J. Schneider, "Rethinking Jehu," *Bib* 77 [1996] 100-07). Is he partnering with Hazael in a Syro-Israelite collusion to eliminate Joram and Ahaziah from power (W. Schniedewind, "Tel Dan Stela: New Light on Aramaic and Jehu's Revolt," *BASOR* 302 [1996] 75-90)? M. White ("Naboth's Vineyard and the Legitimation of a Dynastic Extermination," *VT* 44 [1994] 66-76) speculates that the Naboth-"story" in 2 Kings 9 predates the Naboth story in 1 Kings 21, and further, that the latter is composed to legitimate Jehu's violent revolution.

56. R. LaBarbera, "The Man of War and the Man of God: Social Satire in 2 Kings 6:8-7:20," *CBQ* 46 (1984) 637-51.

57. T. Gaster, *Myth, Legend, and Custom in the Old Testament* (New York: Harper & Row, 1975) II, 620.

58. D. Marcus, *From Balaam to Jonah: Anti-Prophetic Satire in the Hebrew Bible* (Brown Judaic Studies 301; Atlanta: Scholars Press, 1995).

59. G. Yee, "The Anatomy of Biblical Parody: The Dirge Form in 2 Samuel 1 and Isaiah 14," *CBQ* 50 (1988) 565-86.

60. T. Jemielity, *Satire and the Hebrew Prophets* (Louisville: Westminster/John Knox, 1992).

61. Jemielity, 57.

62. Jemielity, 61.

63. Gerald L. Bruns, "Allegory and Satire: A Rhetorical Mediation," *New Literary History* 11 (1979-80) 129.

64. Jemielity, 23.

65. Carl D. Evans, "Naram-Sin and Jeroboam: The Archetypal *Unheilsherrscher* in Mesopotamian and Biblical Historiography," in *Scripture in Context II: More Essays on the Comparative Method*, eds. W. W. Hallo, J. C. Moyer, L. G. Perdue (Winona Lake, IN: Eisenbrauns, 1983) 114.

66. W. Schniedewind ("History and Interpretation: The Religion of Ahab and Manasseh in the Book of Kings," *CBQ* 55 [1993] 656) sees all mention of Jezebel as exilic/post-exilic because he thinks that "the strict condemnation of Jezebel…fits into an exilic and postexilic situation in which the marriage to foreign women threatened the ethnic and religious existence of Israel" (652-53). Such arguments used to be applied to Ruth as well—another foreign woman (*contra* M. S. Moore, *Ruth* [NIBCOT

7; Peabody, MA: Hendrickson, 2000] 296).

67. The story of "Anat's Purge" appears in the larger Baal-cycle and Ugaritologists disagree over how to reconstruct the sequence of tablets upon which these stories are preserved. Dennis Pardee's reconstruction/translation appears in "The Ba'lu Myth," *The Context of Scripture, vol I: Canonical Compositions from the Biblical World* [eds. W. W. Hallo and K. L. Younger, Jr.; Leiden: Brill, 1997] 241-74). Mark Smith's reconstruction/translation appears in *Ugaritic Narrative Poetry* (ed. S. B. Parker; Atlanta: Scholars Press, 1997).

68. For a discussion, see J. B. Lloyd, "Anat and the 'Double' Massacre of *KTU* 1.3 ii," *Ugarit, Religion, and Culture: Essays Presented in Honour of J. C. L. Gibson* (eds. N. Wyatt; W. G. E. Watson, and J. B. Lloyd; Münster: Ugarit-Verlag, 1996) 153-57.

69. See Lloyd, 156-57.

70. J. Gray, "The Blood Bath of the Goddess Anat in the Ras Shamra Texts," *UF* 11 (1979) 315-24.

71. M. S. Smith, *The Early History of God* (San Francisco: Harper, 1990) 64.

72. P. D. Stern, "The 'Bloodbath of Anat' and Psalm XXIII," *VT* 44 (1994) 120-24.

73. P. Craigie, "Deborah and Anat: A Study of Poetic Imagery (Judges 5)," *ZAW* 90 (1978) 174-81. S. G. Dempster ("Mythology and History in the Song of Deborah," *WTJ* 41 [1978] 33-53) sees the Baal-Anat imagery transferred directly to Yahweh-Deborah, but John Day (*Yahweh and the Gods and Goddesses of Canaan* [JSOTSup 265; Sheffield: Shefield Academic Press, 2000] 137-39) is critical of these parallels.

74. M. Smith (*Early History of God*, 6) and K. van der Toorn ("Anat-Yahu, Some Other Deities, and the Jews of Elephantine," *Numen* 39 [1992] 82-3) find little evidence for the existence of an Anat cult in first millenium Phoenicia.

75. Lloyd, 160.

76. In another Canaanite myth, Anat so covets a particular bow she kills its owner and steals it—behavior similar to what we see in Jezebel when she kills Naboth and steals his land (*KTU* 1.18 iv 12-13; 1 Kings 22:5-14).

77. *UNP* 83.

78. S. Olyan, "*Hashâlôm?* Some Literary Considerations of 2 Kings 9," *CBQ* 46 (1984) 652-68.

79. M. Smith in S. Parker, ed., *Ugaritic Narrative Poetry*, p. 167, n. 43.

80. W. J. Murnane, *Texts from the Amarna Period in Egypt* (Atlanta: Scholars, 1995) 31 (text # 7).

81. H. Tadmor, "The Inscriptions of Nabunaid: Historical Arrangement," in *Studies in Honor of Benno Landsberger* (Assyriological Studies 16; Chicago: University of Chicago, 1965) 351–64.

82. J. C. VanderKam, "2 Maccabees 6, 7A and Calendrical Change in Jerusalem," *JSJ* 12 (1981) 52-74; L. H. Schiffman, "Origin and Early History of the Qumran Sect," *BA* 58 (1995) 37-48.

83. E. Otto, *Krieg und Frieden in der Hebräischen Bibel und im Alten Orient* (Theologie und Frieden 18; Stuttgart: Kohlhammer, 1999) 14.

84. Hosea's opinion is obviously not shared by the narrator of Kings (Hos 1:4-5 vs. 2 Kings 10:30). S. Irvine thinks ("The Threat of Jezreel," *CBQ* 57 [1995] 494-503) that the debate between Kings and Hosea has fundamentally to do with whether or not the dynasty of Jehu deserves to continue.

85. Otto, *Krieg und Frieden*, 14.

86. This needs to be underlined because Jehu often gets bad press from contemporary interpreters. Hannelis Schulte, for example ("The End of the Omride Dynasty: Social-Ethical Observations on the Subject of Power and Violence," *Sem* 66 [1995] 133-48) simply puts a contemporary socio-political context over this story and reads it accordingly.

87. Jemielity, *Satire*, 14.

88. R. Knierim, *The Task of Old Testament Theology: Substance, Method, and Cases* (Grand Rapids: Eerdmans, 1999) 120.

89. Yee, "Anatomy of Biblical Parody," 567.

90. In 2 Kings 8:18 she is called a "daughter of Ahab," but in 8:26, "daughter of Omri," a contradiction the versions try to harmonize. LXX's Lucianic recension, for example, changes "Omri" to "Ahab" in 8:26. The Syriac version of 2 Chron 21:6 reads "sister of Ahab."

91. R. J. Leprohon, "Egypt, History of," *ABD* 2.346.

92. W. Durant, *Caesar and Christ* (New York: Simon and Schuster, 1944) 277.

93. Susan Ackerman argues ("The Queen Mother and the Cult in Ancient Israel," *JBL* 112 [1993] 385-401) that Judahite queen mothers enact both official political and cultic roles as counselors and "ordained" representatives of Asherah (the goddess/consort of Yahweh in Baalized Yahwism). Nancy Bowen disagrees ("The Quest for the Historical *Gebîrâ*," *CBQ* 63 [2001] 597-618).

94. This refers to one of the bronze pillars cast by Solomon (1 Kings 7:15-22). Josiah renews the covenant in front of it as well. The royal custom which terrifies Adonijah is David's decision to put Solomon on the royal mule (1 Kings 1:44).

95. S. Mowinckel, *He That Cometh* (Oxford: B. Blackwell, 1956).

96. Euripides, *Medea* 1069-78.

97. *Oedipus Tyrannus* (written by Sophocles, c. 429 BC); Herakles (written by Euripides, c. 416 BC); *Frogs* (written by Aristophanes, c. 405 BC).

98. *The Sixth Sense* (written and directed by M. Night Shyamalan, 1999); *Bringing Out the Dead* (novel written by J. Connelly; screenplay by P. Schrader; directed by M. Scorsese, 1999); *Ghost* (written by Bruce Joel Rubin; directed by Jerry Zucker, 1990).

99. D. Bonhoeffer, *Ethics* (New York: MacMillan, 1955; translated from the 1949 German edition based on manuscripts written between 1940-43) 3.

100. Lewis Carroll's classic fantasy is another subtle critique of capricious monarchy (Philadelphia: Henry Altemus, 1895; originally published in 1851).

101. Still the most penetrating critique of narcotic mind control (via the drug "soma") is A. Huxley's *Brave New World* (New York: Bantam; originally published in 1932).

102. C. Spurgeon, "It Is God That Justifieth (Rom 8:33)," *All of Grace* (CD-Rom; Albany, OR: Ages Software, 1997; reprint of c. 1880 ed.) 15.

CONCLUSION

FINAL FOUR (2 Kings 23:31-25:30)

Tragedy and comedy are different kinds of literature. Only the latter has a U-shaped structure.[1] Both tend to begin the same way, but where the characters in comedies make that critical U-turn the characters in tragedies do not. Saul, for example, clings to his obsessions to the bitter end, even as the Philistines close in and destroy him.[2] Job, however, is a comedy because Yahweh eventually restores him to a higher position than where he began. Many contemporary readers see the Bible as a tragedy, but the Gospel of Christ is not a tragedy. The Gospel of Christ is the quintessential divine comedy: life, death, and resurrection.

In Kings, however, many characters never make that critical U-turn. Solomon, for example, begins his reign on a high plane with the building of Yahweh's Temple, but then ends his life as a devotee of Ashtoreth and Molech. Jeroboam's reign begins on a high plane as well. He hears a powerful Yahwistic prophecy, and he takes responsibility for leading the northern ten tribes away from Rehoboam's tyranny—but then he builds two golden calves and leads Israel into brazen idolatry. Jehu begins his mission with great zeal and conviction, then fails "to keep the law of Yahweh...with all his heart" (2 Kings 10:31). Hezekiah begins his reign with prayer and piety, then ends it trying to cut back-room deals with the Babylonians.

Against this context Josiah's reform stands out like a bright light. After his death Judah's final four kings—Jehoahaz, Jehoiakim, Jehoiachin, and Zedekiah—become broken puppets dangling from shattered hopes. Prior to Josiah Yahweh is "unwilling" to destroy his people (*lo' 'abâ*, 2 Kings 13:23). After Josiah, however, he is "unwilling" to save them (*lo' 'abâ*, 24:4). None of these four kings comes before us as a subject, only as an object of God's wrath, and though we can reconstruct Assyria's fall, Babylon's rise, and Egypt's policy of interference with some precision (*ANET* 294-316), this remains a time of great uncertainty in the ancient Near East. When Nineveh falls in 612 BC the Assyrian king Assuruballit retreats to Haran to make one last stand against the Babylonian-Mede coalition aligned against him.[3] Pharaoh Neco tries to help Assyria by leading an army up the Mediterranean coast, but not so much to save Assyria as to create a buffer zone between himself and the Babylonian army. Nebuchadnezzar, however, stops the Egyptians at Carchemish and scores a decisive victory (Jer 46:2-12). The following year he pushes Neco all the way back into Egypt: "The king of Egypt did not march out from his own country again, because the king of Babylon had taken all his territory, from the Wadi of Egypt to the Euphrates River" (2 Kings 24:7).

Trying to stay afloat in this sea of chaos, Judah bobs about like a soggy cork, her fortunes threatened with every violent wave. On Neco's first trip north Josiah meets him at Megiddo (609 BC) and the Egyptians suddenly (and unceremoniously) kill him. Lamenting this sudden loss Judah turns to Jehoahaz as king, but Neco rejects their choice. Summoning him to Riblah on the Orontes river he sends him off into Egyptian exile and we never hear from him again. Astonished by this turn of events Jeremiah interprets it as a dark omen of things to come: "He (Jehoahaz) will never return. He will die in the place where they have led him captive; he will not see this land again" (Jer 22:11-12). Now fully in charge of Syria-Palestine, Pharaoh Neco installs Eliakim (another of Josiah's sons) on the throne of Judah, changing his name to Jehoiakim ("Yah will raise up"). For the next few years, Jehoiakim compliantly sends tribute to his boss in Egypt, but in the meantime builds himself a luxury palace on the backs of struggling Judahites. This infuriates the prophet Jeremiah, who rants at him:

"Does it make you a king to have more and more cedar?
Did not your father (Josiah) have food and drink?
He did what was right and just,

so all went well with him.
He defended the cause of the poor and needy,
    and so all went well.
Is this not what it means to know me?" (Jer 22:15-16).

Instead of caring for the poor and needy, Jehoiakim becomes an "Oskar Schindler" type of war-profiteer, lining his own pockets at Judah's expense. When another prophet, Uriah, dares to speak out against the king he has him executed (Jer 26:23). The same thing almost happens to Jeremiah (26:24).

Jeremiah and Jehoiakim lock horns most famously through Baruch (Jeremiah's scribe) and Yehudi (Jehoiakim's messenger, Jer 36:1-32). Jeremiah commissions Baruch to write a scroll intended to record all the punishments Yahweh plans to bring upon Judah, and Baruch goes to the Temple to read it aloud. This inaugurates a chain of events which upon close inspection looks eerily familiar. Jeremiah's scroll comes to Jehoiakim just like the Torah scroll earlier comes to Josiah (2 Kings 22:8-11). In each case (a) the written Word is "discovered," (b) a minor functionary shares its message with more powerful functionaries, (c) these functionaries react with fear, and (d) they concoct a political strategy for presenting it to the king.

Yet here the parallels break down because when Josiah hears the words of his scroll he tears his robes in shame and repentance. When Jehoiakim hears the words of his scroll, however, he tries to destroy the scroll itself, cutting it into pieces and burning it in his fireplace. The intertextual contrast cannot be more striking. Josiah's contriteness is the exact opposite of Jehoiakim's arrogance. Josiah's response is "U-shaped." Jehoiakim's is "I-shaped."

After Nebuchadnezzar pushes Neco into Egypt, Jehoiakim puts his finger into the wind and tries to guess which way international power is going to shift. When Nebuchadnezzar fails to conquer Egypt Jehoiakim interprets this as a sign of weakness and rebels against his oppressors (2 Kings 24:1). This proves fatal. Egypt and Babylon quickly call a truce and Nebuchadnezzar marches straight back to Jerusalem to squash the rebellion. Before he arrives, however, Jehoiakim mysteriously dies (assassinated?) and Jehoiachin inherits the throne of David. Nebuchadnezzar then arrives at the gates of Jerusalem and Jehoiachin wisely surrenders the city (597 BC). Nebuchadnezzar accepts his surrender, but instead of demanding tribute (as Sennacherib does with Hezekiah in 701), he throws Jehoiachin into chains and drags him into Babylonian exile.

Then things *really* go bad. Between 597 and 587 Judah suffers the worst decade of its national life. The Babylonians install another of Josiah's sons as king—Mattaniah (Jehoiachin's uncle)—and rename him Zedekiah ("righteousness of Yah"). Nebuchadnezzar throws him into the middle of Judah's crisis and the pressure overwhelms him. For advice Zedekiah consults with the prophet Jeremiah, but this makes his advisers at court so angry they throw Jeremiah into prison. Clinging to their hollow Zionism, these blind "patriots" hold tenaciously to the belief that Yahweh is obligated to rescue them. From their perspective, Jeremiah is a pro-Babylonian traitor—they are patently unable to see anything any longer in non-political terms or categories. Torn between these two positions—prophetic theology vs. political Zionism—Zedekiah eventually caves in to the Zionists and when the Babylonians find out about the change, they don't wait to see how things will turn out. They march straight back to Jerusalem and put it to death. Seeing them coming Zedekiah desperately approaches Jeremiah one last time for counsel and comfort (Jer 37:1–10, 16–21; 38:14–28), but Jeremiah refuses him: "If I give you an answer, will you not kill me? Even if I did give you counsel, you would not listen to me" (Jer 38:15).

Finally, after a two-year siege the Babylonians break through the city walls and round up the remnants of Judah's army. Then they execute all of Zedekiah's sons before his eyes and tear his eyes out of their sockets. The deaths of his children are the last thing he ever sees in this life. Lamentations lists these and many other atrocities in heartbreaking detail—the burning, the looting, the groaning, the cannibalism, the despair, the horrid violence. The "daughter of Jerusalem" becomes a suffering widow (Lam 1:1-2). Judah watches in horror as the Babylonians strip the Temple and torch their beloved capitol.

Intratextual Reflection
Later the Babylonians also release Jehoiachin from prison, but not to lead the exiles back to Judah. Not until Cyrus' decree (538 BC) does a remnant of Jews receive this permission (Ezra 1:1-4). Kings instead ends with Jerusalem in ruins. Judah's enemies destroy everything—temple, city, dynasty, identity—and Yahweh's people have nowhere left to turn, no one to comfort them in the midst of their pain (Lam 1:2). Doubtless some Jews try to convince themselves, as their homes go up in flames, that this failure, too, will be temporary. But those still selling this pablum will be proven horribly wrong. The Exile is the exact opposite of the Exodus. Judah will live in a foreign land for many decades until a priest named

Ezra challenges his fellow exiles to rediscover, with their ancestor Josiah, the resurrective power of the Scroll:

> On the first day of the seventh month Ezra the priest brought the Law before the assembly, which was made up of men and women and all who were able to understand. He read it aloud from daybreak till noon as he faced the square before the Water Gate in the presence of the men, women and others who could understand. And all the people listened attentively to the Book of the Law (Neh 8:1-3).

But for now Jerusalem sits, like Job, on the ash-heap of broken dreams and shattered hopes.

Because Kings is a *tragedy*, what begins with an open hand finally ends with a closed fist. Israel's relationships with her neighbors start off with good intentions, but good intentions are never enough. Solomon's covenant with the foreigner Hiram eventually leads to the foreigner Nebuchadnezzar's invasion. Hiram's "love" for David (1 Kings 5:1) proves only skin-deep. Nebuchadnezzar's capture of Jehoiachin irrevocably shatters this "love." Solomon's construction of the Temple eventually ends with Nebuzaradan's destruction of its buildings. The wisdom-influenced openness of Solomon's reign eventually ends in the cold waters of *Realpolitik*. Kings starts with a blessing and ends with a curse—a curse predicted by prophet after prophet:

> He sent them to destroy Judah, in accordance with the word of Yahweh proclaimed by his servants the prophets (2 Kings 24:2).

> Surely these things happened to Judah according to Yahweh's command, in order to remove them from his presence because of the sins of Manasseh (24:3).

> For he had filled Jerusalem with innocent blood, and Yahweh was not willing to forgive (24:4).

> As Yahweh had declared, Nebuchadnezzar removed all the treasures from the Temple (24:13).

> It was because of Yahweh's anger that all this happened to Jerusalem and Judah, and in the end he thrust them from his presence (24:20).

> So Judah went into captivity, away from her land (25:21).

Prophetic theology always questions the wisdom of trusting foreigners, whether foreign neighbors (1 Kings 5:1-12), foreign women (11:1-13),
foreign religions (2 Kings 9:14-10:36), or foreign resources (1 Kings 7:1-
12). The prophetic mantra is 'Look at what foreigners do to the Temple.
Look at what they do to Jerusalem. Look at what they do to the Davidic
dynasty." This attitude is worlds apart from, say, the book of Ruth or the
Acts of the Apostles,[4] yet this narrator holds out little hope for ecumenical dialogue. The *pressure of violence* trajectory runs parallel to the *pressure of foreigners* trajectory. When we look at the Bible as a whole, Kings
speaks "from the middle of the exile....Whatever hope [the narrator]
holds for the future is an uncertain one. Chronicles, on the other hand,
describes the exile as an event that is past. It is an unpleasant memory
that may serve as a warning for the future, but does not require elabora-
tion. Chronicles holds a great deal of hope for the future."[5]

To end Israel's history here, therefore, would be tantamount to ending the Gospel at the foot of the Cross. Condemning Kings' final four
leaders (Jer 22), Jeremiah nevertheless knows and maintains a fundamental difference between *agency* and *cause* in his oracles of judgment
(Jer 23:1-8). Yahweh is the cause. These "final four" are merely agents of
his judgment, not its cause. Where these agents "scatter" and "drive
away," Jeremiah prophesies, Yahweh still has the power to "gather" and
"bring back." Where Yahweh is the Righteous Judge, Yahweh is also the
Future Deliverer of his broken, defeated people.

Theological Reflection

How do we apply this message to our own time? Today we live in an age
where so many people live in exile, where the temptation is so constant
to view faith as powerless, where so many confuse agency with cause,
where despair constantly threatens to snuff out hope. We see "Babylonians" at the gates and "Zedekiahs" in the pulpits and we wonder what the
future will hold. We wonder about the future of our children. We wonder
about the future of the Church.

In the Gospels this conflict often comes down to one central question: "Who is King?"[6] This question preoccupies Kings too. Zedekiah's
"rotten fig" advisers (Jer 24:8), for example, think that Zedekiah is righteous because he's a genetic "son of David." Jeremiah ridicules this lunacy
for what it is—a counterfeit substitute for faith.[7] Instead, he dares to argue
what Micaiah argues, what Isaiah argues, what all the prophets argue.
Yahweh is Israel's king. Yahweh is the Savior of his people.

When President Kennedy was assassinated I was a gangly fifth-grader sitting in a classroom at Coleman Place Elementary School in Norfolk, Virginia. I can still see the shock on my teacher's face as the intercom blared out the terrible news. After things calmed down I remember walking home that day with my friends and playing football in the back yard. I remember the smell of the leaves in the crisp fall air, the sound of our laughter as we yelled and shouted out plays. I remember the feeling of being grateful for a day off, blissfully ignorant of the tragedy happening all around us.

I remember also the tears on my mother's face as she told me the other important news of the day: "Pawpaw is dead." Puzzled, I remember saying, "It's OK, Mom," thinking that she'd somehow confused the President with my grandfather, Pawpaw. But Mom wasn't talking about the President. She was talking about her father, my grandfather—the warm, bubbly man who taught me how to fish and hunt and look for crayfish in the streams of Oklahoma. Pawpaw died on the same day as President Kennedy—November 22, 1963.

This was more news than I could emotionally handle. Should I mourn the President or the death of my grandfather? One death impacted all of us. The other impacted only my family. Each death brought in its wake its own pain—one distant, one immediate; one national, one personal; one "out there," one painfully "in here." Years later, I learned that C. S. Lewis had died on the same day, too—November 22, 1963—and to this day I cannot read *The Screwtape Letters* without seeing my mother's face or Jackie Kennedy's blood-stained suit. Catastrophes take time to process. They need time to be absorbed. Sometimes we deal with them in a healthy way; sometimes we don't. Sometimes we associate them subconsciously with other events, even as we try to separate them out into neat, manageable piles. So also the catastrophe of Israel's destruction. In one way these stories seem so distant and so irrelevant to our everyday lives. Yet in another way they're so relevant to our lives they make us wince with pain.

The primary purpose of this book has been to focus on these stories in order to draw from this study better tools for working the Faith. A second purpose has been to show that none of these stories stands alone, but on identifiable trajectories which incorporate, revise, and empower them in identifiable ways. A third purpose, though muted, and never clearly stated, has been to demonstrate that biblical prophecy is not what many people say it is. Mark Twain once commented that "prophecies which promise valuable things, desirable things, good things, worthy things, never come true. Prophecies of this kind are like wars fought in a good cause—they are so rare that they don't count."[8] Well some prophecies do foretell gloom and doom, but not all, and certainly not all of the prophecies in Kings. Many can and do "promise valuable things, desirable things, good things, and worthy things" and God is able to make it all "count"—especially when these promises take root in the hearts of believers who dare to practice the Faith under pressure.

Notes

1. W. Whedbee, "The Comedy of Job," *Semeia* 7 (1977) 1-39.

2. See my "Saul's Leadership Style," in *Reconciliation: A Study of Biblical Families in Conflict* (Joplin, MO: College Press, 1994) 142.

3. D. Wiseman, *Chronicles of Chaldaean Kings (626–556 B.C.) in the British Museum* (London: Trustees of the British Museum, 1956) 54–63.

4. See my article, "Ruth the Moabite and the Blessing of Foreigners," *CBQ* 60 (1998) 203-17.

5. S. McKenzie, *The Chronicler's Use of the Deuteronomistic History* (HSM 33; Atlanta: Scholars, 1984) 187.

6. J. Kingsbury, "The Plot of Luke's Story of Jesus," *Int* 48 (1994) 369-78.

7. Note the pun on the root *tsdq* in Jer 23:6. Zedekiah (*tsdqyh*, "Yah is righteous") will someday be replaced by a messianic king whose name will reflect this name: *yhwh tsdqnw* ("Yahweh is our righteousness").

8. *The Autobiography of Mark Twain*, C. Neider, ed. (New York: Harper & Row, 1959) 66.

INDEXES

Subject Index

Author and Name Index